Love and Theft

RACE AND AMERICAN CULTURE

General Editors:
Arnold Rampersad and Shelley Fisher Fishkin

Love and Theft:
Blackface Minstrelsy and the American Working Class
Eric Lott

LOVE
AND
THEFT

*Blackface Minstrelsy and
the American Working Class*

ERIC LOTT

New York   Oxford
OXFORD UNIVERSITY PRESS
1993

Oxford University Press

Oxford New York Toronto
Delhi Bombay Calcutta Madras Karachi
Kuala Lumpur Singapore Hong Kong Tokyo
Nairobi Dar es Salaam Cape Town
Melbourne Auckland Madrid

and associated companies in
Berlin Ibadan

© 1995 by Eric Lott

Published by Oxford University Press, Inc.,

198 Madison Avenue, New York, New York 10016-4314

Oxford is a registered trademark of Oxford University Press

Library of Congress Cataloging-in-Publication Data
Lott, Eric.
Love and theft : blackface minstrelsy and the American working class /
Eric Lott.
p. cm. — (Race and American culture)
Includes bibliographical references.
ISBN 0-19-507832-2; 0-19-509641-X (pbk)
1. Minstrel shows—United States—History and criticism.
2. Working class—United States.
3. United States—Race relations.
4. United States—History—Civil War, 1861–1865.
I. Title. II. Series.
ML1711.L67 1993
791'.12'097309034—dc20   92-41071

Portions of chapter 2 and chapter 6 originally appeared as "Love and Theft: The Racial Unconscious of Blackface Minstrelsy." © 1992 by the Regents of the University of California. Reprinted by permission from *Representations*, no. 39.

Chapter 5 originally appeared as "'The Seeming Counterfeit': Racial Politics and Early Blackface Minstrelsy," in *American Quarterly*, 43, no. 2 (1991). Reprinted by permission.

Quotations from the promptbook manuscript of H. J. Conway's stage adaptation of *Uncle Tom's Cabin* are reprinted courtesy of the Theatre Arts Collection, Harry Ransom Humanities Research Center, The University of Texas at Austin.

19 18 17 16 15 14 13 12 11

Printed in the United States of America
on acid-free paper

To
Susan Fraiman
Judith Lott
Richard Lott

Acknowledgments

Walter Rodney once wrote that the authorial habit of absolving a book's friends and helpers from responsibility for its shortcomings was "sheer bourgeois subjectivism." Fortunately, any errors or nonsense I have committed will scarcely tarnish the example of those whose contributions I do not pardon. I acknowledge, above all, the collective settings in which I have been privileged to work. The Carter G. Woodson Institute for African-American and African Studies granted me a fellowship during which much of this study was written; many thanks to its director, Armstead Robinson, its staff—particularly Gail Shirley and Mary Rose—and its fellows for critical talk, prodding, and jovial abuse. Thanks are due as well to colleagues and students at the University of Virginia and at the Commonwealth Center for Literary and Cultural Change. As the book was taking shape, the UVa Feminist Theory Group was an indispensable space of intellectual and political support and exchange, as, at an earlier stage, were the various Union Square Marxist study groups at Columbia University. I must thank Columbia's Center for American Culture Studies and its director, Jack Salzman, for the chance to try out early notions in various settings. John Short and fellow teachers in the literacy workshops at the Borough of Manhattan Community College's Writing Center provided a formative example of collective academic work.

I owe a great debt to the staffs of the Harvard Theatre Collection, the music, dance, and theater collections of the New York Public Library, the Harry Ransom Humanities Research Center at the University of Texas–Austin, the Free Library of Philadelphia, the Music Collection at the Library of Congress, and the Barrett Collection at the University of Virginia. At Harvard Joe Keller and curator Jeanne T. Newlin provided affable and expert help and advice; at the University of Texas Melissa Miller-Quinlan crucially expedited some microfilming.

I am also grateful to my teachers; it is a pleasure to thank them after all this time. Jackson Lears, Tom Quirk, Albert Devlin, and Robert Bender got me interested in the study of culture, and Ann Douglas enlivened that interest. Steven Marcus made it impossible to think about cultural products separately from history, theory, and society. This study had its beginnings in a seminar paper for Jane Tompkins. Later, Andrew Delbanco, Steven Marcus, and Arnold Rampersad worked with me on the dissertation from which this book has grown, and made invaluable suggestions about its scope, procedure, and method—unawares in many cases.

Several people gave me materials of various kinds, often from their own research and writing, for which I am much in their debt: Bluford Adams, Paul Cantor, Patricia Cline Cohen, Joe Donahue, Ken Emerson, Arnold Fraiman, Barbara Green, Noel Ignatiev, Gail Karp, Hal Kolb, Nancy Loevinger, Mary Mackay and Edward Wheatley, George Rehin, Lucy Rinehart, David Roediger, Jack Salzman, and Lillian Schlissel. Others read all or part of the manuscript and offered extremely helpful criticism, sarcasm, encouragement, and advice: Stanley Bailis, Michael Bérubé, John Blair, T. J. Clark, Carol Clover, Dale Cockrell, George Cunningham, Steve Cushman, Kathleen Diffley, Jonathan Freedman, John Frick, Michael Frisch, Saidiya Hartman, Gary Kulik, Jack Levenson, David Levin, Rip Lhamon, Chris Looby, Karen Lystra, Don Pease, Chuck Perdue, David Roediger, David Scobey, Alan Trachtenberg, Susan Willis, and above all Elizabeth Blackmar, Robert Ferguson, Eric Foner, and Michael Rogin. A grant from the University of Virginia's Small Grants Committee aided me in gathering the illustrations for this book, and a generous subvention from Columbia University's Bancroft Dissertation Prize has been much appreciated. Virginia Germino and Elisabeth Crocker were of enormous help in preparing the manuscript. Liz Maguire and Susie Chang at Oxford University Press provided incalculable support and enthusiasm, and I thank them.

Friends and family kept me going all down the line. The long-standing comradeship of Benj DeMott has taught me much of what I know about moral and intellectual passion. Michael Denning and Hazel Carby have long been advisers and exemplars; my work would have been far more difficult without them. Over the past few years Debbie McDowell has clarified my thinking about a host of matters great and small. Conversations and excursions with Austin Quigley and Pat Denison brought to life the British music hall, close cousin (I subsequently realized) of the minstrel show. Tera Hunter mercifully took this project seriously; Andy Bienen's understanding of rock 'n' roll added dimension to it; Harry Stecopoulos's interest and (constant) interrogation kept me at it. Mark Edmundson and Jahan Ramazani offered a rich fund of encouragement and sage counsel. Late in the day my brother, Brian, joked about the book going into "Chapter 11," for which, as for so much else, he knows he has my thanks.

The dedication barely begins to repay the debt I owe my parents. As for Susan Fraiman, comrade and co-conspirator, she knows this book by heart—which says as much about her heart as it does about her importance in my life and work.

Contents

Introduction, 3

PART I

1. Blackface and Blackness:
   The Minstrel Show in American Culture, 15

2. Love and Theft:
   "Racial" Production and the Social Unconscious of Blackface, 38

3. White Kids and No Kids At All:
   Working-Class Culture and Languages of Race, 63

4. The Blackening of America:
   Popular Culture and National Cultures, 89

PART II

5. "The Seeming Counterfeit":
   Early Blackface Acts, the Body, and Social Contradiction, 111

6. "Genuine Negro Fun":
   Racial Pleasure and Class Formation in the 1840s, 136

7. California Gold and European Revolution:
   Stephen Foster and the American 1848, 169

8. Uncle Tomitudes:
   Racial Melodrama and Modes of Production, 211

Afterword, 234

Notes, 239

Bibliography, 277

Index, 305

Love and Theft

Introduction

It was at this epoch that Mr. T. D. Rice made his debut in a dramatic sketch entitled "Jim Crow," and from that moment everybody was "doing just so," and continued "doing just so" for months, and even years afterward. Never was there such an excitement in the musical or dramatic world; nothing was talked of, nothing written of, and nothing dreamed of, but "Jim Crow." The most sober citizens began to "wheel about, and turn about, and jump Jim Crow." It seemed as though the entire population had been bitten by the tarantula; in the parlor, in the kitchen, in the shop and in the street, Jim Crow monopolized public attention. It must have been a species of insanity, though of a gentle and pleasing kind. . . .

—*New York Tribune* (1855)

Despite their billings as images of reality, these Negroes of fiction are counterfeits. They are projected aspects of an internal symbolic process through which, like a primitive tribesman dancing himself into the group frenzy necessary for battle, the white American prepares himself emotionally to perform a social role.

—Ralph Ellison

The race question is subsidiary to the class question in politics, and to think of imperialism in terms of race is disastrous. But to neglect the racial factor as merely incidental is an error only less grave than to make it fundamental.

—C. L. R. James

Blackface minstrelsy was an established nineteenth-century theatrical practice, principally of the urban North, in which white men caricatured blacks for sport and profit. It has therefore been summed up by one observer as "half a century of inurement to the uses of white supremacy."[1] While it was organized around the quite explicit "borrowing" of black cultural materials for white dissemination, a borrowing that ultimately depended on the material relations of slavery, the minstrel show obscured these relations by pretending that slavery was amusing, right, and natural. Although it arose from a white obsession with black (male) bodies which underlies white racial dread to our own day, it ruthlessly disavowed its fleshly investments through ridicule and racist lampoon. Yet I am not so sure

3

that this is the end of the story. In light of recent discussions of race and subjectivity, we probably ought to take these facts and processes as merely a starting orientation for inquiry into the complexities of racism and raced subjects in the United States.[2] In doing so we shall find that blackface performance, the first formal public acknowledgment by whites of black culture, was based on small but significant crimes against settled ideas of racial demarcation, which indeed appear to be inevitable when white Americans enter the haunted realm of racial fantasy. Ultimately I am after some sense of how precariously nineteenth-century white working people lived their whiteness—a matter of the greatest consequence in the history of America's racial cultures and their material or institutional transactions.

This study grew out of a dissatisfaction with erstwhile modes of racial critique, which in their political disapprobation, dovetailing with aesthetic disdain, were unwilling to engage with the artifacts and social realities of popular life, too ready to dismiss the *mentalité* of the popular classes, finally impatient with politics itself. Cultural critics have recently become more aware of the uneven and contradictory character of popular life and culture, the ambiguities or contradictions that may characterize the pleasures of the masses.[3] It is one of the arguments of this book that in blackface minstrelsy's audiences there were in fact contradictory racial impulses at work, impulses based in the everyday lives and racial negotiations of the minstrel show's working-class partisans. Indeed, there are reasons for thinking of blackface in the years prior to the Civil War as a far more unsettled phenomenon than has been supposed; critics of minstrelsy have too often dismissed working-class racial feeling as uncomplicated and monolithic, and historians of working-class culture have usually concurred—or made apologies.[4] It seems particularly clear that in the pages of recent social history the antebellum potential for a labor abolitionism has not been adequately explored nor its failure accounted for, and that the minstrel show crucially helps address this question.[5]

This agenda may seem an undue burden to place on a "counterfeit" cultural phenomenon such as the minstrel show. One ought, though, to take seriously Ralph Ellison's ironic image of whites racially girding themselves by way of rituals that mirror rather than distance the Other, in which whites are touched by the blacks they would lampoon and are in the process told on, revealed. Studying the most popular entertainment form of the nineteenth century together with its characteristic audience is perhaps the best way to understand the affective life of race in that time and in ours. The minstrel show has been ubiquitous, cultural common coin; it has been so central to the lives of North Americans that we are hardly aware of its extraordinary influence. Minstrel troupes entertained presidents (including Lincoln), and disdainful high-minded quarterlies and rakish sporting journals alike followed its course.[6] Figures such as Mark Twain, Walt Whitman, and Bayard Taylor were as attracted to blackface performance as Frederick Douglass and Martin Delany were repelled by it. From "Oh! Susanna" to Elvis Presley, from circus clowns to Saturday morning cartoons, blackface acts

4

and words have figured significantly in the white Imaginary of the United States.

Without the minstrel show there would have been no *Uncle Tom's Cabin* (1852), no *Adventures of Huckleberry Finn* (1884); investments as various as Norman Mailer's "White Negro" (1957), John Howard Griffin's *Black Like Me* (1961), or certain of John Berryman's *Dream Songs* (1955–69) would likewise have been impossible.[7] Leslie Fiedler's thesis in *Love and Death in the American Novel* (1960) that our white male writers have been obsessed with white male–dark male dyads (Huck and Jim, Ishmael and Queequeg) finds intimate material expression in the blackface performer's assumption of familiarity with "blackness." The early history of motion pictures was bound up with blackface—witness its importance to such major cinematic developments as *Uncle Tom's Cabin* (1903), *Birth of a Nation* (1915), and *The Jazz Singer* (1927)[8]—and the movies have regularly returned to it since then, whether in Fred Astaire's blackface tribute to Bill "Bojangles" Robinson in *Swing Time* (1936), Melvin Van Peebles's ironic *Watermelon Man* (1970), or the egregious post–affirmative action *Soul Man* (1986). Bill Monroe, Jimmie Rodgers, and other early country music stars routinely "blacked up," as did ethnic vaudevillians such as Sophie Tucker; as Armond White has written, "some form of darkie mimicking has been the strongest musical tradition in pluralized American culture."[9] Indeed, in minstrelsy's cultural force, its racial crossings, and what the *New York Tribune* called its pleasing "insanity" (June 30, 1855), its emergence resembled that of early rock 'n' roll. Every time you hear an expansive white man drop into his version of black English, you are in the presence of blackface's unconscious return.

For an index of popular white racial feeling in the United States, one could do worse than minstrelsy. I am concerned in this book with its shape and resonance in the decades before the Civil War. The tone and format of the early minstrel show, with its knee-slapping musical numbers punctuated by comic dialogues, bad puns, and petit-bourgeois ribaldry, should seem familiar to anyone who has seen American television's "Hee Haw." (The resemblance is apparently not coincidental, for one scholar has speculated that the rural white tradition, and its commercial issue in modern bluegrass music, inherited much from the minstrel show—not least the black style of banjo playing on which minstrelsy partly traded.)[10] Although the makeup of minstrelsy changed continually after its emergence at the beginning of the 1830s, it was configured at the height of its popularity as a semicircle of four or five or sometimes more white male performers (there were very rarely female performers in the antebellum minstrel show) made up with facial blacking of greasepaint or burnt cork and adorned in outrageously oversized and/or ragged "Negro" costumes. Armed with an array of instruments, usually banjo, fiddle, bone castanets, and tambourine, the performers would stage a tripartite show. The first part offered up a random selection of songs interspersed with what passed for black wit and japery; the second part (or "olio") featured a group of novelty performances (comic dialogues, malapropistic "stump speeches," cross-dressed "wench" performances, and the like); and the third

5

part was a narrative skit, usually set in the South, containing dancing, music, and burlesque.

This "ethnographic miniature," in Clifford Geertz's phrase, jumbled together a dramatic spectacle based on an overriding investment in the body, a figural content preoccupied with racial marking and racial transmutation, and a social context of white working-class proximity to blacks (21, 444). We might almost call it a precognitive form: not, as in Geertz's study of the Balinese cockfight, a story one people told themselves about themselves, but an encapsulation of the affective order of things in a society that racially ranked human beings. What the minstrel show did was capture an antebellum structure of racial feeling, in Raymond Williams's phrase, "social experiences *in solution,* as distinct from other social semantic formations which have been *precipitated* and are more evidently and more immediately available." Minstrelsy brought to public form racialized elements of thought and feeling, tone and impulse, residing at the very edge of semantic availability, which Americans only dimly realized they felt, let alone understood.[11] The minstrel show was less the incarnation of an age-old racism than an emergent social semantic figure highly responsive to the emotional demands and troubled fantasies of its audiences.[12] By looking at the formal aspects of minstrelsy in the context of its time, we may see its historically new articulation of racial difference.

This articulation took the form of a simultaneous drawing up and crossing of racial boundaries. Minstrel performers often attempted to repress through ridicule the real interest in black cultural practices they nonetheless betrayed—minstrelsy's mixed erotic economy of celebration and exploitation, what Homi Bhabha would call its "ambivalence" ("Other" 18) and what my title loosely terms "love and theft." The very form of blackface acts—an investiture in black bodies—seems a manifestation of the particular desire to try on the accents of "blackness" and demonstrates the permeability of the color line. I depart from most other writers on minstrelsy, who have based their analyses on racial aversion, in seeing the vagaries of racial desire as fundamental to minstrel-show mimicry. It was cross-racial desire that coupled a nearly insupportable fascination and a self-protective derision with respect to black people and their cultural practices, and that made blackface minstrelsy less a sign of absolute white power and control than of panic, anxiety, terror, and pleasure. As it turned out, the minstrel show worked for over a hundred years to facilitate safely an exchange of energies between two otherwise rigidly bounded and policed cultures, a shape-shifting middle term in racial conflict which began to disappear (in the 1920s) once its historical function had been performed.[13] It appears that during this stretch of American cultural history the intercourse between racial cultures was at once so attractive and so threatening as to require a cultural marker or visible sign of cultural interaction. This requirement would eventually wither away, or in any case transmogrify, not least because of the minstrel show's success in introducing the cultures to each other. The blackface mechanism of cultural control, as John

Szwed has suggested, also provided a channel for the black cultural "contamination" of the dominant culture: "The fact that, say, a Mick Jagger can today perform in the same tradition without blackface simply marks the detachment of culture from race and the almost full absorption of a black tradition into white culture" (27). In the mid-nineteenth century, however, culture was "attached" to race with some tenacity; blackface acts both enforced and, in the end, remapped this regime.

As I point out in chapter 1, writing on the minstrel show has been inordinately partial. Minstrelsy, of course, was long enveloped in a reactionary nostalgia that desperately needed debunking; partisans of blackface have always longed for the imaginary day of the strumming Sambo.[14] A superficially similar (and still very questionable) tradition, however, has celebrated minstrelsy for its "blackness," seeing the phenomenon as a public forum for slave culture which might have liberating effects. Constance Rourke's chapter on minstrelsy in *American Humor* (1931), for example, gave modern force to what might be termed a "people's culture" position—one whose sources, as I show, can be found in the writings of Margaret Fuller, Walt Whitman, and others. The revival of this impulse had everything to do with a 1930s reclamation of the "folk," if not, as Warren Susman has suggested, with a new definition of "culture" itself (150–210): the extraordinary success of Marc Connelly's near-minstrel show *The Green Pastures* (1929), the anthropology of Franz Boaz, Ruth Benedict's *Patterns of Culture* (1934), the novels of John Steinbeck, Zora Neale Hurston's *Their Eyes Were Watching God* (1937), James Agee and Walker Evans's *Let Us Now Praise Famous Men* (1941), and so on. Rourke's genial view is a relatively benign, and to that extent unhistorical, one, though it has the virtue of acknowledging both the extensive effect of black cultural practices on blackface performance and the public effects of blackface itself. This position, in fact, was partially defended in Robert Toll's *Blacking Up: The Minstrel Show in Nineteenth-Century America* (1974), and some have ventured it in refurbished form, but it has not been a position to which scholars regularly recur.[15]

Harking back to a tradition of minstrel-show criticism that began with Frederick Douglass's articles in the *North Star*, scholars and writers initiated a long-awaited political revisionism in regard to minstrelsy beginning in 1958 with Ralph Ellison's "Change the Joke and Slip the Yoke" and crystallized—with attitude— in LeRoi Jones's brief remarks in *Blues People* (1963). The most notable instances of this revisionism include Nathan Huggins's powerful chapter on minstrelsy in *Harlem Renaissance* (1971) and Toll's *Blacking Up*. These works can indeed be taken as representative of the reigning view of minstrelsy as racial domination. James Dorman, for instance, writes: "The arrival of Jim Crow was to provide the final ingredient in the total pattern of antiblack prejudice" ("Strange" 118). In retrospect this necessary critique seems somewhat crude and idealist; in reading off from a text the stereotypes that a historical moment is presumed to have

7

required it is typically presentist, and in viewing minstrelsy as the nail in the coffin of cultural containment it is rather narrowly functionalist. Based on a politics of "positive" black images, images meant to replace racist types with what Stuart Hall terms the "essential black subject," this strategy still, in certain instances, offers the terms in which cultural struggle ought to be waged. At the same time, however, the engagement on the part of cultural critics with poststructuralist discourses, and a dismantling of binary racial categories in favor of multiply determined and positioned subjects, has begun to trouble the notion of "racial" representation itself. We must now recognize, as Hall argues, "that the central issues of race always appear historically in articulation, in a formation, with other categories and divisions" ("New" 28). To do so will require a much more sensitively historicist look at the uneven class, gender, and racial politics of forms such as the minstrel show. And it will require as well a subtler account of acts of representation. Where representation once unproblematically seemed to image forth its referent, we must now think of, say, the blackface mask as less a *repetition* of power relations than a *signifier* for them—a distorted mirror, reflecting displacements and condensations and discontinuities between which and the social field there exist lags, unevennesses, multiple determinations. It will take a good deal of decoding to get at the meanings of blackface minstrelsy.[16]

In contrast to both the populist and the revisionist views, which see minstrelsy's politics as univocal, my study documents precisely the historical contradictions and social conflicts the minstrel show opened up. It first reconstructs the antebellum cultural formation in which minstrelsy did its work (part I). One of our earliest culture industries, minstrelsy not only affords a look at the emergent historical break between high and low cultures but also reveals popular culture to be a place where cultures of the dispossessed are routinely commodified—and contested. The heedless (and ridiculing) appropriation of "black" culture by whites in the minstrel show, as many contemporaries recognized, was little more than cultural robbery, a form of what Marx called expropriation, which troubled guilty whites all the more because they were so attracted to the culture they plundered. Indeed, for a time in the late 1840s minstrelsy came to seem the most representative national art. In this way minstrelsy became a site of conflictual intensity for the politics of race, class, and nation.

This interpretation is particularly suggested by my readings of blackface minstrel forms (part II). Each of the last four chapters concerns itself with a particular social and political situation, set of texts, and theoretical problem. Reading minstrel music, lyrics, jokes, dances, burlesque skits, and illustrations in conjunction with working-class racial ideologies and the sex/gender system, I show how blackface minstrelsy embodied and intervened in Jacksonian racial politics. Underwritten by envy as well as repulsion, sympathetic identification as well as fear, the minstrel show continually transgressed the color line even as it made possible the formation of a self-consciously white working class. There was a good fit, for example, between the conflicted nature of the shows and the racial tendencies of their audiences, such that the artisan abolitionist constituency could rather benignly enjoy the same form of leisure that supported racist, antiabolitionist ridicule. This situation was aided by ideologies of working-class manhood, which shaped white men's contradictory feelings about black men. Because of the power of the black penis in white American psychic life, the pleasure minstrelsy's largely white and male audiences derived from their investment in "blackness" always carried a threat of castration—a threat obsessively reversed in white lynching rituals. Notwithstanding that this threat was itself part of the fascination, or at least a price white men appear to have paid gladly in patronizing blackface performances, the minstrel show was constructed along several lines of defense against it. This is not at all to claim that the defenses worked—only that their intermittent failure provided blackface with its longevity and power.

The moment of minstrelsy's greatest popularity (1846–54) was marked by a variety of bitter political controversies: labor struggles in New York and other major cities, the Wilmot Proviso debates over the extension of slavery, the Seneca Falls women's rights convention, the Astor Place theater riot, the Fugitive Slave Law and its aftermath, the Kansas-Nebraska bill, and others. In significant ways this historical moment suddenly made the misappropriations and distortions committed in minstrelsy politically dangerous. The conflictual character of minstrelsy only deepened with the approach of the gravest pre–Civil War threat to the social order of the Union, the debates over slavery that led to the Compromise of 1850. Stephen Foster's "Plantation Melodies" unwittingly conjured up the hydra-headed conflicts; these melodies, and the vast dissemination of *Uncle Tom's Cabin* in various politically divergent blackface theatrical productions—a kind of prelude to civil war on the stage—offer a lens through which to read a political crisis Michael Rogin has called "the American 1848," a revolution on American soil.

Given this formal and historical complexity, it is no surprise that minstrelsy has overwhelmed most attempts to study it in all its variousness and difficulty. The minstrel show was an entertainment form that called in turn on a variety of elements: folklore, dance, jokes, songs, instrumental tunes, skits, mock oratory, satire, and racial and gender cross-dressing or impersonation. From a variety of locales, including city, backwoods, small town, and frontier, it impinged on a history of intense class, racial, national, and gender formation. Scholars understandably most often take one or another aspect of minstrelsy for focused study rather than the whole; and the few comprehensive treatments of the minstrel show have without exception read the printed record (songsters, playlets, and so on) of what was in fact a negotiated and rowdy spectacle of performer and audience.[17] I have restricted this study to the antebellum decades, and to the minstrel show's performance amid the social and political life of (for the most part) New York City. Yet I have also attempted to do justice to minstrelsy's various constituent parts as well as to its audience and its historical role, and in this I make no plea for my own sagacity. I have unquestionably poached on academic territory in which I can claim at best amateur competence. Writing this book has convinced me, however, that such an interdisciplinary attempt is worth the gamble and, especially given the habits of specialists and subspecialists, is an opportunity rather than an embarrassment. In addressing my study to a variety of fields and disciplines, I mean not only to properly portray a complex phenomenon but to help solidify the claims of cultural studies as a practice.

Accordingly, this book has been oriented by several specific debates. One of these is, of course, the discussion of blackface minstrelsy, in particular its political status and effectivity as public performance. Also important are theoretical questions regarding the (post-Freudian) study of humor, the political interpretation of commercial popular music, the uses of folklore, the cultural exhibition of the body, and the political efficacy of melodrama. A related debate concerns the usefulness of film theory in the study of theater, a highly problematic but potentially generative development. Recent theoretical and political investigations of race, especially those oriented by psychoanalysis, are fundamental concerns, as are questions about the place of race in working-class culture and in the development of American nationhood.

Implicit in any work of this kind is also the question of American Studies as a field in (perhaps perennial) crisis and its relationship to cultural studies. The American Studies of a generation ago cast its vision over a wider expanse of American culture than is now sometimes recognized; and it often functioned as a left-liberal "culturalist" alternative to American New Criticism, however much it may now seem like the literary equivalent of the Truman administration. In fact there was a great deal of interchange between the British New Left and certain American Studies scholars, whether in the interested stateside reception of Raymond Williams's and Richard Hoggart's early work or the impact of Leo Marx's *Machine in the Garden* (1964) on the early figures of British cultural studies.[18] Of course, the older American Studies emphasis on "representative" texts and problems is out of date, while E. P. Thompson's (contemporaneous) definition of culture "as a whole way of conflict" ("Long" 33) has offered a decisive reorientation to a generation of cultural studies practitioners, including myself. Indeed, my focus on a highly elaborated if crudely executed popular stage form has arisen from the immense importance, in such a definition of culture, of cultural texts requiring relatively few "inherent resources" such as literacy or education and therefore offering relatively unmediated access to those whose struggles make history.[19] Sorely neglected in the academic study of cultures until very recently, such forms have usually been central to their time—certainly more influential than the great literature so often taken as culturally representative. Although American Studies has in some sense been a pioneer (e.g., Constance Rourke's *American Humor,* Henry Nash Smith's *Virgin Land*), it has restricted itself to addressing what is "most American" and exceptional about such forms rather than the richer questions of how cultures work, are contested, divide and cohere, or how transpersonal historical structures consort with human activity to produce social and political change.[20]

I try in these pages to help reorient the traditions of American Studies by asking questions about the role of culture in the political development of a specific national entity. The challenge here is to resist the tendency in American versions of cultural studies to examine culture apart from political structures and movements—an airless "politics" of the cultural rather than social and political cultures.[21] To this end the significance of current work in cultural studies lies in making it possible to situate the analysis of cultural *forms*, the various sorts of textuality and subjectivity most closely related to human agency, with regard to the analysis of social and cultural *formations*, the organizations, processes, and overdetermined conjunctures that bear most significantly on political life. The greatest yield of this work is an understanding of "historical forms of consciousness and subjectivity," in Richard Johnson's words (43)—as I see it, the chief concern and special ability of cultural studies.

If at this juncture we are to understand anything more about popular racial feeling in the United States, we must no longer be satisfied merely to condemn the terrible pleasures of cultural material such as minstrelsy, for their legacy is all around us. As Antonio Gramsci once remarked, the "starting-point of critical elaboration is the consciousness of what one really is, and is 'knowing thyself' as a product of the historical process to date which has deposited in you an infinity of traces, without leaving an inventory" (*Prison* 324). Only by beginning to inventory the deposits of feeling for which blackface performance has been responsible can we hope to acknowledge the social origins and psychological motives of "racial" impulses, reckonings, and unconscious reactions that lie so deep in most Caucasians as to feel inevitable and indeed natural. An equally urgent outcome of this undertaking will be to make ourselves aware of the resistant, oppositional, or emancipatory accents of the racial bad attitudes residing in American working-class culture today.

Love and Theft is thus perhaps a product of its political times in investigating the ironies of cultural reaction, the potential reversals in a context of defeat.[22] Like much of the recent cultural theory on which it draws, it has been marked by our age of "authoritarian populism," as Stuart Hall has termed it, in its tea leaf–reading documentation of culture-industry contradictions and subversions in the face of overwhelming odds.[23] There is, I would rush to add, justification for this anxious attention: not only was blackface minstrelsy a peculiarly unstable form, but the social realities to which it in part contributed demand careful sorting out. The left has too often construed black Americans as saboteurs of class-based politics, their presence acting as an impediment to "real" social change. No less than writing off white working-class racial feeling, blaming black people themselves for being obstacles in the path of the American experiment has been a nasty habit.[24] The story has usually taken the form of an imagined conspiracy of white liberals and black "extremists" who have foisted civil rights demands on to left initiatives and in the process affronted working-class whites. But, as Adolph Reed and Julian Bond observe, this tale presumes a prior equality between black and white, and consequently "denies the reality of explicitly racial stratification within the working class and a history of white working-class antagonism toward blacks—coexisting, certainly, with many exemplary instances of interracial solidarity—that stretches back through the 1863 New York draft riot" (733–34). This gnarled history stretches back indeed into the antebellum decades I consider here, and I advance a revivifying attention to its contradictions: the competing but sometimes collateral claims of black and white labor. The source of post–World War II conflicts in those of white workers versus black slaves and their abolitionist allies indicates the need to study carefully a moment when a possible interracial labor alliance went awry. Any vision of a renewed socialism demands that we consider race as more than merely "incidental" (as C. L. R. James urges) to the motors of political change. And if it is culture rather than shared work experience that primarily creates the conditions for social movements, one critical task is to achieve a renovated public culture through inquiries into popular forms such as the minstrel show.[25]

PART I

1

Blackface and Blackness:
The Minstrel Show in American Culture

> In the theatrical world, as in the aesthetic world more generally, ideology is always in essence the site of a competition and a struggle in which the sound and fury of humanity's political and social struggles are faintly or sharply echoed.
>
> —Louis Althusser

The current consensus on blackface minstrelsy is probably best summed up by Frederick Douglass's righteous response in the *North Star*. Blackface imitators, he said, were "the filthy scum of white society, who have stolen from us a complexion denied to them by nature, in which to make money, and pander to the corrupt taste of their white fellow citizens," a denunciation that nicely captures minstrelsy's further commodification of an already enslaved, noncitizen people (October 27, 1848). From our vantage point, the minstrel show indeed seems a transparently racist curiosity, a form of leisure that, in inventing and ridiculing the slow-witted but irrepressible "plantation darky" and the foppish "northern dandy negro," conveniently rationalized racial oppression. The culture that embraced it, we assume, was either wholly enchanted by racial travesty or so benighted, like Melville's Captain Delano, that it took such distortions as authentic. I want to suggest, however, that the audiences involved in early minstrelsy were not universally derisive of African Americans or their culture, and that there was a range of responses to the minstrel show which points to an instability or contradiction in the form itself. My project is to examine that instability for what it may tell us about the racial politics of culture in the years before the Civil War.

Writing in Horace Greeley's antislavery *New York Tribune* in 1855, an anonymous advocate of blackface minstrel songs celebrated the "earliest votaries of the colored opera":

> Why may not the banjoism of a Congo, an Ethiopian or a George Christy [one of the most famous blackface performers of the 1840s and 1850s], aspire to an equality with the musical and poetical delineators of all nationalities? . . . Absurd as may seem negro minstrelsy to the refined musician, it is nevertheless beyond doubt that it expresses the peculiar characteristics of the negro as truly as the great masters of Italy represent their more spiritual and profound nation-

15

ality. . . . [And] has there been no change in the feelings of the true originators of this music—the negroes themselves? . . . Plaintive and slow, the sad
soul of the slave throws into his music all that gushing anguish of spirit which
he dare not otherwise express. ("Black" 107)

Surprising lines, these, from a writer sympathetic to the idea of African-American
art. We tend not to associate an approving view of minstrelsy with a determination
to take slave culture seriously, let alone a determination to take minstrelsy *as* slave
culture. Moreover, the writer's egalitarian rhetoric links one of the strongest
antebellum cases on behalf of minstrel songs with a sympathetic (if typically
condescending) attitude toward black people. The motivating idea here is a
Herderian notion of the folk, articulated in the year of *Leaves of Grass* for much
the same reason: to celebrate the popular sources of a national culture. It is
possible, of course, to take such lines as evidence of the incomprehension that
greeted minstrelsy, a position that is certainly defensible. But it does not fully
account for the frequency of responses such as the one just quoted—the ready
imputation of folk authenticity to patently "impure" songs such as "Ole Dan
Tucker," "Jump Jim Crow," and "Zip Coon." Nor does it explain the desire to
put moderate racial attitudes and minstrel shows together.

Indeed, Margaret Fuller spoke in a similar vein about this cultural form. In
"Entertainments of the Past Winter," published in the *Dial* in 1842, she claimed
that Americans were "beggars" when it came to the arts of music and dancing:

Our only national melody, Yankee Doodle, is shrewdly suspected to be a scion
from British art. All symptoms of invention are confined to the African race,
who, like the German literati, are relieved by their position from the cares of
government. "Jump Jim Crow," is a dance native to this country, and one
which we plead guilty to seeing with pleasure, not on the stage, where we have
not seen it, but as danced by children of an ebon hue in the street. Such of the
African melodies as we have heard are beautiful. But the Caucasian race have
yet their rail-roads to make. . . . (52)

We will have occasion to return to the juxtaposition of American blacks with the
idea of governance, particularly in the notion of slaves as poet-legislators. Interesting here, in addition, is the assumption that the only music and dance which
are *not* false coin are those found in blackface minstrelsy, which represents, Fuller
hints, something like the folk culture of an American peasantry. These comments
begin to suggest that when, in the decades before the Civil War, northern white
men "blacked up" and imitated what they supposed was black dialect, music, and
dance, some people, without derision, heard Negroes singing.

Blackface minstrelsy as an African-American people's culture: this may seem
an odd view. But it is one perception of the minstrel show that has been understandably repressed in antiracist accounts of it. Most scholars have yet to appreciate W. E. B. Du Bois's belief that Stephen Foster compositions such as "Old
Black Joe" and "Old Folks at Home" were based on African-American themes;
Du Bois included them in his assertion that black music was the "only real

American music" ("Negro" 231; *Souls* 382). In *Black Manhattan,* James Weldon Johnson similarly remarked that minstrelsy originated on the plantation, and constituted the "only completely original contribution" of America to the theater (87). These judgments appear terribly misguided now, given that blackface minstrelsy's century-long commercial regulation of black cultural practices stalled the development of African-American public arts and generated an enduring narrative of racist ideology, a historical process by which an entire people has been made the bearer of another people's "folk" culture. We ought nonetheless to know how such positive assessments of the minstrel show were possible as well as wrong. Without a fuller understanding of blackface performance, one that includes the intensely conflicted set of responses it called forth, we miss the part it played in the racial politics of its time—the extent to which, for that matter, it *was* the racial politics of its time—from its northern emergence as an entr'acte in about 1830 to the various New York stage versions of *Uncle Tom's Cabin* in the mid-1850s.

In the pages that follow I return the minstrel show to a northeastern political context that was extremely volatile, one whose range can be seen in the antinomy of responses I have identified, themselves anticipatory of twentieth-century debates about the nature of the "popular." On one side there is a disdain for "mass"-cultural domination, the incorporation of black culture fashioned to racist uses; on the other a celebration of an authentic people's culture, the dissemination of black arts with potentially liberating results.[1] Let me suggest that one finds elements of both in early minstrelsy: there is as much evidence to locate in it the public emergence of slave culture (as Constance Rourke argued in *American Humor*) or pointed political protest (as David Grimsted and William Stowe have written) as there is to finger its racism, this last needing little demonstration. Ultimately, however, this stubborn dualism is an impoverished, not to say obsolete, way of thinking about one of America's first culture industries. Our simplistic (and almost completely ahistorical) understanding of minstrel shows comes partly as a result of swinging between one position and the other—or at least of the notion that these are our only choices.

Recent research into popular culture has allowed us to see the popular instead as a sphere characterized by cultural forms of social and political conflict, neither, in Gareth Stedman Jones's terms, entirely the "social control" of the ruling classes nor the "class expression" of the dominated. Because the popular is always *produced*, capitalized, it is hardly some unfettered time-out from political pressures, a space of mere "leisure"—a clear enough distinction in the case of minstrelsy—nor does it arise in some immediate way from collective popular desires. But, as Stuart Hall has insisted, neither does it passively mirror political domination taking place in other parts of the social formation, as though it were only epiphenomenal—a form of dominant-cultural "reinforcement," as commentators on the minstrel show have often said—or, in the Frankfurt School scenario, wholly administered and determined. Since the popular emerges at the intersection of received symbolic forms, audiences' experiences of authority and subordination in workplace, home, and social ritual, and new articulations by various producers of symbolic forms—local teachers and labor organizers, storytellers and journalists, theater managers and actors—it is itself a crucial place of contestation, with moments of resistance to the dominant culture as well as moments of supersession. Talking about the minstrel show this way reveals the most popular American entertainment form in the antebellum decades as a principal site of struggle in and over the culture of black people.[2] This struggle took place largely among antebellum whites, of course, and it finally divested black people of control over elements of their culture and over their own cultural representation generally. But it was based on a profound white investment in black culture which, for a time, had less certain consequences. My study documents in early blackface minstrelsy the dialectical flickering of racial insult and racial envy, moments of domination and moments of liberation, counterfeit and currency, a pattern at times amounting to no more than the two faces of racism, at others gesturing toward a specific kind of political or sexual danger, and all constituting a peculiarly American structure of racial feeling.

So far are we from any idea of what the vagaries of this structure of feeling might have been—the relationship of blackface to "blackness"—that it is useful to generate some sense of the contradictions and ambiguities in blackface representation and its place in American culture. Let me, for instance, elaborate what I mean in calling minstrelsy a popular form by returning briefly to the symptomatic moments of the debate I have sketched. Each position has its partial force, and taken together they define the range of possible forms and effects that could be produced in the minstrel show. To be sure, minstrelsy was an arena in which the efficient expropriation of the cultural commodity "blackness" occurred, demonstrated in what this *Atlantic Monthly* writer (writing in 1867) supposes is a hilarious account of "originator" T. D. Rice's first blackface performance in Pittsburgh around 1830:

> Rice prepared to take advantage of his opportunity. There was a negro in attendance at Griffith's Hotel, on Wood Street, named Cuff,—an exquisite specimen of his sort,—who won a precarious subsistence by letting his open mouth as a mark for boys to pitch pennies into, at three paces, and by carrying the trunks of passengers from the steamboats to the hotels. Cuff was precisely the subject for Rice's purpose. Slight persuasion induced him to accompany the actor to the theatre, where he was led through the private entrance, and quietly ensconced behind the scenes. . . . Rice, having shaded his own countenance to the "contraband" hue, ordered Cuff to disrobe, and proceeded to invest himself in the cast-off apparel. . . . [Onstage] the extraordinary apparition produced an instant effect. . . . The effect was electric. . . .
>
> Now it happened that Cuff, who meanwhile was crouching in dishabille under concealment of a projecting *flat* behind the performer, by some means received intelligence, at this point, of the near approach of a steamer to the Monongahela Wharf. Between himself and others of his color in the same line of business, and especially as regarded a certain formidable competitor called

Ginger, there existed an active rivalry in the baggage-carrying business. For Cuff to allow Ginger the advantage of an undisputed descent upon the luggage of the approaching vessel would be not only to forget all "considerations" from the passengers, but, by proving him a laggard in his calling, to cast a damaging blemish upon his reputation. Liberally as he might lend himself to a friend, it could not be done at that sacrifice. After a minute or two of fidgety waiting for [Rice's] song to end, Cuff's patience could endure no longer, and, cautiously hazarding a glimpse of his profile beyond the edge of the flat, he called in a hurried whisper: "Massa Rice, Massa Rice, must have my clo'se! Massa Griffif wants me,—steamboat's comin'!"

The appeal was fruitless. Massa Rice did not hear it, for a happy hit at an unpopular city functionary had set the audience in a roar in which all other sounds were lost. . . . [Another appeal went unheeded, when,] driven to desperation, and forgetful in the emergency of every sense of propriety, Cuff, in ludicrous undress as he was, started from his place, rushed upon the stage, and, laying his hand upon the performer's shoulder, called out excitedly: "Massa Rice, Massa Rice, gi' me nigga's hat,—nigga's coat,—nigga's shoes,— gi' me nigga's t'ings! Massa Griffif wants 'im,—STEAMBOAT'S COMIN'!!"

The incident was the touch, in the mirthful experience of that night, that passed endurance. (Nevin 609–10)

This passage, in all its woozy syntax and headlong rush, is probably the least trustworthy and most accurate account of American minstrelsy's appropriation of black cultural practices. Indeed this eulogy to the minstrel composer Stephen Foster reads something like a master text of the racial economy encoded in blackface performance. For one thing, it calls on minstrel devices (ventriloquized dialect, racial burlesque) to narrate the origins of minstrelsy, as if this particular narratable event generated or secreted "naturally" the formal means appropriate to it; its multiple frames (minstrelsy within minstrelsy) amount to so many techniques of black subordination. True to form, a diminished, not to say "black-faced" Cuff has replaced Rice as this account's center of attention. And its talk of opportunity and investment, lending and ownership, subsistence and competition is more preoccupied with cultural value than we might have expected. Its social unconscious, we might say, reveals a great deal of anxiety about the "primitive accumulation" it ostensibly celebrates.[3] Perhaps this is also why the passage is fully a third longer than what I have just quoted. The fascination with Cuff's nakedness, moreover, highlights the affair as one of male bodies, in which racial conflict and cultural exchange are negotiated between men. Cuff's stripping, a theft that silences and embarrasses him onstage but which nevertheless entails both his bodily presence in the show and the titillating threat that he may return to demand his stolen capital, is a neat allegory for the most prominent commercial collision of black and white cultures in the nineteenth century. Cultural expropriation is the minstrel show's central fact, and we should not lose sight of it.[4] But it is also a fact that needs explaining, for in itself it establishes little about the cultural commerce suggested by one performer's enthusiasm as he gathered material for his blackface act: "I shall be rich in black fun."[5]

Even in expropriation there was a strong white attraction to the material which surfaced in less malign ways. White people believed the counterfeit, often sympathetically, as I have begun to suggest; the blackface hieroglyph so fully unpacked in the *Atlantic Monthly* account went largely unread. There were, it is true, nudges and winks folded into claims like that of the Apollo Minstrels to be the "only original Negroes travelling," or in the *New York Herald*'s coy references to Christy's Minstrels as "the very pinks of negro singers."[6] But often, in the minds of many, blackface singers and dancers became, simply, "negroes." How else explain the tireless references to "these amusing darkies" (*New York Herald* January 21, 1848), as if the originals had somehow gotten lost? Early audiences so often suspected that they were being entertained by actual Negroes that minstrel sheet music began the proto-Brechtian practice of picturing blackface performers out of costume as well as in (see Fig. 1); and there are several existing accounts of white theatergoers mistaking blackface performers for blacks.[7] Even Mark Twain's mother, at her first (and presumably only) minstrel show, believed she was watching black performers. Like Margaret Fuller (and, as we shall see, Walt Whitman), Mark Twain was himself intrigued by what he called the "happy and accurate" representations of the minstrel show.[8]

Of course, belief in the authenticity of blackface hardly ruled out racial ridicule; the oscillation between currency and counterfeit in the minstrel show was related to but often discrete from the oscillation between sympathy and ridicule toward its representations. Indeed, the wayward valuations attached both to irony toward the fakes and belief in them make the task of gauging audience response a dizzying one. What was the precise mix of irony, false consciousness, interest, and interracial recognition in a white Union soldier's perception that two blacks in his barracks "look[ed] exactly like our minstrels" (Howe 91)? We are back where we began, but with a difference: although minstrelsy was indeed in the business of staging or producing "race," that very enterprise also involved it in a carnivalizing of race, as the range of critical response has begun to suggest, such that the minstrel show's ideological production became more contradictory, its consumption more indeterminate, its political effects more plural than many have assumed. It is worth asking what those effects could possibly have amounted to. Ultimately I would like to make some sense of the dialectical relationship noted in Constance Rourke's observation that "little Jim Crow appeared at almost the precise moment when *The Liberator* was founded" (*American* 98). What was the brief shared history of blackface minstrelsy and racial ideologies of liberation? And was their relationship a story of racist compensation, or were there unsuspected similarities?

Fig. 1. The Virginia Serenaders, 1844.
Courtesy of the Harvard Theatre Collection

A GENEALOGY OF JIM CROW

I begin with a brief genealogy of Jim Crow.[9] This will offer a glimpse of black-face's ambiguous modes of authority based on certain of its earlier, as well as its minstrel-show, manifestations. The virtue of the genealogy, as Fredric Jameson suggests, is that it defamiliarizes the cultural object, revealing from a diachronic perspective, as in an X ray, functional elements in forms such as minstrelsy that probably seem transparent enough (*Political* 139). Although it will be necessary to trace the formal contradictions noted here in the various appearances of blackface through to the American cultural contradictions they figure, this genealogy begins to suggest the range of purposes the black minstrel mask could serve, both onstage and in public. It thus constitutes a certain groundwork for that dialectic of white responses to "blackness" which I believe traversed not only the early minstrel show but antebellum racial feeling as well.[10]

It would certainly be a mistake to see the minstrel types that began to emerge in the late 1820s as continuous outgrowths of slave tales à la Constance Rourke, though there exist certain similarities. They should rather be placed at the intersection of slave culture and earlier blackface stage characters such as the harlequin of the commedia dell'arte, the clown of English pantomime and the clown of the American circus, the burlesque tramp, perhaps the "blackman" of English folk drama. This intersection establishes the political and emotional range within which minstrel songs characteristically worked. The twin infusion of these antecedents in minstrel representations lends a highly uncertain status to an already ambiguous stage tradition.[11] Clowns and harlequins are as often lovable butts of humor as devious producers of it; slave-tale tricksters are frequently (though not always) champions, heroes, backdoor victors for the weak over the strong. Early minstrel figures overlapped with each tradition, tending more or less toward self-mockery on the one hand and subversion on the other. The overlap was registered, first, in British productions such as *Cowardy, Cowardy, Custard; or Harlequin Jim Crow and the Magic Mustard Pot* (1836), which marked a trend beginning in the 1830s of appending the name Jim Crow to all sorts of British clowns and Punch-and-Judy figures;[12] and, second, in the animal tales early blackface performers set to music, not to mention the alleged black derivation of the "Jim Crow" tune itself (about which more in chapter 2).

This contradictory lineage, the stage trickster overdetermined by the slave trickster, highlights some hint of danger in the earliest blackface types which few have been willing to grant them. Consider T. D. Rice's mid-1830s version of "Clar de Kitchen":

> A jay bird sot on a hickory limb,
> He wink'd at me and I wink'd at him;
> I pick'd up a stone and I hit his shin,
> Says he you better not do dat agin.

> A Bull frog dress'd sogers close,
> Went in de field to shoot some crows;
> De crows smell powder and fly away,
> De Bull frog mighty mad dat day.[13]

Such small victories were won continually in early minstrelsy. Small and undoubtedly self-diminishing though they were, the coded triumphs of black men over sinister jaybirds and black crows over patrolling bullfrogs were triumphs all the same, reminiscent indeed of certain slave tales. It might even be said that part of the triumph lay precisely in their recalling slave lore, in which foxes flee roosters, goats terrorize lions, and Brer Rabbit gleefully taunts Wolf.

Other early minstrel characters veered much more toward an intentionally ridiculous blustering, inherited less from the slaves or conventional stage figures than from the Mike Finks and Davy Crocketts of southwestern humor. Whether plantation rustics (Jim Crow) or urban dandies (Zip Coon), these figures of exaggerated strength and overwhelming power, as Lawrence Levine has suggested, have little in common with the slave tricksters' underhanded manipulations and deceits (*Black* 104). There was thus a third tradition infusing the most common characters of antebellum minstrelsy, who, Nathan Huggins argues, were often little more than blackfaced versions of heroes from southwestern humor.[14] Characters based on those heroes, however, sometimes took on "black" lineaments as well (Toll 42); and there was in any case an inherited power that came with the bluster, however culturally fraudulent that bluster may have been. Selected verses from the first song sheet edition of "Jim Crow" (published by E. Riley in the early 1830s) capture this ambiguity:

> Come listen all you galls and boys
> I'se jist from Tuckyhoe,
> I'm goin to sing a little song,
> My name's Jim Crow.
>
> Weel about and turn about
> And do jis so,
> Eb'ry time I weel about
> And jump Jim Crow.
>
> Oh I'm a roarer on de fiddle,
> And down in old Virginny,
> They say I play de skyentific
> Like Massa Pagannini.
>
> • • •
>
> I'm a full blooded niggar,
> Ob de real ole stock,
> And wid my head and shoulder
> I can split a horse block.
>
> • • •

De great Nullification,
And fuss in de South,
Is now before Congress,
To be tried by word ob mouth.

Dey hab had no blows yet,
And I hope dey nebber will,
For its berry cruel in bredren,
One anoders blood to spill.

• • •

Should dey get to fighting,
Perhaps de blacks will rise,
For deir wish for freedom,
Is shining in deir eyes.

An if de blacks should get free,
I guess dey'll fee some bigger,
An I shall consider it,
A bold stroke for de nigger.

• • •

An I caution all white dandies,
Not to come in my way,
For if dey insult me,
Dey'll in de gutter lay.
(Dennison 51–57)

This is hardly the stuff of which revolutions are made; it was easy enough to patronize such happy-go-lucky bravado. Still, references to sectional conflict (Andrew Jackson's 1832–33 nullification fight with John C. Calhoun over states' rights) and to a black desire for freedom (only a couple of years after the Nat Turner insurrection), all in a context of general insolence, were certainly nothing to be laughed off. Like most of the potentially subversive moments of early minstrelsy, they are qualified by "darky" dialect (in the theater) and orthographic derision (on the page); but in the mouth of the very figure who had begun to make the question of national unity an issue, such lyrics could be dangerous, even if it was understood that the singer need not be taken seriously. One ought not immediately assent to the anthropological truism that social formations are always buttressed by the permission of certain experiences not normally permitted. With regard to antebellum minstrelsy so much remains to be seen. As Barbara Babcock-Abrahams notes, "Any form of symbolic inversion has an implicitly radical dimension" (183). We should in any case avoid the essentialist notion that such representations are *inherently* anything, for given the right context, Peter Stallybrass and Allon White imply, they may indeed take on a transformative capacity (14).

These ambiguities were owing in part to the iconography such figures employed—that of blackface and male transvestism—features also commonly found together in public uses of blackface. Quite strikingly, many minstrel performers began their careers in the circus, perhaps even developing American

24

blackface out of clowning (whose present mask in any case is clearly indebted to blackface), and continually found under the big top a vital arena of minstrel performance. Clowning is an uncanny kind of activity, scariest when it is most cheerful, unsettling to an audience even as it unmasks the pretentious ringmaster. Blackface performers, often inspiring a certain terror as well as great affection, relied precisely on this doubleness. Ralph Ellison locates their specifically American resonance:

> When the white man steps behind the mask of the [blackface] trickster his freedom is circumscribed by the fear that he is not simply miming a personi-fication of his disorder and chaos but that he will become in fact that which he intends only to symbolize; that he will be trapped somewhere in the mystery of hell . . . and thus lose that freedom which, in the fluid, "traditionless," "classless" and rapidly changing society, he would recognize as the white man's alone. ("Change" 53)

The black mask offered a way to play with collective fears of a degraded and threatening—and male—Other while at the same time maintaining some sym-bolic control over them. Yet the intensified American fears of succumbing to a racialized image of Otherness were everywhere operative in minstrelsy, continu-ally exceeding the controls and accounting, paradoxically, for the minstrel show's power, insofar as its "blackness" was unceasingly fascinating to performers and audiences alike. This combined fear of and fascination with the black male cast a strange dread of miscegenation over the minstrel show, but evidently did not preclude a continual return to minstrel miming.

Far from simple indulgence, however, the returns began to take on the aura of attempted mastery, of a culture trying to contain what Ellison calls "disorder and chaos" but which could more historically be called intermixture and insurrec-tion.[15] The effete but potent black "dandy" figure incarnated these threats, as in "Long Tail Blue" (1827):

> As I was going up Fulton Street,
>   I hollerd arter Sue,
> The watchman came and took me up,
>   And spoilte my long tail blue.
> • • •
> If you want to win the Ladies hearts,
>   I'll tell you what to do;
> Go to a tip top Tailor's shop,
>   And buy a long tail blue.[16]

"Raw, undomesticated bodily and collective power," as Victor Turner would have it, the blackface trickster, "long tail blue" or not, suggests white men's obsession with a rampageous black penis ("Myth" 580). As Ellison puts it, "The mask was the thing (the 'thing' in more ways than one)" ("Change" 49). Bold swagger, irrepressible desire, sheer bodily display: in a real sense the minstrel man *was* the penis, that organ returning in a variety of contexts, at times ludicrous, at others rather less so.[17] Such contexts were contradictory in any case, invoking the power of "blackness" while deriding it, in an effort of cultural control, through the very convention that produced its power—the greasepaint and burnt cork of blackface.

Transvestism, of course, is subject to similar instabilities, though, as Marjorie Garber has powerfully argued, male cross-dressing can resist the stasis of ambiguity and thoroughly undermine traditional gender categories.[18] Garber herself admits, however, that women often become the target of such humorous disguises. This is certainly the case with minstrelsy's many "wench" characters (played by men at a time when women regularly appeared on the legitimate stage), which offer one of the most revealing discourses on male sexuality in America at midcentury.[19]

Gal from the South.

Ole massa bought a colored gal,
  He bought her at the south;
Her hair it curled so very tight
  She could not shut her mouth.
Her eyes they were so bery small,
  They both ran into one,
And when a fly light in her eye,
  Like a June bug in de sun.

Her nose it was so berry long,
  It turned up like a squash,
And when she got her dander up
  She made me laugh, by gosh;
Old massa had no hooks or nails,
  Or nothin' else like that,
So on this darkie's nose he used
  To hang his coat and hat.

One morning massa goin' away,
  He went to git his coat,
But neither hat nor coat was there,
  For she had swallowed both;
He took her to a tailor shop,
  To have her mouth made small,
The lady took in one long breath,
  And swallowed tailor and all.[20]

This portrait is fairly typical of the representation of black women on the minstrel stage, whether simply narrated or fully acted out; the two modes occurred simultaneously as often as not, the narrative detailing the jokey blazon, the oblivious "wench" ridiculed in person on another part of the stage. The anxieties aroused by such figures are also typical: the empowering insistence of the two "boughts" attempts to cancel the threatening open mouth (later to be "made small"), while the phallic nose and the engulfing, vaginal throat finally wreak revenge on the master.

White men's fear of female power was dramatized with a suspiciously draconian punitiveness in early minstrelsy, usually in the grotesque transmutations of its female figures. It is as if that fear were so fundamental that only a major effort of surveillance—like a dream, revealing its anxieties even as it devises its censors—would do. The widespread prostitution in the theater's notorious third tier, the literal analogue of the song's wish to buy women, comes to seem an ugly kind of compensatory space given the unruliness of these stage figures, if the figures did not themselves contain the female threat.[21] These "female" bodies, it is true, were "also" male, and minstrel performers did not hesitate to flirt with the homosexual content of blackface transvestism (the master's hat on the black "woman's" nose), which no doubt created an atmosphere of polymorphous license that could blur conventional gender outlines (for men). But a flight from such "compromising" subtexts may in fact have produced the reassertion of masculinity in misogynist representations, which usually constituted the reactionary face of a perhaps more "undecidable" racial masquerade.

When we turn from these dramatic roles to the public display of the blackface convention, we find as long a history. Victor Turner defends such displays—in parades, protests, carnivals, processions—as a mode of "public reflexivity," during which societies think in sometimes displaced and condensed ways about their forms and functions. He links them to "times of radical social change," when they can form part of the "repertoire of prophetic leaders who mobilize the people against invaders or overlords threatening their deep culture" ("Frame" 36). For this reason Barbara Babcock-Abrahams has likened stage tricksters to E. J. Hobsbawm's "primitive rebels," those backward, marginal antinomians who demonstrate quite literally that "oppression can be turned upside down" and who inspire myths and legends about their lives (Hobsbawm 24). Natalie Davis has more dialectically described these public performances as both harmless communal "safety valves" that deflect attention from social reality and proposals of new social paradigms or models; they "can on the one hand perpetuate certain values of the community (even guarantee its survival), and on the other hand criticize political order" (97). In conjunction with transvestism, the blackface mask has indeed been worn as an equivocal emblem of popular resistance, on behalf, variously—even simultaneously—of tradition and innovation. (The Boston Tea Party, with its howling "Indians" and "blacks," is only the most famous American occasion.) In her essay "Women on Top," Davis describes several instances of "ritual and festive inversion." In the Beaujolais of the 1770s, for example, "male peasants blackened their faces and dressed as women and then attacked surveyors measuring their lands for a new landlord" (147). The "Whiteboys" of Ireland, for about a decade (the 1760s), dressed in long white frocks and blackened their faces, setting themselves up as an "armed popular force to provide justice for the poor, 'to restore the ancient commons and redress other grievances'" (149); they tore down enclosures, punished greedy landowners, and forced masters to release unwilling apprentices. They referred to themselves as "fairies," and signed them-selves "Ghostly Sally"—prototypes, says Davis, of the Molly Maguires and Rib-bon Societies of the nineteenth century (149).

In each of these instances the "unruly" resonances of blackness and female-ness emerged from the dramatic frame into public, where they were put to new uses by men in a political realm that obviously excluded both blacks and women. Davis observes:

> On the one hand, the disguise freed men from the full responsibility for their deeds and perhaps, too, from fear of outrageous revenge upon their manhood. After all, it was mere women [or mere blacks, or indeed black women] who were acting in this disorderly way. On the other hand, the males drew upon the sexual power and energy of the unruly woman and on her license (which they had long assumed at carnival and games)—to promote fertility, to defend the community's interests and standards, and to tell the truth about unjust rule. (149)

There was no immediate internal racial context for blackface in these examples, but the European slave trade provided the broadest conditions of possibility; and the assumed inferiority, sexuality, license, and perhaps even sense of injustice associated with women were clearly ascribed to black people as well. Davis does not mention whether blackface was seen as representational rather than abstract or "metaphysical" (recall the diabolical associations with blackness that Winthrop Jordan extensively documented in *White over Black*), but there is no question that by the late eighteenth century blackface had taken on representational force, as the many sentimentally "noble" black characters on the British stage illustrate. The dynamic of the processional mask in these instances thus preserves the ascription of certain detested qualities to "blackness" while momentarily paying tribute to their power, a power that even in peasants' or workers' movements is compromised by such ascription. Herein lay the meaning of blackface in the American context of rioting and revelry, though it is perhaps not surprising that in such a conflictual racial scene the mask was increasingly used for reactionary purposes.

Susan Davis has demonstrated that in militia burlesques and Christmas street festivities, public "masking"—the assumption through disguise of a new or in-verted identity—became common in northern American cities after the 1820s, precisely contemporary with the rise of minstrelsy (and over against similar tradi-tions of black pageantry).[22] During carnivalesque Christmas Eve celebrations, for instance, roving young working-class men parodied the militia, marched to the rough music of kitchen-utensil instruments, and brawled on street corners. On one occasion in Philadelphia in 1834, one hundred men in intentionally makeshift uniforms conducted elaborate sham maneuvers, accompanied, one newspaper said, by a masked band of "Indians, hunters, Falstaffs, Jim Crows and non-descripts." Women and blacks, as usual, were the most frequent sources of disguise. While only public transvestism, not blackface, brought a stiff fine—a

28

fact that underscores both the permissiveness of the popular theater and the possible radicalism of men in drag during this period—blackface cross-dressing, as in its extended European history, was a popular favorite. Such disguises appear to have served similarly duplicitous purposes as those of Natalie Davis's peasants, but the American context added an even more troubling dimension. Gang attacks on blacks, mobbings of black churches, and battles between black and white gangs were commonplace holiday occurrences.[23] Other racially motivated mobs repeated the pattern: during the 1834 Philadelphia race riot in the Moyamensing district, some of the antiabolitionist rioters who attacked the homes of well-to-do blacks, burned black churches, and destroyed racially integrated places of leisure wore black masks and shabby coats (Runcie 209).

This "blackface-on-Black violence," as David Roediger has called it, would seem to indicate a fairly direct correspondence between racial hostility, public masking, and the minstrel show (*Wages* 106). In many instances we find this to be the case, but such a notion generally underrates the complexity of both ante-bellum racial politics and minstrelsy itself. Susan Davis suggests of the Christmas celebrations, for instance, that "masking made an ambiguous statement about race despite its violent mocking tone, for blackface found use as a way to play with racial identity, important in a city where black inferiority was taken for granted yet segregation was incomplete" ("Making" 193). Stage blackface was to be called on to negotiate just such contradictions in the culture of the antebellum American popular classes—between "white egalitarianism" and interracial urban prac-tices,[24] or between antislavery and antiabolitionism—called on so frequently, in fact, that its primary purpose appears to have been to provide "imaginary" resolu-tions to intractable social conflicts. Moreover, if minstrelsy was a theatrical cele-bration of how deeply American racism is "embedded into a sense of racial and class affection and even envy" (Grimsted and Stowe 95), this contradictory struc-ture occasionally witnessed unexpected returns of indentificatory desire.[25] At the very least, symbolic crossings of racial boundaries—through dialect, gesture, and so on—paradoxically engage and absorb the culture being mocked or mimicked (Szwed 27–28). Acting black: a whole social world of irony, violence, negotiation, and learning is contained in that phrase.[26]

Minstrel representations, then, were not continuous with either earlier dra-matic blackface figures or the deployment of blackface in rioting and revelry; although in certain cases there clearly were borrowings and affinities, these were scarcely all structurally "the same." Such traditions do, however, highlight a feature of American blackface masking that critics have been slow to recog-nize: an unstable or indeed contradictory power, linked to social and political conflicts, that issues from the weak, the uncanny, the outside. Above all, the slippery political valences of the traditions I have outlined are instructive. For it was with precisely this slipperiness that the minstrel mask resonated: a derisive celebration of the power of blackness; blacks, for a moment, ambiguously, on top.

PEOPLE'S CULTURE OR CULTURAL DOMINATION?

To put it another way, the early minstrel show was a Janus-faced figure for the cultural relationship of white to black in America, a relationship that even in its dominative character was far from self-explanatory. The duplicity of this cultural form is suggested not only by my genealogy, minstrelsy's formal makeup, but also by its role in American racial discourses. In many kinds of racially fraught cultural production—novels, cultural histories, and minstrel commentaries no less than antebellum blackface performance—minstrelsy has been a ground of American racial negotiation and contradiction, based on the antebellum collision course of competing modes of production and the various historical transformations in its aftermath. From this perspective certain representative critical engagements with the minstrel tradition turn out to be little less than furtive serial positions in a debate on American racial politics. The critical problem announced in this section's title—people's culture versus cultural domination—is thus an ideological problem of the broadest import, and it bears so much on the minstrel show's place in American culture that we ought to do what we can to unpack it before we attempt to supersede it. The fact is that these two positions both have their paradigmatic nineteenth-century instances: Mark Twain's vexed relationship to the minstrel tradition and Frederick Douglass's various writings on it in the *North Star*. In their nineteenth-century guises, however, these perspectives are actually more ambivalences than positions, betraying slippages, coming off conflicted. Like the traditions they exemplify, they are worth examining for what they tell us about minstrelsy's role in the racial politics of American culture.

As I have said, the position favoring minstrelsy as a people's culture typically celebrates the minstrel show's folk authenticity, its elevation of black types and black culture through blackface to a place in the national mythology.[27] The rather revealing problem inherent in this position, however, is that it regularly slips into an indulgence of racist typing. Mark Twain's avowed love of minstrelsy—"if I could have the nigger show back again in its pristine purity and perfection I should have but little further use for opera" (*Autobiography* 59)—is contradictory in just this way. Twain first saw rural minstrel productions in early-1840s Hannibal, where they burst on the unwitting town as a "glad and stunning surprise":

> The minstrels appeared with coal-black hands and faces and their clothing was a loud and extravagant burlesque of the clothing worn by the plantation slave of the time; not that the rags of the poor slave were burlesqued, for that would not have been possible; burlesque could have added nothing in the way of extravagance to the sorrowful accumulation of rags and patches which constituted his costume; it was the form and color of his dress that was burlesqued. (*Autobiography* 59)

This perception is far from incautious. Twain even observes that minstrels had "buttons as big as a blacking box," collapsing blackface masquerade, the means of its artifice, and an echo of one of its literal sources—Negro bootblacks—in a single self-conscious figure. His involvement here, however, soon outstrips all moderation:

> The minstrel used a very broad negro dialect; he used it competently and with easy facility and it was funny—delightfully and satisfyingly funny. . . . [Minstrels'] lips were thickened and lengthened with bright red paint to such a degree that their mouths resembled slices cut in a ripe watermelon. . . . The minstrel troupes had good voices and both their solos and their choruses were a delight to me as long as the negro show continued in existence. (*Autobiography* 59–61)

Twain's response marks a real (and perhaps typical) attraction to and celebration of black culture. Indeed, in *Following the Equator* (1897) he notes his love of beautiful black bodies and his disgust for white ones. But when such observations do not fall into derision, they are clearly the patronizing obverse of it, and at the very least signify an unexamined investment in exoticism. Ralph Ellison's remark to the effect that *Huckleberry Finn*'s Jim rarely emerges from behind the minstrel mask is to the point here.[28]

Huckleberry Finn (1884), as more than one critic has observed, was not only written but situated in minstrelsy's boom period. Anthony Berret has argued that this fact accounts for the odd indebtedness of the novel's language, rhetorical strategies, and structure to blackface minstrelsy: the preponderance of comic dialogues between Jim and Huck (much of the comedy at Jim's expense); the burlesques of both elite and popular literature; and the tripartite comic dialogue-olio-burlesque structure.[29] In the spring of 1882 Twain visited George Washington Cable and Joel Chandler Harris in New Orleans, and suggested that they do a lecture tour (which he called a circus or menagerie) to include William Dean Howells and Thomas Bailey Aldrich. As Berret points out, this authorial circus was, in conception at least, little more than the variety acts of a minstrel show; and the reading tour that finally materialized, with Cable's straight man countering Twain's comic, found both authors reading the roles of black characters onstage, Cable even singing songs (Berret 38). It was during this tour that American audiences first heard parts of *Huckleberry Finn*, notably the "King Sollermun" and "How come a Frenchman doan' talk like a man?" passages, scenes whose fit with the minstrel tradition is rather close. These passages may even have been expressly written, after the novel's completion, for readings in just such a context (Woodard and MacCann 5). The ideological complexity of this affair is compounded by the fact that Cable rather remarkably wrote a stinging rebuke of southern racism, "The Freedman's Case in Equity," which appeared during the tour in the same issue of *Century Magazine* that printed an excerpt from *Huck Finn*. But this perhaps collective commitment did not prevent blackface tones from creeping into the readings, or Twain from naming one of his offerings "Can't Learn a Nigger to Argue," a title he changed only at Cable's behest.[30] These events no doubt put a highly ambiguous spin on America's greatest nineteenth-century political novel, but they indicate as well that the contradiction between the book's overt politics and its indebtedness to the minstrel show was much less cumbrous in the nineteenth century. Many antiracist arguments, that is, were unfortunately not so far from the exoticism and hierarchical assumptions of the minstrel tradition. The ideological cement of such a seemingly outrageous yoking was of course nineteenth-century sentimentalism—"romantic racialism," as George Fredrickson has termed it—which underwrote the widespread and arguably radical attraction of an African-American people's culture even as it postulated innate differences between the "Anglo-Saxon" and "African" races.

Regrettably, the recent major histories of sentimental or women's culture find no place for racial categories. Neither Ann Douglas's *Feminization of American Culture* nor Mary Kelley's *Private Woman, Public Stage,* for example, pauses over the centrality of the passive, sentimentalized, often male slave in the mid–nineteenth-century culture of feeling; even Jane Tompkins's soteriological reading of *Uncle Tom's Cabin* deemphasizes the racial component of that novel's power. In fact Tompkins's reading is compelling because the sentimentalist strategies for representing white women and blacks were often identical, each image lending the other emotional and political force. "Blackness" was indeed a primary site of the religious appreciation of the emotions that came with the decline of Calvinism. In the 1830s, Fredrickson observes, theories of Negro personality were in a state of relative flux; the debate was largely one between "environmentalist defenders of a single human nature and proponents of deep-seated racial differences" (*Black* 101). With the emergence of the "American school of ethnology" in the 1840s and 1850s, however, which argued the case for "polygenesis," or the separate creation of the races as distinct species (there were biblical versions of this argument as well), both sides of the dialogue increasingly assumed the fundamental difference of the races. A new kind of theoretical fluidity now entered the picture. On the polygenetic view, blacks were intellectually inferior because in thrall to the emotions. But since this notion was closer to a racial relativism of the Herderian variety—that the various races make contributions of their special "gifts" to humanity—than to a hierarchical racism, both evangelical religion and literary romanticism could virtually recuperate such a belief into an ideology of black superiority. As William Ellery Channing put it in 1840: "We are holding in bondage one of the best races of the human family. The negro is among the mildest and gentlest of men" (50). Like women, blacks were considered creatures of feeling at a time when feeling was paramount in the culture; what fund of emotion the "go-ahead-ative," aggressive Anglo-Saxon lacked, blacks would surely supply. Thus, stereotypes and arguments of this kind already in place in the plantation school of fiction tended to be taken over, but *revalued:* slavery was evil, for example, because it destroyed the great good nature, the blithe innocence, and above all the family structure of, in Methodist Bishop Gilbert Haven's words, "the choice blood of America." Blacks, it came to be argued, were not only exemplars of virtue but natural Christians.[31]

Nor was the antislavery movement exempt from such condescension. Awkward attempts to rewrite what were believed to be natural differences into special racial capacities resulted in notions of racial "variety without inferiority," as Lydia Maria Child, editor of the *National Anti-Slavery Standard,* put it: "Flutes on different keys . . . will harmonize the better."[32] Although the idea was to move "feminine" values to the cultural center, such arguments relied on the black inferiority they sought to displace. Karen Sánchez-Eppler has suggested that this tendency derived in part from the final asymmetry of white women and blacks in such rhetoric. Child's story "Mary French and Susan Easton" (1834), for example, urges the sentimental ideal of equality-in-difference, but can imagine even this outcome only by obliterating the racial lineaments of the good Negro figure, as though blackness, even when feminized, were inferior by definition (Sánchez-Eppler 39). Black leaders themselves, it should be said, did little to contest such unwittingly hierarchical thinking. Martin Delany, perhaps the most vehement of midcentury black nationalists, spoke of his race on several occasions as a repository of natural aestheticism and morality; thus it flourished in music and oratory, while whites "probably excel in mathematics, . . . commerce and internal improvements." Frederick Douglass attributed his implicitly feminized "love of letters" to the Negro ancestry of his mother rather than to his Anglo-Saxon paternity.[33] Such widespread attitudes, Wilson Moses argues, may have been responsible for the emphasis of black leaders from Douglass to Booker T. Washington on specifically industrial training (46).

The key text of explicitly antislavery romantic racialism is of course Harriet Beecher Stowe's *Uncle Tom's Cabin* (1852). With the character of Uncle Tom we are already on our way to the gentle, childlike, self-sacrificing, essentially *aesthetic* slave Mark Twain created in Jim and thought he recognized on the minstrel stage; and it is instructive to remind ourselves that *Uncle Tom's Cabin* and *Huck Finn* were among the most powerful antislavery or antiracist novels of the nineteenth century. All the more remarkable, then, that Tom bears so much resemblance to the many sentimental slaves of Stephen Foster's complacent "Plantation Melodies": Old Uncle Ned, Old Black Joe, and so on. Very little distinguishes the types in such minstrel songs from those in Stowe or Twain. Loosed from Stowe's rhetoric into stage tableaux, they are quite continuous with the minstrel tradition; T. D. Rice, who began his career in the 1830s playing Jim Crow, ended it in the 1850s playing Uncle Tom on the stage. And *Huckleberry Finn,* as Anthony Berret observes, seems nowhere closer to the sentimental ethos of Foster's songs than during Huck's many fictional tales of disunited families, or his returns to the raft and an emotional Jim (42–43). If Foster's "Old Folks at Home" or "Oh! Susanna"—somewhat better versions of staple minstrel themes in the 1840s—depend for their effect on the pathos culled from black families forced to split up or attempting to reunite, Twain's novel relies on similar "familial" reunions whose resonance derives from the stereotyped emotionality of the black slave.

Notwithstanding the desperate ambiguity contained in the sentimental makeover of these black types, in their culture they were capable of wielding enormous power. As William Taylor has written, "To attribute to someone the simplicity of a child, . . . especially in the middle of the nineteenth century, was a compliment of the first order, and dangerous, too, if the child were to be mistreated and sympathy was not the response sought for" (305). Hence the somewhat backhanded power of *Uncle Tom's Cabin* and, in a more vestigial way, *Huckleberry Finn*. And yet, obviously, such a racial philosophy very quickly fell into one of white supremacy. Romantic racialist thinking, George Fredrickson notes, "was one aspect of the retreat from environmentalism and the Enlightenment view of a common human nature" (*Black* 125). At this point the minstrel show rears its ungainly head; but precisely because it reveled in the contradictions I have outlined, unmistakably present in the work of Mark Twain, among others, we must attend to the rather gnarled effects of blackface performance in the context of nineteenth-century racial ideologies.

To be sure, the ambiguity easily empties out of this perspective, and its later nineteenth-century instances represent little more than the ritual, reactionary celebration of an ideologically rigidified minstrelsy meant to counter American antislavery practice.[34] (In intention at least *Huckleberry Finn* is something of an "immanent critique" of this tradition.) In the guise of what has come to be called "scientific racism"—a set of post-Darwinian explanations for the arrested development of blacks—this period's anthropology straitjacketed the relative fluctuations of earlier racial ideologies. Thus legitimized, white historians and memoirists in the nostalgic mood frequently recounted stories of the minstrel show's origins, tales of famous performers, even formal histories of the representation of blacks on stage, assuming (when they thought about it at all) that minstrelsy's scurrilous representations of black people were scrupulously authentic. "Their gibes, their gambols, their songs, their flashes of merriment," wrote one such historian, "still linger in our eyes and in our ears; and before many readers scores of quaint figures with blackened faces will no doubt dance to half-forgotten tunes all over these pages" (Hutton 144). The nostalgia of this view is ultimately for a simpler, pre-emancipation America: "That such [distinguished men] should have appeared at a leading theatre, between the acts, in plantation dress and blackened face, shows perhaps better than anything else the respectable position held by the negro minstrel half a century ago" (Hutton 140). By 1915 Brander Matthews of Columbia University was sadly detailing minstrelsy's decline, which he attributed to the fact that blackface performers were less and less true to life, increasingly "content to be comic without any effort to catch the special comicality of the darky" (758). This emphasis—deriving just as much as Twain's from the idea of blackface as a people's culture—is racist either by default or design, and it has infected its share of modern theater historians. The important point about this tendency is not only that it deserves censure but that it, no less than the others, stands for the historical existence of a certain kind of audience response.

It was thus critical that a revisionist corrective, denouncing minstrelsy's patent inauthenticity, its northern white origins, its self-evidently dominative character, should have come to displace the more complacent views.[35] This critique, inaugurated by Frederick Douglass, later sustained treatments of the minstrel stage in novels such as Paul Laurence Dunbar's *Sport of the Gods* (1901) and Wallace Thurman's *The Blacker the Berry* (1929); both fictionalize black stage performances derived from the minstrel tradition to represent some version of racial false consciousness—in Dunbar the facile, corrupted world of northern urban Negroes, in Thurman an indulgence by color-conscious blacks of racial caricature. In certain ways, however, this position is least satisfactory as historical and cultural analysis when it works best as antiracist politics. This is not to urge a position that, somehow avoiding politics, might get the emphases right for once. On the contrary, the minstrel tradition is still too present for us to take antiracist critiques of it for granted. Rather, we must better historicize the minstrel show, for in fact we remain ignorant of exactly what its antebellum political range happened to be. It strikes me as tautological to catalogue racist stereotypes from a time when slavery existed in fifteen states. In their indispensable focus on minstrelsy's oppressive dimension, revisionist accounts leave perfectly intact the cultural dualism—wholly authentic or wholly hegemonic?—that I want to complicate. Outmoded antiracist strategies of reversal and inversion, of simply turning the polarities of racist discourse around, must give way to a wider recognition of the complexities of white subject formation and subjectivity, and of the multiple determinations that make race such a complex lived social reality.[36]

Among these determinations number primarily social class and the sex/gender system. One might return briefly here to *Huckleberry Finn*. Pap's notorious rant about a "free nigger . . . from Ohio" who, in his wealth, his knowledge of languages, and his right to vote, threatens the status of Pap's own working-class whiteness instances one way in which class overdetermines if not overrules race in my account.[37] Conversely, Twain's sly construction of this scene so that Pap, covered with mud after a drunken night in the gutter, is actually blacker than the hated "mulatter" free man suggests the underlying "racial" equations between black and working-class white men that occasionally called forth in the minstrel show interracial recognitions and identifications no less than the imperative to disavow them. And the fact that Twain's fantasy of racial harmony, of Jim and the adolescent Huck, could occur only by excluding conventional manhood altogether reminds us here of the gender dynamic through which the intersections of race and class, in the minstrel show as elsewhere, were lived. When one notes as well that those who "blacked up" and those who witnessed minstrel shows were often working-class *Irish* men, the complex picture of the blackface institution and its audiences is complete. Minstrelsy's role as a mediator of northern class, racial, and ethnic conflict—all largely grounded in a problematic of masculinity—has much to do with the equivocal character of blackface representations. This conflict can be seen to underlie the minstrel show's most politically productive and politically regressive moments. That moments of each kind occurred has not yet been adequately accounted for.

Certain nineteenth-century revisionists were, however, aware of this complexity. James Monroe Trotter, for example, though cognizant of what he called the "often malicious caricaturing" of the race to which he belonged, posed the "fine *musical* achievements" of the black Georgia Minstrels against "severe and somewhat sweeping" denunciations by other critics.[38] This, too, at the most virulently racist moment (the late nineteenth century) in the history of black representation. The most careful assessment of this kind, however, was also the earliest. As I began with one of Frederick Douglass's disdainful comments from the *North Star,* so I will end with his 1849 article on a short-lived black minstrel troupe, Gavitt's Original Ethiopian Serenaders. I believe he has the clearest sense of any contemporary as to what was at stake in early minstrelsy—its limitations, possibilities, and ultimate importance—and has therefore guided my own interpretations. Douglass begins:

> Partly from a love of music, and partly from curiosity to see persons of color exaggerating the peculiarities of their race, we were induced last evening to hear these Serenaders [in Rochester, New York]. The Company is said to be composed entirely of colored people; and it may be so. We observed, however, that they, too had recourse to the burnt cork and lamp black, the better to express their characters, and to produce uniformity of complexion. (141)

Conscious or not, there is a doubleness in that word "characters" (inner self? dramatic role?) which begins to capture Douglass's insight into blackface performance: that "blackness" is a matter of display or theater, as Melville would dramatize in "Benito Cereno" (1855).[39] It is reiterated in his charge that the Gavitts' singing was "not even a tolerable representation of the character of colored people"; indeed, Douglass signifies, "their attempts at it showed them to possess a plentiful lack of it" (141). "Blackness," then, is not innate but produced, a cultural construction. Douglass inverts the racist logic of minstrelsy and locates its actual function of staging racial categories, boundaries, and types even when these possessed little that a black man could recognize as "authentic." That is to say, Douglass also clarifies the way the blackface convention *disguised* "blackness," marking this black troupe's race first as hearsay ("said to be"), and then as latent possibility ("it may be").[40] But this disguise did not close down the political play of blackface; in a culture where "blackness" was construct and exhibition, blackface kept it on display and up for grabs, politically speaking. Although Douglass does not extend his argument to white performers, he does concede that the production of "blackness" remains a potential source of political advantage:

> We are not sure that our readers will approve of our mention of those persons, so strong must be their dislike of everything that seems to feed the flame of

American prejudice against colored people; and in this they might be right; but we think otherwise. It is something gained, when the colored man in any form can appear before a white audience; and we think that even this company, with industry, application, and a proper cultivation of their taste, may yet be instrumental in removing the prejudice against our race. (142)

Douglass defined blackface minstrelsy, a few months before the 1850 Compromise debates, as a site of political struggle for representation, debased and suspect though it may have been. "Blackness" in the minstrel show indeed generated a conflictual intensity, occasionally unsettling the notion to its roots—as the complexities in the foregoing traditions of response suggest. We might have expected nothing less than conflicted messages from such a cultural mediator, despite the fact that minstrelsy attempted precisely to mute conflict. The story that follows is one of dissension as much as domination, although we will need to specify its outlines, uncover the codes that clashed.

Writing on minstrelsy has failed to move very much beyond the debate over people's culture versus cultural domination. But as my genealogy and close examinations of Mark Twain and Frederick Douglass reveal, this dualism, like that of class expression versus social control, may be a fabrication. Already encoded in these antinomies are the political conflicts and cultural contradictions early minstrelsy was devised to repress. Modern writing on the minstrel show turns out to have been an unwitting accomplice in this repression. By foregrounding the minstrel show's position as one new working-class entertainment industry in the embattled formation of northeastern American capitalist culture, a racially loaded form situated in the most politically explosive moment of the nineteenth century, I hope to show the shifting contours of this racial counterfeit, as well as its currency.

2

Love and Theft: "Racial" Production and the Social Unconscious of Blackface

Motives of race, status, economics and guilt are always clustered here.

—Ralph Ellison

Where, literally, did the minstrel show come from? What black cultural forms did it reference, and how were they taken up and eclipsed by minstrel performances? What social relations were mapped in the blackface mask? One might begin by recognizing that the minstrel show most often glossed not white encounters with life on the plantation (minstrel-show mythographers to the contrary) but racial contacts and tensions endemic to the North and the frontier. The chiefly working-class orientation of cultural interchange in the North and Southwest was responsible both for installing this new entertainment in its northern class context and for the kinds of racial representation to be found there. This regional subtext was ignored, denied, and repressed by its contemporaries (and has been ever since); national divisions soon became too pressing not to find a plantation referent for minstrelsy's displays of "blackness." Fantasies about the Old South certainly shaped white reinventions of black culture as a whole. But southern venues always had a troubled relationship to minstrel performance, some cities in the South even banning it as the slavery controversy escalated in the 1850s. It was largely the industrializing North that was the minstrel show's immediate cultural purview, political referent, and context of performance.[1] So it is to the North—"North of slavery," in Leon Litwack's memorable phrase—that we must turn our attention.

In doing so we necessarily stress cultural practices and racial affect rather than discrete, bodiless texts—an emphasis that will not allow us to study blackface's production of public "blackness" by juxtaposing slave lore with minstrel lyrics and noting the difference. Our subject properly becomes historical forms of white racial subjectivity as they were worked out in various arenas of cultural contact. For blackface artists minstrelized racial encounters into imitative entertainments that were homologous with northern racial feeling. Rather than offer an account

38

of exactly what was black about blackface, a kind of balance sheet of authenticity (a task that has in any case been ably attempted by Hans Nathan and Robert Toll, among others), I want to highlight the social relations of "racial" production, the structural and emotional pressures that helped to produce the cultural commodity "blackness." Of course, to do so will mean developing some sense of the black forms available to white observation, and of the transformations that were worked upon them. We simply need a greater understanding of the conflicts and accommodations that lay behind the transformations, their "social unconscious." Accordingly, I will look at the social spaces that tended to host racial "interaction rituals," as Berndt Ostendorf has termed them, and at the blackface artists who were the major expropriators and beneficiaries of black cultural capital. I take as normative a long, conflicted history of racial exchange that significantly "blackened" American culture as it creolized African cultural imports, a history that in one sense makes it difficult to talk about expropriation at all. Yet it is also true that in the antebellum years a kind of raw commodification lay behind and in turn resulted from cultural exchange; we are dealing, in many cases, with the cultural commodities of human commodities. This commercial context mediated cultural mixing, whatever the latter's routineness or the intentions of the individuals involved.[2]

It is nonetheless crucial to acknowledge the intricacies of the process by which black performative practices were recruited into blackface minstrelsy, a process that is only partly accounted for in the notion of a static and reified "black culture's" removal into the pocketbooks of white imitators. Black performance itself, first of all, was precisely "performative," a cultural invention, not some precious essence installed in black bodies; and for better or worse it was often a product of self-commodification, a way of getting along in a constricted world. Black people, that is to say, not only exercised a certain amount of control over such practices but perforce sometimes developed them in tandem with white spectators. Moreover, practices taken as black were occasionally interracial creations whose commodification on white stages attested only to whites' greater access to public distribution (and profit). At the same time, of course, there is no question that the white commodification of black bodies structured all of this activity, or that the cultural forms of the black dispossessed in the United States have been appropriated and circulated as stand-ins for a supposedly national folk tradition.[3] We merely ought to be clear about the enormous complexity of this process, in which partly shared, partly black cultural practices were circulated as authentically black, with whites profiting outright to the extent that they were in fact black, while obstructing the visibility of black performers in any case. In minstrelsy these practices were fed into an exchange system of cultural signifiers that both produced and continually marked the inauthenticity of their "blackness"; their ridicule asserted the difference between counterfeit and currency even as they disseminated what most audiences believed were black music, dance, and gesture. The first appearance in U.S. history of black culture as property was blackface minstrelsy's marketing of an internally differentiated cultural "blackness." My subject here is its affective sources—an affair of copies and originals, theft and love.

MINSTRELIZATION

Blackface was the most visible part of a process by which black practices were appropriated and regulated in Jacksonian America. I assume less that this "minstrelization" came about as a result of some stark political intention than that its dominative character, already bound up with the kind of familiarity and interest that brought "black" culture to minstrel acts, was also the only way such an interest could possibly have been staged. As Clifford Geertz has written, cultural forms are seldom devised simply to reinforce social hierarchy in societies whose every act proclaims it (448). The minstrel show was, on the one hand, a socially approved context of institutional control; and, on the other, it continually acknowledged and absorbed black culture even while defending white America against it.[4] Just here, then, we are looking for the contradictory motives and conditions of exchange that might have inspired commodified minstrel forms.

Because it was less visible there to whites, black culture in the North had perhaps a lower public profile than southern slave culture; but it was no less present or persistent. The growing importation of Africans into the North in the mid-eighteenth century, writes Ira Berlin, gave new direction to a previously highly creolized African-American culture ("Time" 53). New arrivals provided direct knowledge of West African societies, and, as we shall see, northern blacks adopted a variety of African-derived forms and practices in this period, decisively shaping black life. Because of the greater proportion of whites to blacks in the North, blacks were acculturated more quickly and more completely, but it also gave whites more hegemonic self-assurance, which, along with a variety of segregated practices, offered blacks autonomy to develop their own cultural institutions. The first African Free Schools and African Methodist Episcopal churches, for instance, date from around the turn of the nineteenth century. In addition, the very circumstances of the North, including densely populated urban spaces and residences with separate access, helped generate autonomous black association. By the early nineteenth century free blacks and slaves alike gathered in taverns and dance houses, engaged in festivals and parades, and generally constituted an acknowledged (and occasionally threatening) public presence. Shane White has suggested that distinctively "black" linguistic patterns, naming practices, hairstyles, and physical demeanor—a world of stylistic difference—characterized northern blacks as well as southern ones.[5]

The chances for white involvement in this culture were routine, if rather variable and occasional. The vast quantity of black dialect, habit, and mannerism regularly reported in almanacs and newspapers evinces the variety and frequency of interracial contact, and no doubt provided a readily imitable outline of white fantasies about black behavior; its material extension was indeed the massive output of dime minstrel songbooks that buttressed the theatrical popularity of minstrelsy (see Fig. 2). Print caricature was probably a necessary but not a sufficient condition for racial burlesque, for it lacked the crucial presence of the body. Eileen Southern has broadly and succinctly phrased one view of minstrel performers' theft of black cultural forms:

> To obtain materials for their shows, the minstrels visited plantations, then attempted to recreate plantation scenes on the stage. They listened to the songs of the black man as he sang at work in the cotton and sugar cane field, on the steamboats and river docks, and in the tobacco factories. The melodies they heard served as bases for minstrel songs, and they adapted the dances they saw to their needs.
>
> The musical instruments originally associated with plantation "frolics" became "Ethiopian instruments"—banjos, tambourines, fiddles and bone castanets. (*Music* 91–92)

Although this description overstates the performers' diligence (as I have said, much of their material, and certainly much of its force, came out of northern interracial contexts), it is an advance over those critics who wrongly hew to the line that white minstrels had no investment in black culture, no idea what they were doing. And it captures the physical immediacy of their investment, as well as the diffuse array, perhaps the disarray, of spaces open to cultural exchange. If we substitute northern, mostly working-class places of labor and leisure for cane field and tobacco factory, and more casual and random instances of observation for plantation "frolics," we come closer to actual circumstance. We might say that minstrel men visited not plantations but racially integrated theaters, taverns, neighborhoods, and waterfronts—and *then* attempted to recreate plantation scenes. We will see in later chapters how minstrel-show versions of the South mediated northern political conflicts. Here let me briefly isolate certain activities in postrevolutionary America that made black culture available to whites in a way that permitted its insertion into a burgeoning leisure industry.

Even the purest white "interest" in black cultural practices literalized the financial metaphor: it was always implicitly structured by an economics of slavery. Street scenes such as the white butcher Thomas De Voe witnessed early in the nineteenth century near the lower Manhattan grocery store of Micah Hawkins (author of one of the very first blackface songs, "Backside Albany" [1815])[6] offer ample evidence:

> The first introduction in [New York City] of public "negro dancing" no doubt took place at this market. The negroes who visited here were principally slaves [emancipation came in 1827] from Long Island, who had leave of their masters for certain holidays, among which "Pinkster" was the principal one; . . . then, as they usually had three days holiday, they were ever ready, by their "negro sayings or doings," to make a few shillings more. So they would be hired by

41

Fig. 2. Minstrel Songbook, 1849.
Courtesy of the Butler Library, Columbia University

some joking butcher or individual to engage in a jig or break-down, as that was one of their pastimes at home on the barn-floor, or in a frolic, and those that could and would dance soon raised a collection; but some of them did more in "turning around and shying off" from the designated spot than keeping to the regular "shakedown," which caused them all to be confined to a "board," (or shingle, as they called it,) and not allowed off it; on this they must show their skill; and, being several together in parties, each had his particular "shingle" brought with him as part of his stock in trade. This board was usually about five to six feet long, of large width, with its particular spring in it, and to keep it in its place while dancing on it, it was held down by one on each end. Their music or time was usually given by one of their party, which was done by beating their hands on the sides of their legs and the noise of the heel. The favorite dancing-place was a cleared spot on the east side of the fish market in front of Burnel Brown's Ship Chandlery. (344)

The rather umbral distinction between butchers and other "individuals" in this remarkable passage alerts us to the white working-class connection with paid black performance long before the advent of minstrelsy. Rather more inspiring is the resourcefulness with which these slaves invented and commodified black performative practices for their own gain in an already frightfully commodified setting, momentarily dominating "by the superior powers of grace and invention" a world that attempted to "drain every atom of life and feeling" out of them.[7] But the extensive marketing of "negro sayings or doings"—the services for hire, the raising of collections—is so pressing here as to seem itself a major impetus to blackface acts. While the slaves are certainly playing for some control, it is clear that black culture was frankly on display in the North as well as the South, and that such display adhered to a commodified logic whose roots inevitably lay in slavery and whose outcome was eventually the minstrel show. No amount of evidence as to the affection of white performers and spectators for black people and their culture, or the "authenticity" of minstrel representations, or the generalized (as opposed to racially specific) character of minstrel burlesque can contravene this fact. The passage suggests that turning black forms into "stock in trade" was not merely an unconscious extension of antebellum economics but itself an expression of white interest in black performance; and that interest was indeed a matter of ownership. I will speculate later as to why such rituals were not in this period simply extended to the stage and black performers exploited for white profit. In 1837, for instance, the *New Orleans Picayune* urged "scheming" Yankees to engage that city's most popular black vendor and street musician, Old Corn Meal, promising "a fortune to any man who would start on a professional tour with him" (quoted in Kmen 32); such a move might well have outrun minstrelsy. Instead, complexly commodified blackface acts such as that of J. W. McAndrews made their way to the minstrel stage: McAndrews's "Watermelon Man" skit, his ragged costume purchased and his distinctive cry taken from a black watermelon vendor, paid his rent for over forty years (Leavitt 31). The ironies attending this best-selling counterfeit sales pitch, which continually gestured back to its originator's commodities (watermelon, cry, costume), were only more savage than those of most minstrel appropriations.

This economy, apparently responsible for the first blackface tunes and dances which began to appear after the War of 1812, was played out in somewhat subtler ways in black theatrical performance. To the striking convergences of this period—the twin births of minstrelsy and Garrison's *Liberator* at the beginning of the 1830s—may be added the demise of black theatrical institutions such as New York's African Grove Theatre. If the *Liberator*'s historical relationship to the minstrel show is in the nature of an open question, the shutting down of the African Grove seems a rather more direct result of the caricatures that went some way toward replacing it. Initially an ice cream pleasure garden, the African Grove was opened by William Henry Brown in 1821 in response to the uncongenial atmosphere of most theaters to black patrons (not to say black actors), particularly their restriction of blacks to the upper galleries. Organized around talent such as James Hewlett and Ira Aldridge, the enterprise was for a brief time very success-ful, offering mostly productions of Shakespeare but other pieces as well. As in white theaters, hornpipes were danced and comic songs sung between the acts of *Othello* and *Richard III*. Black men and women immediately crowded the shows, as did whites (many of them hecklers), who were confined to a separate section—because, a handbill said, "whites do not know how to conduct themselves at enter-tainments for ladies and gentlemen of color" (quoted in Ottley and Weatherby 73).

This success apparently inspired a venture that reveals the limits—and dangers—of black performance in this period. Gunning for larger crowds and profits, and "determined to rival the great Park Theatre," the managers of the African Grove hired out the hotel next to the Park for performances of *Richard III*. The *National Advocate* reported:

> The audiences were generally of a riotous character, and amused themselves by throwing crackers on the stage, and cracking their jokes with the actors, until danger from fire and civil discord rendered it necessary to break up the estab-lishment. The ebony-colored wags were notified by the police that they must announce their last performance, but they, defying the public authority, went on and acted nightly. It was at length considered necessary to interpose the arm of authority, and on Monday evening a dozen watchmen made part of the audience. . . . Finally they plead so hard in blank verse, and promised never to act Shakespeare again, that the Police Magistrates released them at a very late hour. (quoted in Marshall and Stock 35–36)

This audience behavior, as we shall see, was indistinguishable from that in white theaters; but the spectacle of revolt loomed large. Neither was the outcome of this enterprise remarkable: according to an 1821 playbill, the African Grove was "the third attempt of this kind in the City, by persons of Colour" (Odell 3:35). Brown's parting blow appears to have been an 1823 production of "the Drama of King Shotaway, Founded on facts taken from the Insurrection of the Caravs in the

Island of St. Vincent, Written from experience by Mr. Brown" (Odell 3:71). The insurrection was put down. At least one more attempt in the 1820s to establish an African-American theater followed; but owing in no small part to the market for minstrelsy—the determination that blacks should profit only from street, not theatrical, performance—there would for some time be no more.[8]

The minstrel show as bulwark against insurrection: if it was not consciously planned, it nevertheless had that effect on the cultivation of public black arts, though with the irony that it became, over the course of two decades, a rather threatening black counterfeit in its own right. The intervention of blackface into the brief early run of black theater may be gathered from the way that whites, incurring a familiar racial debt, were quick to latch onto it. Chief among these was the British actor Charles Mathews, a kind of Rameau's nephew variety star whose American caricatures included black preachers and other such types—the first popular antecedents of blackface acts. Mathews is of interest to us not only for this reason, and for the evidence he offers of the northern black cultural display available to the attentive observer, but also for his trip to the African Grove Theatre, where he allegedly got the idea for one of his foremost caricatures, a lampoon of the black Shakespearean Ira Aldridge. Mathews had happily been picking up scraps of song and dialect from several black sources, usually from the street; on one occasion he allegedly saw a black man driving a stagecoach with the reins around his neck, urging the horses on with his fiddle. But he longed to dig deeper, and complained that his class exemption from spaces of interracial contact hampered the effort: "The stage-driver says, 'Yes, *sir*,' and 'no, *sir*,' to the ostler, but to a question from a person who has a clean neckcloth, he instantly draws up, and, in the most repulsive manner, answers, 'No,' 'ay,' or 'very well.'" Nevertheless, Mathews exulted in his prospects: "I shall be rich in black fun. . . . It is a pity that I dare not touch upon a preacher. I know its danger, but perhaps the absurdity might give a *colour* to it—a *black* Methodist!" (Anne Mathews 1:237, 235, 239). He was answered with a trip to a black church, from which he culled the kind of "stump speech" that would not grace the minstrel stage for another twenty years.[9]

But an African Grove *Hamlet* yielded more enduring results. One account offers this record of the occasion, though it is no doubt closer to the skit Mathews manufactured:

> "To be or not to be, dat is him question, whether him nobler in de mind to suffer or lift up him arms against a sea of hubble bubble and by opossum (oppose 'em) end 'em." At the word Opossum, the whole audience burst forth into one general cry of "Opossum, Opossum, Opossum." On enquiring into the cause of this, Mr. Mathews was informed that "Opossum Up a Gum Tree" was the national air, or sort of "God Save the King" of the Negroes. . . . The cries of "Opossum, opossum" increasing, the sable tragedian [Aldridge] comes forward, and addressing the audience, informs them that he will sing their favourite melody. (quoted in Marshall and Stock 40)

Mathews continued to perform the skit until his death in 1835. He did not say so, but the public assumed that it was a parody of Aldridge, an assumption Mathews did nothing to correct, performing it on occasion in the very theater in which Aldridge happened to be appearing. Aldridge coolly disavowed the imitation: "The truth . . . is that I never attempted the character of Hamlet in my life, and I need not say that the whole of the ludicrous scene so well and so humorously described by Mr. Mathews never occurred at all" (quoted in Marshall and Stock 43–44). Yet what is astonishing about this skirmish is that Aldridge, besieged by whites with requests for the song Mathews had popularized, soon incorporated "Opossum Up a Gum Tree" into his own performances, making himself, in a morbid play on Sartre, of what he had been made. We are thus confronted with the perverse spectacle of one of Mathews's most profitable caricatures becoming one of Aldridge's most profitable performances. Its influence is a foretaste of the way the minstrelization of black practices helped to obscure them.[10]

This process extended to more public kinds of exchanges. For instance, black festivals and pageantry in northern cities were commonly visible even to unadventurous whites. The performative zeal of celebrations such as Pinkster, Election Day, and John Canoe was observed with interest and often recorded (constituting in itself a minor genre of "black" cultural circulation). Pinkster—derived from the Dutch name for Pentecost—was, from around 1750, increasingly a black celebration over several days in early June, during which community restrictions were eased and revelry of all kinds took place. James Fenimore Cooper seems to have been intrigued by Pinkster, and in *Satanstoe* (1845) evokes its atmosphere:

> Nine-tenths of the blacks of [New York City] . . . were collected in thousands in those fields, beating banjoes, singing African songs, drinking, and worst of all, laughing in a way that seemed to set their very hearts rattling within their ribs. Every thing wore the aspect of good-humor, though it was good-humor in its broadest and coarsest forms. Every sort of common game was in requisition, while drinking was far from being neglected. Still, not a man was drunk. (60)

As this seesawing account suggests, white interest in such bodily efflorescence was not untinged with doubt. One critic said of a Pinkster dance in Albany that it "partook so largely of savage license that it gradually came to be shunned by respectable whites" (quoted in Emery 143). Sometime between 1811 and 1813, as if on schedule with Micah Hawkins's "Backside Albany," the Albany Common Council outlawed the gaming and drinking common to Pinkster Day, pretty much consigning it to history.

For its part, Election Day (also dating from about 1750) positively traduced the norms of many communities. On this day blacks chose their own governing officials, who had real power among themselves and, for the space of the celebration at least, symbolic power over whites. Part appropriation of similar white ceremonies, part African survival, this political ritual openly burlesqued the dominant culture. Certain of the festivities of Election Day seem prescient inversions

46

or perhaps even counterparodies of blackface buffoonery, especially of the sort I have observed in white working-class parades and revelries. Amid the usual celebratory excess, culminating in the election of black kings, governors, and judges, blacks enacted rituals of reversal in which they lampooned their masters, wore their masters' clothes, and mounted their masters' horses. Some of these events must have seemed quite unnerving; an 1853 description of a Hartford Election Day—safely set in the seventeenth century but borrowing its force from contemporary example—depicted "a troop of blacks, sometimes an hundred in number, marching sometimes two and two on foot, sometimes mounted in true military style and dress on horseback . . . with drums beating, colors flying, and fifes, fiddles, clarionets, and every 'sonorous metal' that could be found, 'uttering martial sound'" (Stuart 49). As with Pinkster, however, whites indulged and even participated in such events. For this reason Ira Berlin has suggested that the celebrations were perceived as less dangerous than their southern counterparts, which were in fact outlawed ("Time" 54). Yet if the widespread negative reactions to Election Day are any indication, the practice unsettled even as it fascinated whites. At the very least, these events set off a train of racial burlesque and counterburlesque that surely helped inspire blackface miming, a less efficient control of independent black practices than proscription, perhaps, but more lucrative and engaging.[11]

Most of the antagonism and negotiation that occurred here, however, was based on increasingly routinized white familiarity with black culture. In northern cities, or on the levees of northern and southwestern frontier towns, working-class whites and blacks in many instances shared a common culture of jokes, games, and dances. The Five Points section on the Lower East Side of Manhattan was one such milieu of mixed-race enthusiasms; river ports in the West, where, for example, black and white boatmen both knew "Opossum Up a Gum Tree," were another (Woodson 10; Nathan 48). Long before emancipation, writes Eric Foner, lower-class subcultures in northeastern cities saw extensive elbow-rubbing among apprentices, servants, slaves, journeymen, sailors, and laborers; bullbaiting and footracing, masques and street fighting were indulged in by black and white together. The Philadelphia grand jury, at a loss for language to describe the mixed-up goings-on in that city, often complained that "many disorderly persons" were wont to gather at the courthouse, "and great numbers of negroes and others sit there with milk pails, and other things, late at night, and many disorders are there committed" (Foner, *Paine* 48–50). This kind of activity was especially common in frontier towns—not coincidentally the most important early centers of blackface innovation.[12] Whether in Louisville, Pittsburgh, or Cincinnati, the first performances of blackface's "originator" T. D. Rice, the musical education of minstrel-show innovator Dan Emmett, and the first attempts at composition by Stephen Foster all took place in these settings. The minstrel show is one instance in American commercial culture of an outland form exported to the northeastern city, rather than vice versa; and its cultural logic—its "mulatto" character, its imitative thrust—owes much to the interracial embrace of the milieu from which it originally sprang.[13]

Lafcadio Hearn captures something of this culture in his postwar transcriptions of black Cincinnati stevedores' songs, which include a variation of the blackface verse I have already quoted:

> Jay-bird sittin' on a swinging limb,
> Winked at me an' I winked at him.
> Up with a rock an' struck him on the shin,
> G——d d——n yer soul, don't wink again.
> (224)

Perhaps these black workers appropriated the minstrel verse; the admitted plausibility of this direction of cultural exchange has sustained a tradition of racist commentary bent on proving black culture's ultimate derivation from white.[14] Or perhaps the verse was black to begin with and remained so even after its widespread dissemination in blackface acts. Either alternative, or indeed the possibility that such songs were interracial inventions, makes the point about the racial contact common to frontier cultures. So does the fact that Cincinnati Negro singers could, as Hearn notes, "mimic the Irish accent to a degree of perfection which an American, Englishman or German could not hope to acquire" (226). Or that, according to a scornful circus manager, Dan Emmett learned to play the black style of banjo from a white man named Ferguson, "a very ignorant person, and 'nigger all over' except in color" (quoted in Nathan 110). As Robert Cantwell writes, wherever "social and economic marginality had created conditions favorable to cultural interpenetration . . . the racial barriers so familiar to us, which closed so suddenly and so resoundingly after Emancipation, had, by the middle of the nineteenth century, begun to dissolve in the American heartland" (259).

Victor Turner has argued that cultural performance originates in "social drama" such as I have outlined and continues to draw force and meaning from it, constituting, in essence, "performances about performances" (*Anthropology* 107). This notion is particularly helpful in thinking about a context in which the original dramas themselves held such a complicated mix of racial impulses, interracial imitations, and economic facts. The development of blackface miming out of primarily working-class rituals of racial interaction suggests that blackface performance reproduced or instantiated a structured relationship between the races— racial difference itself as much as black cultural forms. This relationship included its share of interest and fascination, but it was built on an antebellum racial economy, not to mention a nimbus of racist ideology, as the minstrel show, true to the character of the culture industry, proceeded to make quite plain. Its circulation of black cultural practices—more accurately the racially mixed forms that both did and did not read as "black"—operated through burlesque or humiliation, that is, the metaphorical restriction of them to the white man's shingle. For this reason Susan Willis has written of the blackface mask as precisely a figuration

48

of the commodity, a sort of trademark assigned to the "black" images white people paid to see (189). In sum, the cultural logic of blackface preserved that of the spaces I have surveyed, opening to view the culture of the dispossessed while simultaneously refusing the social legitimacy of its members, a truly American combination of acknowledgment and expropriation.

THE WHITE NEGRO

> "Lucy Long" was sung by a white negro as a male female danced.
> —*New York Tribune.* (1853)

Minstrelization did not give rise in any immediate way to developed forms of racial mimicry. It was left to a small class of eccentric performers, galvanized by cultural interchange, to work up symbolic ideological articulations that, following Pierre Bourdieu, we should see as "doubly determined" ("Symbolic" 81)—owing not only to the class milieu that encouraged cultural exchange but also to the specific interests of the men who devised blackface caricatures. While I am ultimately interested in a white working-class structure of feeling, it will not do to dismiss the particular concerns of minstrel performers themselves. For though these artists called on common ways of feeling, thinking, and living their white-ness, they also inflected it with a specific set of attitudes and preoccupations before giving their racial fantasies back to the class arena from which they had been drawn. The reader will have noted that much of the cultural negotiation I have outlined depended on encounters between a white man and a black man: master and slave, white minstrel and black vendor, Charles Mathews and Ira Aldridge. A certain dynamic of masculinity or, conversely, "unmanning" seems to have been at work here, making the theft of black forms more urgent, if not indeed more pregnant. Codes of black and white manhood gave the exchange its force, a fact enlarged upon in the minstrel show itself. A look at white minstrel performers reveals that a gendered logic of exchange, a kind of commerce be-tween men, facilitated the cultural expropriation central to blackface minstrelsy.[15]

One might first remark, however, that the men who began to "black up" in the years around 1830 were in some cases close to the center of Jacksonian political power. Thus, the temptation has been to read the minstrel show as a fairly pat instance of cultural manipulation in which the prejudices of benighted audiences are secured from above by a fully administered form of leisure. There is, to be sure, a "Frankfurt School" case to be made here, and Alexander Saxton has made it most persuasively.[16] Saxton surveys the social origins of certain major minstrel figures, among them T. D. Rice, Dan Emmett, E. P. Christy, and Stephen Foster. Many of the major innovators were northerners of urban origin (none from New England) who were raised in families with intimations of upward mobility. All of them rejected the Protestant ethic and escaped into the latitudes of the entertainment world. In the course of such escape they came into contact with the music and dance of slaves and free blacks, and first tasted theatrical success in blackface performances. While these "professionals" were sometimes class mutineers, passing up opportunities at a clerkship or better to immerse themselves in the underground world of blackface theater ("initiated into the mysteries of cork," as one contemporaneous theater historian put it),[17] they nevertheless shared with their families certain political ties to the elite of the Democratic party, the party of Andrew Jackson, antimonopoly, expansionism— and white supremacy. Henry Wood of Christy and Wood's Minstrels was the brother of Fernando Wood, southern-sympathizing mayor of New York; another brother served three terms as a Democratic congressman from Buffalo and one term as a state senator. Stephen Foster belonged to a family of ardent Democrats related by marriage to President James Buchanan's brother, and Foster himself helped organize a local Buchanan for President club. On the basis of such evidence, Saxton and other writers have rather hastily denied the political contra-dictions self-evident in minstrelsy, by which of course I mean more than the many examples of Whig (specifically pro-Henry Clay) songwriting, although these ex-ist.[18] And while connections tell only a partial story, there were also other connec-tions: the black nationalist editor, organizer, and novelist Martin Delany, a physi-cian and the first black to attend Harvard, began his medical studies in the 1830s under Dr. Andrew McDowell, Stephen Foster's future father-in-law (Austin 68).

Moreover, as I have begun to suggest, evidence from performers themselves points to a more complex dynamic in which such dominative tendencies coexisted with or indeed depended on a self-conscious attraction to the black men it was the job of these performers to mimic. Billy Whitlock, a banjo player with Dan Em-mett's Virginia Minstrels, on his first tour of the South would, as the *New York Clipper* put it, "quietly steal off to some negro hut to hear the darkeys sing and see them dance, taking with him a jug of whiskey to make them all the merrier" (April 13, 1878). More revealingly, the performer Ben Cotton claimed that he would sit with and study blacks on Mississippi riverboats: "I used to sit with them in front of their cabins, and we would start the banjo twanging, and their voices would ring out in the quiet night air in their weird melodies. They did not quite understand me. I was the first white man they had seen who sang as they did; but we were brothers for the time being and were perfectly happy" ("Interview"). Self-serving as this account is, it indicates that a major strain of American bohemia has its origins in blackface performers and enthusiasts. So much the worse for bohemia, perhaps; but in addition to the minor disasters bohemia has perpetrated, from Walt Whitman to Carl Van Vechten to Jack Kerouac, there is in its activities an implicit tribute to, or at the very least a self-marginalizing mimicry of, black culture's male representatives. To say this hardly addresses the social *results* of such activities, which may be more or less harmful than the exoticism that gener-ated them. But with antebellum blackface performers a set of racial attitudes and

50

cultural styles that in America go by the name of bohemianism first emerged, and there was a utopian or emancipatory moment in their often clumsy courtship of black men. I am not interested in romanticizing these performers. While I believe they were to some extent drawn to "blackness," this fact should also interrogate the racial logic usually hidden in our romantic notions of the bohemian, the Beat, the hipster. We ought to recognize, in other words, the degree to which blackface stars inaugurated an American tradition of class abdication through gendered cross-racial immersion which persists, in historically differentiated ways, to our own day.

Histories of American bohemia, among them Albert Parry's engrossing *Garrets and Pretenders* (1933), have always disregarded this racial and sexual narrative. Though occasionally sensitive to the declassing that underlies bohemia's "spirit" of revolt, they follow Henri Murger's *Scènes de la vie de bohème* (1851) in emphasizing, as Parry puts it, the literary tradition of "vitriolic criticism with a frankly personal tinge and twist, of making taverns into rendezvous of arts, and of dying drunk and delirious in a gutter, an attic, and the backroom of a saloon" (7). Minstrel performers and writers not infrequently lived up to such a script, the most spectacular being E. P. Christy, who in a fit of madness threw himself from a high window in 1862. But this definition amounts to a formalism of dissipation. T. J. Clark, for example, has pinpointed the class content of midcentury French bohemia:

> The Bohemian caricatured the claims of bourgeois society. He took the slogans at face-value; if the city was a playground he would play; if individual freedom was sacrosanct then he would celebrate the cult twenty-four hours a day; *laissez-faire* meant what it said. The Bohemian was the dandy stood on his head: where the dandy was the bourgeois playing at being an aristocrat (hence his pathos), the Bohemian was the bourgeois playing at being a bourgeois. . . . (*Image* 34)

Minstrel performers gave this pattern an American spin. Most of them were minor, apolitical theatrical men of the northern artisanate who pursued a newly available bourgeois dream of freedom and play by paradoxically coding themselves as "black." Marginalized by temperament, by habit (often alcoholism), by ethnicity, even by sexual orientation, these artists immersed themselves in "blackness" to indulge their felt sense of difference. It was an avenue that allowed them certain underground privileges (and accrued many demerits) which a more legitimate course would not have provided. Indeed, if for men sexuality is where freedom and play meet, "blackness" was for antebellum bohemians its virtual condition—that fascinating imaginary space of fun and license outside (but structured by) Victorian bourgeois norms.[19]

Coming from areas of much cultural commerce, the men who became blackface minstrels had many opportunities to engage the black practices to which they were drawn. According to legend—the closest we are going to get to truth in the matter—T. D. Rice used an old black stableman's song and dance in his first "Jim

Crow" act. Dan Emmett had left his Mount Vernon, Ohio, home by the age of eighteen (in 1834) and joined the military, where he learned to play the infantry drum from a man nicknamed "Juba"—a black name, if not a black man, perhaps earned for the style of drum he played. Appearing as a banjo player in various circuses, Emmett very soon teamed up with the dancer Frank Brower, who had learned his dances directly from black men (Nathan 107, 110). Stephen Foster no doubt had contact with black wharf workers and boatmen in his hometown of Pittsburgh, but according to his brother, he experienced black church singing firsthand through a family servant, Olivia Pise, "member of a church of shouting colored people."[20] Ralph Keeler, who ran away from his Buffalo home at the age of eleven, wrote that as a dancer with Johnny Booker's minstrels in the 1850s he "wandered all over the Western country" (77), keeping continual company with that troupe's black baggage handler, Ephraim. E. P. Christy reportedly drew material in the late 1830s from One-Legged Harrison, a black church singer in Buffalo; Christy said the two had often traded "down home talk" (Toll 46). Within the institution of minstrelsy itself, as we will see, the renowned black dancer Juba (William Henry Lane) provided a link between the cultures, figuring centrally in many challenge dance contests between black and white dancers. The tableau reiterated in many of these scenes—a white man and a black man becoming, as Ben Cotton put it, "brothers for the time being"—is the bohemian encounter that interests me here. It shows up often enough to be a defining interest of these "white Negroes," and we might pause over its enabling role in cultural theft.

What appears in fact to have been appropriated were certain kinds of masculinity. To put on the cultural forms of "blackness" was to engage in a complex affair of manly mimicry. Examples of this dynamic since the heyday of minstrelsy are ready enough to hand—Elvis, Mailer—but in the early nineteenth century it had yet to be given an available public form. To wear or even enjoy blackface was literally, for a time, to become black, to inherit the cool, virility, humility, abandon, or *gaité de coeur* that were the prime components of white ideologies of black manhood.[21] Rice, said his friend F. C. Wemyss, in the event of an empty house fell into a kind of black homespun when negotiating with theater managers, as if indeed into a black-white dyad that reproduced his own felicitous exchanges with black men: "Lookye here, my master, this has been a bad job—I don't think you ought to suffer to this tune; live and let live is a good motto—hand over ———, and I will give you a receipt in full, and wish you better luck another time" (*The Life* 179). How interesting that Rice should assume this humbled sense of masculinity precisely at the guilty moment of receiving payment for expropriated goods, in the process authenticating his claim on the material.[22] And how fitting, too, that this disturbing moment of conventional masculinity in the public sphere—the hard bargain, the deal—could, with a ventriloquial shift, be evaded or at least better managed.

It is worth remarking the way minstrelsy marketed racialized images of masculinity if only because they have become so familiar, indeed ritualized. In *North Toward Home* (1967), white Mississippian Willie Morris remembers "a stage, when we were about thirteen, in which we 'went Negro.' We tried to broaden our accents to sound like Negroes, as if there were not enough similarity already. We consciously walked like young Negroes, mocking their swinging gait, moving our arms the way they did, cracking our knuckles and whistling between our teeth" (81). I would maintain that this dynamic, persisting into adulthood, is so much a part of most American white men's equipment for living that they remain entirely unaware of their participation in it. The special achievement of minstrel performers was to have intuited and formalized the white male fascination with the turn to black, which Leslie Fiedler describes this way: "Born theoretically white, we are permitted to pass our childhood as imaginary Indians, our adolescence as imaginary Negroes, and only then are expected to settle down to being what we really are: white once more" (*Waiting* 134). These common white associations of black maleness with the onset of pubescent sexuality indicate that the assumption of dominant codes of masculinity in the United States was (and still is) partly negotiated through an imaginary black interlocutor. If this suggests that minstrelsy's popularity depended in part on the momentary return of its partisans to a state of arrested adolescence—largely the condition to which dominant codes of masculinity aspire—one must also conclude that white male fantasies of black men undergird the subject positions white men grow up to occupy. This dynamic is, further, one whose results are far from given; its appropriations of "black" masculinity may or may not have racist results. But in thus mediating white men's relations with other white men, minstrel acts certainly made currency out of the black man himself, that obscure object of exchangeable desire. The stock in trade of the exchange so central to minstrelsy, that is to say, was black culture in the guise of an attractive masculinity.[23]

In contrast to such homosocial relationships, as Eve Sedgwick has termed them[24]—exchanges that buttressed the social relations of patriarchy, however variable their racial results—there is evidence that performers and audiences also found in blackface something closer to a homoerotic charge. Sedgwick has argued that nineteenth-century bohemia was a space not of infinite heterosexual appetite but of ambiguous sexual definition, through which young bourgeois men passed on their way to the "repressive, self-ignorant, and apparently consolidated status of the mature bourgeois *paterfamilias*" ("Beast" 251; emphasis in original). Something of this situation applied in the case of minstrel men, certain of whose female impersonations appear, in the context of rough-and-tumble Jacksonian manliness, to have grown out of a sense of sexual ambiguity. The actress Olive Logan wrote that "some of the men who undertake this ["wench"] business are marvellously well fitted by nature for it, having well-defined soprano voices, plump shoulders, beardless faces, and tiny hands and feet. Many dress most elegantly as women" (698). Although she is referring here to postwar female impersonation—which as an American show business tradition may have gotten its start in minstrelsy—there is no reason to believe that the wide renown of antebellum "wenches" (George Christy, Barney Williams) owed any less to their aptitude for or predisposition to such roles. And while it is inaccurate simply to read off homosexuality from effeminacy or indeed transvestism, same-sex desire does seem to have been registered by these performers (see chapter 6). "Heaps of boys in my locality don't believe yet it's a man in spite of my saying it was," said a Rochester critic of Francis Leon, the most famous postwar female impersonator. Leon was seductive enough, this writer remarked, "to make a fool of a man if he wasn't sure."[25]

Other performers evinced homosexual attractions more obliquely. "A minstrel show came to town and I thought of nothing else for weeks," said Ben Cotton ("Interview")—this from the man who recalled the brotherhood of black and white singers. George Thatcher, a well-known performer later in the century, said of his first encounter with blackface performance in Baltimore: "I found myself dreaming of minstrels; I would awake with an imaginary tambourine in my hand, and rub my face with my hands to see if I was blacked up. . . . The dream of my life was to see or speak to a performer" ("Only"). We might speculate a little as to the referent of the imaginary tambourine; the fantasy of racial conversion enacted in blackface seems to gesture at least toward sexual envy of black men (tambourine as penis), if not desire for them (tambourine as anus). The fantasy may indeed direct us to a process I will explore later, in which homosexual desire is deflected by identifying with potent male heterosexuality. Perhaps the fantasy indicates only the usefulness of blackface in mediating white men's desire for other white men. In any case, though it overlapped with appropriations of the sexualized mantle of black masculinity, this was a "feminizing" outcome of cultural exchange. Of course it did nothing to redirect myths of black masculinity, not to mention white men's attitudes toward women; and it only confirmed black men's status as bearers of black culture or objects of exchange. But it brings to the surface a more submerged motive for racial intercourse, and it was probably one aspect of most white men's enjoyment of black caricature.

Norman Mailer's essay "The White Negro" (1957), a text whose mythologies are as telling as its analysis, is of course the twentieth-century reinvention of these homosocial and homosexual fascinations. Mailer codifies the renegade ethic of male sexuality, conceived out of and projected onto black men—and always "compromised" by white men's evident attraction to them—which constituted the more than metaphorical racial romance of the minstrel show. Early minstrel performers would not have been able to articulate it, but Mailer's dream of the black male may stand as a fairly close description of their own fascination:

> Knowing in the cells of his existence that life was war, nothing but war, the Negro (all exceptions admitted) could rarely afford the sophisticated inhibitions of civilization, and so he kept for his survival the art of the primitive, he lived in the enormous present, he subsisted for his Saturday night kicks, relinquishing the pleasures of the mind for the more obligatory pleasures of the

> body, and in his music he gave voice to the character and quality of his existence, to his rage and the infinite variations of joy, lust, languor, growl, cramp, pinch, scream and despair of his orgasm. (314)

Mailer and other white Negroes down the years inherited a structure of feeling that no doubt preexisted but was crystallized in the responses of the first minstrel performers to the allure of black men. Underwritten by various kinds of public cultural interaction, minstrel men appropriated styles of racialized masculinity as much as any particular cultural product, a gendered obsession easily converted into profitable minstrel-show counterfeits. Its modern resonance is articulated in white guitarist Scotty Moore's remark to Elvis Presley at one of the recording sessions in which Elvis first found his voice: *"Damn,* nigger!"[26]

BEGINNINGS

Contrary to expectation, perhaps, the production of the minstrel show out of gendered commodity exchanges, or what I have called its social unconscious, tended often to disrupt nineteenth-century perceptions of blackface. Most commentators believed minstrelsy to have derived at least in part from slave culture, and found affinities between the two that effectively displaced the differences. Given this perception of origins, anxieties arose about the precise nature of the cultural relationships encoded in minstrelsy, a problem that was fleeting and murky but unmistakably present to most of those who wrote about the minstrel show. "How much of the wonderful success and popularity of the negro minstrel is due to the minstrel, how much to the negro melody he introduced, and how much to the characteristic bones, banjo, and tambourine upon which he accompanied himself, is an open question," wrote the theater historian Laurence Hutton, rather typically (144).[27] It was in the obsessive accounts of minstrelsy's origins that these anxieties were most extreme. In what follows I hope to convey something of the beginnings of blackface, not by means of yet another mystified account of them, but by looking at how even offhand contemporaneous narratives of the minstrel show's origins attempted to legitimate or resolve pressing ideological questions raised by their subject. For all positions on the origins and makeup of blackface minstrelsy implicitly or explicitly rely on a theory of the racial politics of American culture.[28]

In these tales of minstrelsy's "ancestry," the moment of "racial" exchange between white and black men returns with a vengeance. We should understand this fixation as the desire to hold the object of study in the moment of its emergence, as if to uncover the pure thing (unadulterated by later, superfluous changes or events) were finally to grasp its essence. The great nineteenth-century narratives of origin all rely on this kind of depth model, whether Marx's work on capitalism, Engels's account of the industrial city, James Fenimore Cooper's and Frederick Jackson Turner's narratives of the frontier, or Nietzsche's books on morals and tragedy. Properly speaking, writes Edward Said in *Beginnings*, what such narratives pursue are principles of difference or *differentiation* rather than essences, which make possible or inaugurate the "knowledge" they intend (51). The slightly ridiculous return of such principles of differentiation in tales of the origins of minstrelsy nevertheless highlights the kind of project taking place there: narratives of cultural acknowledgment by one race of another, the development of a discourse on cultural "blackness," accounts of a relatively trivial cultural form that find themselves worrying the minstrel show's racial economy. They reveal how white performers and audiences conceived of what they were doing in minstrelsy, and the extent to which ventriloquized cultural forms confronted them with a rather more troubling prospect than has been recognized.

The moment that interests me in these narratives is the one in which black sounds fill the air and fascinated white men understand for the first time that there is fame and money to be made. We have already seen an account of Rice's first performance, but the same *Atlantic Monthly* writer fixes this earlier moment as well:

> As [Rice] sauntered along one of the main thoroughfares of Cincinnati, as has been written, his attention was suddenly arrested by a voice ringing clear and full above the noises of the street, and giving utterance, in an unmistakable dialect, to the refrain of a song to this effect:—"Turn about an' wheel about an' do jis so, / An' ebery time I turn about I jump Jim Crow." Struck by the peculiarities of the performance, so unique in style, matter, and "character" of delivery, the player listened on. Were not these elements—was the suggestion of the instant—which might admit of higher than mere street or stable-yard development? As a national or "race" illustration, behind the footlights, might not "Jim Crow" and a black face tickle the fancy of pit and circle, as well as the "Sprig of Shillalah" and a red nose? Out of the suggestion leaped the determination; and so it chanced that the casual hearing of a song trolled by a negro stage-driver, lolling lazily on the box of his vehicle, gave origin to a school of music destined to excel in popularity all others. (Nevin 608–9)

Rice is credited here with the higher development or logical conclusion of the culture of street and stable yard. Minstrelsy is claimed as the *completion* of black culture, its professional emergence—"like the music of the Bermoothes [coming alive under] the magic wand of Prospero," as another account has it.[29] For all the belief in the minstrel show as authentic "national illustration," then, there is also in this account a submerged melting-pot version of American culture *avant la lettre*, of cultural intercourse almost unconsciously acknowledged, and hastily forgotten. These narratives, in other words, are riveted by the moment of cultural expropriation, and we should look to them, as Pierre Macherey's work suggests, as much for what they do not say as for what they do—for the way they construct, and then sometimes blur, racial boundaries.[30]

The cultural mixing in these narratives, however, usually takes place, as it were, *en l'air;* there is rarely any actual meeting between racial representatives (unlike the exceptional, harrowing, and probably fanciful account of Rice and

56

Cuff in chapter 1). When there is such a meeting, issues of ownership, cultural capital, and economics arise (as in the Rice and Cuff account). These are the two narrative paradigms of minstrelsy's origins: one in which mixing takes place by an elision of expropriation, through absorption (in both senses); the other in which it takes place by a transfer of ownership, through theft (or occasionally payment). In the accounts I have come across the story is nearly always told one way or the other—obvious attempts to master the relationships I have just sketched. Both paradigms, it is safe to say, share an anxiety over the fact of cultural "borrowing." And both, I suggest, have as their purpose the resolution of some intractable social contradiction or problem that the issue of expropriation represents. That of the first is miscegenation; that of the second slavery itself. If, as Joseph Litvak has suggested, "anxiety itself has a narrative (i.e., implicitly history-making) structure," both anticipating and deferring the "deconstructive cancellation of its sustaining techniques" (127), these narratives of love and theft are manipulations of historical anxiety meant to overcome the threatening implications of their primary concerns.[31]

It should hardly seem strange that miscegenation is suggested (if in oblique and displaced form) in accounts of white men's fascination with and attraction to black men and their culture, for these are accounts in which the cultures merge. The logic of such accounts is that fascination may be permitted so long as actual contact is avoided; that is the way the passage just quoted works. The white man is "arrested" and "struck" by a voice only. At the end, when we do finally see the black man "lolling lazily on the box of his vehicle" (by what means? through whose eyes? where was he before?), this suggestive appearance indicates the reason for his absence throughout: black male sexuality is one component of his arresting voice. In accounts like this we read a relatively transparent white male attraction to and repulsion from the black penis, for which the preoccupation with miscegenation serves as a kind of shorthand. These two concerns—a jealous guarding of the prized white female body and a fascination with black male sexual potency that either precedes or follows it—amount in any case to the same thing: the twitchy "love" of this chapter's title. The discussion by James Kennard, Jr. (in an 1845 *Knickerbocker*) of the racial mixing attendant upon minstrelsy (he is careful to say that it happens "by proxy," i.e., in blackface performance) clarifies the nature of the threat. A brief account of the origins of T. D. Rice's "imitative powers" is given, and then whimsy turns to distressed irony:

> From the nobility and gentry, down to the lowest chimney-sweep in Great Britain, and from the member of Congress, down to the youngest apprentice or school-boy in America, it was all: "Turn about and wheel about, and do just so, / And every time I turn about I jump Jim Crow."
> Even the fair sex did not escape the contagion: the tunes were set to music for the piano-forte, and nearly every young lady in the Union, and the United Kingdom, played and sang, if she did not *jump*, "Jim Crow." . . . [Negroes themselves] were not permitted to appear in the theatres, and the houses of the fashionable, but their songs are in the mouths and ears of all. . . . (332–33)

"Contagion" indeed. The author's peremptory desire later in the article for the ubiquitous minstrel music (personified as "Dan Tucker") to disappear altogether runs against the same problem, here too anxiety-inducing to avoid its representation:

> Depend upon it, he will do no such thing, so long as the young ladies speak to him in such fascinating tones, and accompany their sweet voices with the only less sweet music of the piano. Dan takes it as an invitation to stay; and doubtless many a lover would like to receive a similar rejection from his lady-love; a fashion, by the way, like that in which the country lass reproved her lover for kissing her: "Be done, Nat!" said she, "and (*soto voce*) begin again!" (335)

For some, the mixing of minstrelsy apparently meant the eroticized return of Nat Turner. If only it had been the "young ladies" who could not resist.

No wonder, then, that in this first paradigm minstrelsy's origins are ordinarily so displaced and disembodied; talk of cultural merging is too dangerously close to a discourse of "amalgamation." A bizarre "amalgamaphobia" infects even the briefest of accounts: "These songs, spawned in the very lowest puddles of society, at length found their way, like the frogs of Egypt, into places of admitted respectability. On so *dark* a subject it can hardly be expected that we should be quite precise in reference to dates" ("Obituary" 118). The repetitive, even obsessive insistence on black sexuality in these encounters and in descriptions of their "offspring" has a vaguely unconscious or unmotivated quality; it is less a rhetorical tic or standard reference than something that has slipped by. In an article sympathetic to minstrelsy, one writer imagines "the hum of the plantation":

> I listen with attentive ears—for I know by experience the gratification in store for me—and soon catch the distant tones of the human voice—now more faintly heard, and now entirely lost. . . . [N]ow, anew, I hear the sound of those manly negro voices swelling up upon the evening gale. Nearer and nearer comes the boat, higher and higher rises the melody, till it overpowers and subdues the noise of the oars, which in their turn become subservient to the song, and mark its time with harmonious beating. ("Negro Minstrelsy— Ancient and Modern" 76–77)

If black men could do this with their voices, imagine what they could do in the flesh! But they remain voices, without presence, imaginative projections, and these accounts seem to require that they remain so, even as the black male is referred to compulsively. The accounts all suggest fears and desires in the shape of a social narrative involving overpowering black men. That narrative surfaces in many contexts, but refers us in the end to the unresolved—and, to these writers, fascinating—threat of intermixture suffusing the minstrel phenomenon. Emblems of a relationship between the races that has been culturally repressed, minstrel songs, like the mulatto child of Thomas Jefferson in William Wells Brown's *Clotel, or The President's Daughter* (1853), returned to haunt the most respectable of places.

But miscegenation and/or homoerotic desire is not the only kind of relationship whites would rather have forgotten. The other narrative paradigm that organizes tales of the origins of minstrelsy expresses an overriding concern with exchange value, the economics of race, with slavery itself. Recall that in Robert Nevin's *Atlantic Monthly* account Rice gets the minstrel idea without meeting any black man; it is only later that "Cuff's" clothes come in handy, and the issue of ownership, and value generally, emerges. (This is the only account containing both paradigms.) The central issue of the second paradigm is so pressing that a later writer, in retelling Nevin's account nearly word for word, nevertheless amends it in a striking way. Nevin writes that "Cuff was precisely the subject for Rice's purpose. *Slight persuasion* induced him to accompany the actor to the theatre" (609; emphasis added). Amidst an almost verbatim account, H. P. Phelps writes that "a darkey . . . was induced, *for a slight consideration*, to go with the actor to the theatre" (166; emphasis added). Given the monotony and the cheerful plagiarism of the general run of these accounts, such minute shifts are quite revealing, slips of the tongue in a public discourse. And what they disclose is white guilt or anxiety about minstrelsy as a figure for the plundering of black culture. I hinted just now that whites would like to have imagined the expropriations of minstrelsy to be nonanalogous to those of slavery, to have forgotten or displaced the latter in accounts of the minstrel show—a form, after all, meant to reassure them that everybody was happy down on the plantation. That is indeed what occurs in the payment imagined by Phelps, and it happens in other ways as well. While occasionally the minstrel show becomes a narrative substitute for slavery, a comfortable alternative to the idea of free black labor, generally the intention of this second paradigm is a denial or forgetting of the unremunerated labor of slavery, a denial often difficult to sustain as repressed economic facts return.

In the most benign of these accounts, there can be no meeting between racial representatives without some kind of reparation made by whites to blacks:

> One spring season of the Louisville Theatre, on a clear, bright morning, during the rehearsal of some play in which Mr. Rice had but little to do, as he was standing on the stage, at a back door that looked out upon the rear of a stable-yard, where a very black, clumsy negro used to clean and rub down horses, he was attracted by the clearness and melody of this negro's voice, and he caught the words, the subject of his song; it was the negro version of "Jump, Jim Crow." He listened with delight to the negro's singing for several days, and finally went to him and paid him to sing the song over to him until he had learned it. (Ludlow 392)

This is obviously a legitimating story of cultural "borrowing": all accounts have been paid in full. The mention of a "negro version" of "Jim Crow" is no doubt a nice touch, implying as it does the neutrality and simple difference of versions. But its willful reversal of the cultural relationship here—its reading of blackface songs as originary and black songs mere versions—reveals, even as it attempts to disguise, precisely the *difference* of versions, the implied inaccuracy of blackface minstrelsy's appropriating "delineations." Even in accounts that would deny the notion of imbalance, whether in the evaluation of cultures or in cultural indebtedness, that imbalance, perhaps inevitably, returns.

Since, as we have seen, the cultural commodities of blackface were defined by this difference, references to the monetary or commodity status of minstrel songs, as well as that of their black "inventors," are routine in these narratives. Most accounts take up at some point the issue of minstrelsy's authenticity, and are therefore littered with defenses against or assertions of its "counterfeit" nature: "Base counterfeits as they are, they pass current with most people as genuine negro songs" (Kennard 336). Hence the false currency implied in the same writer's quip that "white men have blacked their faces to represent [Negroes], [and] made their fortune by the speculation" (333). The disapproval of this practice suggests an uneasiness with the surplus value thus generated; its falseness seems to stem from the fact that its black "owners" are not equal buyers and sellers on the market but are "represented," bought and sold by brokers. And yet the disapproval may not have to do directly with slavery. A distrust of the "speculation" of minstrelsy may be only a cautious approach to the main chance, made risky in the aftermath of the panic of 1837 perhaps. But though the "blackness" that minstrelsy peddles may be a commodity like any other, it ultimately derives, as these references continually remind us, from a certain southern commodity: "Those of us who have for so many years been looking anxiously forward to the advent of the coming poet who is to take away from America the sin and the shame of never having produced an epic, or a lyric, commensurate with Niagara and the Rocky Mountains, will do well to get up a subscription and buy the author of [these songs], if his owner can be persuaded to part with him."[32] The cultural nationalism of Young America notwithstanding, one wants to reply that the sin and shame lie somewhere else. The underlying suggestion, in any case, is that blackface minstrelsy figured less as a palliative to the economics of slavery than as an uncomfortable reminder of it.

In this context we should recall the most horrific of the accounts organized by this second paradigm. It is Nevin's narrative in which outright theft and public embarrassment are indulged; but here too, as I have suggested, simply narrating the "primal scene" introduces issues of economy, value, and ownership almost behind the author's back. A great deal of space is allotted to Cuff's mode of subsistence, too much in fact for the part he plays as the lender of his "blackness" to Rice. He carries passengers' trunks from steamers to shore; he is, moreover, in active competition for business with another black man, Ginger. Revealingly, it is midway through Rice's performance in Cuff's clothes that the "near approach of a steamer"—Cuff's livelihood—intrudes and requires the song somehow to end. And it must end because, as Nevin writes, "liberally as [Cuff] might lend himself to a friend, it could not be done at that sacrifice" (609). This allegorically suggestive scene—suggestive against the grain of what its author wants to convey—is yet marked by certain complex displacements. The first is the odd overemphasis on

60

Cuff's free labor, here located not in slaveholding Louisville but in Pittsburgh, a swerve away from most other accounts, such as those of Noah Ludlow, T. Allston Brown, and Edmon S. Conner, which make the cultural "donor" a Louisville slave. It is as if, in this first displacement, the fact of slavery is jettisoned in favor of industrious black men "liberal" enough to "lend themselves" to white friends. But the shape of that last phrase, in which black people offer up their selves like the talking commodities in *Das Kapital* or in Theodore Dreiser's *Sister Carrie*, already suggests the slave economy that "lending" exists to cover over.[33] And indeed the scene as a whole, with its successive subordinations of Cuff in Rice's minstrel performance and in Nevin's use of dialect, enacts a second displacement, this time from the free labor by which the passage initially sought to distance itself from slavery. It narratologically reenslaves a black man who has evidently turned out to be more competitive and enterprising than he should be. This rather desperate shifting indicates the ambivalence that minstrelsy's debt to black cultural production called forth—and which this origin paradigm, I believe, was invented to mediate or "manage."

But we have yet to deal with the most curious detail of this scene, that in which Cuff "let[s] his open mouth as a mark for boys to pitch pennies into"— suspiciously close to white fantasy, but possibly observed. Then again, perhaps Nevin had read Melville's *Confidence-Man* (1857). In the third chapter Black Guinea, a "grotesque negro cripple, in tow-cloth attire and an old coal-sifter of a tambourine in his hand," makes his appearance:

> Shuffling among the crowd, now and then he would pause, throwing back his head and opening his mouth like an elephant for tossed apples at a menagerie; when, making a space before him, people would have a bout at a strange sort of pitch-penny game, the cripple's mouth being at once target and purse, and he hailing each expertly-caught copper with a cracked bravura from his tambourine. To be the subject of alms-giving is trying, and to feel in duty bound to appear cheerfully grateful under the trial, must be still more so; but whatever his secret emotions, he swallowed them, while still retaining each copper this side the oesophagus. And nearly always he grinned, and only once or twice did he wince, which was when certain coins, tossed by more playful almoners, came inconveniently nigh to his teeth, an accident whose unwelcomeness was not unedged by the circumstance that the pennies thus thrown proved buttons.
>
> While this game of charity was yet at its height, a limping, gimlet-eyed, sour-faced person . . . began to croak out something about his deformity being a sham, got up for financial purposes, which immediately threw a damp upon the frolic benignities of the pitch-penny players. (17–18)

By the end of the scene we realize with a jolt that this is probably a blackface performance;[34] the attentive reader recognizes another of the confidence man's disguises. This is more than the *Fidele*'s passengers do. Hence the dramatic irony here: Melville lifts the mask for the reader only. Indeed, a "purple-faced drover," by implication a slave trader, actually hints at capturing what he takes to be a black man (thus casually linking minstrelsy with the human traffic of slavery). The accusation of fraud extends only to Black Guinea's lameness. Melville here exposes the minstrelization of Cuff in Nevin's account: what these passengers and Nevin himself take as "blackness" Melville reveals to be part of a white discourse undergirding the minstrel phenomenon.

This turn, however, takes place only when the limping man levels his accusation. Before that the reader sees a pitiable cripple doing his best amid a brutal "game of charity," though Ann Douglas has rightly noted that our sentimentalized pity is itself being savaged here (361). (Melville, I need hardly note, was not one to truck in "benevolence," northern or southern, as Captain Delano in "Benito Cereno" makes perfectly clear.)[35] We soon pay the price in embarrassment, but Melville briefly tries to make us as sympathetic as he possibly can. For all its fakery, the passage just quoted is mightily effective. We have no way of knowing that Black Guinea's "secret emotions" are probably those of a white man pretending to be black, and so we are shocked, drawn in. His is an act of blackness as "target and purse," object of derision and repository of market value. Only then does the accusation break up the illusion: "got up for financial purposes." But that, of course, is what Melville has himself been so careful to construct—a sham that works, if only to embarrass—and he has done it by commodifying the blazes out of Black Guinea. In a curious echo of the black shingle dancers in lower Manhattan, the consciousness of black commodification which the writing forces on us works all the more to make blackness into a marketable object of white interest, this time for the reader. In order for the passage to possess any effect, the racial economy so bitterly exposed here must arouse before it is revealed. Commodification is, in a sense, Black Guinea's *attraction;* it is what seems "blackest" about him. It is precisely what is calculated to evoke the foolish pleasure of our pity, and Melville's grim irony only confirms that the attempt to reveal minstrelsy's financial purposes has itself proved to be an act of minstrelization.

Blackface here is one more con game. But Melville's rejection of it accords in striking ways with the thing itself. Far from a happily secured distribution of cultural needs and desires, in other words, racial counterfeiting in Jacksonian America appears actually to have defeated the efforts to master it—whether by mystification or by exposure—no less than it haunted its partisans. The writings I have surveyed were variously ineffectual plays for control of the questions minstrelsy apparently raised and tried to resolve. What these narratives seem to have realized is that the minstrel show flaunted as much as it hid the fact of expropriation and its subtexts, enslavement and intermixture. Such seemingly coherent and purposive accounts, in short, constituted part of a volatile discourse on "blackness"—examples in themselves of "racial" production's social unconscious.

3

White Kids and No Kids At All: Working-Class Culture and Languages of Race

> This may be the music
> for the million, hurly burling,
> We will not hear it
> for a million sterling.
>   —anonymous

As the minstrel show situated itself in the urban North, its debased cultural position, no less than its racial economy, made its representations politically volatile. Its racial meanings were inextricable from its class argument, and one must therefore attend to the shifting class formations, and minstrelsy's shifting place within them, in the antebellum North. It was in rowdy theatrical spaces that an emergent racial politics was both registered and created, and that the racial feeling underlying and shaping but many times eluding the official narratives of race in these years began to appear. Rather than locate in disembodied minstrel types some coherent, intentional politics (derived from our present notions of nineteenth-century racial matters), one ought, as Gareth Stedman Jones's work suggests, to examine the complications in the minstrel show's languages of race with reference to antebellum social and political developments (*Languages* 8). The popular theater was itself an increasingly crucial though less and less respectable part of those developments, and for a time this status enabled minstrelsy to become an oppositional, almost underground cultural form. As a result, it told a story less articulate yet perhaps more revealing than the taunts and ripostes of polemicists.

To get at this story I will sketch the outlines of a new kind of "popular" sphere in the urban Northeast (primarily in New York) that began to emerge after 1830. The disparate meanings of blackface found their material basis in the various concrete ways certain popular domains engaged black culture, in the physical spaces and cultural institutions where it was produced for and enjoyed by predominantly working-class audiences. Leaving to one side the minstrel show's more baroque transgressions, I am after some sense of why this suitably racist

63

cultural form generated so much disdain, why its critics found it so distasteful, an objection that often had little to do with race. Rather, in its appropriations of "blackness" the Jacksonian popular theater—along with the penny press, the saloon, and the public museum—appears to have reproduced and revitalized a set of class values. It was the way it *staged* class that was most often the objection, the way the stale patter and bad puns and achieved grotesquerie kept sliding from racial burlesque into class affiliation or affirmation. It was through "blackness" that class was staged, and to some observers, at least, the combination could not have been more irksome.

THE GREAT DIVIDE

The minstrel show, eclectic in origin, primitive in execution, and raucous in effect, virtually announced itself as one of our first popular institutions. The nineteenth-century debate about it seems familiar perhaps because minstrelsy helped constitute a break (and thus an anxious discourse about that break) between elite, genteel, and low cultures which would be fundamental by our century. In fact, the dual emergence of the first remarkable body of (black and white) American imaginative literature and of such notable popular phenomena as minstrelsy, melodrama, and the dime novel neatly demonstrates Fredric Jameson's point about the dialectical interrelatedness and opposition of high and low cultural forms; in capitalist societies they presuppose and depend on each other, are twin responses to a common, class-divided history ("Reification" 133–34). Many writers (such as the dime novelist George Lippard) put a broadly class-related face on the opposition in terminologies of the scandalous "upper ten" and the abused "lower million." Indeed, by the early 1840s minstrelsy—alongside lower-million amusements such as the public lecture, the public museum, and melodrama—was ranged explicitly against the opera, the "legitimate" theater, and the concert hall, the American beginnings of what Andreas Huyssen has called the "great divide."[1] In this sense minstrel shows actually resembled the nineteenth-century dime museum, as George Rehin has observed. On the one hand, they constantly deflated the pretensions of an emerging middle-class culture of science, reform, education, and professionalism, while on the other, they disseminated information about technology and urban life for working people very often new to the city: "Minstrel 'darkies' were conned and swindled, run down by trolleys, shocked by batteries, and jailed for violating laws they didn't understand."[2] They ultimately assuaged an acute sense of class insecurity by indulging feelings of racial superiority.

Yet minstrel companies unquestionably had a defiant sense of both their own and their audiences' compromised cultural position. Part of a general emergence of artisan culture into national view, the minstrel vogue, along with mass political parties and the penny press, helped to create or organize a new public whose tastes the popular amusements now represented for the first time (Henderson 103). As one popular song put it:

> Music now is all de rage;
> De Minstrel Bands am all engaged;
> Both far and near de people talk
> 'Bout Nigger Singing in New York.
> • • •
> Barnum's Museum can't be beat:
> De Fat Boys dar am quite a treat.
> Dar's a Big Snake too, wid a rousing stinger;
> Likewise Pete Morris, de Comic Singer.
> • • •
> De Chatham keeps among de rest—
> Entertainments ob de best.
> In public favor dis place grows,
> 'Specially on account ob *Mose.*
> • • •
> De Astor Opera is anoder nice place;
> If *you* go thar, jest wash your face!
> Put on your "kids," an fix up neat,
> For dis am de spot of de *eliteet!*[3]

By the time this song was published in 1849 (it was probably performed somewhat earlier), the minstrel show had long since found its urban northeastern audience: the Bowery milieu whose more vehement representatives rioted at the Astor Place Opera House later that year. We might, in fact, take this variety of song as a rallying cry for that event, inasmuch as both riot and songs marked the end of an earlier fluidity and intermixture of class-identified entertainments and institutional sites.

One does not quite yet find this song's sentiments consolidated in, for instance, the early 1830s (though of course blackface always bore a fiercely popular stamp). First performed in those years between the acts at "respectable" theaters, minstrelsy in New York steadily retreated over the next decade to lower Broadway, and lower-class, houses. The long-accepted (and somewhat permeable) internal division of theater audiences into cheap gallery, fashionable box, and middling pit seats—the so-called gods, gentlemen, and groundlings—gradually became rough external divisions between class-specific theaters. In 1820 the "internal situation" of a Boston house still looked this way to one patron:

> It appeared that the gallery was the resort of the particoloured race of Africans, the descendants of Africans, and the vindicators of the abolition of the slave trade; that the tier of boxes below it in the center was occupied by single gentlewomen who had lodgings to let, and who were equally famous for their delicacy and taciturn disposition. The remainder of the boxes, I was given to understand, were visited by none but the dandies, and people of the first respectability and fashion; while the pit presented a mixed multitude of the lower orders of all sorts, sizes, ages, and deportments.[4]

"Africans," "vindicators of abolition," and "mixed multitude," one surmises, are shorthand for the rabble; but the rabble (at least its white members) soon had its own playhouses, and made its triumphant mark on existing ones. This division was not a simple matter of newly specialized theaters, as Raymond Williams has reminded us; the specialization itself was produced by, and in a range of ways mirrored, the social structure and tensions in metropolizing northeastern cities ("Social" 131). Exemplars of a new cultural sphere, minstrel shows were unrelentingly self-conscious, continually inscribing audiences' allegiances in the form of the show: *you* would never go to the Astor Place Opera because you came here (recall that Margaret Fuller hadn't actually gone to the theater to hear those "African" melodies). The result, however, was in one sense to equate "low" audiences with the racial ritual that defined their cultural position, that is, implicitly to identify the Bowery constituency with the blackness they "put on."

They were, in any case, understood to inhabit the bottom. The *Philadelphia Public Ledger* (May 16, 1849) conceded the class character of the audience for minstrelsy and melodrama in its response to the Astor Place riot: "It leaves behind a feeling to which this community has hitherto been a stranger—an opposition of classes—the rich and poor—white kids and no kids at all; in fact, to speak right out, a feeling that there is now in our country, in New York City, what every good patriot has hitherto considered it his duty to deny—a *high* class and a *low* class." If this is vague sociology it is better cultural geography. For not only in the theater but in the public sphere generally, as Peter Buckley has shown, a bifurcation had indeed occurred between the 1830s and 1849. From the late 1820s, when audiences and entertainments were still broadly representative of the social totality, northern urban culture had begun to develop along two lines—in New York, one following Chatham Street and then up the Bowery, the other marching fashionably up Broadway to the Astor Place Opera House. "These two cultural axes were not initially in opposition," Buckley writes, "yet gradually there developed, especially after 1837, two distinct idioms, two audiences and two versions of what constituted the 'public' sphere of communication and amusement" (31). In 1849 the cultures clashed where the axes nearly met, at Astor Place.

The Astor Place riot proved a full-scale eruption of national and class tensions into the sphere of culture. With some help from the press, and from nativist Bowery agitators such as the dime novelist Ned Buntline (E. Z. C. Judson), himself a direct link between the new culture of amusements and growing social fissures, a lengthy rivalry between the British "legitimate" Shakespearean actor Charles Macready and the air-sawing American Edwin Forrest entered a new register as the two actors portrayed Macbeth in concurrent New York productions. To their respective constituencies this was a struggle for political legitimation fought out in the cultural terms that the "great divide" had made available. If Forrest had for more than twenty years created various incarnations of a Jacksonian hero (Metamora, Jack Cade, Spartacus),[5] Macready, as the feud developed, came to signify an aristocracy of "taste," the "upper ten," the Dickens of *American Notes*. On May 7 Macready's New York opening at Astor Place was interrupted by boos, a hail of rotten lemons, and ultimately a row of chairs thrown by a conspiratorial claque of Forrest's Bowery "b'hoys." A published list of signatories (including Washington Irving and Herman Melville) quickly responded, vowing order and urging Macready to continue his performances. Three nights later similar demonstrations plagued Macready's *Macbeth;* refusing to be bullied, however, and buttressed by some well-placed police, Macready pressed on. A crowd of over five thousand, further angered by admission restrictions and the show of police force, now gathered outside the opera house, assaulting the structure with paving stones and yelling slogans such as, "Burn the damned den of the aristocracy!" and "You can't go in there without kid gloves on!" The militia, two hundred anxious troops, readied themselves for this assault, which was soon turned against the troops themselves. First they fired over the heads of the crowd, and then directly into it; twenty-two were killed, over one hundred and fifty wounded. As Buckley puts it, "The Astor Place riot appeared to be a moment when the mob became a class and when the classes seemed in irreconcilable opposition."[6] The minstrel show, in other words, inhabited—and began actually to signify—not an undifferentiated "mass" culture but a class-defined, often class-conscious, cultural sphere.

But while the broadest structural outlines of minstrelsy's class character are sharp enough, the details are rather less so. One should note, for instance, that its audience's class makeup was often contradictory; while the audience was made up predominantly of young male workers, there was also a fair number of men and women from other classes, not only in the more mixed audiences of the 1830s but later as well. The journeyman craftsmen and semiskilled or unskilled workers (teamsters, boatmen, barbers, and so on) who increasingly constituted the minstrel show's audience when theater prices plummeted after the 1837 panic were often joined by people from "contradictory class locations," to use Erik Olin Wright's term (19–63): shopkeepers, clerks, small master artisans. Regarding even the class-bound audiences of the 1840s, there was some confusion among commentators about just who was out there in the pit and the gallery. As I will argue later, one of minstrelsy's functions was precisely to bring various class fractions into contact with one another, to mediate their relations, and finally to aid in the construction of class identities over the bodies of black people. Emerging splits within the working class (between artisans and proletarianized workers, for instance, or between "natives" and immigrant Irish) were often made manifest in terms of these groups' differential relations to racial privilege, even as the formation of a northern working class depended on a common sense of whiteness. In short, the new milieu that blackface occupied came unevenly into being, cutting across the popular classes and constituting in itself a field of conflict over which "public" would in fact turn out to define it. Nor was the minstrel show simply created out of nowhere; consisting partly of appropriations of extant institutions, partly of new inventions, it grew up right alongside the more respectable entertainments.[7]

These unevennesses were enough to tilt the "lower million's" rhetoric of class in the direction of a populist sensibility, as the phrase itself suggests, but they hardly mitigated the minstrel show's class basis. As David Montgomery has observed of the people who were minstrelsy's adherents: "The praise they bestowed on the 'honest mechanics' of their communities echoed through the popular songs and dime-novel literature of the day. . . . Although this culture was infused with a populist, rather than a strictly class consciousness, it clearly separated the nation into 'the producers' and 'the exploiters'" ("Labor" 94). Ideologically the minstrel show was a "popular" or "producer's" form, mightily class-inflected but unstable in its class ideologies and shifting in its class makeup; structurally it was a working-class form, firmly grounded in the institutional spaces and cultural predispositions of workers.[8] Christy's Minstrels had their longest New York run at a theater named Mechanics' Hall. Working-class values and desires were aired and secured in the minstrel show. Its racial "narrative" dovetailed with its class sources in surprising and sometimes confusing ways. Theatrical displays of "blackness" seemingly guaranteed the atmosphere of license so central to working-class entertainment in this period. And blackface provided a convenient mask through which to voice class resentments of all kinds—resentments directed as readily toward black people as toward upper-class enemies. But as we have seen, there was also a historical logic in glossing working-class whites as black, given the degree to which large sections of these groups shared a common culture in many parts of the North. Certain minstrel forms attested to this fact; moreover, as David Roediger has shown, many popular racial slurs both onstage and off ("coon," "buck") also referred to whites (*Wages* 97–100). Occasionally these facts resulted in positive identifications between black and white, however quick the minstrel show usually was to forestall them.

All of which evidence may begin to suggest that blackface, in a real if partial sense, *figured* class—that its languages of race so invoked ideas about class as to provide displaced maps or representations of "working-classness." Thus it was said of T. D. Rice's English tour that his burlesque skits were "vulgar even to grossness," and captivated "the chimney sweeps and apprentice boys of London, who wheeled about and turned about and jumped Jim Crow, from morning until night, to the annoyance of their masters, but the great delight of the cockneys."[9] The submerged equation here of slaves and white workers (apprentices and perennially blackened sweeps ranged against their "masters") was not at all unusual; it was popularized, as we shall see, in radical artisans' rhetoric of "wage slavery." Nor was the implicit (and opposing) claim that caricatures of blacks culturally represented workers above all. Blackface quickly became a sort of useful shorthand in referring to working men. New York's Castle Garden, noted the *Journal of Music*, nightly featured a variety of distinguished musical offerings, "and two or three songs by ANNA ZERR, who (shame to say) stooped to pick up one night and sing 'Old folks at home,' for the b'hoys; one would as soon think of picking up an apple-core in the street."[10] Indeed, the overlapping of racial and class codes probably made the minstrel show's audiences seem more homogeneously working class than they actually were; in this way as in others, minstrelsy helped resolve internal differences within plebeian culture, creating notions of white working-classness and blackness at one and the same time.[11]

Certainly this rhetorical situation only hardened observers of the theater against blackface's constituency. "There must be some . . . place for a certain class of people to effervesce in their excitements of pleasure," said one wit of the Chatham Theatre, a primary site of minstrelsy and by all accounts the "lowest." "It has been useful as a kind of sewer for the drainage of other establishments" (Northall 152–53). The sporting paper *Spirit of the Times* produced a clipped taxonomy: "Firemen, butcher-boys, cab and omnibus drivers, 'fancy' men, and b'hoys, generally" (February 6, 1847). Yet while the minstrel show was too mediated or overdetermined a form to have been simply the creation of a workers' culture, or enjoyed solely by it, the "sheer weight of numbers," as Gareth Stedman Jones has argued of the English music hall, "the preoccupations and predilections of workers" did impose a "discernible imprint" on minstrelsy's racial imagery (*Languages* 9–10). Conversely, racial rhetoric became instrumental to ideas about working people themselves. How, exactly, did this situation come about?

Historians agree that American culture in the Northeast underwent profound changes between 1825 and 1835. Among other things, a bourgeoisie worthy of the name came into being. As many recent historians have in different ways constructed this history, an unprecedented separation and discrete self-definition of classes occurred after the mid-1820s. For Burton Bledstein, an emerging "professionalism" constituted the "cultural process by which the middle class in America matured and defined itself" (ix); for Karen Halttunen, antebellum sentimentalism was "central to the self-conscious self-definition of middle-class culture" (xvii). Mary Ryan's account places the family at the center of middle-class formation—the child-rearing practices, familial values, and domestic ideologies that became, in her striking phrase, the "cradle of the middle class." Paul Johnson and Paul Boyer, like David Brion Davis before them, both see a culture of moral reform as crucial to the middle class's self-making; as Boyer has it, a phalanx of temperance reformers, advocates of industrial morality, and the like, concerned to instill good Christian principles in an undisciplined work force, in fact helped "an embryonic urban middle class define itself" (61). This work undoes an earlier historiographic tradition (the "consensus school"), still alive in the writing of scholars such as Sacvan Bercovitch, which saw a hegemonic culture of liberalism at work in all walks of American life, summed up in Louis Hartz's remark that America is "a kind of national embodiment of the concept of the bourgeoisie" (51). As Stuart Blumin has argued, "However broad the bourgeois consensus may have been in comparison to European societies, it was not so broad that it precluded the formation of distinct classes within American society" ("Hypothesis" 304). For what is implied in the notion of middle-class formation is precisely the formation of a distinctive working-class culture or way of life— though of course the development of each class (and its class fractions) was uneven, halting, not necessarily synchronous with the others.[12]

The specific results of working-class formation, particularly with regard to popular racial consciousness, will necessarily be foregrounded in my readings of the minstrel show in part II. Here, however, the broadest social effects on male workers of a new free-labor economy may be briefly noted. The crafts were fairly quickly proletarianized, splitting formerly self-sufficient artisans into masses of wage workers on the one hand and select groups of industrious mechanics and industrial entrepreneurs on the other; control over the trades went to merchant capitalists who had in some cases been artisans themselves. The word *boss* was coined in these years, Paul Johnson observes, a sign that the interests of master and worker were now different and opposed.[13] In many trades, de-skilling accompanied this keener sense of social hierarchization, and increasingly rigid practices of industrial discipline were instituted. Making and selling for the first time became distinct activities; employees in the front rooms of, say, shoemakers' shops were separated from—and as "clerks" came eventually to occupy a higher class than—the artisans who made the shoes.[14] Housing practices mimicked these new divisions. Master craftsmen, men on the way up, moved away from their places of business and into residential neighborhoods, while workers moved themselves and their families out of their masters' homes—if, that is, they had been lucky enough to live in them in the first place. In a host of new journeymen's societies and more informal collectives, workingmen implicitly set themselves off from a supposedly harmonious community of "the Trade." Massive Irish and German immigration soon segmented that community even further, transforming the American working class, by the mid-1850s, into a largely foreign-born population.[15]

The minstrel show's cognitive equation of black and white working class had its origins here. In *Policing the Crisis*, Stuart Hall and others argue that disarticulations of hegemony accompany periods of extreme capitalist crisis, generating fresh repertoires of domination. The strained class relations that resulted from the explosion of capitalist energies in early nineteenth-century America produced various such languages and practices. A new discourse of crime and lower-class criminality in these years was one example, although journals such as the *Police Gazette* also admitted of more populist, "republican" accents, resulting in a war of definition between, as Dan Schiller puts it, "rogues" and the "rights of men" (377). Similarly, a new discourse of race, employed largely by workers themselves, also helped mute newly created class conflicts, particularly in the postdepression 1840s.[16] The insecurity that attended class stratification produced a whole series of working-class fears about the status of whiteness; working-class white men, Richard Slotkin points out, began to perceive "the form of labor degradation in racial and sexual terms," rejecting such degradation by affirming positions of white male superiority (150).

Sandwiched between bourgeois above and black below, respectable artisans feared they were becoming "blacker" with every increment of industrial advance, and countered with the language and violence of white supremacy. But the very vehemence of their response indicated the increasing functional and discursive interchangeability of blacks and working-class whites. The neighborhoods to which white workers moved, for example, were often racially integrated, effectively negating the cushion of difference, and this condition, along with workers' fears of being displaced from work by blacks, seems to have given rise to much of the racist violence in the antebellum United States.[17] Likewise, "blackleg" was used to describe what later strikers would call a "scab," its racial overtones further evidence of black and white working-class competitiveness and interchangeability, for blacklegs were in fact in some cases black. An extreme instance of working-class "blackening" was that of the immigrant Irish, whom antebellum native whites widely equated with blacks as an alien, subhuman, and brutal species.[18] The rhetoric of race that was a specific product of antebellum America's capitalist crisis thus equated working-classness with blackness as often as it differentiated between them, an antinomy with properly equivocal results. For while it gave "the cutting edge of racial feeling," Slotkin writes, to working-class disdain for both Lords of the Loom and Lords of the Lash, it also produced "artificial and ultimately destructive distinctions within the working classes" (150). Blackface minstrelsy, I would argue, was founded on this antinomy, reinstituting with ridicule the gap between black and white working class even as it reveled in their (sometimes liberatory) identification.

This dynamic surfaced not only in the minstrel show but in a variety of popular domains of discourse[19]—largely because they constituted one major way in which working people resisted the constricting demands of metropolitan industrialization. It should come as no surprise that social conflicts in which race and class interpenetrated and contradicted each other were acutely registered in the cultural forms and spaces that arose to ease them.

DOMAINS OF DISCOURSE

In the early 1830s changes in the northern American class structure urged the need for a discrete sphere of working-class sociability just as an urban culture industry started to emerge. The classes began to forge social lives independent of one another; drinking became a staple of working-class boardinghouses as abjuring drink became a badge of respectability. Goaded by these developments and accelerating them in turn, amusements of all kinds sprang up in New York's Bowery. Unsympathetic observers noted the connection, and one blamed boardinghouse life itself for the upsurge in New York amusements. "There is no bond of union among the lodgers of a boarding-house," wrote the popular playwright William K. Northall; in the absence of fireside enjoyments boarders were forced on their own resources, and "public places of entertainment offer the readiest means to these poor undomesticated animals" (7). At least the animals appear to have gotten what they wanted. Although the city had decided in 1823 to regulate an already alarming array of novelty acts in the commercial summer gardens, Peter Buckley speculates that these restrictions only drove such "minor" amusements onto the commercial stage (141). The Bowery Theatre opened in 1826; and while it had begun with "legitimate" fare, by 1830 its innovative manager, Thomas Hamblin, was booking melodrama, performing animals, jugglers, minstrel acts, and more—that theater's contribution to a whole new downtown milieu. Scores of cheap dance halls, billiard rooms, saloons, and amphitheaters for bare-knuckle prizefights and cockfights, as well as prime minstrel show sites such as the Olympic, Franklin, and Chatham theaters, had all established themselves by the late 1830s, more or less in spite of the panic. Not only theater managers but also entrepreneurs such as P. T. Barnum revolutionized commercial forms of leisure. Barnum developed in his Great American Museum the variety acts that were coming to characterize many downtown "vaudevilles." The first organized minstrel troupe in New York City, Dan Emmett's Virginia Minstrels, grew out of this context in 1843; while accounts conflict, the troupe was probably born in a hotel across the street from the Bowery Theatre.[20]

These domains of popular discourse together constituted a new, largely masculine ideological field separate from both bourgeois culture and that of the trade unions, as Sean Wilentz suggests, in its own way connecting "workingmen's pride, resentments, and simple pleasures to the language of republican politics" (263)—a sensational street version of the radical artisan's emphasis on liberty, egalitarianism, and cultural independence.[21] The uses of race in this anti-authoritarian culture, however, have not been properly examined; labor historians have done little, beyond apologizing for white workers' racial attitudes, to clarify the affective results of American "freedom's" dependence on American slavery and racism.[22] The fact is that these new amusements were also primary sites of antebellum "racial" production, inventing or at least maintaining the working-class languages of race that appear to have been crucial to the self-understanding of the popular classes, and to others' understanding of them as well. In minstrel acts and other forms of "black" representation, racial imagery was typically used to soothe class fears through the derision of black people, but it also often became a kind of metonym for class. Even then it usually referenced only a cherished working-class relationship to its objects of fun; yet one occasionally finds in this imagery the tones of racial sympathy. Indeed, the popular theater, the saloon, the museum, and the penny press—to name the institutions I look at here—prominently displayed the ambiguities that resulted from the grounding of much racial discourse in working-class culture.

72

It is difficult to capture both the unevenness and the peculiar coherence of this popular sphere in the antebellum years. The character of the minstrel show in particular appears to have shifted slightly at least once in each of the three decades under consideration, and these shifts refer us not only to changing historical formations or conventions of racial representation but also to the earliest development of the culture industry itself. Beginning as an entr'acte affair of solo songs and dances in legitimate theaters and certain popular sites, minstrelsy remained an art of brief burlesque and comic relief throughout much of the 1830s. But from its development into a full-fledged show in the post-panic early 1840s until its partial absorption into the *Uncle Tom's Cabin* melodramas in the early and mid-1850s, minstrelsy formed one major part of urban popular culture, settling into a rather lifeless, and enormously profitable, institutionalization in the late 1850s.

Produced in theaters that hosted the whole range of popular amusements, blackface performance was marked by the new styles of staging and commercial organization that were only one example of this theatrical culture's internal continuity. In 1839 Mitchell's Olympic Theatre, mid-panic, halved its admission prices; and it focused almost exclusively on what William Mitchell described as "tragico-comico-illegitimate" productions—essentially travesties of local events and amusements (Buckley 383). These innovations sustained minstrel companies as well. Their topical commentary, Shakespearean or operatic burlesques, and stock companies (useful in generating familiarity between actors and audiences) resulted in extended runs. Shakespearean burlesque proved particularly long-lived, so intimate were even popular audiences in the antebellum years with what one minstrel parody called "de Bird of Avon." Shakespeare's plays became *Hamlet the Dainty*, "Bad Breath, the Crane of Chowder," *Julius Sneezer*, "Dars-de-Money"; while, as Lawrence Levine has shown, Shakespeare was truly an author for the million, such travesties defined even more clearly this culture's difference from that of the upper ten. One *Hamlet* parody refused to distinguish between hawk and handsaw:

> Oh! tis consummation
> Devoutly to be wished,
> To end your heartache by a sleep;
> When likely to be dished,
> Shuffle off your mortal coil,
> Do just so,
> Wheel about and turn about
> And jump Jim Crow.

Owing to the popularity of such fare, theaters devoted solely to blackface began to appear by the late 1840s, and many troupes eventually, if briefly, supported their own "Ethiopian Opera Houses."[23]

The coherence of this class-based culture, as I have noted, was also to be found in its self-conscious relationship to its own amusements. Many minstrel songs amount to little more than narratives of the audience's preferred entertainments, and much of the playing time of productions such as Benjamin Baker's wildly popular *A Glance at New York in 1848* was taken up, Peter Buckley notes, with the "vigorous consumption of popular amusement and commodities—the popular fiction, the 'waudevilles,' . . . corner rolls and fried liver" which defined this culture's everyday life (390). Like other popular plays in this period, *New York As It Is* (1848), an updated version of *A Glance at New York*, features scenes set at the Chatham Theatre itself, as well as a bout of "nigger" dancing reminiscent of the black Catherine Street shingle dancers. This commercial self-consciousness was, like minstrelsy, one result of an aesthetic of local travesty; it was also an obvious product of culture-industry cunning, a self-serving roll call of brand names. But it served, again, to equate working-class audiences with the arts, notably blackface, that they patronized—the most immediate reason, perhaps, for the overlay of racial and class imagery. As the Young America writer Cornelius Mathews was one of the last to point out, the more popular pleasures and their characteristic audiences were in some sense interchangeable metaphors for each other. In *A Pen-and-Ink Panorama of New York City* (1853), Mathews boards a Hudson River steamer and is soon surrounded by a "group of Bowery pit inhabitants" who "begin to dance to the banjo and triangle" (89). (A plantation frolic on the Hudson!) By 1853 the signifying chain linking workingmen to Bowery amusements and through these to blackface performance was little more than a cliché of social observation. What concerns us here are the chain's uncertain racial outcomes.

Perhaps its strongest link, in these times of temperance, was alcohol. As early as the 1820s, saloons and grocery-grog shops had become the centerpiece of an emergent culture (Wilentz 53), despite the attempts of protoindustrialists and other elites to police working-class habits and amusements through the revival, the Sunday school, and the temperance society—that "middle-class obsession," as Paul Johnson calls it (55). It is true that drinking was so central to this culture that journeymen and laborers hardly needed a separate place to indulge the pastime. E. P. Thompson remarked the "alternate bouts of intense labour and of idleness, wherever men were in control of their own working lives" ("Time" 73), and although employers were increasingly in a position to insist on abstemious codes of industrial behavior, shop-floor traditions such as brandy tippling and hangover-induced, inoperative "Blue Mondays" provided the readiest means of worker control (Gutman 33–39). Yet saloons were not simply more and better space for saturnalia; they were semiofficial working-class institutions. Their function was often proclaimed in various bold inscriptions hung above the entrance:

1. *King*—I govern all.
2. *General*—I fight for all.
3. *Minister*—I pray for all.
4. *Laborer*—And I pay for all.[24]

74

Custodians of a sometimes overtly politicized cultural style, tavernkeepers nourished camaraderie, mutuality, and solidarity among their patrons. For immigrant workingmen especially, friendly saloons were upholders of traditional customs and rituals, or political halfway houses; the Irish nationalist Daniel O'Connell was a regular toastee. Major figures of immigrant life, among them the prizefighter Yankee Sullivan and politician David Broderick, organized constituencies and maintained their position by owning saloons. Broderick actually named his The Subterranean after the radical news sheet of his friend, firebrand Mike Walsh.[25]

A wide variety of amusements was to be found in the saloon, from cockfights to minstrel acts; for every T. D. Rice making his fortune on the stage, we might suppose several or even dozens of imitators worked the local taverns. Some of these, like the men who formed the Virginia Minstrels in 1843, went on to fame of their own; and many of the taverns began an upgrading to the status of "concert saloon" by the late 1840s. Yet the presence in this particular milieu of a Mike Walsh—who, however radical in his class sympathies, went so far as to form an alliance with proslavery Calhoun Democrats in the early 1840s—perhaps affirms the racist intentions behind the casual presence of blackface in the saloon.[26] It is nevertheless clear, as we will see in chapter 4, that Repealer O'Connell and Liberator William Lloyd Garrison frequently corresponded in the 1840s, attempting for a time an "internationalist" labor abolitionism that could not have left many Irish-American saloon patrons untouched though it ultimately failed in its project. Indeed, writes Bruce Laurie, one tavern in Philadelphia sported a placard with a bust of O'Connell and a snippet from Byron's *Childe Harold* that may have permitted a variety of political investments: "Hereditary bondsmen! who would be free, / Themselves must strike the blow" ("Nothing" 100), instancing again the potentially positive equation of white working-class and black. (Significantly, Frederick Douglass appended this couplet to the end of the Covey chapter [chap. 17] of *My Bondage and My Freedom* [1855]; he also used it to argue in favor of black enlistment in the Civil War [*Life* 339].) The conflicted intimacy American racial cultures shared is certainly present in a detailed account of saloon life later in the century, in which a black man is said to have sung songs "of many kinds, comic, sentimental, pathetic, and silly," inducing tears and a respectful hush with his "strange, wailing refrain" (Harrison 178–88). This response was of course only another kind of condescension, and it set the terms of interracial association, but in the mid-nineteenth century productive working-class political ties across racial boundaries usually had no other base of support.

If the saloon was a more "organic" component of this culture, the museum marked the extent of early American "cultural industrialization." Future University of Michigan president Henry Tappan in 1851 delineated the difference between its British and American versions: *"Museums—a place for the Muses,"* he wrote, a "fit appellation" for an institution such as the British Museum. In New York, however, the word denoted only "a place for some stuffed birds and animals, for the exhibition of monsters, and for vulgar dramatic performances—a mere place of popular amusement" (quoted in Harris 33). Although we should be much more careful in assessing the attraction of landmarks such as Barnum's American Museum, this remark indicates, from the point of view of the educated classes, the adjectives they called forth. Yet they were of no slight lineage. Historians have emphasized the importance of such plebeian places of learning to revolutionary-era artisans, rationalist Paineites whose thirst for knowledge was slaked by scientific exhibits and astronomical lectures. From a certain angle, indeed, the story of the museum is one of declension, Jeffersonian republicanism vulgarized into Jacksonian democracy.[27] Neil Harris, however, has argued that Barnum's relation to his audiences was underwritten by an "operational aesthetic," an active intellectual responsiveness on the part of patrons who were delighted with issues of truth and falsity and were as ready to be fooled by an ingenious humbug as to be thrilled by a genuine curiosity. Yet, as Peter Buckley argues, this more sympathetic view still tends toward an ahistorical idea of undifferentiated cultural predisposition. "Barnum's pieces of management," rather, "were concrete responses to the need to create a paying reliable public at a time when this 'public' was a contested political category and when the market for popular amusement was typed by its plebeian origins and attitudes" (489). Barnum was helping this popular sphere define itself, that is to say, by putting it in his pocket. A new public was being won over in every sense by the same culture-industry innovations it was beckoning into existence.[28]

Race figured prominently in the spate of amusements the museum offered, most obviously in blackface acts but in other productions as well. One way to evade the genteel prejudice against theatrical vice was to provide the same entertainments under the roof of a seemingly more respectable institution. Henry James, one of Barnum's early customers, later wrote that Barnum's "'lecture room,' attached to the Great American Museum, overflowed into posters of all the theatrical bravery disavowed by its title" (162). Barnum, whose early enterprises (dwarfs, minstrel dancers, foreign jugglers) planted him firmly within the Bowery setting, was himself a sometime blackface performer, and, he wrote, "to my surprise was much applauded" (90). The showman's first major success was the exhibition of a blind, paralytic black woman named Joice Heth, a slave Barnum purchased in 1835—a particularly gruesome instance of the economics of minstrelization. Barnum claimed Joice Heth to be one hundred and sixty-one years old, and to have been the nurse of George Washington. "She was apparently in good health and spirits, but from age or disease, or both, was unable to change her position; she could move one arm at will, but her lower limbs could not be straightened; her left arm lay across her breast and she could not remove it." Yet she was "pert and sociable," Barnum wrote, often breaking suddenly into hymn (74–75). His display at New York's Niblo's Garden of the gnarled old woman, who combined patriotic appeal (she spoke of dressing "dear little

George") with circus monstrosity, brought Barnum an estimated $1,500 a week (Werner 31). It was in Barnum's use of such appalling spectacles that the tastes of his plebeian audiences were represented—in the sense both of satisfying their desires and of raising them to public view.

Joice Heth was only the beginning of Barnum's intrigues with "blackness." He exhibited a skillfully constructed mass of animal parts as the "Fejee Mermaid" in 1842; he hosted blackface acts throughout the antebellum years; and in the 1850s the American Museum ran stage productions of Harriet Beecher Stowe's *Uncle Tom's Cabin* and *Dred.* Like his audiences, Barnum seems to have been fascinated with the mystery of color. In 1850 he hired a black man who claimed to have discovered a weed that would turn Negroes white. True to form, Barnum the future Republican trumpeted this discovery as the solution to the slavery problem, while newspapers daily reported any changes in the black man's hue.[29] Barnum takes obvious relish in mimicking this very process in his enlarged autobiography, *Struggles and Triumphs* (1869). Someone mistakes the young Barnum for a querulous black man after one of his blackface performances and makes a move for his revolver; nothing daunted, Barnum, as he wrote, "rolled my sleeve up, showed my skin, and said, 'I am as white as you are, sir.' [The man] dropped his pistol in positive fright and begged my pardon" (90). These instances of imaginary racial transmutation literalize one train of thought responsible for the minstrel show.[30] They are less articulations of difference than speculations about it. They imagine race to be mutable; very briefly they throw off the burden of its construction, blurring the line between self and other, white workingman and black. (Here blackface actors approached certain fictional uses of the mulatto figure.)[31] They obviously devalue blackness, canceling racial boundaries only to (triumphantly) reinstitute them: through biology with the weed, through makeup with blackface. But they perform this whole operation with a kind of ludic, transgressive glee. One also finds this spirit in, for instance, minstrel-show stump speeches, themselves a species of inflated Barnum-speak. Indeed, stump speeches occasionally parodied certain popular practices devoted to the fixing and classifying of racial boundaries—phrenology, for instance, or the midcentury "science" of racial ethnology.

There was indeed a revealing continuity among these discourses. The Egyptologist George Gliddon, who in *Ancient Egypt* (1844) argued that the greatness of the Egyptians owed to their Caucasian (not Negro) origins, made lecture tours carrying an extensive collection of Barnum-like artifacts; Samuel Morton's *Crania Americana* (1839), which gauged the mental capacity of different races by skull size, was at least as indebted to phrenological techniques as to controlled experiment. The class-based character of blackface performance went some way toward making these discourses seem absurdly similar, or just plain absurd. "On dis side ob me, you may obserb, I hab a cast ob de head ob a gemman ob color; on de udder side, I hab a cast ob de head ob a common white feller," goes a "lecture" on phrenology. A series of perambulatory speculations follows, coming to rest in the observation that all great men are "brack": blacklegs, blackguards, and so on. As to the difference, finally, between the two specimens, "Julycum Cezar Pompy Dan Tucker" and the "dam white rascal": "You see den, dat clebber man an dam rascal means de same in dutch, when dey boph white; but when one white and de udder's brack 'dat's a grey hoss ob anoder color'" (*De Susannah* 80, 83–84). It is no doubt remarkable to discover in a minstrel act an inquiry into the construction—by language, no less—of racial difference; but this speech and the minstrel show generally share with Barnum's antics an urge, nonetheless real for its derisive humor, to investigate the boundaries of race established by "respectable" science, to play with, even momentarily overturn, their placement. This was so even when there was fundamental accord as to that placement: lower-million impatience with the discourses of learned authority, not to mention the complexities of working people's everyday negotiations with race, might result in assaults on the color line itself.

Class prickliness usefully inflected the production of "race" in the penny press as well, which was sometimes capable of outright contradiction. New York newspapers such as the *Transcript* and the *Sun*, for instance, often printed both self-consciously egalitarian antislavery material and lurid accounts of white assaults on blacks.[32] Perhaps the most interesting product of this culture's racial paradoxes was the urban journalist Walter (subsequently Walt) Whitman. As a reporter for the *New York Aurora* in the early 1840s (where he was, in fact, a colleague of Mike Walsh), the author of a temperance dime novel *Franklin Evans; or, The Inebriate* (1842), a columnist at the *Brooklyn Star* in the mid-1840s, and, shortly after, a many-hatted editor at the *Brooklyn Daily Eagle*, Whitman stands out in his attention to the various modes and media of "racial" representation, from minstrelsy to painting to politics itself. He too registered the contradiction between white supremacy and staunch egalitarianism, and while it can scarcely be said that Whitman always found himself on the better side of this problem, he at least has the virtue of having wrestled with it. There were surely complacent moments, such as the racialist-gothic subplot of *Franklin Evans* in which the protagonist, after a drunken binge, finds himself married to a Creole woman, herself a figure for his profligacy. Worse yet, "Is not America for the Whites?" Whitman wrote in 1858. "And is it not better so?" On the other side were Whitman's antislavery views, his celebrations of black English (about which more later), and his praise of William Sidney Mount's paintings of black life, which, he wrote in William Cullen Bryant's *New York Evening Post*, "may be said to have a character of Americanism."[33] Falling somewhere between these instances was Whitman's interest in blackface minstrelsy.

Whitman was a great lover of the minstrel show, seeing in it an American example of what he had found in opera, but he could never quite decide whether it represented the best or the worst America had to offer in the way of a national art. He avidly attended blackface performances, as he did many Bowery productions, and he praised them in print. One troupe, the Harmoneons, said Whitman in 1846, proved that much could be done with "low" material: "'Nigger' singing with them is a subject from obscure life in the hands of a divine painter: rags, patches and coarseness are imbued with the great genius of the artist." Before long I hope to clarify what nourishment our democratic poet might have gotten out of blackface coarseness and obscurity; he certainly seems to have taken them for a people's culture, representative not only of black life but of the Bowery pit as well. Yet Whitman later excoriated minstrelsy, not for its racism but for its vulgarity—"I must be pardoned for saying, that I never could, and never will, admire the exemplifying of our national attributes with Ethiopian minstrelsy"—a judgment whose evident distaste for black people themselves reflects a somewhat common split in working-class culture between antislavery beliefs and personal abhorrence of blacks, not to mention of abolitionism as a movement. (There were also, of course, other sorts of disjunctions and contradictions.) We do know that at the time of Whitman's greatest enthusiasm for the minstrel show he was extensively engaged in Free-Soil politics, that late 1840s challenge to the pro-southern Democracy which would shortly grow into the Republican party. But the ambiguities of Whitman's culture inhered even in the relatively egalitarian Free-Soil movement, for, as Eric Foner observes, it was ideologically broad enough to encompass those opposed to slavery on moral grounds as well as those opposed to the presence of Negro slaves in newly acquired territories and those worried about fugitive slaves fleeing North—in short, "the most vulgar racists and the most determined supporters of Negro rights, as well as all shades of opinion between these extremes." Whitman is a salutary reminder that there is no simple correspondence between individual racial feeling, cultural predisposition, and political ideology. In this he is perhaps a representative case; and he is representative as well in demonstrating both the potential and the real limits of class egalitarianism as a wellspring for antiracism.[34]

It is an ambiguity one finds even in working-class forms such as the dime novel. Although black characters (and black writers) were seldom featured in such fiction, Michael Denning has argued that certain of its favorite class plots could result in surprisingly radical racial stories. George Lippard's *New York: Its Upper Ten and Lower Million* (1853) uses the familiar trope of a lowly mechanic's inheritance to narrate the fortunes of one of its black protagonists, Randolph Royalton. Born of a black slave mother, Randolph is the half-brother of the white Harry Royalton. Both have a claim on the Van Huyden inheritance; seeking it for himself, Harry hires a slave catcher to abduct Randolph and his sister into slavery. The inheritance takes on symbolic weight when Lippard reveals that Randolph's mother was the daughter of a great "leader of the American people"—Thomas Jefferson, perhaps, since stories of his purported slave children were well known (William Wells Brown called on them the same year in *Clotel*). The story thus becomes, writes Denning, "an allegorical assertion of the Black Randolph's rightful share in the inheritance of the Republic" (*Mechanic* 116); derived from stories of noble white mechanics, the plot suddenly accommodates a sympathetic tale of black people's fate in America. (Neither Randolph the black hero nor Arthur Dermoyne the white mechanic receives his inheritance.) Lippard certainly shared the racism of much of the antebellum labor movement, and in his novel *The Quaker City; or, Monks of Monk Hall* (1844) he uses race as a metaphor for corruption: the swindling, pretended southern aristocrat Colonel Fitz-Cowles turns out to be the son of a Creole slave. But the lineaments of Randolph's story reveal that when structured along acceptable class lines—when, that is, there was an implicit twinning of blacks and working-class whites—black characters in such writing, as in popular culture at large, could be portrayed in liberatory ways. As it turned out, the converse was equally true: more than once, and increasingly as the 1840s went on, the presence of "blackness" in this culture would pose a significant class threat.

"No Dainty Kid-Glove Business"

It was, most of all, as a "culturalist" class ideology, a manifestation of class values in audience rites and cultural self-presentation, that blackface sponsored a sense of incipient class trouble. The social tenor of the new amusements very quickly became fodder for the critics, who began to light on the defining—ideological— behavior of this emergent "public." Even as early as the 1830s, T. D. Rice's performances of "Jim Crow" at the Bowery Theatre routinely brought crowds onto the stage (see Fig. 7):

> When Mr. Rice came on the stage to sing his celebrated song of Jim Crow, they not only made him repeat it some twenty times, but hemmed him in so that he actually had no room to perform the little dancing or turning about appertaining to the song; and in the afterpiece, where a supper-table is spread, some among the most hungry very leisurely helped themselves to the viands. It was a rare treat, indeed, to the audience.[35]

Now this was theater for the million. Even when they did not partake of stage viands, audiences made their demands plain. The *New York Mirror* noted of one 1833 Bowery performance:

> A few evenings since [the orchestra] were performing an overture, which did not exactly suit the cultivated taste of some worthies in the pit. "Yankee Doodle," being more in unison with the patriotic ideas of propriety, was loudly called for, and its melting tones forthwith breathed forth in mellifluous harmony. The pit were gratified, and evinced their satisfaction by a gentle roar. (quoted in Buckley 156–57)

This is by no means the last we will see of such demonstrations; nor is it the last of stage reports whose irony, in a kind of homeopathic reaction to the events they describe, is barely under control.

Yet as many have pointed out, it is at first baffling that such audience activities should in the 1830s have taken on class-related signification, for they had marked the experience of theatergoing as early as the turn of the nineteenth century. In 1802 Washington Irving (as Jonathan Oldstyle) was assailed by "thunderbolts" from the gods in the gallery:

> Some how or another the anger of the gods seemed to be aroused all of a sudden, and they commenced a discharge of apples, nuts & gingerbread, on the heads of the honest folks in the pit. . . . I can't say but I was a little irritated at being saluted aside of my head with a rotten pippin, and was going to shake my cane at them; but was prevented by a decent looking man behind me, who informed me it was useless to threaten or expostulate. They are only *amusing themselves* a little at our expence, said he, sit down quietly and bend your back to it. My kind neighbour was interrupted by a hard green apple that hit him between the shoulders—he made a wry face, but knowing it was all in joke, bore the blow like a philosopher. (12)

So there was nothing especially new about the "gentle roar" of later years. Why, then, the access of irony in accounts of theater in the 1830s? As in so many instances, the irony says less about theatrical events than about the ironists themselves, particularly their increasing social distance, both within the theater and without, from an emerging self-conscious class culture unheedful of the vulgarity of racial display. Theater audiences and performances were becoming more differentiated, not more rowdy.[36]

By the 1840s rowdiness had begun to seem a working-class style. If "legitimate" productions in this period aspired to a new restraint, popular amusements cultivated a sort of demonstrative excess through which cultural allegiances were formed and class values negotiated. This ethos was briefly crystallized in the post-panic street and stage appearance of the Bowery b'hoy (see Fig. 3), that "compound of East Side swell, gutter bum, and volunteer fire laddie," in Richard Dorson's words, who parodied the styles of the "upper ten" and posed the greatest cultural challenge to uptown mandarins (288). Termed "Mose" after the stage character that set forth his popular image, the b'hoy affected a brusque manner, peculiar lingo, and extravagant costume, often capped by hair in "soaplocks" plastered to the temple and a shiny stovepipe hat. In many ways he exemplified the first U.S. working-class subculture—the volunteer fireman bent on class travesty, the butcher wise in the ways of cultural bricolage. Although the b'hoy's rubric invoked Irishness, no single ethnic profile defined him, nor was he (contrary to later myth) a partisan of nativism. As one member of the subculture later recalled: "I was at that time what was known as a 'Bowery Boy,' a distinct 'gang' from either the 'know-nothing' or 'Native American' parties. The gang had no regular organization, but were a crowd of young men of different nationalities, mostly American born, who were always ready for excitement, generally of an innocent nature" (quoted in Buckley 316). "Generally," of course, makes room for the Astor Place riot—a phenomenon not only concurrent with the emergence of the b'hoys but in many ways a result of their conscious cultural self-

Fig. 3. Mose and Lize, 1848.
Courtesy of the Library of Congress

definition. By about 1847 their arrival was being announced in various fictional forms, but it was secured by *A Glance at New York in 1848,* one of the greatest melodramatic successes of the nineteenth-century New York stage.

"Mose's" reception on opening night made it clear that the b'hoys' time had come. As a near-contemporary wrote:

> He stood there in his red shirt, with his fire coat thrown over his arm, the stovepipe hat . . . drawn down over one eye, his trousers tucked into his boots, a stump of a cigar pointing up from his lips to his eye, the soap locks plastered flat on his temples, and his jaw protruded into a half-beastly, half-human expression of contemptuous ferocity. . . . Taking the cigar stump from his mouth and turning half-way round to spit, he said:
> "I ain't a goin' to run wid dat mercheen no more!"
> Instantly there arose such a yell of recognition as had never been heard in the little house before. . . . Every man, woman, and child recognized in the character all the distinctive external characteristics of the class.[37]

A Glance at New York and sketches like it were riotously egalitarian, offering a kind of plebeian heroism against the dangers of downtown New York. As with Davy Crockett, one of Mose's frontier antecedents, pugilism was his avocation: "I'm bilein' over for a rousin' good fight with some one somewhere. . . . If I don't have a muss soon, I'll spile" (Baker, *Glance* 15). But the urban (and often pugilistic) business of fire fighting was his central preoccupation:

> Seys I, "What's de matter, good woman?" Seys she, "My baby's in de house, and it's burnin'!" Seys I, "What!"—I turned my cap hindside afore, and buttoned my old fire-coat, and I went in and fetched out dat baby. . . . Ever since dat time I've had a great partiality for little babies. The fire-boys may be a little rough outside, but they're all right here. (*Touches breast.*) It never shall be said dat one of de New York boys deserted a baby in distress. (20)[38]

The figure of Mose, with his "g'hal" Lize or his partner Sykesy, focused an urban style that gave visible, class-resistant expression to the Bowery milieu.[39] Yet few writers have noted how much this expression owed to the accents of race.

I have mentioned that productions such as *A Glance at New York* did not stint on narratives of leisure time. One scene finds Lize on her way to work; she and Mose meet, and the two plot the evening's fun:

Mose: Say, Lize, you're a gallus gal, anyhow.
Lize: I ain't nothin' else.
Mose: What do yer say for Waxhall [the Vauxhall] to-night?
Lize: What's a-goin' on?—is de wawdeville plays there?
Mose: No—there's goin' to be a first-rate shindig; some of our boys will be there.

• • •

Lize: . . . I'd rather go to Christy's. Did you ever see George Christy play the bones? ain't he one of em?
Mose: Yes, he's some.

(22)

Lize proceeds to sing one of the Christy's Minstrels' songs, to Mose's demotic approval, thus attesting again to the frequency with which blackface was used in nineteenth-century discourse to locate white working people. And it is almost predictable that minstrel acts would appropriate Mose himself, one of the many figures of white American humor that underwent a telling sea change on the minstrel stage.[40] The b'hoy appears not to have been compromised by this disguise. Mose's mechanic accents already tend toward the dialect represented as black on the popular stage; some minstrel songs merely blackened a Mose conforming in all other respects to the outlines of the stage b'hoy:

> Wake up, Mose! De Fire am burning;
> Round de corner de smoke am curling.
> Wake up, Mose! the engine's coming;
> Take de rope and keep a running!

"Fire, Fire, Fire" (1848) moves the titular conflagration to the plantation for heroism in black; "Work! Niggers, work!" (1849) celebrates b'hoy culture in sepia tones:

> I like to see de engines fly
>   Through streets and ober ditches;
> And when de b'hoys get in a row,
>   Dey fight like sons of—Freedom![41]

Such were the ready class associations of "blackness" that even this transmutation came with little effort. As the *Journal of Music* wrote, "What magnificent basses and tenors may be heard among our firemen, when making merry together and singing [blackface songs such as] "Uncle Ned," "Old Dan Tucker," or "Lovely May!" ("Letter from A. W. T." 170). To be sure, the rowdiness that gave rise to chants of freedom was achieved by way of oppressive racial caricature, and in this the minstrel show mimicked Jacksonian social relations all around. What is surprising is the degree to which the blackness of the oppressed could itself become an idiom of class dissent—a fact that implied some sense of cross-racial identification. The danger was, of course, that the b'hoys' blackface conquest of the theater foretold greater disasters than those at Astor Place.

   An indication that "black" practices routinely conveyed this kind of danger appears in an 1849 account of saloon dancing by George Foster, the most famous urban chronicler of nightlife and amusements in this period. Retracing Dickens's steps (in *American Notes*) on a Saturday night slumming trip to New York's depressed Five Points section, Foster describes the entertainment at Pete Williams's saloon, now renamed Dickens's Place. The performers are black, not blackfaced; they number a fiddler, a trumpeter, and a bass drummer. The dancers are racially mixed: "Thieves, loafers, prostitutes and rowdies, as well as . . . honest, hard-working people" (*Gas-Light* 73). The orchestra strikes up a blackface minstrel tune, "Cooney in de Holler":

> The dancers begin contorting their bodies and accelerating their movements, accompanied with shouts of laughter and yells of encouragement and applause, until all observance of the figure is forgotten and every one leaps, stamps, screams and hurras on his or her own hook. Affairs are now at their hight [*sic*]. The black leader of the orchestra increases the momentum of his elbow and calls out the figure in convulsive efforts to be heard, until shining streams of perspiration roll in cascades down his ebony face; the dancers, now wild with excitement, like Ned Buntline at Astor Place, leap frantically about like howling dervishes, clasp their partners in their arms, and at length conclude the dance in hot confusion and disorder. (74)[42]

The point here is not merely that black cultural forms and their minstrel counterfeits evoked the riotousness that had lately riven the city. It is also that the language of revolt and the language of amusement were impossible to separate; they bled into each other, the same words referring effortlessly to two, now necessarily related, phenomena. What Foster is describing is in fact the riot—a fling beginning merrily enough and descending, urged on by the leader, into hot confusion and disorder. If the Astor Place riot had itself manifested social divisions in the sphere of culture, it now made a language of eruption available for revolutionary cultural events. The inference that blackface forms, despite all appearances, might have been included among these is hard to resist, given that the revolution then brewing under William Lloyd Garrison's slogan "No Compromise with Slaveholders" was adding a racial component to the threat of social breakup. Fervid cultural forms, often "black" ones, sustained the sense of blood and revolution that came to be associated with Astor Place.

It is clear at least that high-toned commentators directed a broad vocabulary of distaste at these possibly insurrectionary developments. Following the riot, the *Home Journal* wrote that if Macready wished to see those he had offended, he had only to "follow a well-dressed idler down Broadway and observe the looks he gets from *Mose* and the soap-lock-ery as he goes along." The article went on to say: "Let but the more passive aristocratic party clearly select a favorite . . . and let there be but a symptom of a handle for the B'hoys to express their dissent, and the undercurrent breaks forth like an uncapped hydrant" (May 12, 1849). But the b'hoys themselves found the "aristocratic party" far from "passive." Said one speech maker at a rally the day after the riot: "For what—for whom was this murder committed? . . . To please the aristocracy of the city, at the expense of the lives of inoffending citizens . . . to revenge the aristocrats of this city against the working classes."[43] These were, perhaps, the same "sons of freedom" that blackface acts were so apt to celebrate. In any case, such talk kept the class ardor of this plebeian culture in full view, even before the riots. The standard account of Bowery patrons usually repeated the familiar metaphors, which, though they very quickly assumed the status of narrative convention, lost little of their power to disturb. Whitman, whose early journalism, if not his early poetry, is in the b'hoy manner, late in his life celebrated the 1830s Bowery Theatre:

> Pack'd from ceiling to pit with its audience mainly of alert, well dress'd, full
> blooded young and middle-aged men, the best average of American-born
> mechanics . . . the whole crowded auditorium, and what seeth'd in it, and
> flush'd from its faces and eyes, to me as much a part of the show as any—
> bursting forth in one of those long-kept-up tempests of hand-clapping peculiar
> to the Bowery—no dainty kid-glove business, but electric force and muscle
> from perhaps 2000 full-sinew'd men. ("Old" 595)

And in 1847 the *Spirit of the Times* observed

> a vast sea of upturned faces and red flannel shirts, extending its roaring and
> turbid waves close up to the foot-lights on either side, clipping in the orchestra
> and dashing furiously against the boxes—while a row of luckier and stronger-
> shouldered amateurs have pushed, pulled and trampled their way far in ad-
> vance of the rest, and actually stand with their chins resting on the lamp board,
> chanking peanuts and squirting tobacco juice upon the stage. (February 6,
> 1847)

What, finally, are we to make of howling dervishes, uncapped hydrants, elec-
tric force, turbid waves? First, this was indeed a "manly" preserve, a sphere of
traditional male prowess and bravado whose turf loyalties were as likely to result
in individual or gang violence as in the camaraderie of the saloon.[44] There is no
doubt that it was a newly contested space: since it drew its focus from leisure
activities rather than the experience of work, it had to make a certain amount of
new room for "its" gals; and a gay male subculture was just beginning to come
into view in the Bowery, as Christine Stansell has noted (90–92). But its masculinism traversed the minstrel show's representations of women and black men
both. Whitman's account captures the homoerotic moment of the usually misogynist male bonding that took place—over women's bodies, between the men onstage and those in the audience—in the minstrel show's "wench" characters.
This homosexual-homosocial pattern persisted all through minstrelsy's antebellum tenure, structuring in white men's "imaginary" relation to black men a
dialectic of romance and repulsion.[45] If minstrelsy was based on an extreme
though contradictory white fascination with black(faced) men, there was no less a
white male solidarity over against them that obviously inspired racist ridicule. In
any case, we shall see how insistently blackface performance concerned itself with
matters of the body—gender anxieties, unconventional sexuality, orality—which
mediated, and regulated, the formation of white working-class masculinity.[46]

Second, we ought to take seriously the more or less explicit threat regularly
imputed to this culture, despite the temptation to see its collective fervor, like the
violence at Astor Place, as little more than American farce to European tragedy—
all we could muster, perhaps, in the way of revolutionary barricades. This view is
unfortunately encouraged by the influential typology Alan Dawley and Paul Faler
devised to account for the range of nineteenth-century working-class cultural
predispositions. Charting workers' varied responses to an increasingly rigid code
of industrial morality, Dawley and Faler found a basic cleavage between "tradi-

86

tionalists" and "modernists." Traditionalists were those men we might expect to see in minstrel theaters; they "refused to give up their casual attitudes toward work, their pursuit of happiness in gaming and drinking, and the raucous revelry that accompanied fire and militia musters." Modernists, by contrast, shunned the "warm sociability of the drinking club [and] the 'wasteful' amusement of the circus and the Jim Crow show," whether they were "rebels" who involved themselves in industrial militancy or "loyalists" who in the name of respectability held aloof from both spirits and class conflict (468).

Yet, as Sean Wilentz has stressed, there was intentionality even in the b'hoys' traditionalist vehemence. Wilentz does not see in their pursuit of pleasure the passivity of workers dulled by a consolidating culture industry and uninterested in radical organizing; on the contrary, he construes "the republicanism of the Bowery and the republicanism of the unions" as "different but at times overlapping expressions of the journeymen's fears and aspirations—one focused on the economic and political sources of inequality and exploitation, the other stressing cultural autonomy and manly independence" (270). In many ways the b'hoy was a rebel in traditionalist disguise; and this is a matter worth being clear about, given the advent in the postdepression 1840s of apparently more "cultural" responses to class conflict (nativism, temperance, and so on) and the decline of organized, 1830s-style class militancy. Certainly one sees a marked class accent in most minstrel acts' racial representations. The dictates of autonomy readily enough produced blackface butts of derision for white men on the bottom; yet, perhaps as a result of minstrel figures' sexual or sentimental power, they were occasionally objects of white male envy as well, even figures of interracial identification, providing in imaginary ways the labor abolitionism that failed to materialize in the Northeast before the Civil War. Minstrelsy's use of racial license to map class revolt was one gesture in the sphere of culture toward what remained undone in the realm of politics.

With the eruption of class into the cultural arena—in the modality of race— the lower million had certainly shattered the mirror held up to nature, the universally representative character of "the" theater. As the actor William Davidge complained in 1866 (in a ritual mode by then at least twenty years old), "The rapid increase in the population in newly formed cities, produces a style of patrons whose habits and associations afford no opportunity for the cultivation of the arts" (202). In 1850 that would have been far the best face to put on it. By then the minstrel show was offering class turbulence with a racial accent, one element of a cultural revolution that made correlate use of grave racial conflicts. Minstrelsy was a prime example of the sometimes contestatory character of plebeian culture, articulating class difference, intentionally or not, by calling on the insurrectionary resonances of black culture. To put this another way, popular entertainments in which race was foregrounded yielded up a sense of unrest waiting to be tapped at its class source. For a brief time in the nineteenth century it seemed that the blackface impulse, based so firmly on the association of "blackness" with the white working class, was backfiring. As certain traditions of racial exchange were "elevated" into an art of black humiliation, that art fed in turn off class energies which resisted containment—and which had the unintended effect of marking the public threat of black culture. There was no other conclusion, wrote an exasperated *New York Herald* in 1848: "There is a revolution going on in theatres. The legitimate drama is down for ever, buried and entombed twenty feet under ground" (January 3).

Culture was now politicized in the most spectacular ways. The class anger of the Astor Place riot was strangely confluent with the struggles over slavery that were coming, that same year, to characterize the state of the Union. And this twin threat was no mere satire of the Paris June days. It was, in a sense, our 1848. In just what sense, exactly, is the subject of the next chapter.

4

The Blackening of America:
Popular Culture and National Cultures

American opera—put three banjos (or more?) in the orchestra. . . .

—Walt Whitman

Jim Crow and Zip Coon seemed unlikely candidates for a national cultural form. And yet, as the *Democratic Review* admitted in 1845, the idea had a certain plausibility. "The lowest description of American farce," to be sure, "still in its elements, not without originality, considerable invention, and a rich vein of bur- lesque humor, is the Æthiopian drama" ("American" 219). (Perhaps an ortho- graphical adjustment would take care of everything.) In what possible way could a host of white men in blackface and motley rags, given to unvarnished obscenity and anticipating the phallic hucksters of *Huckleberry Finn's* Royal Nonesuch, be considered representative of a national art form? This question was bound to be debated in the 1840s, the years of blackface minstrelsy's greatest popularity as well as of an intense investment on the part of many Americans in the idea of cultural and political nationalism.

Unfortunately, the American theater was much slower than the country's literature to develop what one might call a postcolonial sensibility. While Irving, Bryant, and Cooper could already be said to have given unique expression to America in the major literary genres, playwrights, as David Grimsted has empha- sized, sustained themselves mainly through rewritings of August von Kotzebue and other European melodramatists. America had its players (Edwin Forrest, Charlotte Cushman) and its thematic and formal proclivities (Forrest's Jackso- nian stalwarts; antiarriviste comedies of manners such as Anna Cora Mowatt's *Fashion*), but little that could stand as distinguished national drama. The appear- ance of Mose on the Bowery stage, as we have seen, was no consolation to anyone but the class of New Yorkers he purported to represent; and to parvenu Whig fashioners of bourgeois taste such as Nathaniel P. Willis, the whole Bowery scene was a bad dream the country might never shake off. The Whiggish preference for imported opera and the general influx of European talent, including Ole Bull and Jenny Lind, only reiterated the dearth—and were rivaled anyway by less respect-

89

able competition. "While even [the] attempt to establish an Italian Opera here, though originating with the wealthiest and best educated classes, has resulted in bankruptcy, the Ethiopian Opera has flourished like a green bay tree," *Putnam's Monthly* sardonically observed. "The only places of Amusement where the entertainments are indigenous are the African Opera Houses, where native American vocalists, with blackened faces, sing national songs, and utter none but native witticisms" (February 1854). The main misfortune was perhaps that the confirmed social divisions in American culture produced lively popular theatrical forms at the very moment when nationalist fervor was reaching its highest peak.

It appears rather self-evident to us, as it did to antebellum partisans of the slave narrative, that slavery and race were matters which particularly defined America, and which might have been expected to furnish it with politically expedient and emotionally charged cultural material. That the minstrel show took up these issues at all is perhaps more significant than that it did so in an objectionable way; yet the fact that it shoved racial matters to the fore made it even less palatable to elites than the usual run of "low" comedy. The legitimate stage's colonial hangover looks from this perspective like avoidance and suppression rather than inadequacy of talent or ambition, for it broached such matters only in minor or superficial ways until the 1850s. But it must also be said that this avoidance was part of a generalized inverse provincialism in midcentury American life, characterizing even those intellectuals most engaged in defending a new kind of national democratic culture. Andrew Ross observes that a major component of the national culture in the United States has in fact been its dependence for cultural authority on borrowed foreign capital, owing to the absence of intellectual "formations of prestige" relatively independent of the canons of European taste (*No* 62–63). This situation had more specific results than Emerson's failed "original relation with the universe," most notably an intelligentsia unable to address the elements of its own national-popular culture. Thus, in the battle between the *Knickerbocker* writers and the striplings of Young America over the definition of an "American" culture, the antagonists—excepting Melville—were united in looking to Europe for legitimation, whether the particular quest was for "Rabelaisian" wit or intellectual Teutonism.[1]

Melville was nearly the only elite cultural figure to recognize the centrality of racial conflict to whatever national culture might be on the horizon. For the most part, addressing the American dilemma was left to less legitimized cultural spheres, such as genteel women's fiction (*Uncle Tom's Cabin*) or popular entertainment forms (the minstrel show), themselves united in *Uncle Tom's* stage tenure. This is one context also for the brief engagement with race by that least respectable of now canonical writers, Walt Whitman. It seems to me no accident that the writer who took up literary nationalism just as Young America was abandoning it did so partly through an encounter with the cultural politics of race—helped, perhaps, by the fact that he would have been quite out of bounds in Evert Duyckinck's library in Clinton Place.

Indeed, the project of cultural nationalism was finally to be tripped up by the racial difference it had repressed, a difference registered most insistently and popularly in the minstrel show. But this issue was complicated even more by a brief flourishing of competing national cultures. With the massive swell of immigrants from famine-ridden Ireland in the mid-1840s, subcultural institutions set up to organize Irish concerns (among others the Catholic church), not to mention varieties of nativist resistance to them, gave new visibility to nationality and ethnicity. Later in the decade, Martin Delany and other black nationalists, in political tracts and projected African expeditions, began urgently moving toward some new sense of black nationhood. In a kind of postcolonial chain, "Anglo-Saxon" Americans distanced themselves from Britain as new ethnic formations combated one another in their turn. Far from being abstract inquiries, however, these movements were lived by working people who were bound up with the culture in which blackface moved and had its being. The point is that this jostle of cultures opened a national-popular space that was to be vigorously contested in the 1840s, quite fiercely as it turned out, and often in the arena of blackface minstrelsy. Ultimately, the measure of its cultural power in this period is the claim the minstrel show made, against all the odds, on the idea of a national culture.

THE NATIONAL POPULAR

In his great essay on the British music hall singer Marie Lloyd, T. S. Eliot raised certain issues vital to the notion of what Antonio Gramsci called a national-popular culture.[2] Eliot refused to see her popularity as mere commercial success: "It is [rather] evidence of the extent to which she represented and expressed that part of the English nation which has perhaps the greatest vitality and interest" (172). Lamenting the "listless apathy" characteristic of viewers of the "rapid-breeding cinema," Eliot (in curiously Whitmanesque tones) argues that the "working man who went to the music-hall and saw Marie Lloyd and joined in the chorus was himself performing part of the act," engaged as he was in "that collaboration of the audience with the artist which is necessary in all art" (174). Embedded in these already atypical reflections is a passage that is worth quoting at length:

> It was her understanding of the people and sympathy with them, and the people's recognition of the fact that she embodied the virtues which they genuinely most respected in private life, that raised her to the position she occupied at her death. . . . I have called her the expressive figure of the lower classes. There is no such expressive figure for any other class. The middle classes have no such idol: the middle classes are morally corrupt. That is to say, their own life fails to find a Marie Lloyd to express it; nor have they any independent virtues which might give them as a conscious class any dignity. (173)

If there is here a certain degree of *nostalgie de la boue,* these remarks, venom and all, strike me as a largely persuasive formulation of the place of successful popular arts in the life of the popular classes and of the relation of both to "respectable" society. Although I have no impulse to champion the minstrel show in similar terms,[3] Eliot's essay suggests at least two major emphases in regard to that phenomenon, emphases my whole study is concerned to investigate. First, black-face artists did give voice (if not in unitary or stable ways) to the most private "virtues" of the popular classes, regarding not only race but a whole range of meanings and values. This is the fairly straightforward sense in which minstrelsy offered a national stage for conflicts and concerns peculiar to some of the people who suffered most immediately the effects of the industrializing metropolis in the earliest years of its development. Second, however, the minstrel show's adherents also occupied, culturally, something of the position of Eliot's middle classes, for their values were expressed through figures drawn not from their own lives but from another part of the social formation. The blackface performer is in effect a perfect metaphor for one culture's ventriloquial self-expression through the art forms of someone else's.

To say so seems merely to state the obvious. Perhaps the sheer strangeness of this predicament is—after the Jazz Age, after early rock 'n' roll—now lost to us. Some of its reasons, or at least some of its effects, will, I hope, eventually become clear. What I mean to suggest about the character of popular culture in America is how unstable an entity it has been—a site of conflicting interests, appropriations, impersonations, indeed "nationalities," even in its allegedly national forms. Little wonder, then, that the question of whose "national" culture best expressed American life emerged around the popularity of the minstrel show, or that one sees a constant struggle for control—encompassing black, white, immigrant Irish, and other cultures—within blackface forms themselves. The problem of min-strelsy and national cultures at midcentury, that is to say, comprised both a continual struggle over and an unceasing struggle within the popular. The contest between cultural forms for national hegemony was matched only by that among various "national" cultural elements for control of particular forms. If the issue of the national culture is, as I believe it should be, at the center of U.S. cultural studies, this volatile engagement and internal self-differentiation of cultures, rather than consensus models of cultural assimilation or unity-in-difference, must become our focus.[4] Popular forms and popular audiences are less fixed referents than sites of continual reconstitution, the popular less an object than a space: in the case of blackface acts the most accessible place of public interaction and conflict between and among dominant, subordinate, and enslaved "national" cultures at a crucial moment in our history.[5] This tangle of involvement occurred at many levels: blackface performers' relations with the black artists from whom their material was "collected"; these (often Irish) performers' engagement with the material itself; the mix of white material and black material; the reception of this mixed material by variegated white audiences; those audiences' attitudes toward the small number of black performers; and finally, the struggle between minstrelsy and other contenders for the status of national art form. It is important to stress the conflictual nature of these relationships, which has for the most part been neglected. The complexity of the conflicts is evident above all in the way competing "national" vernaculars were housed within the minstrel show, around which certain lines of historical force begin to emerge.

One must beware the figural status of national entities—those "imagined communities," in Benedict Anderson's phrase. This is not to say that they are "inauthentic," or always irredeemably hypostatized; any community whose members are not immediately present to one another is necessarily constituted by some idea of itself, indeed by elaborate performative strategies of rhetorical self-constitution. As Anderson puts it, "Communities are to be distinguished, not by their falsity/genuineness, but by the style in which they are imagined" (15). In nineteenth-century post-Herderian vogues of the folk, this "style" most often included raising a "people's" vernacular to view, usually in print, but also in popular songs and theatrical forms. (The dubiousness of the claims for authentic "folk" culture need not detain us here; I will return to this question later in the chapter.) As has often been argued, the part played by the invention of "folk" cultures in the constitution of nationality cannot be overestimated, and is a chief means by which "indigeneity" may be constructed by postcolonial societies.[6] It was in the nineteenth century, as Hugh Seton-Watson shows, that the vernacularizing drive was linked to the florescence of European nationalisms; and it was in this period as well (not immediately after the 1776 Revolution) that the United States went through a peculiarly "European" phase of vernacular self-discovery. True to the nation's internally contradictory makeup, however—or to the contradictions of any national self-definition, as Homi Bhabha suggests ("DissemiNation" 299, 301)—America witnessed a simultaneous *hybridization* and *proliferation* of vernaculars, in which frontier lore, European elements, and various local or regional forms merged into an "American" vernacular even as the outlines of each of these elements sharpened—in, for instance, Major Jack Downing broadsides, the stage Yankee, southern Cavalier mythology, immigrant Irish and German stories and songs, Davy Crockett almanacs, and slave culture's oral and performance genres. Indeed, if the newspaper is a distinctive factor in the organization of national self-consciousness, the expansion of the penny press in America in the 1830s, with its broad emphasis on artisan concerns, as well as its splintering into ethnic, political, and racial publics, is another instance of this dual phenomenon.[7] The minstrel show was a major exponent of such simultaneously creolizing and individuating developments. Based, however uneasily, on the blending of "national" cultures—offering indeed a primary channel for cultural interchange—minstrelsy, with its perceived "blackness," became a competitor for control of the national popular.

This ambiguity gave minstrelsy much of its resonance. For the play of vernaculars *within* the form of the minstrel show helped make it a mediator of ethnic conflict in the antebellum North, which in turn reinforced its formal polyphony. This, it seems to me, is the best way to map what is usually seen as its cultural "mix." The mix itself is genuine. As we know, some minstrel performers claimed they did "fieldwork" among southern blacks while on tour, though in fact this required at most a trip to the East River waterfront; it was to their professional advantage to make such claims. In any case, there was no reason for performers not to lift black material when they came across it. The constant public references to minstrel performances as "unique" can probably be accounted for by this blending of black and white elements (Toll 43–45). The researches of Hans Nathan, Robert Toll, and others suggest that the minstrel show's humor, songs, and dances were so culturally mixed as, in effect, to make their "racial" origins quite undecidable—black lore interspersed with southwestern humor (itself often an interracial creation); black banjo techniques and rhythms interrupting folk dance music of the British Isles (as it had been taken up by whites in the United States); the vigorous earth-slapping footwork of black dances warring with the Irish lineaments of blackface jigs and reels.[8] The very instrumentation of minstrel bands followed this pattern: the banjo and jawbone were black, while the fiddle, bones, and tambourine (derived perhaps from an instrument called the bodhran) were Irish (Cantwell 258). Most critics, then and now, agree that a certain amount of mixing characterized the music and the dances, but much less the lyrics on which most of the burden of racial burlesque rested.[9] In T. D. Rice's act alone one might have seen some version of a predominantly black dance style performed to manifestly European (often Irish) music, with lyrics of a more or less satirical and racist nature.[10] The creolized character of black forms themselves, of course, not to mention their casual and undocumentable influence on white ones, muddies this whole question considerably and makes all cultural labeling a provisional matter. Indeed, the heated debate about black secular music's "origins" (as with minstrelsy) turns up highly speculative, straining, even bizarre arguments as to its definitive (white or black) "source," arguments that unmask nothing so much as the arguments themselves, self-evident plays for rhetorical (and racial) mastery over a very confused and confusing history of cultural intermixing.[11]

As they became entrenched in a rough and rowdy urban sphere, particularly after the first halting decade of entr'acte performances and theatrical experiments, such miscegenated minstrel acts came to negotiate interethnic tensions among working-class Irish and blacks, the history of which could in part be written from the history of minstrelsy. This history incidentally displaces both the binary emphasis on "the" black-white relationship in America and romantic models of ethnic pluralism in favor of black-ethnic white relations, and highlights the *necessarily* exploitative making of the Irish as "white" even as that privileged category often oppressed the Irish themselves. These tensions, of course, would finally prove disastrous in the bloody 1863 draft riots, when Irish draftees, angry at a conscription law that allowed men of means to buy their way out of military service, unleashed their frustrations on New York City's blacks. But there was in fact a quite ambiguous history of Irish-black relations behind this violence. Indeed, evidence exists that in these years blackface provided a means of displaced immigrant self-expression; another strain of white ventriloquism through black art forms begins to make sense here.

Even before the vast waves of immigration (one came in the late 1820s, another in the mid-1840s), Irish and black tended to share the same class niche, resulting in conflicts of all kinds, but also in interracial friendships and even marriages. Robert Cantwell observes that "smoked Irishman" was nineteenth-century rural slang for "Negro" (262)—a phrase that indicated the fundamental affinity in the popular mind between these groups. As this phrase also suggests, there were surely uncharitable equations of black and Irish: during her stay on a Georgia plantation, the actress Fanny Kemble wrote in her diary of the remarkable resemblance between the "low Irish" and southern slaves (105), an equation exploited, as Dale Knobel points out, in stage productions such as William Macready's *Irishman in London* (1853), in which Murtoch Delaney finds his perfect match in "grinning Cuba," the African (93). More sympathetically, however, Frederick Douglass once remarked that the only songs which came close to the pathos of slave songs were those he had heard in Ireland in 1845–46, during the famine.[12] Some of these strains may have infected the work of the many Irish-American minstrel composers and performers—Stephen Foster, Dan Emmett, Dan Bryant, Joel Walker Sweeney, George Christy, and others—who were also on intimate terms with local black cultural forms. (To take but one example, Foster's family's consciousness of its heritage kept alive the poems and songs of Thomas Moore, whose sentiments would inform Foster songs such as "Old Folks at Home" [Hamm 214–15].) The Irish elements of blackface, including the fact that minstrel characters were surely influenced by Irish low-comedy types from the British stage, no doubt made possible the Irish ascendancy within the minstrel show, affording immigrants a means of cultural representation from behind the mask. They probably account as well for the ease with which blackface songs and skits incorporated Irish brogues and other ethnic dialects, with absolutely no sense of contradiction; blackface, bizarrely enough, was actually used to represent *all* ethnicities on the antebellum stage prior to the development of ethnic types (Flynn 426). The classic expression of this racial-ethnic overlap would come with the postwar skits of the Irish team Harrigan and Hart, but the frequency of titles such as "Tis Sad to Leabe Our Tater Land" (early 1850s) and "Ireland and Virginia," or of blackface Irish nationalist tunes, attested to the potential embrace of Paddy and Jim Crow.[13]

As Fanny Kemble herself remarked, however, the closer the affinity, the greater the hostility between Irish and black. The violent confrontations of these years point to less cheery interpretations of Irishmen's involvement in minstrelsy. An English observer noted in 1833 that "nearly all of [the Boston Irish], who have resided there any length of time, are more bitter and severe against the blacks than the native whites themselves. It seems as if the disease were more virulent when taken by inoculation than in the natural way" (quoted in Runcie 198). Many antiabolitionist and anti–black temperance riots in the 1830s and 1840s (particularly in Philadelphia) have been seen as angry correctives on the part of Irish and other workingmen to their own sense of political powerlessness and economic disenfranchisement—their resemblance, in both class and ethnic terms, to "blackness." At the polls the Irish typically resisted this resemblance by voting for proslavery Democrats and decrying abolition as "niggerology."[14] This evidence would appear to support Robert Cantwell's notion that blackface acts had the effect of promoting socially insecure Irishmen (actors as well as audiences), an "Americanizing" ritual by which they distanced themselves from the people they parodied (265). Yet I have shown that the class aura of minstrel shows was scarcely elevating; and performers' contradictory relations with those from whom they appropriated black arts, and their social proximity to black culture, considerably complicate Cantwell's idea.

As with their relationship to American blacks generally, a social antinomy characterized Irish immigrants' involvement in minstrelsy. Its clearest political analogue was the equivocation of Irish nationalists in regard to antislavery. In the 1840s the Garrisonians, on the basis of the nationalist and antislavery prestige of Daniel O'Connell's anticolonial Repeal movement, tried to forge an alliance that would garner immigrant Irish support for abolitionism. In the mouth of Wendell Phillips, the equation of the sorry conditions of Irish peasants and southern blacks became an emancipatory strategy. While this effort was briefly successful (with Hibernian Anti-Slavery Society enthusiasm riding high), the Garrisonians' entrepreneurial outlook, and what Gilbert Osofsky terms the "dilemmas of romantic nationalism," finally alienated immigrant workers necessarily more attuned to the wage envelope and (for all their sympathy with Ireland) their own position within the American nation—hardly a concern of the Garrisonians. As Irish miners in Pennsylvania put it: "We do not form a distinct class of the community, but consider ourselves in every respect as CITIZENS of this great and glorious republic."[15] The immigrant Irish identification with both marginal and "native" Americans epitomized by this episode was institutionalized in, for example, the Catholic church, which, as Mike Davis argues, joined plebeian ethno-religious commitments to a liberal republican nationalism so as to acculturate "millions of Catholic immigrants to American liberal-capitalist society while simultaneously carving out its own sphere of sub-cultural hegemony" (24). Minstrelsy's mix of "national" vernaculars was situated at the precise juncture of these conflicts; it resolved the contradictory "national" impulses into a popular art form. Blackface was at one and the same time a displaced mapping of ethnic Otherness and an early agent of acculturation. A song such as "Ireland and Virginia" depended on an expression of Irishness through the medium of "blackness," itself also an institution of "Americanizing" whitening.[16]

The irony, however, is that this conflictual sphere was so often taken as the domain of a newly fascinating "negro" or "African" culture, and in this guise blackface minstrelsy threatened to lay claim to the title of native American genius.

> Oh, white folks, I'll revibe to you,
>   Dem good old songs dat once was new;
> De fust I'll name, was all de go,
>   'Bout de dancing nigger dey call Jim Crow
>   • • •
> But de greatest one in de sable crowd,
>   Was a rich old man dey called him proud;
> He made great Norway Ole Bull stutter,
>   For a champion ob de string, was ole Dan Tucker[17]

With its cool inscriptions of racial difference ("Oh, white folks") and national chauvinism (against Ole Bull), such material launched "black" culture into the nationalist fray. No matter how distorted or weak this material may appear, one must take seriously the frequent public perception of the minstrel show as black. For it was in this way that it became not just an ethnic mediator but a civic presence—to some a foretaste of revolution. ("The basic paradox" of people's attachment to a nation, writes Slavoj Žižek, is that it is "conceived as something inaccessible to the other, and at the same time threatened by it" [54].) Notwithstanding the sometimes withering irony of the blackface counterfeit, its troubling, or just as often attractive, "black" aspects competed for public attention. We have already seen several accounts of the minstrel show as a black "people's culture," as in Margaret Fuller's "African" melodies; German observer Moritz Busch similarly took certain blackface songs for a genuine black *Volkslied*, capable, moreover, of culturally representing America as a whole.[18]

It is further striking that blackface performers became "negroes" in the playbills, daily newspapers, and song sheets that registered their careers. In all but the most self-conscious of discourses, it was always implied that *black* men now nightly purveyed black dialect, dance, music, and humor in a theatrical form invariably called "negro minstrelsy." It must have been these tropes that accounted for the belief of many early observers that they were in fact watching blacks onstage. The power of blackface, indeed, must be understood as in part a media creation:

> The performances at the New York Museum are unparalleled in the annals of exhibition. For the sum of one shilling you see Master Frank Diamond [white dancer Francis Lynch], the great negro dancer, Mr. Alden, the unrivalled Ethiopian melodist and banjo player, Mr. Nellis, the wonder of the world, born without arms, Miss Rosalie, the lovely songstress, Mr. Delarne, the much admired mimic, and Mr. Collins, the popular comic singer.[19]

We must ask why in the world a culture so fearful of "blacks on top" would indulge that very fantasy in reports of the stage. The phenomenon of minstrelsy itself was an admission of fascination with blacks and black culture. Why then rub it in with this suspension of disbelief? From the beginning there seems to have been a general forgetting of the fact of white impersonation, a thrilling pretense of breaking the taboo against black performers on the popular musical stage which prevailed into the 1850s. In effect, this meant trading one equivocal cultural relationship for another: momentarily preserving the idea of blacks onstage as the price of denying one's own mimicry of them. This was hardly a satisfactory trade; if it was mesmerizing, it was also perilous, as we shall see. But it was compelling in any case, or this fiction of black performers would not have been extended into the daily papers, effectively creating for the first time a sense of popular black cultural representation.

In spite, that is, of the greater or lesser hegemonic intentions of the types, and in spite of audience awareness of the counterfeit, the advent of minstrelsy was still read as a new infusion of "blackness" and black cultural practices into American life. Perhaps the journalistic convention of referring to blackface "negroes" merely paid conflicted tribute to that infusion. As for the types, they probably could not have taken a very different shape. I have noted the ideological ferment around racial theories in this period (perhaps more complex than "scientific racism" later in the century); nevertheless, a set pattern of racial traits tended to be present in representations of black people. The traits themselves were hardly open to question. What were debated were the kinds of explanation (religious, metaphysical, anthropological, and so on), and indeed valuation, given those traits.[20] As for the counterfeit, it is clear enough from the evidence that consciousness of the copy did not foreclose on a variety of responses to its "blackness."

Indeed, if by the mid-1840s it was generally held true, as Whitman wrote in the *Brooklyn Daily Eagle*, that "the subtlest spirit of a nation is expressed through its music—and the music acts reciprocally upon the nation's very soul" ("Thought" 345), then a minstrel-loving America was caught in something of a cultural hailstorm. As we have seen, part of the tony disgust that grew up around minstrelsy was simply a revulsion against the popular, the vulgar and sentimental tastes of what J. S. Dwight rather typically referred to as the "clapping classes" ("Music" 94). In his *Journal of Music,* Dwight on one occasion tried to deflect his critics' (accurate) charges of Europhilia: "Why assume that the term 'German' was applied to [a piece of music under review] by way of *praise?"* he feinted. His logic is somewhat tortuous:

> To have said nothing would but have left the door open to the inference that the piece had a style new and original, peculiarly its author's, or peculiarly American; which would have been true only in a limited degree. Indeed the motive of the term "German" partly was to save it from the questionable praise of classification with what are commonly understood to be songs of the American stamp, that is to say "negro melodies," or namby-pamby sentimental ditties. . . . ("Complaint" 94)

Apparently the demotic "American" came inevitably to mind as the inverse of European; though Dwight had high hopes for a national music, he was no Young

American. On the contrary, there is an interesting set of equations here, of American music with "negro" music, and of "American" with debased art forms generally, as if minstrelsy were the most natural example of both.[21] Many commentators implicitly relied on this kind of equation in lamentations to the effect that American culture was turning out to be not only "questionable" but black.

"The Jim Crows, the Zip Coons, and the Dandy Jims, who have electrified the world," trumpeted *Knickerbocker* writer J. K. Kennard in 1845, "from them proceed our ONLY TRULY NATIONAL POETS" (332). Kennard, like many Anglophiles, was less than sanguine about the prospects of a national culture. By seizing on the newly available "black" idioms of the minstrel show as the most typically national cultural form, he intended to lampoon Young America's quest for a national art with what he (probably correctly) assumed was its logical consequence. By their logic, Kennard implies, a *truly* national culture—in his terms provincial, untutored, and close to the soil, after the manner of Robert Burns—would be made by slaves. The article's mismanaged reactionary irony reaches straight to the heart of the problem, fueled inexorably by cultural anxiety and dread. For the outcome of such a national culture, as Kennard demonstrates, would amount to little less than insurrection. Finally mastered by his own irony, Kennard echoes Shelley:

> The popular song-maker sways the souls of men; the legislator rules only their bodies. The song-maker reigns through love and spiritual affinity; the legislator by brute force. Apply this principle to the American people. Who are our true rulers? The negro poets, to be sure! Do they not set the fashion, and give laws to the public taste? Let one of them, in the swamps of Carolina, compose a new song, and it no sooner reaches the ear of a white *amateur,* than it is written down, amended, (that is, almost spoilt,) printed, and then put upon a course of rapid dissemination, to cease only with the utmost bounds of Anglo-Saxondom, perhaps of the world. (340)

This strange piece is absolutely unflinching: it imagines, negatively and somewhat convolutedly, the very end of antebellum America's attraction to black culture as it was presented in the minstrel show—a national culture owing to "Ethiopia," not Europe.[22]

Kennard was only the most hysterical observer of this "blackening of America."[23] Dwight notably reprinted an article from London (no doubt echoing American concerns) citing "the great grievance of the metropolis—it is inundated by the 'blacks.'" Part of the article's interest is its utter confusion of blackface and blackness in describing the great grievance—an indication itself of national blackening. While "'blacks'" probably referred only to blackface performers, it is not clear whether actual black people are being invoked. The reference to an increase of "nigger minstrels" and "sable musicians from America" (as indeed in the newspapers' "negroes") thus functioned as a dominant-cultural figuration of black people that covered up the people themselves; it collapsed blacks into itself and held them captive, both suggesting and withholding their presence. This doubleness indeed seems pretty much to have been the mode of the inundation. Cities experienced cultural blackening as a vast profusion of ambiguous signs that, like the minstrel mask itself, offered the experience of "blackness" even as they absented it.

> They [the referent is unclear] infest our promenades and our concert halls like a colony of beetles. If we avoid their presence in street or music-room, their names and designations stare us out of countenance from dead walls, boardings, lamp posts, and the interior of omnibuses. If we read the advertising columns in the journals, our eye is arrested by a long list of musical performances to be given, after the most approved fashion, by these ebony artists from the regions of the sun. . . . The great Derby race is run amid a salvo of bones and banjos, and the Surrey and Middlesex Stakes are contested to the accompaniment of "Dandy Jim from Caroline," or "My old massa tol' me so."[24]

Blacks were suddenly everywhere—captive countenances paradoxically on the loose, bringing dead walls to life and crowding the omnibuses. It is no wonder that in these years Whitman the budding poet speculated in his notebooks on the ideal number of banjos to be included in an American opera orchestra, or felt compelled to sketch a modification of English pronunciation, suitable for a "native grand opera in America," to be based on what he called "nigger dialect."[25] Sometimes it was remarked with hysteria, sometimes with interest, but it was always remarked: "blackness," despite the extremely compromised form in which it was represented, had made inroads into the national culture. The poet Bayard Taylor caught the mood:

> The Ethiopian melodies well deserve to be called, as they are in fact, the national airs of America. Their quaint, mock-sentimental cadences, so well suited to the broad absurdity of the words—their reckless gaiety and irreverent familiarity with serious subjects—and their spirit of antagonism and perseverance—are true expressions of the more popular sides of the national character. They follow the American race in all its emigrations, colonizations and conquests, as certainly as the Fourth of July and Thanksgiving Day.[26]

The invocation of minstrelsy together with American national expansion amid the cataclysms of 1850 was no idle conceit; as we shall see, the two were unexpected intimates.

POPULAR COUNTERFEITS

In the preceding chapters we have seen how minstrelsy's crude racial appropriations entered a conflictual male class arena and almost became shorthand for a national-popular culture. Let me briefly review what I think was going on here, and then gesture toward the historical and political shape of part II.

It is insufficient, I have been arguing, merely to read off racial oppression from minstrelsy's inauthenticity. As with all popular forms, I am concerned with what is best thought of as a realm of counterfeits—contradictory popular constructions that were not so much true or false as more or less pleasurable or politically efficacious in the culture that embraced them. Popular culture, as Gramsci once remarked, "takes the place of (and at the same time favors) the fantasizing of the common people": a realm neither of populist desire nor of commercially imposed distraction, but a stage on which appropriated goods and manufactured daydreams are transformed into culture.[27] It is true that, while blackface sometimes seemed an authentic instance of black culture, its "black" simulations were even less a populist product than popular arts usually are. Yet we have also seen that its dominative intentions were continually compromised by the return of unwanted meanings, gestures, and relationships. Indeed, according to Gramsci's formulation, this will always be the case with the "popular"; in steering us away from its status either as failed "folk" art or as "mass" cultural manipulation, he suggests we focus on the social fantasies and historical conflicts that the minstrel show inspired and to which it gave a temporary home.

The minstrel show was a signal instance of the popular because its black materials, or at least its black models, were worked over, transformed, reinvented, and re-presented by its white practitioners and adopted by white, mostly male and working-class audiences with some familiarity with the culture being represented. What was on display in minstrelsy was less black culture than a structured set of white responses to it which had grown out of northern and frontier social rituals and were passed through an inevitable filter of racist presupposition. What is vitally important is that minstrel performers reproduced not only what they supposed were the racial characteristics of black Americans (minstrelsy's content) but also what they supposed were their principal cultural forms: dance, music, verbal play.[28] In their rise to popularity, blackface actors let loose an iconography of racial difference, clearly graphing difference as inferiority, but at a time when difference itself could be a dangerous fact, particularly when set down in a class-inflected sphere of belly laughs and brawling. The social complexities of this counterfeiting, however, only rate minstrelsy among many other forms of the popular. Where critics have gone wrong is in assuming that the political designs so apparent in the minstrel show were unique to it. It is no doubt astonishing that for a period of more than one hundred years white people were so politically, historically, emotionally, and sexually bound up with black culture that they directly mimicked and displayed it for their own enjoyment (and, in various ways, still do). But popular culture in capitalist societies is always so "produced." It begins in the reprocessing and containment from above of traditional, oral, or "folk" cultures, but at certain historical conjunctures it can have untoward effects. Stuart Hall puts the matter this way:

> There is a continuous and necessarily uneven and unequal struggle, by the dominant culture, constantly to disorganise and reorganise popular culture; to enclose and confine its definitions and forms within a more inclusive

101

range of dominant forms. There are points of resistance; there are also
moments of supersession. This is the dialectic of cultural struggle. ("Notes"
233)

The minstrel show's commercial prominence gave it the widest possible berth for
doing its work. Born of social conflict, blackface sometimes usefully intensified it;
based on the social violence of cultural caricature, it paradoxically resulted in the
blackening of America.

I hasten to add that it is obviously in the interest of the dominant classes to
have a measure of control over the culture of those they dominate, especially
when other forms of control threaten to evaporate, as seemed to be happening in
these years. And here, whatever the short-term effects, the minstrel show had
disastrous consequences—particularly since black people had little room to contest publicly the social meanings generated out of their culture. Yet we might as
well acknowledge the peculiarly unstable way in which these meanings *were*
generated. The process of counterfeiting can never be a simple matter of bread
and circuses, activities dreamed up by state functionaries to ensure that sub-
alterns stay in their places. Varieties of appealing ventriloquism are most effective;
indeed, had the minstrel show not pleased, it could not have achieved even its
worst effects. An instance in white culture of this ventriloquism was the popular
Davy Crockett almanac, in which, as Carroll Smith-Rosenberg has demonstrated, Whig publicists used frontier dialects to tell lurid tales underwritten by
bourgeois mythologies for "vernacular" readers (108), and which, it is pertinent
to note, also gave authentic headaches to many an earnest moral reformer.[29] I
would define the minstrel show precisely as a case of popular racial ventriloquism,
which, because it was spoken in vernacular accents, could never be counted on to
stifle undesirable responses. Despite the often hegemonic intentions or beginnings of popular forms, they can occasionally retain subversive dimensions, or for
a time be invested with them. That is why the hegemony of what Gramsci termed
the historical bloc is never secure, has constantly to be reconquered, and why
there is a continual state of play in and over the popular sphere. Blackface
performers, voices of the dominant racial culture, had to take care in these volatile
years to check the subversive elements of their art—the mischief or ire that
inhered in an appropriated black song or set of images; the wayward, often
disturbing fantasies that clung to many attempts at black caricature—even as they
amused the million. Nevertheless, there were excesses, overflows, resistances to
the intended containment of the form, both in the material it reworked and in the
responses of its popular audiences.[30]

This instability has been obscured by a refusal to recognize in the minstrel
show the sort of cultural mediations with which we are very familiar. For one
thing, cultures of the people, even "folk" cultures, are always constructed, in this
particular case by a postromantic ideology of the folk—hence the characteristic
comparison in nineteenth-century discourse of minstrelsy and black secular song
to the English ballad tradition.[31] It is of course essentialist to ignore the extent to

which our understanding of any culture is determined in the first place by a particular ideology of culture. Just such an ideology worked to make the elements of black culture purveyed in minstrelsy—watered down, humiliated, but unmistakably present—seem all the more naturally elements of a national "folk." Moreover, ideologies of culture have most often been produced by those who do not belong to the culture that is defined, variously, as folk, traditional, popular, or oral. Which is to say that cultures of the dispossessed usually, for better or worse, come to us mediated through dominant-cultural filters, whether it is Thomas Percy's compilation of *Reliques of Ancient English Poetry* (1765), Henry Rowe Schoolcraft's renderings of Chippewa poetry in his influential history *Indian Tribes of the United States* (1851–57), or even Carlo Ginzburg's resurrection of a sixteenth-century miller, "Menocchio," in *The Cheese and the Worms* (1976), distanced once by the court records of the Inquisitors who finally put him to death and then again, as Stanley Aronowitz has suggested, by Ginzburg's bourgeois novelistic devices.[32] As with these efficacious documents, minstrelsy mediated elements of a vernacular tradition, bringing to the surface, like some nonscientific anthropology, the culture of black people. Given this period's *scientific* anthropology, one is hard-pressed to choose the lesser medium. That this is so indicates the counterfeit's potential to have disturbed when it most sought to soothe.

My assumption that the new centrality of "black" forms and representations in American culture precipitated a corresponding instability in American racial feeling might seem somewhat dubious. For the dominant culture today is quite at home with the visibility of certain forms of black culture, in athletics and entertainment, for example, or in advertising. The ways in which envy, affection, and sentiment are folded into racist modes of feeling are of course prominent; negrophobia and negrophilia, as Berndt Ostendorf has remarked, are not at all contradictory (81). By the same token, however, it is clear that certain kinds of cultural conquest—Jackie Robinson's entrance into major league baseball, Elvis Presley's explicit dismantling of "racial" music—are far from harmless allowances on the part of white-supremacist capital.[33] They amount to cultural struggle, and one must be wary of foreclosing on them, for the spectacle of revolution, as T. J. Clark has observed, does occasionally lead to revolution proper: "[T]he circuitry of popular art in capitalist society does appear to be delicate, and therefore to stand in need of fairly constant overhaul if it is not to produce undesirable effects. . . . What begins as a process of control and containment is too often liable to end in mob rule" (*Painting* 227, 229, 236).

In the long run, of course, black repossession of the means of cultural representation was a tragically halting affair. The historical evolution of the contexts in which blackface did its work unquestionably diffused the struggle to redeem black cultural forms. Yet this matter is a complicated one, shot through with fakery and organized around reappropriation rather than redemption. Particularly after minstrelsy, but also because of the nature of the national popular in America, there could be no simple restoration of black authenticity. Such were the circumstances of nineteenth-century racial ideology that even when black performers took the stage after the Civil War, black representation was not immediately returned to self-present fullness. Robert Toll makes it clear that blacks in blackface, far from providing an immediate corrective to minstrel types, actually reinforced them, lent them credibility, no doubt because the newcomers had to fit the ideological forms the minstrel show had itself helped to generate, but also because of the impact of racial ideology on even black performers (196, 228). One thinks again of the black shingle dancers in lower Manhattan; and nothing in Frederick Douglass's account of black performers in 1849 suggests that "inauthenticity" was merely white men's share. We lose no quotient of historical outrage in recognizing these conditions of popular counterfeiting, which in the case of blackface depended as much on American racial ideologies as on the political tendencies of popular culture. Such a recognition does require us finally to see the fallen character of culture—culture as agonistic, not a preserve of purity—in which political outcomes are by no means guaranteed in the forms of popular culture or in their historical conditions.

This recognition might also help us resist the widespread tendency to project white racial hostility onto the working class, the duped "masses." Hence the thrice-obvious conclusion that, as a counterfeit popular form indulged by the vulgar mind, blackface stroked its audiences' racist common sense. Consider, as an extreme case, the words of an Irish-American leader of the interracial New Orleans longshoremen's strikes of 1907:

> I wasn't always a nigger-lover. I fought in every strike to keep Black labor off the dock. I fought until in the white-supremacy strike your white-supremacy governor sent his white-supremacy militia and shot us white-supremacy strikers full of holes. . . . [T]here was a time when I wouldn't even work beside a nigger . . . You made me work with niggers, eat with niggers, sleep with niggers, drink out of the same water bucket with niggers, and finally got me to the point where if one of them . . . blubbers something about more pay, I say, "Come on, nigger, let's go after the white bastards."[34]

Allowing for regional and historical differences, this statement captures something of the racial complexity we find in the antebellum United States. Presenting sequentially what was probably a simultaneous and overlapping set of responses, it clarifies white workers' privileged and yet disenfranchised relation to capital, and the racial perspectives that followed from it. The displacement of solidarity from white, cross-class alliances to interracial ones was a tortuous affair, continually made and then unmade, replete with unevenness and scarcely limited to concerted activity such as strikes. It was complicated by workingmen's perceived position in the sex/gender system as wage-earning patriarchs whose "manliness" was perpetually at stake, and in terms of which racial conflicts were usually fought out. This variable compromise formation, involving masculinity, class, and racial feeling, was responsible for the initial potential and ultimate failure of an interracial labor radicalism in Jacksonian America, and its contours are still virtually unexamined. Alongside casual working-class racism, in other words, one must insist on the complex racial negotiations that took place in the everyday lives of working people, negotiations foreign to denizens of the counting room, the study, and the front office. The minstrel show is one legacy of those negotiations.

Minstrelsy therefore briefly became an object of "live social intelligibility," to borrow V. N. Volosinov's notion of the ideological sign, an internally riven form whose *"inner dialectic quality"* bursts fully into the open "only in times of social crises or revolutionary changes" (23; emphasis in original). America's crisis came in the form of what I call (after Michael Rogin) the American 1848. The minstrel show had no little part in the crisis.

The American 1848

It is worth pondering to what extent the national-popular conflicts in and around the minstrel show—above all its creation of a sense of popular "black" cultural representation—helped foster the struggles of America's midcentury "revolutionary turn" (in Karl Marx's phrase): the Wilmot Proviso debates, the 1850 Compromise, Bleeding Kansas, the Civil War.[35] Certainly this situation was worthy of the name 1848. Michael Rogin has demonstrated the similarity the Compromise of 1850 bore to the class struggles in Europe, particularly France.[36] As Marx wrote that history, the "beautiful revolution" of February, when the monarch was deposed in the interests of political equality, was shattered during the "ugly revolution" of the June days, when the working class took the rhetoric of equality seriously and went to the barricades to fight for it. In June, as "the fireworks of Lamartine . . . turned into the war rockets of Cavaignac" (*Class* 57), the interests of civil society were definitively revealed to underlie the "imagined content" of the political sphere (39); the proletariat was challenging the class character of "political equality" and demanding that it extend beyond the confines of the bourgeoisie. That challenge, of course, was finally stifled and social order restored in 1851, when the accession of Louis Bonaparte solidified the interests of the middle class, still in the guise of political equality.

In America a similar struggle took place, and the similarity did not go unremarked. "[S]et off the names of Cavaignac and Cass, of Ledru-Rollin and Van Buren . . . [of] Napoleon . . . [and] Webster," wrote the *Democratic Review* in 1852, "and the histories of the French and American republics for these four years . . . have been identical." In the political arena, the expansionism of the Polk administration embroiled the United States in the Mexican War in 1846, a war meant to conquer territory for an enlarged national entity. Manifest Destiny, it appeared, was egalitarian ideology gone west. As in France, however, this "beautiful" evasion of both wage labor in the North and slavery in the South, a political solution to conflicts in civil society, only served to open those conflicts all the more, for it posed in ever starker form the question of whether the new territories would be slave or free. In a telling irony, the myth of potentially endless frontier expansion actually exposed rather than disguised patterns of class conflict and racial oppression which American democracy was supposed to have done away with. Civil war loomed: with slavery an issue even in the masterless West, the rhetoric of Manifest Destiny and California gold was every bit as ominous as that of secession.[37]

The crisis began with the 1846–47 debates around the Wilmot Proviso, Pennsylvania Representative David Wilmot's bill urging that all land newly acquired from Mexico—namely California and much of the Southwest—be considered territory for nonslaveholding white men. Sectional tensions immediately ran high, opposing Wilmot supporters and Young America expansionists against southern secessionists and conservative, proslavery Unionists, while various strained crosssectional coalitions rushed to counter them. In 1848 a group of radical Democrats and antislavery Whigs bolted their respective parties and formed the Free-Soil party, based largely on Wilmot's proposals; Martin Van Buren was their (unsuccessful) presidential nominee. Hardly the antiracist vanguard, the Free-Soilers at the very least threatened the stability of the party system. Certainly there was room in the Free-Soil party for dangerously radical sentiments. Wrote one Barnburner Democrat, *"Shall we, in view of these struggles of all Europe, with our model before them, renounce the doctrine of our fathers, and the sentiment of the civilized world, that slavery is an evil?"* (quoted in Schlesinger 462; emphasis in original). This moment witnessed the greatest threat to social order the United States had ever experienced, analogous to the turmoil in France but centered on the politics of slavery, as well as class struggles such as the 1849 Astor Place riot and the 1850 New York tailors' strike. Whitman split several differences at one stroke in language that clinched the interpenetration of race and class—*"the grand body of white workingmen, the millions of mechanics, farmers, and operatives of our country,* with their interests on the one side—and the interests of the few thousand rich, 'polished,' and aristocratic owners of slaves at the South, on the other side" (*Gathering* 1:208; emphasis in original). Very shortly, of course, America had its own Louis Bonaparte. The Compromise of 1850 (passionately advocated by Daniel Webster) and the enactment of the Fugitive Slave Law in 1851 (tantamount to the federal sanction of slavery) temporarily preserved the social order of the Union. But disorder would continue to erupt, in 1854 with the Kansas-Nebraska Act (the fight over the right to take slaves west), in 1857 with the Dred Scott decision (which ruled that blacks were not to be considered U.S. citizens), and finally in 1861 over the future of the Union.

In the broadest political sense we might say that blackface artists all at once found themselves staging a sort of unintended play about the slavery crisis, a play that pointed up rather than papered over cracks in the historical bloc of midcentury America. The ground beneath the minstrel show shifted quickly. From the beginning minstrelsy was an arena in which class conflict and racial strife continually intersected and contradicted each other. In a variety of clashes in the 1830s and early 1840s—pervasive rioting, abolitionism and its counterresponses, labor strikes—class resistance and racial feeling were imbricated in displaced and distorted ways that the minstrel show duly registered. The depression following the 1837 panic, however, deflected these complex energies into more "cultural" responses: temperance, evangelicalism, nativism. The "industrial" character of 1830s class conflict was increasingly displaced in the 1840s onto struggles against "preindustrial" foes, in Paul Faler and Alan Dawley's terms, whereby workers who had fought their masters now allied with them against backsliders and foreigners (477). As a result, the minstrel show abutted and addressed what had become, by the mid-1840s, a somewhat more racially hardened audience of "white egalitarians," journeymen and small masters both, who sought to preserve the republic against preindustrial incursions of all kinds. As we have seen, class antagonisms that persisted could now be mapped as ethnic, moral, or indeed racial matters, and it was here that minstrelsy found one of its major historical uses.

Yet with the crises of 1848 this racially homogeneous cross-class alliance produced as it were its opposite. The most visible cultural signifier of northern white egalitarianism, the rush to California, suddenly signified a sectional breach that pitted northern capitalists and western farmers against southern slaveholding landowners. In the partial transformation of class conflict into racial and ethnic struggles against preindustrial drags on capital formation, the South became the chief "preindustrial" foe, and blackface performers found themselves invoking a national controversy—on behalf of the North—which they had always intended to elide. The urban dandy Zip Coon and the rustic slave Jim Crow now doubled as sectional types, not the kindest fate for an art form that had sought to stifle such matters. The centrality of "black" arts to the national culture had a political referent after all. The minstrel show's intimations of American expansion were no longer innocent celebrations of Manifest Destiny; they were a portent of the war to come. This was only the largest of the authenticating ironies that attended the blackface counterfeit.

PART II

PART II

5

"The Seeming Counterfeit": Early Blackface Acts, the Body, and Social Contradiction

Jim Crow . . . is made to repeat nightly, almost ad infinitum, his balderdash song . . .

—Philip Hone

In January 1831 William Lloyd Garrison founded the *Liberator* in Boston, setting in motion one of the great radical movements in American history. A little more than a year later, twenty-four-year-old T. D. Rice toured the northeastern seaboard with his celebrated "Jim Crow" act, landing in New York in November 1832.[1] These twin instances of white racial discourse, one middle class and one working class, were dialectical partners not only in their literal coincidence but also their shared ambivalences. For just as Garrison's abolitionism was marred by a good deal of paternalist condescension toward the people he wished to liberate, so Rice's blackface acts mixed equal parts of ridicule and wonder in regard to blacks and black culture. Both ambivalences, moreover, arose from class as much as racial feeling, and it was indeed the way these social categories merged with and repelled each other that defined the political moment in which abolitionism and blackface minstrelsy appeared.

As the blackface acts of Rice, George Washington Dixon, and others hit northeastern cities, they began to register and reaccent the varieties of social unrest that were already the hallmark of industrializing centers. The decade that followed, as historians have constructed it, was one of virtual class war, marked especially by working-class militancy—vehement, collective responsiveness to a class structure that was rigidifying at an alarming rate. In this setting minstrel representations in their inaugural fifteen years after 1830 told a complex tale of gendered class and racial subjectivity. Before the depression at the turn of the 1840s helped mute and redirect class resentment, white male workers targeted both employers and black workers, reformers (often wealthy or evangelical whites) and their "fashionable" black associates—the historical referents of minstrelsy's oft-remarked capacity to ridicule upward in class as well as downward in

111

racial direction.[2] Yet these very spatial metaphors inscribe the interpenetrations of race and class that, as we have seen, constituted the political struggles of this period no less than minstrelsy's mediations of them; indeed, it was never completely clear just who at any given moment was being combated. Even in the antiabolitionist rioting that gives this decade another claim on our attention, concerns of class and race were jumbled together. In fact, the political confusions of these years seem to me largely ones of representation, and I will argue that the complexities of minstrelsy are to be discovered in its distorted attempts to graph a situation finally quite resistant to such attempts.

By the same token, the distortions and displacements of minstrel representations acknowledged the possibility of a working-class racial radicalism even as they diagnosed the factors making it unlikely. A central figuration of this unlikelihood in public discourse and in minstrelsy, as we shall see, was the urban black "dandy," an ideological fiction through which certain of this decade's conflicts were lived. The broadest context for all of this, however, was the simple, undeniable presence of "black" male bodies in the public sphere, and it is with this new presence that I begin.

THE WORLD'S BODY

Until the first blackface band formed in 1843, minstrelsy was an interstitial art: performers appeared between the acts of "respectable" theatrical productions, or as afterpieces to them; they also shared the stage with many comic acts in the pleasure gardens, circuses, museums, and "vaudevilles" newly sprung up to meet the demands of a growing urban working population. Accordingly, the phenomenon consisted largely of solo dancers, banjoists, singers, burlesque playlets, comic impersonations, and various kinds and combinations of duos.

Yet we have seen that for all their scattered presentation, minstrel acts immediately secured "blackness" a public hearing. The urgency that attended its appearance is notable in P. T. Barnum's tussle with the blackface convention in 1841. Thomas Low Nichols (Walt Whitman's editor at the *New York Aurora* in the early 1840s) tells the story of the blackface dancer John Diamond's quitting Barnum's organization and leaving the cultural entrepreneur, early in his career, with a problem:

> In New York, some years ago, Mr. P. T. Barnum had a clever boy who brought him lots of money as a dancer of negro break-downs; made up, of course, as a negro minstrel, with his face well blackened, and a woolly wig. One day Master Diamond, thinking he might better himself, danced away into the infinite distance.
>
> Barnum, full of expedients, explored the dance-houses of the Five Points and found a boy who could dance a better break-down than Master Diamond. It was easy to hire him; but he was a genuine negro; and there was not an audience in America that would not have resented, in a very energetic fashion, the insult of being asked to look at the dancing of a real negro. To any man but

> the originator of Joyce Heth, the venerable negro nurse of Washington, and
> the manufacturer of the Fiji Mermaid, this would have been an insuperable
> obstacle.
>
> Barnum was equal to the occasion. Son of the State of white oak cheeses
> and wooden nutmegs, he did not disgrace his lineage. He greased the little
> "nigger's" face and rubbed it over with a new blacking of burnt cork, painted
> his thick lips with vermillion, put on a woolly wig over his tight curled locks, and
> brought him out as the "champion nigger-dancer of the world." Had it been
> suspected that the seeming counterfeit was the genuine article, the New York
> Vauxhall would have blazed with indignation. (369–70)

It is easy to remark here that blackface was simply less objectionable than the
appearance of black people onstage, particularly given the caricatures that resulted. Yet I would emphasize two things: not only that the idea of black representation had definite limits, was considered offensive or outrageous, worked against
the grain; but also that it was possible for a black man in blackface, without a great
deal of effort, to offer credible imitations of white men imitating him. That is to
say, some blackface impersonations may not have been as far from this period's
black theatrical self-presentation as we tend to believe—and so much the worse,
the reader might add: no doubt the standard was set by whites. On this occasion,
however, far from easily falling into a prefitted stereotype, the hired black "boy"
seems to have been Juba (William Henry Lane), who would a few years later
become the most famous—and, significantly, nearly the only—black performer to
appear in white theaters in the mid-1840s (see Fig. 4). Dickens celebrated him in
chapter 6 of *American Notes* (1842) as the best popular dancer of the day; even
"Master Diamond" (after an 1844 dance competition with Juba that left Diamond
the loser) believed him to be the preeminent dancer in antebellum America
(Winter 47).

The primary purpose of the mask, then, may have been as much to maintain
control over a potentially subversive act as to ridicule, though the double bind was
that blackface performers' attempts at regulation were also capable of producing
an aura of "blackness." The incident suggests the danger of the simple public
display of black practices, the offering of them for white enjoyment. The moments at which the intended counterfeit broke down and failed to "seem," when
the fakery evaporated, could (as we have seen) result in acts of unsettling authenticity, even if a white man were inside. From this perspective we might say that the
elements of derision involved in blackface performance were not so much its
raison d'être as an attempt to "master" the power and interest of black cultural
practices it continually generated. As a figure for early blackface acts, "the seeming counterfeit" is perfectly apt. To the extent that such acts merely *seemed*, they
kept white involvement in black culture under control, indeed facilitated that
involvement; but the power disguised by the counterfeit was also often invoked by
it, suggesting the occasional ineffectiveness, the mere seeming, of the counterfeit
itself.

It is well known that Diamond, Rice, and other early blackface performers laid

"JUBA," AT VAUXHALL GARDENS.

Fig. 4. Juba (William Henry Lane).
Courtesy of the Harvard Theatre Collection

claim to such power through the predominantly black dances in their acts. Even those most skeptical of the blackface phenomenon commonly accepted the authenticity of the dances (though these too, as we have seen, were predictably miscegenated). We should notice, however, that whites subtly acknowledged the greater power of the genuine article, a fact that also illuminates the purpose of the diminished copy. Again, the counterfeit was a means of exercising white control over explosive cultural forms as much as it was an avenue of racial derision (though to say the one is perhaps also to say the other). Advertising himself as the "BEST DANCER LIVING," Diamond boasted in early 1840s playbills of his "skill at Negro Dancing," which audiences surely enjoyed more than mocked. But in challenge dance contests he would tempt only "any other *white* person" (perhaps foreseeing his defeat by the expert Juba), a particularly good way of regulating the black threat to his own reputation and to that of his profession while making a living from just that threat. It was paramount that the culture constantly being called up also be kept safely under wraps. This was made plain in a playbill for a New York performance in 1845, by which time Juba's already legendary stature allowed him to appear regularly on the stage: "The entertainment to conclude with the Imitation Dance, by Mast. Juba, in which he will give correct Imitation Dances of all the principal Ethiopian Dancers in the United States. After which he will give an imitation of himself—and then you will see the vast difference between those that have heretofore attempted dancing and this WONDERFUL YOUNG MAN."[3]

This performance seems, and probably was, astonishingly bold: the trusted counterfeiters mocked in return by a representative of those from whom they had stolen; a public display of black irony toward whites, all stammers and jerks and gracelessness, who had tried to become better blacks. Yet it also foregrounds minstrelsy as a safely imitative form: the notion of the black dancer "imitating himself" indicates minstrelsy's fundamental consequence for black culture, the dispossession and control by whites of black forms that would not for a long time be recovered. Dickens catches this simulacral dilemma almost unawares in his account of Juba when he says, in a final flourish, that the dancer "finishes by leaping gloriously on the bar-counter, and calling for something to drink, with the chuckle of a million of counterfeit Jim Crows, in one inimitable sound!" (139). It was hard to see the real thing without being reminded, even unfavorably, of the copy, the "cover version" that effectively did its work of cultural coverage.[4] Nor, just as surely, could the copy be seen without reminding one of the real thing; as Eileen Southern has remarked, "No one forgot that the black man was behind it all" (*Music* 92). This simultaneous production and subjection of black maleness may have been more than a formal consequence of wearing blackface; it may indeed have been the minstrel show's main achievement, articulating precisely a certain structure of racial feeling. The very real instability of white men's investment in black men, however, seems often to have exceeded this happy ambiguity, giving rise to a good deal of trouble. Much of the trouble, as in Dickens's account, had to do with the black male body.

Dickens, among many others, marked the male body as the primary site of the power of "blackness" for whites. All that separates his record of Juba from other such commentary (on both white and black performers) is literary skill, by which I mean the ability to disguise his own skittish attraction to the dancer's body. In New York City, circling toward the center of the wretched Five Points district, Dickens "descends" into Almack's, "assembly-room of the Five Point fashion-ables" (138). A lively scene of dancing begins to flag, when Juba makes his appearance:

> Suddenly the lively hero dashes in to the rescue. Instantly the fiddler grins, and goes at it tooth and nail; there is new energy in the tambourine; new laughter in the dancers; new smiles in the landlady; new confidence in the landlord; new brightness in the very candles. Single shuffle, double shuffle, cut and cross-cut; snapping his fingers, rolling his eyes, turning in his knees, presenting the backs of his legs in front, spinning about on his toes and heels like nothing but the man's fingers on the tambourine; dancing with two left legs, two right legs, two wooden legs, two wire legs, two spring legs—all sorts of legs and no legs—what is this to him? (139)

The brilliant dancing calls forth a brilliant mimetic escalation: a sharp focus on simple steps of the feet shifts to jump cuts of fingers, eyes, knees, legs, and bodies that blur into fingers, then to curious industrial metaphors (legs of wood, wire, spring) for the dynamo energy of this "heroic" display. All of it is of course a tribute to such display; the escalation is one of enlarging circles or areas of kinesis. But the energy and artistry are finally distanced; the escalation is *away* from the dancing; the metaphors dwarf what they are called on to describe. The whole passage reads as though Dickens did not really know what to do with such energy, where to put it. He ends up producing an account that lacks an immanent purpose. All he will venture is that the dance is so dazzling that everything finally seems like something else, not itself—body into fingers, legs into no legs. And once this move is made, the black man's body has been contained even as it is projected into public, something minstrel performers themselves had somehow to accomplish.

The "black" body's dangerous power was remarked by nearly all observers of the minstrel phenomenon; it was probably mainly responsible for minstrelsy's already growing reputation for "vulgarity." Those conscious of minstrelsy's counterfeit, for example, resorted to suggestive language to describe its distance from the true coin. The actress Fanny Kemble, in her plantation memoirs of the 1830s, clinched such an observation—that "all the contortions, and springs, and flings, and kicks, and capers you have been beguiled into accepting as indicative of [blacks] are spurious"—by ending the list of adjectives with the inevitable sexual parry "faint, feeble, impotent—in a word, pale Northern reproductions of that ineffable black conception" (96). It required little imagination from the audience

116

to make blackface itself "ineffable," for dancers made much of the sexual exaggeration that came so easily to such performances, and song sheet illustrations unfailingly registered, in muted form, this recurring preoccupation. Dancers relied on vigorous leg- and footwork, twists, turns, and slaps of toe and heel. The body was always grotesquely contorted, even when sitting; stiffness and extension of arms and legs announced themselves as unsuccessful sublimations of sexual desire (see Fig. 9). (In "Coal Black Rose" [1827], the cuckolded lover sings, "Make haste, Rosa, lubly dear, / I froze tiff as poker waitin here.")[5] Banjos were deployed in ways that anticipated the phallic suggestions of rock 'n' roll (see Fig. 5). Kemble's frank fascination with what "these people [slaves] did with their bodies" (96) was carried to the stage, where, for instance, dancers would exploit the accents of sexuality and of sexual ambiguity; the "jaybird wing," perhaps similar to a frontier dance of the same name, was considered highly indecent for someone in skirts—perhaps even more so if this someone were male (Nathan 91).

We are justified in seeing early blackface performance as one of the very first constitutive discourses of the body in American culture. Certainly minstrelsy's commercial production of the black male body was a fundamental source of its threat and its fascination for white men, anticipating Harriet Beecher Stowe's famous "vision" that the whipping of Tom would prove the most potent image of *Uncle Tom's Cabin.* The problem this cultural form faced was how to ensure that what it invoked was safely rerouted, not through white *meanings*—for even the anarchic, threatening associations of black male sexuality were created by white cultural meanings—but through a kind of disappearing act in which blackface made "blackness" flicker on and off so as simultaneously to produce and disintegrate the body. Nineteenth-century observers of the minstrel show offer a clue to this dialectic. After a flurry of evidence documenting the authentic nature of early minstrel songs, theater historian T. Allston Brown suggests that most of them ("Long Tail Blue," "Sich a Getting up Stairs") "were taken from hearing the darkies of the South singing after the labor of the day was over on the plantation. The verses and airs were altered, written and arranged as I have described" ("Origin" 6). Another commentator believed minstrel songs to be the "veritable tunes and words which have lightened the labor of some weary negro in the cotton fields, amused his moonlight hours as he fished, or waked the spirits of the woods as he followed in the track of the wary racoon" [*sic*].[6] The fact is that minstrel songs and dances conjured up not only the black body but its labor, not only its sexuality but its place and function in a particular economy.

The body, Richard Dyer has argued, becomes a central problem in justifying or legitimating a capitalist (or indeed slave) economy. The rhetoric of these economies must insist either that capital has the magical power of multiplying itself or that slaves are contented, tuneful children in a plantation paradise; in reality, of course, it is *human labor* that must reproduce itself as well as create surplus value. In these societies the body is a potentially subversive site because to recognize it fully is to recognize the exploitative organization of labor that struc-

Philadelphia Published by G.E.Blake No:13 south Fifth street.

Fig. 5. *Courtesy of the Free Library of Philadelphia*

tures their economies. Cultural strategies must be devised to occlude such a recognition: reducing the body purely to sexuality is one strategy; colonizing it with a medical discourse in which the body is dispersed into discrete parts or organs is another. Shackling the body to a discourse of racial biology is still another, and in western societies the black body in particular has, in Dyer's words, served as the site of both *"remembering and denying* the inescapability of the body in the economy," a figuration of the world's body and its labor, easily called up and just as easily denied.[7] In antebellum America it was minstrelsy that performed this crucial hegemonic function, invoking the black male body as a powerful cultural sign of sexuality as well as a sign of the dangerous, guilt-inducing physical reality of slavery but relying on the derided category of race finally to dismiss both.

The minstrel show as an institution may be profitably understood as a major effort of corporeal containment—which is also to say that it necessarily trained a rather constant regard on the body. Indeed, performers still took care to deflect the wayward valences of the body as they were offered, for there was certainly more at stake than flushes and heavy breathing. Specifically, there were the twin

118

threats of insurrection and intermixture, the consequences, to white men's minds, of black men's place in a slave economy. Blackface performers accordingly devised further strategies to counter the various bodily powers they wanted to, and did, evoke.

It will surprise no one familiar with minstrel-show origin tales that insurrection and intermixture effectively mapped minstrelsy's transgressive range. Early minstrel songs simultaneously produced and muted the physical power of black men coded by such events. Exaggerations or distortions of dialect, for example, or gestures meant to underscore the complete nonsense of some songs might effectively dampen any too boisterous talk, such as that which characterizes one of the earliest versions of "Jim Crow." And all of the unspoken connotations of this bodily power were clearly wedded to an "inferior" people, played moreover by white men who could easily demarcate the ironic distance between themselves and their personae. Still, the power was made quite available, and could be provocative. "Ching a Ring Chaw," or "Sambo's 'Dress to He' Bred'rin" (1833), in a caricatured West Indian dialect, marks a white fascination with the insurrectionary imperative:

> Broder let us leabe, Bucra lan for Hettee [Haiti].
> Dar you be receibe Gran as La Fayette;
> Make a mity show, wen we lan from steamship
> I be like Munro, You like Louis Philip.
> • • •
> Oh dat equal sod, hoo no want to go-e
> Dare we feel no rod, dar we hab no fo-e
> • • •
> No more carry hod, no more oister ope-e,
> No more dig de sod, no more krub de shop-e
> • • •
> No more barrow wheel all about de street-e,
> No more blige to teal, den by massa beat-e.[8]

I am not one of those critics who see in a majority of minstrel songs an unalloyed self-criticism by whites under cover of blackface, the racial parody nearly incidental. Nevertheless, it is hard to resist seeing this invocation of the Haitian republic (whose revolution in the 1790s resonated long after as "a symbol of wild retribution," as T. W. Higginson termed the Nat Turner insurrection ["Nat" 326]) as anything but a kind of ineffectually controlled historical anxiety; and the song is structured by a burden of "no mores," not a form designed, it would seem, to control the fantasies of revolt it probably unleashed. A contemporary ominously said of it that it had "the ringing sound of true metal" ("Black" 107): currency again. This is one of the frankest early minstrel tunes about the weight of slavery, more a reminder than a denial of the black male body in the economy.[9]

More often the reminders came in sexual form. White men were routinely encouraged to indulge in fantasies about black women—which, however, highlighted, and implicitly identified them with, the salacious black male characters who "authored" the fantasies, confusing the real object of sexual interest. Consider the tantalizingly titled "Jumbo Jum" (1840):

> There was a nigger wench and I thought I'd die,
> For when she looked at me she give such a sigh,
> I made an impression on the wenches feeling,
> That I set the coloured lady in a big fit a reeling.
> She dropt right down on the floor,
> In a state of agony you know,
> I kissed her gently on the chin,
> Says she pray do dat agin.
>
> (Dennison 79)

It might be difficult to add any more insinuations of orgasm than already pack these two stanzas. No doubt performers were adroit at manipulating their bodies in order to bring forth the sexual weight of black men's "impression" on "colored wenches" (played, again, by men). Song sheet illustrations captured the phallic sources of such lyrics over and over by showing coattails hanging prominently between characters' legs, and personae were often pictured with sticks or poles strategically placed near the groin or with other appendages occasionally hanging near or between the legs (see Fig. 6; see also Fig. 11).

However strong the attempts at suppression, then, and whatever the ostensible song content, black men were conjured up for the various delectations of white male audiences (even the female characters offered an ambiguous sexuality). Implicit or explicit appreciation of black male sexuality could always slip into homoerotic desire. But the very fact that virulently heterosexual "black" stand-ins were pictured here, and in the theater committed such acts on behalf of the audience, tended further to complicate the whole business. Their potency may have been momentarily attractive (or merely racist typing); but it often shaded inevitably into a suggestion of the "wrong" kind of miscegenation, as in one version of "Zip Coon" (1834): "O my ole mistress is very mad at me, / Because I wouldn't go wid her and live in Tennessee" (Dennison 61). And in the famous "Long Tail Blue" (1827), a song that refers to the "Uncle Sam" coat of the black dandy, the persona sings:

> Some Niggers they have but one coat,
> But you see I've got two;
> I wears a jacket all the week,
> And Sunday my long tail blue.
>
> Jim Crow is courting a white gall,
> And yaller folks call her Sue;
> I guess she back'd a nigger out,
> And swung my long tail blue.[10]

Safe enough pieces of language to us, perhaps; but anyone who has sifted through minstrel song sheets and songbooks knows the seeming scandal, the jealous white

120

Fig. 6. *Courtesy of the Free Library of Philadelphia*

male fears, of miscegenation. And since the black male seems the real object of scrutiny here, it is difficult (perhaps even pointless) to distinguish those fears from homosexual fantasies, or at the very least envy, of black men. I have remarked before that white men's investment in the black penis appears to have defined the minstrel show. As in "Jumbo Jum," however, that investment took varied and overlapping forms, encompassing homosexual attraction, male identification, and male rivalry, for which the apparent concern with miscegenation is a kind of summa. Ideologies of miscegenation were indeed the primary defense against this psychic tangle, and they surfaced in minstrel songs so often as to suggest repeatedly the unconscious material they strained to master.

Worse yet, stage devices such as malapropism, used to control the black male body's threat, could themselves become threatening agencies. Given the popularity of women and blacks as sources for public masking, it is interesting that stage malapropism has historically been associated with working-class white women and black men. From Sheridan's Mrs. Malaprop in *The Rivals* (1775)—"Sure, if I reprehend any thing in this world, it is the use of my oracular tongue, and a nice derangement of epitaphs!"—to minstrel-show stump speeches, malapropism figures as a kind of witless orality signifying nothing beyond itself. But such self-conscious orality usually has a sexual subtext, as in Mrs. Malaprop's remark; and the real interest (though perhaps not the literal sense) of this blackface "lecture" on phrenology is fairly transparent: "Colored frens, dar's one bump dat ought to be on toder side ob de head. (*pointing to the nose.*) Now, sir, if you keep yourself perfectly docile, I will felt ob your semi-intellectual organs ob your organic, galvanic, elifantic, horse-marine, mud-puddle, flounder-flatten, sculpology."[11] Working-class women (white and black) and black men in bourgeois cultural fantasy are figures for a thrilling and repellent sexual anarchy. If in an age of separate spheres women were responsible for household order and spiritual hygiene, all that was dirty, disruptive, and disorderly was projected onto working-class women. The 1870s cross-class relationship of Arthur J. Munby and a domestic servant, Hannah Cullwick, which fully exploited men's erotic interest in social domination, female dirtiness, and sexual debasement—not least in Cullwick's occasional blacking up for Munby, the man she called "Massa"—amply demonstrates the attraction of this kind of Otherness.[12] If in an age of industry men were supposed to be frugal and productive, black men quite evidently came to represent laziness and license, the determining factor in white men's dread of miscegenation; Faulkner's Quentin Compson in *Absalom, Absalom!* is probably America's greatest literary product of this obsession. Onstage these fantasies were partly represented by a vexing and unmeaning linguistic creativity, a proliferation of huge, ungainly, and onomatopoeic words that were meant to ridicule the speaker but which also called attention to the grain of voices, the wagging of tongues, the fatness of painted lips. Through them could be relived the forgotten liberties of infancy—the belly and the sucking of breasts, a wallowing in shit. And while the equation of sexual anarchy with political disorder is an overworked and easy one, it is nevertheless true that minstrelsy's liberties had varied social and political effects. Which is to say that one of the devices that was supposed to dissolve the more threatening, chaotic, and subversive aspects of the black body could instead provide an avenue through which they returned.

CONTORTED ARTISANS

It is equally clear, however, that the cultural form responsible for the insurrection had a built-in structure of disavowal. If the black threat became too grave, audiences merely amplified the insult. A continual acknowledgment of minstrelsy's counterfeit obviously accompanied the illusion of "blackness" onstage—not only accompanied it but was politically *necessitated* by it. As Philip Cohen has written in another context, denigrated features (like the reduction of black men to sexuality) could all too easily become secret sources of male identification, cultural myths reversed into male fantasy; the irony of the counterfeit was therefore necessary to construct and preserve the hegemonic "misrecognition" of black people.[13] The desperate racial ambivalence that minstrelsy's audiences shared, in other words, *depended* on ridicule to counter the sort of attraction or fear we have repeatedly witnessed. To get at the structure of racial feeling exemplified by this dialectic of response, it is first necessary to clarify it, and then to find a social history to account for it.

In the third chapter of Melville's *Confidence-Man*, as I have noticed, a splenetic, limping man accuses the beggar Black Guinea of being a counterfeit. Several chapters into the book the confidence man, now disguised as a collector for a "Widow and Orphan Asylum," engages the accuser in a tête-à-tête, defending what we suspect is one of his earlier disguises:

> "Tell me, sir, do you really think that a white could look the negro so? For one, I should call it pretty good acting."
> "Not much better than any other man acts."
> "How? Does all the world act? Am *I*, for instance, an actor? Is my reverend friend here, too, a performer?"
> "Yes, don't you both perform acts? To do, is to act; so all doers are actors."
> "You trifle.—I ask again, if a white, how could he look the negro so?"
> "Never saw the negro-minstrels, I suppose?"
> "Yes, but they are apt to overdo the ebony; exemplifying the old saying, not more just than charitable, that 'the devil is never so black as he is painted.'"
> (39)

Moments such as this recall Harry Levin's remark that Melville's novel is structured like a cross between the minstrel show and Lucian's *Dialogues of the Dead* (192). I for one am not sure that the limping man trifles at all. It is indeed this novel's strategy continually to dissolve the various meanings of "act" into one another, such that all doers become fakes, role players in a competitive marketplace.[14] But in an aporia that locates the power of blackface counterfeits, this very logic undercuts the man's argument: if all doers are mere masqueraders, minstrels are no different from anyone else; their falseness is the only reality there is. The confidence man's argument likewise self-deconstructs, for he cites the impossibility of a convincing minstrel performance (the ironic "overdo the ebony") in order precisely to suspend disbelief in his own earlier such performance. The man of spleen who disbelieves the con man's fakery succeeds in proving the minstrel show's possibility; the man of irony who argues its impossibility succeeds in proving minstrelsy's power.

This scene is, one might say, an allegory of audience response: mordant irony and suspension of disbelief were simply inextricable moments of white participation in the minstrel show. The racial predispositions loosely attached to those moments, I would suggest, were disavowal or ridicule of the Other and interracial identification with it, though belief in the authenticity of blackface called forth ridicule easily enough; indeed, the valuations and subject positions tend to multiply when one attempts to sketch them out. I am interested precisely in this "play of pronoun function," which film theorists insist characterizes our experience of the cinema, as we successively identify, across gender lines, with logical screen representatives of ourselves (heroes, victims), then with seeming adversaries (villains, killers), and so on: a destabilized structure of fascination, a continual confusion of subject and object.[15] The blackface phenomenon was virtually constituted by such slippages, positives turning to negatives, selves into others, and back again. There was in minstrelsy an unsteady but structured fluctuation between fascination with (or dread of) "blackness" and fearful ridicule of it, underscored but not necessarily determined by a fluctuation between sympathetic belief in the authenticity of blackface and ironic distance from its counterfeit representations—within a single audience, and even within individual audience members.

An illustration has come down to us that suggests this pattern in more concrete and historically specific fashion. It is an engraving of T. D. Rice "jumping Jim Crow" at the Bowery Theatre in 1833, very early in the minstrel show's history (see Fig. 7). The illustration is evidence of a most telling kind—audience response about audience response—and indicates the complex, interrelated interests called forth by such performances. Indeed, to call it a drawing of Rice already understates the case. With only a fiddler by his side, Rice performs center stage. He is the only "black" person in the theater. A crowd has thronged to the foot of the stage and overflowed onto the boards. It is a crowd of some variety, except for the almost total absence of women: workers in smocks and straw hats rub elbows with militiamen; clerks ape the betters they hope one day to become; a few respectable men intervene in scuffles that have broken out in two places on the stage. The picture frame is tightly packed with spectators; the frame extends beyond the boxes on the left to include four more tiers of people. The crowd has become both background and foreground—it is not too much to say that it has become the spectacle itself, so much is Rice dwarfed by the crowd's interest in its own activities. For the singular thing about this audience is that many members of it do not seem to be looking at Rice at all.

There is a circle of attention directly surrounding Rice, and down in front there are scattered faces turned in his direction. Beyond them, however, all is up

Fig. 7. T. D. Rice as "Jim Crow," 1833.
Courtesy of the New-York Historical Society, New York City

for grabs. Much of the crowd is interested in the brawl at stage left, or in conversation among themselves; some of those conversations seem concerned with the brawl, not Rice. The worker behind Rice's fiddler being held back from the fight suggests either an artistic confusion about the real matter of interest or a trick of the pen meant to unsettle us about it: his legs point directly, foursquare, toward Rice, while his torso is turned full toward the fight. It is an impossible contortion even were verisimilitude a secondary goal here. The fight indeed attracts as much if not more attention than Rice's act, as does the confusion stage right, a grand collective lunge toward the performer which has itself taken on theatrical interest. In the lunge, a stout gentleman has been put in the dark by the descent of his top hat over his eyes; the lunge's theatricality has allowed a dandy to appropriate the stage for himself.

One of the earliest pictorial appraisals of this startling new theatrical phenomenon—the caption says this was Rice's fifty-seventh night in his "original and celebrated extravaganza of JIM CROW"—is thus extremely interested in its audience's contradictory responses. In this rendition at least, blackface minstrelsy hosts a variety of attentions. While some frankly indulge in Rice's "blackness," others involve themselves in the class values articulated through what dime novels sometimes called a "fistic duel."[16] Most striking is the illustration's assertion, literalized in the contorted worker, that this audience is seeing the performance and performing onstage at the same time, indulging both in "blackness" and in a kind of ironic self-presentation or self-promotion. It is as if the two indulgences were quite compatible—as if the minstrel show encouraged white audiences to find themselves represented in it.[17] As I have already hinted, two moments of white participation are apparent here: both have to do with minstrelsy's status as a predominantly male arena, preoccupied with matters of the body; and both have roots in working-class culture and ideology.

Take the "fistic duel," for example. What is the significance of working-class brawling onstage at a blackface performance? Why should it be *this* that sums up Rice's fifty-seventh night? One might say, with Tocqueville, that "[i]n written productions the literary canons of aristocracy will be gently, gradually, and, so to speak, legally modified; at the theater they will be riotously overthrown" (85). Yet there is more going on here than mere riotousness. Several social historians of the nineteenth century have determined the importance of physical "manliness" and bravery to working-class life, viewing it as an ambiguous force of "lived" class resistance.[18] Women no doubt bore the brunt of this kind of physical pride; the construction of masculinity in a capitalist dynamic where power in the body substituted for power in the workplace was obviously only partly transgressive.[19] The same can be said for its racial import. Philip Cohen has suggested that working-class men live their class subjection by dissociating themselves from the structural position of their labor and assuming "imaginary positions of mastery linked to masculine 'prides of place'" (27). This assumption is clearly one moment of the drawing: the fighting workingmen assert their mastery and define their superiority in relation to, and over the body of, a "black" man.

Black men, however, lived their subjection in quite similar ways, which white men recognized and wildly exaggerated in their fantasies of black male aggression. The quarrel between two black men, for instance, was a staple of many early minstrel songs and playlets; often the quarrel was over a woman, as in "Coal Black Rose" (1827) or Rice's burlesque playlets *O Hush! or, The Virginny Cupids* (1833) and *Bone Squash* (1835) (see Fig. 8). Mark Twain's chief pleasure in minstrel productions as he remembered them was indeed the "happy and accurate imitation of the usual and familiar negro quarrel" (*Autobiography* 60). The important point is that if white and black men assumed mastery and superiority through similar mechanisms of male rivalry, such similarity, in Cohen's words, implied "some recognition that black and white [were] peers of the same proletarian public realm" (27). The very activities white male workers used to assert that they were not at the bottom, that they were somebody, could produce instances of solidarity with black men. That is the second moment of the drawing—the fascination with Rice—and it is the second moment of early minstrel productions generally. White workers evinced split perceptions in regard to race, identifying, for example, with individual black men and tolerating various kinds of interracial practice, but disavowing ideally, and ideologically, all modes of intercourse with black people, from "amalgamation" to abolitionism, although this is not the only split one might construct on the basis of the evidence.[20] The minstrel show was a form that at some "imaginary" level negotiated and attempted to resolve such contradictions in antebellum American culture, contradictions that stalled organized interracial labor radicalism in the 1830s and early 1840s. Not only were both moments of the contradiction present in minstrelsy, as we have seen in the equivocal character of its representations; but they were also responsible for and infused the ambiguous form of the show itself.[21]

This view might help reaccent recent debates around white working-class racial tendencies in the years of these first minstrel productions. I have already pointed up a seemingly direct correspondence between public masking rituals, minstrelsy, and the widespread racial hostility among working-class white men. It has been a commonplace of antebellum labor history that such hostility was generated in part out of the extreme competition for work in the earliest stage of "initial proletarianization" in America, though it is now clear that the myth of black competition was a cover story for white workers' precipitous descent in the class structure.[22] Cover story or not, white workers labored to preserve the dignity of work by keeping out the "degrading" presence of blacks. This is one context for the beating of the soon-to-be fugitive slave Frederick Douglass in a Baltimore shipyard by a group of white workers fearful that blacks "would soon take the trade into their own hands" (*Narrative* 100). It is also one context for antebellum violence such as the 1834 New York antiabolitionist rioting, much of which

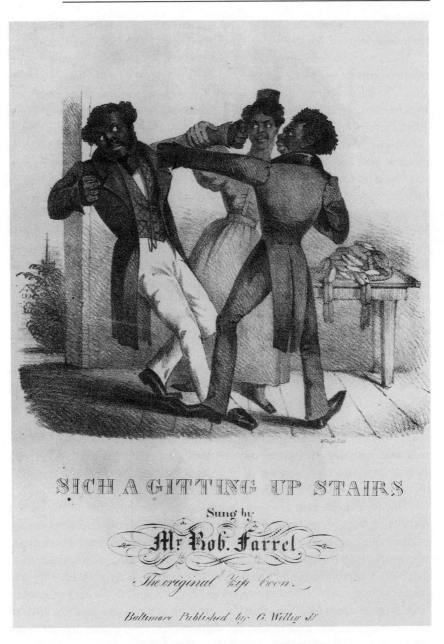

Fig. 8. *Courtesy of the Free Library of Philadelphia*

involved young male workers.[23] And it is of course one context for the minstrel show. Several historians, however, have complicated such notions of working-class racism with subtler inquiries into the contradictions of labor's racial attitudes and ideologies.

A new phrase crept into political discourse in the 1830s to describe the condition of at least the artisan portion of the working class: "wage slavery." Eric Foner observes that this succinct overlapping of racial and class codes embodied fears about a diminished respect for labor, a loss of economic independence, and the emergence of "European" social conditions, all of which tore at the central ideas and values of artisan radicalism—liberty, democracy, equality. Moreover, Foner says, this term's metaphorical equation of northern workers with southern slaves carried within it a "critique of the peculiar institution as an extreme form of oppression," only one indication that the "entire ideology of the labor movement was implicitly hostile to slavery" ("Abolitionism" 61). While such rhetoric was to be put to less emancipatory uses in the hard times of the 1840s, a decade which also witnessed an alliance between Mike Walsh's "shirtless democracy" and proslavery Democrats, evidence for this earlier period suggests it was a useful strategy.[24] The only public New York defense of the Nat Turner insurrection, for example, was published by George Henry Evans's *Daily Sentinel,* an organ of the Workingmen's party: "They were deluded, but their cause was just." In words that evoke the concept of wage slavery, Evans goes so far as to argue that

> we have been negligent in relation to [the slaves'] cause, and our only excuse is, that the class to which we belong, and whose rights we endeavor to advocate, are threatened with evils only inferior to those of slavery. . . . [W]e are now convinced that our interest demands that we should do more, for EQUAL RIGHTS can never be enjoyed, even by those who are free, in a nation which contains slaveites enough to hold in bondage two millions of human beings.[25]

Working-class newspapers (and certain minstrel songs) may have been merciless in their ridicule of wealthy evangelical abolitionists such as the Tappan brothers, but, when not distracted by the class makeup of some abolitionist organizations, they were quite ready to hear the merits of antislavery.

Indeed, the largest single group advocating immediate abolition in the 1830s was that of artisans, not professional reformers; artisans were far more widely represented in abolitionist organizations than in antiabolitionist rioting.[26] Key figures of "artisan republican" ideology such as Robert Dale Owen and Frances Wright were, after all, well-known antislavery advocates. Jacobin radicalism predisposed labor toward abolitionism, as did evangelical religion, though the latter was a limited source of antislavery support and in some cases worked against it.[27] Generally speaking, the hostility to the equation of workers and slaves came as often from the abolitionists, who saw no oppression in northern labor conditions, as from workingmen. The very first issue of the *Liberator* attacked the New England Association of Farmers, Mechanics, and other Workingmen for unnecessarily exciting the working classes against the "more opulent," whereas William West, president of the New England Association, wrote in 1831: "I think there is a very intimate connection between the interests of the workingman's party and [the abolitionists'] own."[28] If minstrelsy had another, more positive moment besides or in addition to racial ridicule, this sympathetic identification between black and white, represented by an inchoate artisan abolitionism, was its political correlative. The minstrel show no doubt supported and was supported by working-class racism; and even an advocacy of abolitionism did not preclude individual racist responses. But opposition to abolitionism did not necessarily mean an acceptance of slavery, either, and minstrelsy also rested on certain kinds of lived interracial identification. These two tendencies within working-class culture were both to be found in blackface, and they shaped the double political valence of the form.[29]

It is plausible but mistaken to suspect that this duality was a mark of the class unevenness of the minstrel show's audience, of racial feeling unequally distributed by class fraction, rather than of generalized racial ambivalence. It could also be objected that contradictions in working-class racial feeling owed simply to Alan Dawley and Paul Faler's cultural and ideological antinomy of "rebels" sympathetic to radical organizing and "traditionalists" indifferent or opposed to it; minstrelsy might then be seen as a form catering not to the restless rebel minority, who rarely went to the theater anyway, but to the traditionalist racist majority—perhaps, in this view, the same men who perpetrated New York's antiabolitionist riots. Actually, however, there was more contradictory race and class feeling here, which it was minstrelsy's task to mediate; at least one of those arrested at the scene of the 1834 riots, for example, was a trade union member, and union men were not unfamiliar with the Bowery milieu (Wilentz 264, 270).

The dichotomy of pro- and antiabolitionist workers was itself shot through with ambivalence. The first working-class penny daily newspapers, as I have remarked, voiced highly contradictory attitudes in regard to slavery. Despite their typical advocacy of Democratic party policy, which championed national expansion in alliance with southern slaveholders, papers such as the *New York Transcript* and the *New York Sun*, not unlike the Democrats nationally, were split in their views on racial issues—the same kind of split visible in white workers who attended minstrel performances.[30] The *Transcript*, for example, hurled angry denunciations at antislavery agitators while also defending their freedom of speech. The *Sun*, as abolitionism gathered force, on the one hand printed various kinds of antislavery material and on the other printed anecdotes about racial brawls in which white men were scornfully victorious. What interests me about such ambivalences is that they disallow simplistic ascriptions of racism to the working class and discourage easy dichotomies of working-class culture. They also capture the structure of feeling that made an interracial labor movement falter. Certainly it is this kind of complexity that gives historical concreteness to the equivocations and ambiguities we have seen in the minstrel show.

It bears reiterating that abolitionism's Whiggish association with wealthy merchants (such as Arthur Tappan), precisely those who were held responsible for the erosion of working conditions, was a major reason for working-class ambivalence toward the movement.[31] Also, the association of abolitionism with the evangelical impulse (most frequently in the person of Arthur Tappan's Sabbatarian brother, Lewis) was read as the "Church and State Party's" cabal to reform Tom Paine's republic out of all recognition.[32] Neither Tappan hesitated to use his socioeconomic power for purposes of coercion. On one occasion, when a tailor would not sign Lewis Tappan's petition against Sunday mail delivery, Tappan threatened the artisan that he would get no more business from his brother Arthur's mercantile firm.[33] The Tappans had also founded the New York-based *Journal of Commerce*, a staunch foe of the trade unions. Artisan ambivalence toward abolitionism was in part a case of class resistance overdetermining and blocking what appears, from the evidence of the minstrel show at least, to have been a real, if tenuous, interest in black people; it was also, of course, merely racist, an expression of white cultural fears. But the sources of identification remained, and were implicit even in minstrelsy's critiques of antislavery reform. True to the popular anticlericalism of which they formed a part, minstrel songs made frequent reference to the supposed amalgamative tendencies of a "Tappan"—it mattered not which—and rumors flew for a decade that one of the Tappans was about to marry, had married, or was encouraging others to marry, a black.[34] Even so, early minstrelsy left occasional interracial recognitions intact by grasping this class resistance to reform even as it took racial parody for granted. This is, as a matter of fact, a succinct way of stating the social complications that wrecked the potential for a labor abolitionism in these years.

THE BLACK DANDY

Perhaps the severest test of my argument about such contradictions was the seemingly unalloyed racism of the infamous 1834 antiabolitionist riots. If minstrelsy could negotiate the contradictions I have outlined, the riots made for far rougher going; yet the same ideological complexities were at work in both social texts. Indeed, blackface minstrelsy illuminatingly glosses this other bit of riotousness from the Bowery crowd.

Occurring in the midst of a long year of violent public disturbances throughout the Northeast, the New York riots witnessed four nights of extensive violence in a variety of locations.[35] More than seven churches—those associated with "amalgamationist," that is to say abolitionist, ministers—and a dozen houses, many of them belonging to blacks, sustained damage. Skilled "native" workers, rather than the more prominent mercantile and professional men recent historians have fingered as perpetrators of much antebellum rioting, seem to have been largely responsible for the violence.[36] On one night of the riots (July 9) there were three separate disturbances that contemporary observers (among them a former mayor, Philip Hone) believed to have been not only linked but attributable to the same mob.[37] That perception demands our attention; it amounts to a kind of narrative. Early in the evening a crowd of two to three thousand gathered at the Chatham Street Chapel (an old theater that Arthur Tappan had converted into a church for Charles Grandison Finney) to break up an integrated antislavery meeting; when the meeting did not materialize (the group had been forewarned),

131

certain of the crowd broke into the chapel and passed resolutions in favor of Negro deportation (one young man, wrote *The Man*, preached "in mock negro style" while his fellows "struck up a *Jim Crow* chorus").[38] Then a number of them left for the Bowery Theatre, intending to ruin a benefit for its English stage manager, George Farren, whose allegedly anti-American remarks had become associated with Britain's attacks on American slavery and with British aid to the Tappans' American Anti-Slavery Society. Meanwhile, a separate mob of about one hundred had converged upon the home of Lewis Tappan himself, smashing windows and doors and burning artwork and fine furniture in the street. One rioter discovered a portrait of Washington, and when a friend insisted, "For God's sake, don't burn Washington," the portrait was gently put aside (Harlow 292). This crowd met the overflow of the Chatham Street crowd at the Bowery. Four thousand people finally stormed the theater, and five hundred to a thousand of them broke in and drove Edwin Forrest and the cast of *Metamora* from the stage. The rioters were calmed only when the theater manager, Thomas Hamblin, ran in from the wings apologizing for the Farren benefit, waving two American flags, and summoning a performer to sing "Yankee Doodle" and "Zip Coon" (Wilentz 265).

It does not trivialize the violence and destructiveness of the riots to see them as complex events, essentially like all cultural forms: intentional, overlapping weaves of social codes and signifying systems whose larger, "narrative" designs transcended the goals of single individuals. The New York riots were indeed purposive, their targets carefully chosen; they were planned and undertaken with consequence, though abolitionist artisans, together with editors such as George Henry Evans, claimed they merely united the "head" and "tail" of society, revealing the "aristocracy of the North" (merchants and politicians) to be in league with the "penniless profligates." Some have taken this very perception by "rebel" mechanics to signify their break not only with the elite but also with "traditionalist" workers suddenly using age-old mobbing practices against their own rightful allies.[39] Yet there did emerge from the rioters' actions a complicated tale of republicanism, blending "traditionalist" racism and "rebellious" class resistance in distorted and allegorized ways—a tale related to the ones that occurred in minstrelsy.

The principal part of the night of rioting I have recounted involved three main sites: Lewis Tappan's house, the Chatham Street Chapel, and the Bowery Theatre. The class logic behind the juxtaposition of these sites ought to be clear from the foregoing pages. And the "recapture" of the Bowery Theatre not only mimics the rowdiness one had come to expect from the shows that played there but also yokes minstrelsy to the ugly purposes of the mob in the form of "Zip Coon." One should note, too, the variousness of the signs conjoined in the rioters' expressions of white supremacy, class resistance, and plebeian patriotism: colonizationist speeches (performed in near-blackface in "amalgamationist" churches), Washington's portrait, "Yankee Doodle," "Zip Coon." Washington in this context

132

seems a familiar artisan-republican standard, as does "Yankee Doodle," talismans meant to keep the British and reformist, that is to say class as well as abolitionist, threats to the republic at bay. Colonizationist speechifying, "in character," directly controverts abolitionist ideology. But the logic of these anti-amalgamationist rioters' being calmed by one of the several minstrel songs about the miscegenating proclivities of black "dandies" is somewhat unfathomable. What are we to make of the odd contiguity of celebrated black dandies ("Zip Coon") and hated "amalgamationist" reformers (the Tappans)? What was the regulative social type of the dandy, who was widely rumored to have been on the loose during the riots advancing racial intermarriage, a figure for—aside, indeed, from amalgamation? What was amalgamation itself a figure for? As with "Jim Crow," there was certainly racist confirmation here, as if the song sealed the fate of the rioters' black targets. But we have seen that such racial feeling was part of a more complex dynamic, and I would argue that the early minstrel show provides the best clue to its inner workings. If the riots confirm our suspicion that the amalgamationist prospect of blacks on top, so often played with in minstrelsy, was an intolerable threat in antebellum America, it is also true that minstrel productions such as burlesque playlets clarify the wayward impulses generating the riots.

In these short dramatic interludes, black mechanics combat self-satisfied black dandies who have begun to consider themselves better than the rest. In the most popular playlet, Rice's *O Hush! or, The Virginny Cupids* (first presented at the Bowery Theatre in 1833),[40] a bootblack named Sambo Johnson who has won the lottery becomes an object of scorn for the "'spectable," hardworking bootblacks who rally behind their boss, Cuff (played by Rice). They ridicule Johnson for putting on airs and reading the newspaper (upside down); Johnson's first riposte to them is to read (that is, pretend to read) an ad for some bootblacks on Canal Street who are underselling them. In what becomes another male-rival plot, it turns out that both Cuff and Johnson are courting Rose (the plot derives directly from the song "Coal Black Rose"). Cuff hides in Rose's cupboard when Johnson comes to call, and foils the visit by tumbling down from a high shelf—covered with flour—when Johnson tries to kiss Rose. Rose protests to Johnson that Cuff (now unrecognizable) is "noffin's else but trash . . . a runaway from de nullifying States," so Cuff shows his free papers, fights with Johnson, and is hit on the head by Rose with a frying pan. When the men are pulled apart, everything seems settled and all begin to dance. As Rose and Johnson dance, however, Cuff breaks a fiddle over Johnson's head, Rose faints, and, as the final stage direction has it, "CUFF stands with uplifted hands."

This is obviously in part a fantasy about social class, in which honest mechanics are vindicated at the expense of those who taunt them with cheap threats and class insults. The dandy who hints that the bootblacks are being undersold is defeated in the end, as is the woman who dismisses Cuff as a slave. It is not too difficult to recognize here the kind of cross-racial identification we have seen before; though the respectable mechanics are black, the plot invokes certain aspects of the "republicanism" so central to white working-class culture—independence, virtue, equality, and so on. There is even an oblique play on "wage slavery," a charge against which Cuff vigorously defends himself; his "free" papers are more a certification of "manly" integrity than a document of status. The plot in fact underscores the identification of black stage mechanic with white audience mechanic in certain of its devices: Cuff's momentary whiteness by way of the flour; the pugilistic male rivalry; and the wish fulfillment of sudden riches through the lottery (variants of which, in inheritance plots and millionaires incognito, would become central to the dime novel). Yet this curious figuration of white class conflict through black characters, a formal recognition that white and black cohabited the "same proletarian public realm" (Cohen 27), is even more complex than it may appear, and takes us straight to the riots.

The class object of this narrative of hostility has a racial component that is far from self-evident. The class animus is directed not, as we might expect, at Cuff the boss but at someone outside the master-journeyman nexus, Johnson the black dandy. This racial object certainly illustrates the class limit to interracial identification—and insofar as it echoes the rioters' call for "Zip Coon" it is an excuse for racist fun. But I believe this character's condensation of race and class to be a figuration of the antislavery reformer; if the class counterpart of Cuff is the white mechanic, the class counterpart of Johnson is a "Tappan," the only current social type combining a superior class position with racial overtones. Johnson the dandy indeed occupies the structural position given to the Tappans in many minstrel songs; "amalgamationist" threat, he interposes himself between Rose and the rightful suitor, Cuff. And the association in the rioting of abolitionism with black dandies, not to mention amalgamation, was so strong as to mark a confusion of one hated object with another. For weeks preceding the New York riots there circulated rumors of two basic kinds: one that charged abolitionists with promoting amalgamation, and one that charged black dandies with the wooing of white women.[41] Even if the black dandy figure referenced an increasing population of middle-class blacks in the urban Northeast, the animus toward it was not only racial but also class-fueled—a substitute, as one black newspaper put it, for less permissible outlets of class hatred.[42] The black dandy literally embodied the amalgamationist threat of abolitionism, and allegorically represented the class threat of those who were advocating it; amalgamation itself, we might even say, was a partial figuration of class aspiration.[43] Hence the dandy's downfall in the playlets and in the rhetoric of the riots, and hence his song at one of the riots' conclusion. Ironically, the rioters' targeting of the dandy seems to have achieved one desired outcome: merchants and professionals withdrew from abolitionism in droves, leaving the movement for the most part to artisans and shopkeepers.[44]

Apparent here, as in the other texts, are the ways in which white men lived an antebellum structure of racial feeling: interracial solidarity was briefly and intermittently achieved through male rituals of rivalry; such solidarity was hampered by the cultural presence of class superiors removed from these rituals, whether in the guise of a wealthy reformer or a black "dandy"; and such solidarity, in any case, was always tenuous and fleeting. We do well to remember, in addition, that even the emancipatory moment of the blackface act was conducted in the realm of male mastery—courtship plots at best, misogynist joking at worst—in other words, over the bodies of women. The plots, types, and disguises to which this structure gave rise might properly be termed minstrelsy's "dream-work of the social," in Michael Denning's phrase, its fantastic figurations of the racial tendencies in antebellum culture (*Mechanic* 81). In condensed and somewhat displaced form, minstrel productions suggested the class obstacle to a labor abolitionism while they relied, in making that suggestion, on an interracial identification it was the purpose of the riots to negate. Riot and blackface both scapegoated the figure of the black dandy because the latter, I would submit, glossed not only the racism that was one response to the political tensions of antebellum New York, but also the working-class hatred of reformers seen as responsible for the republic's impending ruin. Here anticapitalist frustrations stalled potentially positive racial feelings and significations, revealing in the end the viciously racist underside of those frustrations. Yet minstrel productions symbolically and momentarily resolved these contradictions of antebellum white racial feeling.

Readers of Edmund Morgan will have noted a final turn of the screw: the black dandy, in another sense a representative of black maleness as such, was scapegoated to foster the bond between journeyman and master, essentially the argument of Morgan's *American Slavery—American Freedom*. This aspect of minstrel productions, of course, was never absent. It returned as if to refute the burgeoning cross-racial interest so manifest in blackface performance in the 1830s. And it leaves us with a question that would be answered in the next decade: to what extent would white workingmen identify with their masters, and to what extent was it possible to do so with their potential black allies?

6

"Genuine Negro Fun":
Racial Pleasure and Class Formation
in the 1840s

The discovery that one has it in one's power to make someone else comic opens the way to an undreamt-of yield of comic pleasure and is the origin of a highly developed technique.

—Sigmund Freud

Sometime in the winter of 1842–43 four irregularly employed circus and minstrel men, in one of the numberless small hotels that lined the Bowery, hit upon the idea of a blackface minstrel band. The band would soon be called the Virginia Minstrels, and it was the first troupe of its kind to form in New York City. Although the story is variously told, all accounts agree that this happy occurrence came about quite by accident. Sitting in the North American Hotel, Dan Emmett, Billy Whitlock, Dick Pelham, and Frank Brower one day decided to descend upon the Bowery Circus with fiddle, banjo, tambourine, and bones and treat one of its proprietors to what Emmett termed a "charivari." "Without any rehearsal," according to Emmett, "with hardly the ghost of an idea as to what was to follow," they crossed the street and "'browbeat' Uncle Nate Howes into giving them an engagement, the calculation being that he would succumb in preference to standing the horrible noise" the men made. Intrigued, Howes challenged them to sing a song, whereupon they lit into "Old Dan Tucker," Emmett singing and the others joining in the chorus. "The four minstrels were as much surprised at the result as was Uncle Nate," Emmett later told the *New York Clipper*. "After singing some more songs for him, they returned to the North American, where they resumed their 'horrible noise' in the reading-room, which was quickly filled with spectators."[1]

Suspect as such accounts typically seem, Emmett's tale immediately roots us in the culture of early 1840s New York—not least in its crowding of the reading room with the culture of amusements. Above all it situates the activities of the minstrel show in a tradition of "rough music" and charivari that we associate with a moral economy of "natural rights," the right to bread and work, and a time-

136

honored misogyny dedicated to regulating women's courtship and sexual practices.[2] Regarding the first of these, the minstrel show appears to have taken form most immediately as a response to unemployment, as a means of importuning a prospective employer for a job. Although the response of Emmett and his fellows was undoubtedly influenced by a recent trend toward larger minstrel groups, not to mention "singing families" such as the Hutchinsons, its accidental nature suggests that they simply cast about for the best possible solution to a pressing need. The depression following the 1837 panic had indeed devastated theatrical employments as well as most of the trades. One of the Virginia Minstrels, Billy Whitlock, had once been a printer's compositor; now the second of his chosen employments was in jeopardy (Rice 12).

It is fitting that the minstrel "show" began in this way, for its institutional popularity may be said to have sprung up as part of the crisis of hegemony brought about by the forward march of capital in the early republic. If early minstrelsy's contradictory appeal had been subtended by the class warfare that marked most of the 1830s, its plots and types already hinted at the uses of minstrel acts for whites insecure about their whiteness. Working people hit hard by economic disaster in the 1840s were to turn even more urgently to the new minstrel shows. Because the economic slump came amid the enormous shocks that northeastern capitalist consolidation was dealing to the apprentice system of labor, it fostered a profound sense of unease among the popular classes. Their response was a much muted sense of class resistance, an attempt to shore up "white" class identities by targeting new enemies such as immigrants, blacks, and tipplers. This decade's chiliastic sects, its working-class subcultural styles, its nativist and temperance movements are cited by historians as products of a turn to what David Montgomery calls "cultural politics" in the 1840s. The minstrel show was a key player in the turn, and served a crucial new social purpose.

I focus here on the role of blackface in what one might call, after Gramsci, the production of racist consent. I am after the ways in which a new formal achievement in New York entertainment answered and helped promote an 1840s shift in the structure of racial feeling which had emerged with the onset of metropolitan industrialization. Blackface acts did not merely confirm an already existent racism—an idealist assumption that ignores the ways in which culture is reproduced. Social feelings and relationships are constantly generated and maintained, regulated and fought over, in the sphere of culture and elsewhere, and giving due attention to the minstrel show reveals the straitened contours of racial feeling it helped produce in the hard years of the early 1840s. For even as the new shows continued to sponsor a variety of social contradictions, they began to ease the friction among various segments of the working class, and between workers and class superiors, by seizing on Jim Crow as a common enemy. The alliance at which Rice's burlesque playlets had hinted in their effigies of the black dandy soon became commonplace in policing the capitalist crisis of the post-panic years.[3]

Not only had early blackface acts confronted less extreme ideological demands, but they had taken much of their inspiration from class struggle, implicitly coupling the interests of plebeian black and white while mirroring the ways in which class fissures helped destroy interracial coexistence. The minstrel show, as it developed into a night-long entertainment in its own right, met the crisis of the early 1840s with an intensified white egalitarianism that, for all its real instability, buried class tensions and permitted class alliances along rigidifying racial lines, a vital need in this period of seeming disintegration. In what follows I specify the formal and social mechanisms in blackface performance that were congenial to this complex development. If the minstrel show was invented at the very moment when workingmen's nativist, prosouthern, and temperance groups began to form, we shall see that it fostered this chilly climate with an unusual set of racial and sexual fantasies and representations. To address the other aspect of Emmett's charivari, we must indeed attend to the intersecting lines of class and race as they were worked out across the body, often in transvestism. And while we shall also see that the new acts, many of them, were not as racially clear-cut as the white egalitarian alliance might have wished, they ultimately turned matters of the body to racist account.

The Spectacle of Vulgarity

From the start it appeared that a sort of general illicitness was one of the organized minstrel show's main objectives. So much is suggested, at least, by the lengths to which reviews and playbills typically went to downplay (even as they intimated) its licentious atmosphere:

> First Night of the novel, grotesque, original, and surpassingly melodious ethiopian band, entitled the VIRGINIA MINSTRELS. Being an exclusively musical entertainment, combining the banjo, violin, bone castanetts, and tambourine; and entirely exempt from the vulgarities and other objectionable features, which have hitherto characterized negro extravaganzas.[4]

One wants to know more about those other objectionable features. Whatever they were, nobody took very seriously their alleged absence from the minstrel show, as an 1843 song sheet illustration of the Virginia Minstrels only begins to suggest (see Fig. 9). Brower the bone player with legs splayed wide; Pelham on the verge of forced entry of the tambourine; Whitlock in ecstasy behind a phallic banjo: unlike in the engraving of Rice, there is no attempt at realism here. The whole scene has rather the air of a collective masturbation fantasy—accurate enough, one might guess, in capturing the overall spirit of the show. That spirit depended at the very least on the suggestion of black male sexual misdemeanor. And the character of white men's involvement in this institutional Other of genteel culture bears some scrutiny, for as often as not, audiences were themselves inscribed in

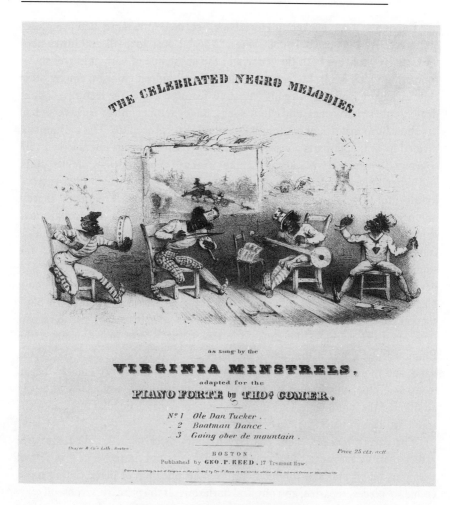

Fig. 9. The Virginia Minstrels, 1843.
Courtesy of the Harvard Theatre Collection

advertisements of companies such as the Virginia Minstrels, the "able delineators of the sports and pastimes of the Sable Race of the South . . . who have won for themselves a popularity unprecedented and the patronage of the elite of Boston" (quoted in Nathan 121). What, in these years, did this spurious "elite" get out of blackface? And what should we make of the obfuscations here, the hints and denials of vulgarity, or the strained attempts to code the popular classes as elite?

The form of the early minstrel show gives us some necessary clues. What the early show was not is as important as what it was. Narrative, for instance, seems to have been only a secondary impulse, even though Rice's burlesque afterpieces had been tremendous successes in the 1830s. In their first performances the Virginia Minstrels gave what they termed "Negro Concerts," containing certain burlesque skits, to be sure, but emphasizing wit and melody; the skits themselves, like Emmett's "Dan Tucker on Horseback," seemed little more than overgrown circus acts. An 1844 playbill publicizing a "Vocal, Local, Joke-all, and Instrumental Concert" conveys both the tenor and the substance of early minstrel shows (quoted in Odell 5:33). In "sporting saloons" and indeed circuses, among other Bowery leisure sites, the Virginia Minstrels featured burlesque lectures, conundrums, equestrian scenes, and comic songs, finally settling into an early version of the show form that would become standard minstrel procedure. The evening was divided in two; both parts consisted mainly of ensemble songs interspersed with solo banjo songs, and were strung together with witticisms, ripostes, shouts, puns, and other attempts at black impersonation. There was as yet no high-minded interlocutor at whom some of the jokes were later directed. Frequently at least one of the songs was sung by a female impersonator, a figure that would prove enormously popular in the 1840s.[5] Very soon the program's first part came to center on the now institutionalized northern dandy, while its second put the southern slave at center stage. In the late 1840s and early 1850s, as the first part began to be devoted to more sentimental music (sometimes performed without blackface), Emmett's and other companies added a stirring middle or "olio" section containing a variety of acts (among them a stump speech), the third part then often comprising a skit situated in the South. Seated in a semicircle, the Emmett troupe placed the bones and tambourine players at either end of the band, and though originally all were comic performers, these two endmen began to assume chief importance in most minstrel companies, particularly after the addition of the interlocutor—genteel in comportment and, popular myth notwithstanding, also in blackface.[6]

The early emphasis, then, was on what film theorists have called spectacle rather than on narrative. The first minstrel shows put narrative to a variety of uses, but relied first and foremost on the objectification of black characters in comic set pieces, repartee, and physical burlesque. If the primary purpose of early blackface performance had been to display the "black" male body as a place where racial boundaries might be both constructed and transgressed, the shows that developed in the mid-1840s were ingenious in coming up with ways to fetishize the body in a spectacle that worked against the forward motion of the show, interrupting the flow of action with uproarious spectacles for erotic consumption, as Laura Mulvey has suggested of women in cinema (19). With all their riot and commotion, contortion and pungency, performers in these first shows exhibited a functional unruliness that, in one commentator's words, "seemed animated by a savage energy," nearly wringing minstrel men off their seats—their "white eyes roll[ing] in a curious frenzy" and their "hiccupping chuckles" punctuating the proceedings (*Ethiopian* 22). Here was an art of performative irruption, of acrobatics and comedy, ostensibly dependable mechanisms of humorous pleasure.[7] "Black" figures were there to be looked at, shaped to the demands of desire; they were screens on which audience fantasy could rest, and while this purpose might have had a host of different effects, its fundamental outcome was

140

to secure the position of white spectators as superior, controlling figures. "I am stating a simple fact," wrote an early admirer of Christy's Minstrels,

> when I say that so droll was the action, so admirable the singing, so clever the instrumentation, and so genuine was the fun of these three nigger minstrels, that I not only laughed till my sides fairly ached, but that I never left an entertainment with a more keen desire to witness it again than I did the first Christy Minstrel concert I had had the pleasure of assisting at. . . . The staple of E. P. Christy's entertainment was fun—mind, genuine negro fun . . . the counterfeit presentment of the southern darkies they personally wished to illustrate, and whose dance and songs, as such darkies, they endeavored to reproduce. (quoted in Nathan 145)

Assertions of the genuine fun these vulgar counterfeits inspired turn up with some frequency in the commentary on blackface, and they offer compelling evidence of the kind of pleasure minstrelsy afforded—so supremely infectious that it begged to be repeated. While we know a fair amount about the overt ideological meanings produced in blackface acts, their more immediate and embodied effects remain poorly understood, as does the relationship of these pleasurable effects to ideology itself. It is not always the case that pleasure, what Roland Barthes once called the "formidable underside" of cultural products (*Pleasure* 39), entirely coincides with ideological intention: it has an underestimated ability to take its captives in wayward political directions, as we have seen, and this held true throughout the antebellum years of the minstrel show. Behind all the circumlocution going on in descriptions of mid-1840s blackface performance, where the celebrations of "fun" and the aspersions against "vulgarity" intersect, we must begin to glimpse the white male traffic in racial degradation whose cardinal principle was yet a supreme disorderly conduct—a rather equivocal means of racial containment. In this affair "blackness" provided the inspiration as well as the occasion for preposterously sexual, violent, or otherwise prohibited theatrical material—material that could result in a somewhat unsettling spectacle of black power, but which, in this social climate, went a great distance toward the subjection of "blackness." Indeed, such material and the guilty pleasure it permitted helped clinch popular racist feeling in these years, if unevenly, and in no area was it so bold and unguarded as in minstrelsy's greatly elaborated staple element, humor.

The function of race in blackface comedy has tended to defeat critics of the minstrel show, particularly when it comes to the subject of racist pleasure. So officially repugnant now are the attitudes responsible for blackface joking that the tendency has been simply to condemn the attitudes themselves—a suspiciously respectable move, and an easy one at that—rather than to investigate the ways in which racist entertainment was once fun, and still is to much of the Caucasian population of the United States. It will hardly do to nod toward ideology as a sufficient explanation for such pleasure, as though it were inherently enjoyable to have one's prejudices confirmed, or indeed as though cultural products were mere reiterations of ideology. The sources of minstrel acts were more complex than that; and the complexity of racist pleasure was precisely that it was labile enough occasionally to outwit Jacksonian ideological prescription. This observation is, by the way, intended to make it perfectly clear that racial feeling was intrinsic to minstrel joking; more than one misguided critic has seen blackface as an only incidentally racialized example of the burlesque impulse.[8] While it is true that audiences in the mid-1840s appear to have been drawn principally to the scabrous fun, it is also true that a special kind of racial pleasure proved so irresistible to minstrel-show audiences. That racist pleasure has proven so resistant to analysis is perhaps only symptomatic of the scandal of pleasure itself, which is notoriously difficult to domesticate and very often goes against the grain of responsible social practice. In pursuing the neglected roots of minstrelsy's offensive humor, therefore, we should also be prepared to find in and alongside them certain dangerous moments of pleasurable disorder that sometimes offended the racial regime of antebellum America. It might even be said that such titillating ambiguity as to the place and proper function of minstrel comedy was one source of its extreme popularity in the mid-1840s, though this ambiguity was, as I say, increasingly circumscribed. And the promise of racially suspect pleasure for whites in the ostensibly right-minded black comedy of our own time is perhaps blackface humor's legacy and equally scandalous analogue, an area of complicitous fun whose formation and sedimentation is mightily clarified by investigating the minstrel show.[9]

Let me emphasize first that the implicitly triangulated, derisive structure of minstrel comedy, in which blackface comic and white spectator shared jokes about an absent third party, usually resolved to a configuration of two people, the joker personifying the person being joked about. The central component of mimicry in minstrel acts was just this aggressive triangulation (the basic situation in Freud's account of the joking process) masked as an intimate but no less objectifying affair of two. "Entering the theatre," wrote the *Knickerbocker* of a T. D. Rice performance, "we found it crammed, from pit to dome, and the best representative of our American negro that we ever saw, was stretching every mouth in the house to its utmost tension. Such a natural gait!—*such* a laugh!—and such a twitching-up of the arm and shoulder! It was THE negro, par excellence. Long live JAMES CROW, Esquire!"[10] Distensions and all, this comic strategy was vital in generating salacious interest in "our" Negroes. Such responses, moreover, begin to point to the affective origins of racist pleasure—the degree to which the scarifying vision of human regression implicit, for whites, in "blackness" was somewhat uneasily converted through laughter and humor into a beloved and reassuring fetish.[11]

The *Knickerbocker* is clearly delighted with "blackness" as spectacle, a delight that, in nineteenth-century terms, might border on benignity, but which here seems unpalatable even in those terms. The intermittent illusion of black performers' presence was especially convenient because in this way white ridicule could be passed off as "naive" black comedy, the sort of comedy, according to Freud, in which spectators indulge in lost moments of childish pleasure evoked by the antics of children, or of "inferior" people who resemble them (*Jokes* 182–89). The great *infectiousness* of minstrel performances, I maintain, owed much to these childish sources. For a good deal of the minstrel show's "vulgarity" approximated life in the nursery, whether it was the nonsense in songs and puns or tirelessly absurd physical antics. Minstrelsy's stump speeches reached back to long-prohibited pleasure in nonlogical modes of thinking and speaking, or simply to the child's helplessness before its bodily demands: "Den I 'gin to sweat so . . . I sweat half de clothes off my back—tumbled ober a sweat-cloth—took a bite ob dar steaks in de bottom ob my pocket—and absquatulated, just for all de world like a California feverite when he's bound for de gold region!"[12] Elsewhere Freud remarks that children tend to expect homonyms to have the same meaning (*Jokes* 120)—not the worst definition of minstrel puns, which on the page are so weak (Mark Twain professed great exasperation with them) that only the most wizened professional could have brought them to life, let alone to a high pitch of naughtiness:

> Why is a fiddle like a handsome young lady? Because it ain't no use without a bow—(*beau.*)

> Why can a ship's crew always have fresh eggs when they are out at sea? Because the captain can make the ship lay-to whenever he pleases.[13]

The oversized clothes performers typically wore, their enormous shooting collars and shoes several sizes too big, had the infantilizing effect of arresting "black" people in the early stages of childhood development.

This is the sense in which "the African," a "child in intellect" and a "child in faith," in the words of one *Journal of Music* minstrel-show fan ("Songs" 51), might become an object of screaming fun and games, as in Emmett's extraordinarily popular "Old Dan Tucker" (1843):

> I come to town de udder night,
> I hear de noise den saw de fight,
> De watchman was a runnin roun,
> Cryin Old Dan Tucker's come to town,
>
> So get out de way!
> Get out de way!
> Get out de way! Old Dan Tucker,
> Your too late to come to supper.
>
> Tucker is a nice old man,
> He use'd to ride our darby ram,
> He sent him whizzin down de hill,
> If he had'nt got up he'd laid dar still.
>
> Tucker on de wood pile—can't count 'lebben,
> Put in a fedder bed—him gwine to hebben,

His nose so flat, his face so full,
De top ob his head like a bag ob wool[14]

Those who have heard this plantation trickster's song know that it conveys the inspired abandon of childhood. What it wished most to provide for its first audiences was the giddiness reliably generated by "Negro" high jinks. Its contribution to racist ideology, like the jokes just cited, is therefore obvious; yet since, as Freud says, naive comedy requires taking the "producing person's psychical state into consideration, put[ting] ourselves into it and try[ing] to understand it by comparing it with our own" (*Jokes* 186), one attraction of such joking seems to have been its ability to reduce not only black people but white spectators themselves to children.

This effect perhaps explains the regularity with which observers resorted to the word "fun" to describe their enjoyment of blacks and of blackface acts, a repetition which, congruent with repeated returns to the minstrel show, may suggest (in Freud's words) "the child's peculiar pleasure in constant repetition" that is a primary wellspring of jokes (*Jokes* 226). In fact the disorder conjured out of wayward portrayals of "black" regression also exuded a certain danger; the evidence indicates that spectators duly arrested in infancy experienced something of its terrors as well as its pleasures. This experience comes through, for instance, in Twain's reminiscences of blackface. The way in which he chooses to celebrate the "genuine nigger show"—he devotes an entire chapter in his autobiography to it—is through a complicated narrative that involves escorting his mother to a Christy's Minstrels performance in St. Louis. This doubled comic situation, in which Twain pays tribute to the fun of blackface acts with a dose of superadded humor at his mother's expense, not only places Twain himself in the position of son but also evokes from him a certain amount of oedipal hostility. His mother is an adherent of the church, and while she delights in all sorts of novelties, she must also square these with her religious proclivities. She is, writes Twain, "always ready for Fourth of July processions, Sunday-school processions, lectures, conventions, camp meetings, revivals in the church—in fact, for any and every kind of dissipation that could not be proven to have anything irreligious about it" (*Autobiography* 62). Twain means to immerse his mother in some real dissipation—a desacralizing impulse on the part of the son inspired by the unease minstrelsy has provoked in the writer.

Twain gets his mother and one Aunt Betsey Smith to go to the minstrel show by telling them it is an exhibition of African music by some lately returned missionaries:

> When the grotesque negroes [Twain here gets carried away with his own conceit] came filing out on the stage in their extravagant costumes, the old ladies were almost speechless with astonishment. I explained to them that the missionaries always dressed like that in Africa.
> But Aunt Betsey said, reproachfully, "But they're niggers." (62)

Of course the novices are soon merrily enjoying themselves, "their consciences
. . . quiet now, quiet enough to be dead," Twain writes. They gaze on "that long
curved line of artistic mountebanks with devouring eyes" (63), finally reinvigorat-
ing with their laughter the whole house's response to a stale joke from the
endmen. As is so often the case in accounts of the minstrel show, Twain's actually
reproduces standard elements of blackface joking, here at the expense of blacks
and women both. Indeed, the linking of these humorous objects is registered in
the syntactical ambiguity as to who possesses the devouring eyes, and this double
threat, along with the aggression Twain aims at his mother, points toward the
sources of pleasure involved. Twain's enjoyment of blackface fooling and funning
arises from a source of humor Freud calls "degradation to being a child" (*Jokes*
227). This, of course, was neither the first nor the last time white male affection
for blacks, (self-)degradation, and infantile pleasure were conjoined by way of an
imaginary racial Other.

This ambivalent atmosphere quite evidently lent itself to a widespread preoccupation in minstrel acts with oral and genital amusement. One might speculate
with Melanie Klein, for example, that Twain's infant sadism owed to blackface's
engendering of a longing for oral bliss whose absence he felt was his mother's
fault and the "devouring" privilege of which was hers alone (267–77, 282–338).
Twain stands out neither in his veiled rage nor in his distinct uneasiness. Carl
Wittke reports that there was among some blackface performers a superstition
regarding the makeup of the mouth, whether painted red or left a sharp, un-
painted circle of white around the lips; if this bit was badly managed it was bad
luck to take the stage (141). This anxiety not only instances again the mystic or
tabooed air that clung to blackface evocations of "blackness" but also attests to
the importance the minstrel show accorded certain strategic bodily zones. Fat
lips, gaping mouths, sucks on the sugarcane; big heels, huge noses, enormous
bustles: here is a child's-eye view of sexuality, a "pornotopia," these fetish images
recurring so dutifully that minstrelsy comes to seem nothing less than a carnival
space devoted precisely to excesses outgrown in the service of workday rationality
(see Figs. 5 and 9).[15] Twain has Jim sing the protuberant "Lubly Fan Will You
Cum Out To Night?" in a book for boys, *Tom Sawyer* (chap. 2), a scene which
again conjoins the naked powers of blackness and femaleness: Jim sings the song
as he discovers Tom painting his aunt's fence in punishment for his truancy. The
black and female goads to this childlike ambivalence naturally came together in
blackface representations of black women, who generally fared far worse than
Twain's mother. The reader will recognize "Lubly Fan" (1844) as "Buffalo
Gals," though not, perhaps, its original lyrics:

> Den lubly Fan will you cum out to night,
>   will you cum out to night,
>   will you cum out to night,
> Den lubly Fan will you cum out to night,
> An dance by de lite ob de moon.

> I stopt her an I had some talk,
>> Had some talk,
>> Had some talk,
> But her foot covered up de whole side-walk
> An left no room for me.
>
> • • •
>
> Her lips are like de oyster plant,
>> De oyster plant,
>> De oyster plant,
> I try to kiss dem but I cant,
> Dey am so berry large.[16]

The singer on the Musical Heritage Society's collection of popular American music gets the ambiguous, almost uncontainable edge of that rising last phrase exactly right.[17] *Dey am so berry large:* allusive promise and exaggerated threat; desire so deep and consequential that it scarcely bears uttering, revulsion so necessary that utterance is ineludible.

What Mikhail Bakhtin called "grotesque realism," which in *Rabelais and His World* provides the occasion for so much antibourgeois celebration, here offers up its less than liberatory effects. This song is, to be sure, antibourgeois, but it is again black people, black *women*, who are the world's body. While minstrel grotesquerie surely had some hand in constructing a raceless popular community ideal of the "low" and vulgar, it was in this sense more historically useful to some of the people than to all of them. Whether because images of black women abetted the return of rowdy audiences to the pleasures of childhood—to the totalizing, and thus terrorizing, connectedness of pre-oedipal bliss—or because their excess, troubling enough in itself, seemed additionally activated by black male potency, blackface performers tilted their staves at the black female power they simultaneously indulged. To appreciate the force of those charges of "vulgarity," one must attend to the way certain material—and, we should recall, performers themselves—pressed home a sort of violent corporeal reality:

> The other day while riding
>> With two ladies by my side,
> I hardly knew which one to chose
>> To make my happy bride;
>
> • • •
>
> I took them into Taylor's shop
>> To get some ginger beer—
> They flirted up and down the room—
>> The white folks they looked queer.
> One swallow'd six milk punches,
>> Half a dozen eggs as well;
> But fore de bill was brought to pay
>> This darkey thought he'd shell.
> The other ate six mince pies,
>> Twelve juleps quickly sped;

> And when dey axed me for de tin,
> Now what do you think I said?[18]

The immediacy of the object supervising a loss of the spectatorial subject—the horror of engulfing female bodies, gorging women depleting the bankbook—seems immanent in the most extreme minstrel representations. Here, it seems, the extraordinary energy of antebellum misogyny, perhaps even that contempt for white women intermittently repressed through men's "protection" of them from savage black manhood, was displaced or surcharged onto the "grotesque" black woman. These images indeed make Klein's point that the child's longing for union with the absent mother—a longing both precipitated and symbolized, it seems to me, by certain blackface images—is inextricable from its primitive desire for vengeance against her, in this case the black woman as the *world's mother.*[19] Yet even within its oppressive outlines, minstrelsy clearly marketed certain "objectionable features" (to recall the first shows of the Virginia Minstrels) which, for all their aggression, were conducive to frightful disorder if not to racial or gender harmony. Why might this experience have been pleasurable at all?

Fredric Jameson has noted that "the aesthetic reception of fear . . . the enjoyment of the shock and commotion fear brings to the human organism" ("Pleasure" 72), is well-nigh central to the experience of pleasure. From eighteenth-century notions of the sublime to Barthes's *jouissance,* Jameson argues, the dissolution of the subject in a paroxysm of threatened menace constitutes one way of transforming "sheer horror" into "libidinal gratification." How much more must this have been the case when, as in minstrelsy, the horror itself was based on a libidinal economy; when the threat of blackface acts was precisely their hint of pre-oedipal suffocation, or their promised undoing of white male sexual sanctity. If all the hilarity here seems suspicious, it is perhaps because it was both a denial and a pleasurable conversion of a hysterical set of racial fears. Images of the body may be of particular help in this project, offering a symbolic map of psychic, spatial, and social relationships, or a site for the concerns of these realms to be secured or dissolved.[20] By way of the "grotesque" (black) body, which, in the words of Peter Stallybrass and Allon White, denied "with a laugh the ludicrous pose of autonomy adopted by the subject" and reopened the normally repressive boundaries of bodily orifices (183–84), the white subject could transform fantasies of racial assault and subversion into riotous pleasure, turn insurrection and intermixture into harmless fun—even though the outlines of the fun disclose its troubled sources. Minstrelsy's focus on disruptions and infractions of the flesh, its theatrical dream work, condensed and displaced those fears, imaged in the "black" body, that could be neither forgotten nor fully acknowledged.

Yet we ought not overlook an equally present historical referent of the "ecstatic surrender," in Jameson's phrase, of blackface minstrelsy's fearsome pleasure in the early and middle 1840s. The overt rudenesses of minstrel performance

147

seem to me calculated recollections of the pleasures workingmen were at least putatively required to abandon in a society experiencing overwhelming industrial change and an emphasis on workplace discipline and abstemiousness. Whether through coercion or suasion, employers increasingly insisted on the "morality" of their workers.[21] The blackface body figured the traditional, "preindustrial" joys that social and economic pressures had begun to marginalize.[22] Minstrelsy's subversively joking focus on bodily degradation, which tainted white spectators themselves, rubbed their noses in foul fluids and anointed them with mud and manure, were splendid transformations of a constricted world into images of imaginary communion and raging excess. The tortured and racist form of this pleasure indicates the ambivalent attitude toward enjoyment itself that industrial morality encouraged.

In rationalized societies such as the one coming into being in the antebellum years, the Other is of prime importance in the organization of desire. Whites' own "innermost relationship with enjoyment," writes Slavoj Žižek, is expressed in their fascination with the Other; it is through this very displacement that desire is constituted. Because one is so ambivalent about and represses one's own plea-sure, one imagines the Other to have stolen it or taken it away, and "fantasies about the Other's special, excessive enjoyment" allow that pleasure to return. Whites get satisfaction in supposing the "racial" Other enjoys in ways unavailable to them—through exotic food, strange and noisy music, outlandish bodily exhibi-tions, or unremitting sexual appetite. And yet at the same time, because the Other personifies their inner divisions, hatred of their own excess of enjoyment necessi-tates hatred of the Other.[23] Ascribing this excess to the "degraded" blackface Other, and indulging it—by imagining, incorporating, or impersonating the Other—workingmen confronting the demand to be "respectable" might at once take their enjoyment and disavow it. Hence indeed the air of sheepish degrada-tion that hangs over so much of this "fun." All the standard elements in the repertoire of inversion—filth, scatology, racial marking itself—returned here to assault the white subject whose self-possession had been constituted by their disavowal. The material capacity of burnt cork or greasepaint, mixed with sweat and smearing under the flickering gaslights, to invoke coal, dirt, or their excre-mental analogues was often acknowledged, as in Tom's humiliating escape, for instance, in the "Whelp-hunting" chapter of Dickens's *Hard Times* (1854), a blacking-up that is a not-quite tarring and feathering. Likewise, it was said of Rice that his reputation depended "upon his blackface; and how he contrives to keep it white, might be matter of grave debate, begrimed as it has been for the last ten years, at least three hours in each of the twenty-four."[24] The pleasurable force of minstrelsy's suffocating degradation was an ambivalent protest against the new moral order.

Chief among the dissenters were the immigrant Irish, with whom such "black" behavior was already widely associated; removed from the land and from less rigidified rural work rhythms, and cramped in the most crowded sections of northern cities, the Irish clung to old habits and customs by way of entertainments such as brawling, drinking, and minstrelsy. Newly arrived, uncertainly "industrialized" Irish workers appear to have relished and identified with the stage peccadillos they necessarily projected onto blacks.[25] Moreover, if, as Paul Gilje suggests, antebellum working-class racism was sometimes only a more focused instance of disgust with unskilled workers and their work habits, then traditionalist practices paraded as "black" in the minstrel show helped displace tensions within the working class even as they made certain objectionable pleasures available to its least reformed members (165–66). In any case, white pleasure in minstrelsy was a kind of social responsiveness; difficult as it may be to acknowledge, this cheap racist libidinal charge was also a willed attempt to rise above the stultifying effects of capitalist boredom and rationalization, especially when the latter meant not increasingly meaningless work but no work at all. It was a rediscovery, against the odds, of repressed pleasure in the body—vulgar enough in taste, and worse in politics, but nonetheless a measure of what Jameson calls the "deeper subject," the "libidinal body . . . and *its* peculiar politics, which may well move in a realm largely beyond the pleasurable in that narrow, culinary, bourgeois sense" ("Pleasure" 69). Codes of industrial morality, or indeed any kind of morality, were utterly negated. I would, however, certainly pause before identifying the pleasure of racist impersonation as some utopian prefiguration; the important point about minstrel-show vulgarity, rather, is that it inevitably connected a local struggle for working-class freedom with the politics of American pleasure. Minstrel comedy forces us to recognize the extent to which comic fun in America is bound up with intimate crises of racial demarcation.

These minstrel types, that is to say, were also black, and much of the disorder was peculiarly orderly after all. If the minstrel show's "black" body offered a terrible return to the gorging and mucus-mongering of early life (witness, indeed, the lingering resonance of the black mammy figure), it did so in the form of "Othered" images of exhibition. As much as blackface types were sometimes menacing vehicles of fantasy, they were made, even in the terms of menace itself, into levers of mere vulgarity and fun. This may recall the common charge, leveled most compellingly by Nathan Huggins in *Harlem Renaissance,* that minstrel characters were simply trash-bin projections of white fantasy, vague fleshly signifiers that allowed whites to indulge at a distance all that they found repulsive and fearsome. I would take this line of thinking much further; for, as Stallybrass and White argue, "disgust bears the impress of desire" (77), and, I might add, desire that of disgust. In other words, the repellent elements repressed from white consciousness and projected onto black people were far from securely alienated; they are always already "inside," part of "us." Hence the threat of this projected material, and the occasional pleasure of its threat. (I do not assume that black people escape such splits, only that these occur by different means.) It is important to grasp that for white Americans the racial repressed is by definition retained as a (usually eroticized) component of fantasy. Since the racial partitioning so necessary to white self-presence opens up the white Imaginary in the first place, the latter's store of images and fantasies is virtually constituted by the elements it has attempted to throw off. Which is to say that white subjectivity, founded on this splitting, was and is (in the words of Stallybrass and White) a "mobile, conflictual fusion of power, fear and desire" (5) absolutely dependent on the Otherness it seeks to exclude and constantly open to transgression, although, in wonderfully adaptive fashion, even the transgression may be pleasurable. And if only to guarantee the harmlessness of such transgression, racist "Othering" and similar defenses must be under continual manufacture.[26] *This* is the color line Du Bois was to speak of a half century later, more porous and intimate than his graphic metaphor allowed, and it is the roiling jumble of need, guilt, and disgust that powered blackface acts. It should therefore come as no surprise that minstrel comedy took great strides to tame the "black" threat through laughter or ridicule, or that, on the contrary, the threat itself could sometimes escape complete neutralization. Blackface representations were something like compromise formations of white self-policing, opening the color line to effacement in the very moment of its construction. Three further examples, two based on songbook images and one on the dynamics of theater spectatorship, will make my meaning plain.

The real urgency of white self-policing is evident in the outright aggression of many blackface jokes. Even the ugly vein of hostile wish fulfillment in dime minstrel songbooks reads as a sort of racial panic rather than confident racial power (though, to be sure, the result was hegemonic enough). We are still in the world of the child, the fantasies of omnipotence barely concealing the vulnerability they mask. One notes in particular the relentless transformation of black people into things, as though to clinch the property relations these songs fear are too fluid. The sheer overkill of songs in which black men are roasted, fished for, smoked like tobacco, peeled like potatoes, planted in the soil, or dried and hung up as advertisements is surely suspicious; these murderous fantasies are refined down to perfect examples of protesting far too much. Here is "Gib Us Chaw Tobacco":

> Natur planted a black baby,
> To grow dis weed divine,
> Dat's de reason why de niggers
> Am made a 'baccy sign.
> (*Negro* 90)

Although this verse comes on in the mimed accents of a cut-rate Aesop, self-buttressing fairy tales such as this one are so baroque that one imagines their concoction requiring a considerable amount of anxious attention. They are not unlike the "atrocious misrepresentations" (as John Quincy Adams called them) in the infamously rigged 1840 U.S. Census, its imagined North populated with frightful hordes of black lunatics and idiots (quoted in Litwack 45). Indeed, in

"My Ole Dad," another oedipal scenario, the ridiculous titular figure mistakenly throws his washing in the river and hangs himself on the line; he goes in after his clothes but drowns. His son subsequently uses fishing line to catch him, a bloated ghost who returns at song's end, interestingly enough, to haunt his mistress (*Negro* 30). In the realm of blackface impersonation, one might say, the house was always haunted; the disavowals were never enough to halt the (parental) Other's encroachment on white self-identity. The continual turn to the mask itself, its obvious usefulness, suggests as much.

Some songs came even closer to the heart of the matter. More successfully prophylactic than "My Ole Dad" is "Ole Tater Peelin":

> Oh, yaller Sam, turn'd a nigger hater,
> Ah, oo! ah, oo!
> An' his skin peeled off like boiled potatoe,
> Ah, oo! ah, oo!
>
> (*Negro* 102)

The protagonist of this little rhyme is called "Tater Peelin"; blacks snub him because he becomes colorless, neither "yellow, blue, nor black." Finally hogs eat him, and plant his bones. (The end result of this particular planting is not specified.) It is difficult to say whether one's speechlessness before this sort of thing owes more to its merciless brutality or its perverse inventiveness—both significant elements, in my recollection, of schoolyard culture. Again, that is to say, there is the imprint of the panicky child. The concern with fluid, not to say skinless, ego boundaries, together with the imagined introjection of objectified black people, acknowledges precisely the fragility of the racial boundaries the song attempts to police. Obviously the dilemma of "race" is a matter of the marking not of white people themselves but only, in particular, of the liminal "yaller" man produced by intermixture, signifier of the crossed line, of racial trespass. In such songs it is as though whites were at a loss for a language to embody the anxiety that in effect constituted the color line, and indicates how extreme the consequent defensiveness must have been.

Racial defensiveness was imaged in this period in more disguised ways as well. Minstrelsy's obsession with the penis and with the world's mother seems to have given rise to an inordinate amount of anxiety and fantasy regarding the threat of castration. Blackface fetish images indeed substituted in complex ways for the threat of the (b)lack.[27] Especially instructive examples in this regard are the many songs in which black women get their eyes put out, as in "Old Blind Josey," whose violent protagonist is already (perhaps revealingly) blind:

> But den one night he [Josey] danced so high,
> He run his heel in a black gal's eye—
> Oh! Golly me, but didn't she cry!
> Unlucky Old Blind Josey.[28]

Repeated ad infinitum, such representations signify, if we are to take seriously Freud's connection of Oedipus' blinding and castration. It is perfectly clear, moreover, that this fantasy resonated against the erotic white male looking inherent in "black" theatrical display. So variable are the possibilities of spectator identification in the theater, however, that we might inquire as to just whose castration was being constantly bandied about. On the most immediate level, collective white male violence toward black women in minstrelsy not only tamed an evidently too powerful object of interest, but also contributed (in nineteenth-century white men's terms) to a masculinist enforcement of white male power over the black men to whom the women were supposed to have "belonged." Indeed, the recurrence of this primal scene, in which beheeled black men blind black women, certainly attests to the power of the black penis in American psychic life, perhaps pointing up the primary reason for the represented violence in the first place. Yet it is still puzzling that black *women* were so often "castrated," even if, to follow the metaphor, they were allegorical stand-ins for white men whose erotic looking was undone by the black men they portrayed as objects of their gaze. (No doubt this racial undoing, phallic competition and imagined homosexual threat both, was the fear that underlay the minstrel show *tout court*.) Or perhaps, if one may extrapolate from Lacan, to castrate the already "castrated" woman was to master the horrifying lack for which she stood.

The elastic nature of spectator identification suggests another possibility, one which does not contradict the general air of male vulnerability being managed or handled here. The blackface image, I have suggested, constituted black people as the focus of the white political Imaginary, placing them in a dialectic of misrecognition and identification. And this dialectic was achieved by a doubled structure of looking; black figures (male and female) became erotic objects both for other characters onstage and for spectators in the theater, with a constant slippage between these two looks. It follows that white men found themselves personified by "black" agents of desire onstage, as in Rice's *O Hush!;* and this was of course an equivocal ideological effect because, in allowing white men to assume imaginary positions of black male mastery, it threatened an identification between black men and white men that the blackface act was supposed to have rendered null. "Old Blind Josey," conversely, uses white men's imaginary "blackness" to *defend* them against black male power. The song calls on tricks of (cross-racial) disguise that Michael Denning has shown to be endemic to working-class cultural production in order to make the black male figure of "Old Blind Josey" a representative of white men—already unfortunately castrated, as I have noted—striking out at a black woman who seems not only female but also a cover for black maleness.[29] Her typically jutting protuberances and general phallic suggestiveness bear all the marks of the white-fantasized black men who loomed so large in racialized phallic scenarios. It makes perfect sense that castration anxieties in blackface would conjoin the black penis and the woman, as not only in "Old Blind Josey" but "Gal from the South" and other songs. Another referent for whites of Lacan's threatening (m)Other, Frantz Fanon argued, is precisely the black male—an overlap too pressing to ignore in songs such as these (161).

152

Thus the "castration" scene played out so often in minstrel songs of the 1840s was an iterative, revealingly compulsive rebuttal of black men by momentarily empowered white men. Such dream-work disguises are telling proof of minstrelsy's need to figure black sexual power and white male supremacy at one and the same time. In fact, their imaginary resolutions speak perfectly to the structure of feeling behind them: the violence against black women vicariously experienced but also summarily performed; the spectacle of black male power hugely portrayed but also ridiculed and finally appropriated. Just as attacker and victim are expressions of the same psyche in nightmares, so were they expressions of the same spectator in minstrelsy. This dynamic of mastery was both the genesis and the very name of pleasure in the minstrel show.[30]

One might, after Laura Mulvey, call this dynamic the "pale gaze"—a ferocious investment in demystifying and domesticating black power in white fantasy by projecting vulgar black types as spectacular objects of white men's looking. This looking always took place in relation to an objectified and sexualized black body, and it was often conjoined to a sense of terror. But the political character of the mid-1840s seems to have held the terror in check. The pale gaze reigned supreme: by 1847 the *Spirit of the Times* rated the increasingly popular Ethiopian Serenaders, recently returned from serenading English royalty, far below the Christy troupe, who were firmly entrenched down at Mechanics' Hall:

> The performance of the Ethiopians as a delineation of Negro eccentricities is a failure. It is entirely too elegant. The singing is very fine and very agreeable for a time, but its very excellence is an objection to it. . . . [W]e listen and are pleased, but leave with little desire to return. At the Mechanic's Hall [*sic*], we listen and laugh, and have a desire to go again, and again. (October 9, 1847)

POLICING THE CRISIS

The theater historian George Odell expressed legitimate surprise that performers of modest talent, best suited for the circus, could within a few years' time occupy center stage in blackface minstrel acts (4:478). Odell's perplexity is a useful reminder that the localizing of "vulgarity" in minstrel shows and other popular forms coincided with their gain in visibility and importance toward the mid-1840s. It should also remind us that nothing *intrinsic* to minstrelsy accounted for its popularity; it was less the performers than working-class demands and preoccupations that brought blackface into the limelight. The chief reference point for such matters was the depression and its effect on the popular classes.

Historians have long held that the depression, unlike its twentieth-century counterpart, temporarily quieted the claims of class struggle. In contrast to the class vehemence of the 1830s, which resulted, for example, in General Trades' Union strikes in several cities in 1835–36 and furnished a broad lexicon of class disgust at evangelical reformers and other usurpers of the republic, the post-panic 1840s produced different antagonisms, other investments. David Mont-gomery has argued that the Philadelphia working class in the mid-1840s divided along ethnic and religious rather than class lines; a "counterpoint of class and ethnic conflict" found disaffected nativist workingmen more often than not siding with their masters against Irish workers, and Irish workers with their masters against nativists rather than "the Catholic weaver, the Methodist shoemaker and the Presbyterian ship carpenter [uniting] as members of a common working class" ("Shuttle" 45, 52, 68). Others have similarly noted the coincidence in this decade of working-class proletarianization—new depredations of "outwork" (piecework done in the home, often for middlemen) and divisions of labor—and the disruption by ethnic segmentation of class militancy.[31]

Yet, as historians have also acknowledged, class resistance hardly went away. It was injected into popular movements such as land reform, temperance, public education, and "self-improving" mutual aid societies which usually brought to-gether participants from a diversity of class positions. Sean Wilentz has deftly shown how class energies both fueled and bifurcated these movements, a phe-nomenon that ought to make us attentive to the way racial, ethnic, and other preindustrial conflicts actually masked and provided displaced terrain for the ever-volatile politics of class. To be sure, reform movements such as nativism and temperance did, in Wilentz's words, define "a new mood in the [New York] trades, an apparent quieting of the class turbulence of the 1830s and a more conservative approach to social and personal problems" arising from workers' "fears of dependence, from the search for an adjustment to what looked like permanent hard times." But the decline of mass trade unionism amid reformist impulses indicated only "a change in emphasis and a loss of apparent unity—a return, in most instances, to the broader terms of social conflict, of 'producer' versus 'nonproducer' rather than of workers versus employers, compounded by a deflection of purpose and new ethnic stratification and tensions" (324, 357). The appearance of lowered class consciousness after the panic was in large part just that, an appearance marred by Mose at the Olympic Theatre, seriously threat-ened by the b'hoys at Astor Place, and abolished altogether by striking New York tailors in 1850.

In these years of evangelical crusades and ethnic hatred, however, most working-class people were not disposed to look toward an exclusively workers' millennium, or were but in the name of other enthusiasms. It is thus possible to speculate on the sources and cultural usefulness of the minstrel show's pleasures. The social contradictions of the 1830s, in which class conflict both permitted and overruled certain radical racial impulses, here became an even more complex bog of social needs, tensions, and feelings. Minstrelsy's markedly elaborated form in the 1840s amounted to racial rather than more multiply determined aggression; it is interesting, for example, that the interlocutor, that "codfish aristocrat," was not yet a permanent fixture.[32] The minstrel show, as with other kinds of cultural politics in this period, brought various classes and class fractions together, here

154

through a common racial hostility. Minstrelsy was still propelled by, and in many ways hosted, the angry energies of class disaffection; indeed there was always the chance that class disdain might become a liberatory alliance across racial lines against capitalist elites. But there is also a good deal of evidence that in these years, unlike in the 1830s, even the class anger capable of disrupting the white egalitarian alliance was directed at racial targets.[33]

Certainly the tensions between labor and abolitionism had never been so great; the early and mid-1840s offer a depressing narrative of failed schemes and scuttled allegiances. The entrepreneurial outlook of most antislavery activists made for distinctly uneasy relations between opponents of slavery and opponents of capital.[34] The notion of slavery as a metaphor for both black and white oppression, which in the form of "wage slavery" had seemingly harbored much antiracist potential in the 1830s, increasingly led to the ranking of oppressions, distancing rather than relating the conditions of slaves and workers. Wendell Phillips, for instance, would have no part of the idea of wage slavery, perhaps understandably, because for him the condition of slaves was not analogous to that of the masses of workingmen; freedom meant precisely self-ownership. When in 1843–44 the abolitionist John A. Collins, a socialist, began to insist that slavery was only symptomatic of a deeper ill—private property—Garrison and Douglass both heaped scorn on what Douglass later termed his "communistic ideas" (*Life* 228). Abolitionists were hardly the sole culprits. Working-class politics had so little room to maneuver in hard times that racial sympathy was shoved aside. In a famous 1844 public correspondence with the abolitionist Gerrit Smith, labor reformer George Henry Evans spoke for many labor leaders when he declared himself "formerly" an advocate of abolition: "This was before I saw that there was *white* slavery." Figures such as Robert Owen and Horace Greeley were saying much the same thing. Indeed, in the mid-1840s, as David Roediger has shown, "white slavery" came to displace "wage slavery" in labor rhetoric, a figure concerned less with twinning the plight of white worker and slave than with privileging the former over the latter.[35] The tenor of the times was evident in one thoroughgoing attempt at a labor abolitionism, Nathaniel P. Rogers's proposed alliance of northern and southern workers against all the exploiters of labor, which unfortunately gave more attention to the northern capitalist than to the slave owner, perhaps confirming the suspicions of the abolitionists. Workers were rarely proslavery, but, for a variety of reasons, abolitionism was less and less their chosen reform.[36]

These incidents highlight the familiar ways in which class oppression hampered working-class abolitionism. Yet in these years such class-resistant impulses were very often expressed or lived as racial distaste and white self-validation, a convenient displacement of class anger not at all unlike the nativist or temperance versions of class collaboration. In contrast to the previous decade, there was now little worker abolitionism to offset such a result, and it had to compete in any case with alliances such as that between the working-class rebels behind Mike Walsh and proslavery Calhoun Democrats (no matter that low-tariffism and anti–Van Burenism helped this alliance along [Wilentz 333]). What class rhetoric remained, moreover, was vented as much at abolitionists as at other class enemies. The general result was to substitute racial hostility for class struggle, which at least temporarily, and in at least this sense, settled accounts between artisans and laborers, ethnics and natives, workingmen as a class and their employers: a crucial development amid the disarticulation of capital in antebellum America.[37]

In the racial chill, then, two main working-class impulses were nourished. On the one hand there was an assumption of broad cross-class agreement on racial tenets, on the other a sense of class disaffection that in the present climate had lost its capacity to extend across racial lines. These impulses marked the relations not only between workers and those above them but also between various fractions of the working class. The minstrel show appealed to workingmen because it relied on a shared (though largely empty) "whiteness" even as its rowdiness differentiated worker from bourgeois. Workers on the very bottom may have negotiated the cementing of their class position beneath the artisan class by denying that position through celebrations of their free-white status as well as embracing it through unseemly—and unrepublican—activities such as racist mobbing and other forms of public racial antagonism.[38] Thus did popular racism aid the formation of the white working class: "whiteness" was capacious enough to allow entry to almost any nonblack worker, and resilient enough to mask the class tensions that were worked out in the modality of race. Racial hostility in itself was no badge of class difference; quite the contrary. But the *way* in which racism was manifested may have helped mark such differences as were coming to characterize the white-egalitarian world of American workingmen no less than the American republic.

It was just here that the first minstrel shows were situated. Insisting on the whiteness of all upstanding workers, blackface minstrelsy still occupied a very uneasy class space—as we saw in chapter 3, the "dark" side of working-class culture. For while minstrelsy began to issue a sort of racial rallying cry across the classes, it stressed its "vulgarity" in ways that made class difference, and therefore the whole business of class formation, uncomfortably apparent. The grasping after the label "elite" in minstrel playbills and newspaper ads suggests that working-class identities in these years of muted class expression were established not only in the realm of race and other non–class-based associations but by way of variable relations to entertainment forms that bore the marks of class. Minstrel-show partisanship, in other words, had class-related implications, however monochromatic its racial design. One might claim one's rowdy allegiance, or finesse it through the language of respectability, but one's ultimate class relationship to such forms could not be ignored. A significant amount of jostling among the classes occurred in the officially homogeneous medium of minstrelsy's racial representations.

156

In light of these developments, one begins to remark another sort of spectacle going on in minstrelsy, one that showcased the vulgar themselves. Spectatorship, we might even say, was bound up in the early minstrel show with surveillance. Blackface's sponsoring of what we have seen to be white as well as black infantilization had its analogue in the way it displayed not only "black" figures but white working-class spectators as well. This exhibition, surely, was the point of the whole genre of journalistic theater-crowd observation which proved so valuable in fixing the class allegiances of the minstrel show. Its often ironic discourse was dedicated precisely to locating working-class "pathologies" of theater behavior. Recall the *Spirit of the Times*'s portrait of the Bowery pit as

> a vast sea of upturned faces and red flannel shirts, extending its roaring and turbid waves close up to the foot-lights on either side, clipping in the orchestra and dashing furiously against the boxes—while a row of luckier and stronger-shouldered amateurs have pushed, pulled and trampled their way far in advance of the rest, and actually stand with their chins resting on the lamp board, chanking peanuts and squirting tobacco juice upon the stage. (February 6, 1847)

The body on display here is white; and class is on display in the form of bodies and bodily behaviors. Such writing serves not only to localize class values in theatrical spectacles of the body such as the minstrel show, but to scrutinize the way working-classness itself was lived in the body—scandalous enough in an age bent on devising bourgeois codes of self-abnegation.[39] The minstrel show's display of spectators' bodily activity had the effect of securing rowdy class meanings and significations in a context which pressed for their absence, for if the body is notoriously an object of regulation and control, the form and placement of activities such as spitting, eating, or yawning may become areas of refusal to conform to the dictates of propriety. Norbert Elias observes that such "personal" habits and behaviors, while seeming the most natural and automatic things we do, are in fact the most "cultural" (150). Which is to say, of course, that there are class modes of these behaviors, shaped by their relation—their opposition—to other class modes. Given that most minstrel playbills warned audience members against spitting, chewing loudly, or "beat[ing] time with their feet, as it is unpleasant to the audience and interrupts the Performers," one must guess that the prevalence of these displays attested to the persistence of working-class self-definition by means other than labor activism.[40]

The reported outrageousness of working-class spectators in accounts such as the one from the *Spirit of the Times* is attributable to the roving eye of the distanced bystander who speaks either for the shocked bourgeoisie (the high-minded quarterly, the cultural reformer) or the respectable portion of the working class (the penny press). If such accounts involve a good deal of class projection in their details, they also capture a significant and self-conscious set of audience rituals. In fact they describe a certain fraction of theatergoers who know their behavior is under scrutiny, and who agree that the spectacle of minstrel comedy includes their own performance. We must, then, read this critical genre itself as a class break—a break disguised in the context of early 1840s reformist politics. Pierre Bourdieu has drawn our attention to different class-inflected modes of spectatorship; where bourgeois (or bourgeois-aspirant) involvement is often pure disembodied gaze, working-class involvement often takes the form of demonstrative engagement (*Distinction* 4). One sees precisely this break in journalistic accounts of minstrel-show audiences. It is a break that minstrelsy both encouraged and bridged. For not only did blackface performance give class meanings a local habitation at a time when ideologies of reform denied them a name; but for the length of a night, at least, it resolved the contradiction between the working-class push against the master and the post-panic impulse toward an alliance with him. Purveying racial ideologies over which the classes could bond, the minstrel show offered them in a guise and in a place that all but the most abject of respectable men might find troubling.

As for these men in contradictory class locations—artisans on the rise into the master class, clerks with working-class cultural links—not all of them, of course, were put off by new developments such as blackface minstrelsy. Working-class culture and minstrelsy both were more complex and multilayered than that. The diversity of the minstrel show's audience depended in part on the fact that upwardly mobile men retained some "low" cultural associations even as they kept a necessary distance from the rites of workingmen. T. J. Clark has detected a kind of knowing connoisseurship in nineteenth-century French petit-bourgeois café-concert spectators, an attitude that helped establish a useful irony toward working-class cultural forms while clearly depending on a oneness with and delight in the forms themselves (*Painting* 237). Embourgeoisement is in fact undertaken in relation to cultural choices, through, among other things, a "superior" appreciation of popular forms such as blackface—a perspective that in antebellum America was constructed by the "elite" view in the ironic press account. To read the protestations of respectability in minstrel ads is indeed to witness the process of class formation. Having a place in which to *be* "elite" was a petit-bourgeois necessity; as if in response to this need, popular theatrical forms hosted rituals of class differentiation as well as class solidarity. When the b'hoys screamed that they were "sons of freedom," the shopkeeper raised a shout he may have retracted with a raised eyebrow. Amusement at the antics of the vulgar distanced them; petit-bourgeois mastery of minstrel-show spectatorship, which included taking in the spectators as part of the show, was precisely the power of one class over another. This dynamic was a theatrical correlative of the contradictory class politics of the 1840s. Indulging the racial vulgarity, small masters and other respectables masked their own social mobility by playacting working-classness among their former associates. Enjoying the show at one remove, they just as surely reveled in the injuries of class.[41]

ACTING THE WENCH

We must now turn to blackface transvestism, the supreme form of "vulgarity" in the popular theater and the most difficult to assess. The immense popularity of cross-dressing in the blackface theater suggests that this was one "objectionable feature" no self-respecting troupe of vulgarians could do without. We have already seen many instances of minstrel-show misogyny, and in part the blackface "wench" character was just a more extravagant form in which to achieve the same result. According to one commentator, the female impersonator had "a hair-trigger sort of voice" and an "unholy laugh" capable of hurrying "little innocent children . . . into premature graves" and convincing wicked unbelievers that "there must, at least, be a hell." This observer further comments that such performances featured fiendish dances, much show of leg, and silly confidences uttered in parody of womanhood, extending to imitations of popping corks, descriptions of the size of "her" last meal, and tales involving hapless boyfriends who must pawn their clothes. In fine, the female impersonator, this expert notes, "makes you wish the journey of life were ended and you were laid away in a nice, cozy little tomb somewhere under the weeping willows."[42]

As this rather extreme account indicates, however, burlesque was wrested from a good deal of anxiety. This is the language of defensiveness, and the first of its referents is the apparently profane and murderous power of women. One outcome of the class formation we have been witnessing was indeed a reorganization of gender roles in and out of the home. "In a period when the productive household economy [men and women working side by side in the patriarchal home] was disappearing and the family wage economy [the pooled earnings of men, women, and children from their separate spheres] had yet fully to take shape," writes Christine Stansell, many forms of gender strife constituted "a great renegotiation of what, exactly, men and women owed each other" (81). Because the "shocks of the wage system" were so often registered in the form of familial adjustments, she argues, some of the most painful effects of the emerging order were lived as rearrangements in the expectations for men and women (77). Ill-paid, irregular, or nonexistent work made husbands ineffectual breadwinners, weakening cherished patterns of patriarchal control, while wage work offered women some new means of self-support; such developments helped set in motion an epochal battle for rule of the home. Workingmen many times sought to redress the erosion of their authority with abusiveness and violence. Quarrels over household arrangements, domestic service, family loyalty, even female drunkenness pitted self-styled male disciplinarians against "their" women. Tenement women were partially fortified against male hegemony by their extensive involvement in one another's lives—from neighborly rounds of drinks and shared domestic tasks to emergency eavesdropping on battered wives. As it turned out, says Stansell, certain masculinist traditions were loosening: young women on the Bowery, for example, flaunted a newfound sense of power by way of stylistic excesses that paralleled the cult of the b'hoy. Counterparts of Mose's Lize, indifferent to bourgeois decorum, they not only dressed in "fancy" clothes—"a light pink contrasting with a deep blue, a bright yellow with a brighter red, and a green with a dashing purple or maroon," wrote a bemused George Foster—but pursued the city's parks, promenades, and amusements (including the theater), using commercial leisure to redraw the boundaries of male privilege and ultimately forcing some enlargement of the proletarian public sphere.[43]

Men threatened by these developments at least had the solace of the minstrel show's popular misogyny. The "wench" role was made famous in the 1840s by performers such as Barney Williams and George Christy, who vied for the title of originator; many performers (such as a "Master Marks" of Charley White's Minstrels) probably engaged in similar displays. The most renowned of "wench" performances centered on the song "Miss Lucy Long" (1842), of which there were numerous variations, the most prominent being that of Williams. As best one can tell, the "wench" (despite a "hair-trigger" voice) usually did not sing the songs she starred in; the songbook headnote to Charley White's version, "The Dancing Lucy Long," for instance, says that the piece was danced by Master Marks and sung by the band, and Ralph Keeler remembered dancing rather than singing "Lucy Long."[44] The "wench" became the lyric and theatrical object of the song, exhibiting himself in time with the grotesque descriptions. The earliest version of "Lucy Long" includes these verses:

> I've come again to see you,
> I'll sing another song,
> Jist listen to my story,
> It isn't very long.
>
> Oh take your time Miss Lucy,
> Take your time Miss Lucy Long.
> • • •
> Oh! Miss Lucy's teeth is grinning,
> Just like an ear ob corn,
> And her eyes dey look so winning
> Oh! would I'd ne'er been born.
> • • •
> If she makes a scolding wife,
> As sure as she was born,
> I'll tote her down to Georgia,
> And trade her off for corn.

An 1848 version interpolates this verse:

> Miss Lucy, when she trabels,
> she always leaves de mark
> Ob her footsteps in de gravel,
> you can see dem in de dark.[45]

In such performances coquette was reduced to coon and scolding wife "mastered," though just what it meant to have footprints that were visible in the dark is anyone's guess.

It is interesting to note that psychoanalysts consider one form of cross-dressing in men to be a way of warding off castration anxiety, of recovering the phallus for heterosexuality. Having experienced a "feminizing" disturbance in early life, some men allay fears of castration by paradoxically enacting a fantasy in which they become a woman who is genitally male. This identification with the "phallic" woman (the mother) who once threatened them is an attempt at mastery; there is no desire to be a woman, only to "prove" that feminization will not take away their maleness, that there can be such a thing as a woman with a penis. Unlike gay cross-dressers, they wear women's clothes as a fetish substitute for the (hetero)sexual object, never losing sight of the fact that they are male: on the contrary, they do it to preserve male potency. As Robert Stoller writes, "If females are evidence [to the transvestite] of a state of penislessness, the cause is not hopeless if there are women with penises. What better proof can there be of this than if one is such a creature oneself?"[46]

Even if it were plausible, as it probably is not, to suggest that blackface "wenches" were so motivated, we must ask whether this logic appealed to their fans. Evidence that it might have is to be found in the kind of pornography that caters to transvestites. It comprises primarily representations of the "phallic" woman—physically large and strong, with gigantic appendages and oversized shoes or boots, the insignia of maleness peeping through the womanly pretense. It is not too far from this preoccupation to spectatorial interest in the theatrical female impersonator, the "funny ole gal" of the minstrel show. "Clad in some tawdry old gown of loud, crude colors," writes Olive Logan, "whose shortness and scantness display long frilled 'panties' and No. 13 valise shoes . . . the funny old gal is very often a gymnast of no mean amount of muscle, as her saltatory exercises in the break-down prove."[47] This description practically insists on the "phallic" womanhood of the blackface cross-dresser, who, as in the pornographic fantasy and the transvestite's private behavior, converted men's gender anxiety into a source of pleasure, in this case comic pleasure. The attraction of all such representations appears to consist in portraying "masculinized," powerful women, not in order to submit but, through the pleasurable response, to take the power back. The "wench" figure, beyond its rather obvious gender insults, salvaged "potency, power, and masculinity from an originally castrating event" (Stoller 206, 214): offering up a "woman with a penis," the "wench," as in other areas of blackface minstrelsy, deflated the threatening, "castrating" power of women.

The theatrical effects the "wench" reached after, however, were sexually variable. The retreat from women into drag tended, of course, to compromise the masculinity that was so hard-won. Indeed, even without female dress the economy of white male looking in blackface spectatorship was apt to convert sexual defensiveness into same-sex desire. This important fact, as I have suggested, asserts itself long before one encounters such desire in cross-dressing. Freud's suggestive notion that jokes allow access to culturally prohibited sources of pleasure may mean that another of the minstrel show's purposes was to allow something besides racism onto the American stage (*Jokes* 101). Antebellum whites scarcely needed a separate institution to indulge their racism; and that racism appears often to have provided the occasion for a wider preoccupation with sexuality, not least homosexuality. Black male genitalia were invoked readily, if coyly:

> I don't like a nigger,
> I'll be dogged if I do,
> Kase him feet am so big
> Dat he can't war a shoe.
> • • •
> Oh, I does hate a nigger,
> Tho' its colour ob my skin,
> But de blood ob dis nigger
> Am all white to de chin.
>
> I war coloured by de smoke,
> In de boat war I war borned,
> And de gals say my gizzard,
> Am as white as de corn.
> (*Negro* 70–71)

These were not the most common lyrics of "Boatmen Dance"—along with "Lubly Fan" and "Old Dan Tucker" one of the most frequently performed songs of the mid-1840s. But in throwing Victorian caution to the wind, they may have gestured toward minstrelsy's true purposes, in "Boatmen Dance" and elsewhere.

Nowhere was this clearer than when minstrel writers verged on pornographic representations of black men, as in "Astonishing Nose," which depicts "an ole nig wid a bery long nose":

> Like an elephant's trunk it reached to his toes,
> An wid it he would gib some most astonishing blows
> • • •
> No one dare come near, so great was his might
> • • •
> He used to lie in his bed, wid his nose on de floor,
> An when he slept sound his nose it would snore,
> Lik a dog in a fight—'twas a wonderful nose,
> An it follows him about wherever he goes.
>
> De police arrested him one morning in May,
> For obstructing de sidewalk, having his nose in de way.
> Dey took him to de court house, dis member to fine;
> When dey got dere de nose hung on a tavern sign.
> (Fox 74–75)

This song is a very nice example of what Freud calls "smut." Freud attributes the genesis of such sexual joking to the social taboo on seductive language directed by men to women. In Freud's frankly speculative originary scenario, a man wishes to seduce his object of desire through sexual language but is prohibited by the woman—who, Freud avers, objects to such language—as well as the presence of a male third party. Owing to the prohibition of this situation, there arises sexual joking among men in which this "original" situation is called up to those who partake of it; significantly, however, the jokes are told by the former seducer to the formerly inhibiting man, who now becomes his partner in ridicule of the former love object. As Freud says, "[T]he desire to see what is sexual exposed is the original motive of smut" (*Jokes* 98). Not only has derision replaced desire, but so has looking replaced the desire to touch. And this activity is *restructured* as an affair between men. In songs such as "Astonishing Nose," one has, it seems to me, a situation in which white male desire for a prohibited object has been converted to ridicule, which reveals all too clearly the desire it seeks to mask. Furthermore, behind the display of black men for white male consumption, a joking relation in which looking and exposure stand in for desire, one begins to make out the presence of a different speculative (though historically specific) transaction. The joking triangle, in which white men share a dominative relationship to a black man which is based above all on looking, seems to me the northern analogue of black men on the auction block. Melville had something similar in mind when he wrote the various exchanges between Stubb and Pip, and Stubb and Fleece, in *Moby-Dick* (1851). These dialogues, of course, are essentially and intentionally minstrel-show feints and jabs: Melville has Pip close the "Doubloon" chapter with a snippet of "Old King Crow" (1843), one of the most popular minstrel songs in the 1840s, and Fleece comes forth with a sermon straight out of the minstrel show. Their ironic import lies in the special, if mundane, power Stubb has over Pip, spelled out before Pip tumbles from the whaleboat a second time: "We can't afford to lose whales by the likes of you; a whale would sell for thirty times what you would, Pip, in Alabama. Bear that in mind, and don't jump any more" (524).

In other words, regardless of the attempts to demystify black men's sexuality, if not indeed amidst them, white male desire for black men was everywhere to be found in minstrel acts. Of course there was very little attempt generally to disguise the fact that uncontrollable black desire was one of the minstrel show's chief attractions, whether in lubricious dances, jokes, gestures, or lyrics. The hunch that white men might momentarily have taken black men themselves for imaginary sexual objects is borne out in the homosexual moments that begin to mark blackface songs in the 1840s, as in "Sally Is De Gal for Me" (1850):

> Oh, Sally is de gal for me,
> I would'nt hab no udder,

> If Sal dies to-morrow night,
> I'll marry Sally's brudder.
> (*De Susannah* 67)

It is true enough, as the reader will no doubt object, that this lyric attributes homosexuality to black men, comfortably "emasculating" them; but there is nothing here that suggests a conformity on the part of the audience to conventional codes of masculinity. These songs allowed white men to imagine same-sex desire even more freely than when virile black men were represented. Consider "Nigga, Put Down Dat Jug" (early 1850s), in which a considerable amount of sucking goes on:

> My mouth around him cling,
> Close as de rum ole friend.
> • • •
> Niggar put down dat jug,
> Touch not a single drop,
> I hab gin him many a hug,
> So dar you luff him stop.
> (*Negro* 41)

It was perhaps the good and proper "vulgarity" of veiled homoerotic desire that was the jewel in minstrelsy's crown, ensuring crowded houses night after night; there is reason enough to think so, given the drawing power of blackface "wenches."

"Acting the wench" was wildly popular not only, I would guess, because of the riotous misogyny in which it indulged. While I have found no evidence of the sort of loving milieu that formed around stars such as Francis Leon later in the century (taking drag that seriously seems to have been a postwar blackface development), the association of a Barney Williams or George Christy with this particular talent may indicate a covert agreement between actor and audience that camping it up would be part of the play. One might posit here an unsteady oscillation in "wench" acts between a recoil from women into cross-dressing misogyny and a doubling-back from the homoeroticism that this inevitably also suggested, with the misogyny serving as a convenient cover story for or defense against the homoerotic desires aired in the process of achieving it. In any case, there is no question that the "wench" brought homosexual desire to the stage, as in "My Love He Is A Sailleur Boy" (sung by a cross-dressed Dan Bryant in blackface):

> My love, he is a sailleur boy,
>   so galliant and bold,
> He's as tall as a flag-staff,
>   scarcely nineteen years old,
>
> For to cruise around this wide world,
>   he has left his own dear,

And my heart it is a busting,
  because he is not here.

  For his spirit was tre-men-du-ous,
    And fierce to behold,
    In a young man bred a carpentier
    Only nineteen years old

His parents they bounded him
  for to be a carpentier,
But a sea-faring life
  he did very much prefer—

My bussom it is a tossing,
  just like the rolling sea,
For fear that his affections
  don't still point to me
            • • •
And it's oh for my lover
  I grieve and repine,
For fear that this young man
  can never be mine. . . .
                (Moreau vol. 1)

The whiff one gets here of absurdly debased John Donne nevertheless conveys the jokey homoeroticism on which the song trades. There is the frank evocation of the lover who has set out for sailors; and there is the beloved's fairly obvious genital obsession. There is even a veiled reference to the public impossibility of this sort of love. Such relatively unadorned moments recall recent speculations about the Elizabethan theater—that women's roles were played by boys on the English Renaissance stage (unlike anywhere else in Europe at the time) because Shakespeare's audiences wanted to see same-sex desire portrayed there.[48] Since women were a major presence in the "legitimate" midcentury American theater, one must surmise that cross-dressing in the minstrel show intended to clear a space in which homoeroticism could find halting, humiliated, but nonetheless public expression.

This expression often achieved its desired effect. The *New York Clipper*, for example, circulated one story of an elderly gentleman who became "desperately enamored of inimitable [Francis] Leon," whom he supposed to be a "dashing brunette of the gentler sex":

> The symmetry of form, the dash and easy, graceful manners of the actor in his guise of a young lady, were irresistible to the old gentleman, and his affections went out in one spontaneous gush. A gentleman who was sitting beside him was the recipient of sundry nudges and whispered words of admiration for the fair one, but with heroic fortitude he maintained his equanimity till after the performance. (May 16, 1874)

Whatever the provenance of this tale, it seems attentive to the male "actor's" centrality to womanly masquerade, and to the transferability of the affections he

165

inspires to a neighbor male—recipient of nudges and whispered words if not of the old gentleman's helpless gush. As Lillian Schlissel has remarked, female "disguise did not diffuse sexuality," as Robert Toll and others have argued. Rather, the "game of sexual identity took on new intensity when the players were 'masked.'" "Wench" performances were rituals of what Schlissel calls "genital guessing," which, as we know one observer noted, might "make a fool of a man if he wasn't sure."[49]

Again recourse to Mark Twain is suggestive. In the 1901 Underwood edition of *Huckleberry Finn,* Huck's brief foray into cross-dressing earns an E. W. Kemble illustration in which Huck flounces around expertly in the foreground (see Fig. 10); the vertical plane of his body intersects that of a horizontal, grinning Jim in the background, Huck's head overlapping and partially obscuring Jim's crotch. The picture brings into contiguity the precise terms of homosexual desire in blackface "wench" acts—white male cross-dressing on the one hand, black male sexuality on the other. It also reiterates the spectatorial terms in which blackface transvestism mapped this desire, with "black" men watching and singing the "praises" of the cavorting "woman" at center stage. Two consequences in particular of this doubled structure of looking (the black male characters' look and the audience's look) interest me here. First, this configuration allowed a displacement of interest from the ambiguously gendered "wench" to her male admirers. Figuring black male heterosexual desire alongside the "wench" offered alternative, and safer, bearers of the audience's look such that more "compromising" desires—for the man under the skirt—might be deflected or remain unacknowledged. This was of course only one moment or possibility in a mass of dangerous options, for who was to say that the "black" male singers were not themselves pursuing gay desire, and who was to guarantee that identifying with them didn't flip over into homoeroticism? At the very least, the recurrence of this specific theatrical structure surrounding the "wench" suggests that she inspired thoughts and feelings that needed containing.

This configuration offered up a second possibility. In acts such as "Lucy Long," the misogyny occurs through the degradation of the male singer who expresses his love for such a distasteful object of desire; he praises Lucy's huge feet and corncob teeth. In the broadest sense, the blackface male's desire for his "wench" acknowledges or represents the relation of the white audience to blacks generally. The blackface male is after all a figure for the audience's looking, however ridiculous he is made to appear; the "wench" encompasses in her person male and female both; and the relationship between the two figures is foregrounded. The singer's most ridiculous impulse is indeed to proclaim his love for such an unworthy object as "blackness." The familiar (and familial) irony is that the act derided white America for its fascination with blacks while at the same time it marketed that fascination. Surely this structure of feeling evidences again the precariousness or dissonance or conflictedness that marked white people's sense of their own whiteness.

166

Fig. 10. Jim and Huck, by E. W. Kemble.
Courtesy of the Alderman Library, University of Virginia

It was, of course, the internal "racial" ghosts that minstrel-show "vulgarity" was meant to exorcise. Exorcism is a drastic resort, and minstrelsy's growing popularity in these years suggests it was an only partly successful one. No doubt its pleasures were peculiarly conducive to a political climate that demanded racial complacency as well as class-coded public arts. Yet we shall see that as time went on, minstrel performers found themselves backed steadily into a corner. That predicament is now known as the slavery crisis, and it was about to erupt.

7

California Gold and European Revolution: Stephen Foster and the American 1848

We follow the descending sun, to that land where the light reigns, while Europe is covered with darkness—to the new Eldorado, which was so recently the golden prize of American prowess, and has already become the apple of discord to the victorious States.

—*Southern Quarterly Review* (1850)

An extraordinary confluence of forces destroyed the minstrel show's hermetic self-satisfaction. The hedging politics of reform were overshadowed in the late 1840s by the slavery issue, and class-consciousness played an unpredicted role in its return. The manner in which social change was registered and produced in public discourse was itself changing, saturated by a consolidating "sentimental" ethos not unrelated to women's rights agitation for female control of the public sphere. The inescapable synecdoches of plantation, factory, and home signified not only a slowly clarifying historical predicament of outrageous proportion but also, perhaps not paradoxically, a highly confused and contested one; each of these images, for instance, often contained significant admixtures of the others. Indeed, so visible were the social contradictions in American life from the start of the Mexican War in 1846 to the enactment of the Fugitive Slave Law in 1851 that earnest analogies and casual representations, generic conventions and allegorical flights of fancy—social figurations of almost every kind—threatened a formidable visitation of unwelcome meanings and resonances. Markers of historical change too convoluted to comprehend fully, such figurations frequently overwhelmed the intentions of their putative users.

This was the burden of an 1850 article in the *Southern Quarterly Review* titled "California Gold and European Revolution."[1] Attempting by analogy to distinguish American prospects from those of a class-riven Europe, it evinced obliquely and against its will the internal shocks and divisions over slavery that had accrued to the wresting of California, the new Eldorado, from Mexico. In crowded Europe, wrote the anonymous author in reference to 1848, "the spell of modern civilization has evoked a devil, which it is powerless to lay, and which yields not to its exorcisms" (297). The "passion for gold" has reduced the citizen of yore to a

169

"slave of the Dollar," pitting greedy capitalist against starving worker (282–83). By contrast, following the descending sun to the ample American West, one finds a "new land of promise . . . the Canaan of mammon," where the "light reigns" (304). "While the scale of Europe descends, that of America must ascend"; the "golden city" of San Francisco "has arisen as rapidly as rose by enchantment the single palace of Aladdin," but as for the Old World, "only a paroxysm of [its] disease" can follow upon the discovery of gold in California (303–5). Working toward a conclusion, the writer remembers a story from childhood:

> . . . the story of that enchanted rock, in the Indian Seas, which attracted to itself the bars and bolts, the rivets and the nails, of the vessels that sailed over the surrounding waters. The luckless mariners were drowned—the dissevered spars, deprived of all bonds of cohesion, floated at the mercy of the waves. Such a rock may California prove to Europe in her advancing dissolution. (312)

As Michael Rogin has observed, this remarkable piece points to California as in every way an enchanted rock for America, not Europe (*Subversive* 105). It is America's "passion for gold" and America's "slaves" that are being worried in the guise of European dissolution. The article's critique of Europe so resembles the South's critique of northern wage slavery, in fact, that it invokes the sectional conflict western emigration not only failed to dispel but—in reopening the question of whether the occupied land would be slave or free—actually revivified. The author's metaphors generally get the better of him. Light does not reign where the sun descends, and "the Canaan of mammon" is a suitably contradictory figure for the United States's imperial subsumption of California gold and the ensuing events, since it implicitly yokes promise with depravity, continental expansion with political convulsions over slavery, unfettered white social desire with the threat of sectional division.

These events, and the article's unwitting attempt to manage them, are emblematic of the American 1848. While blackface minstrelsy was the privileged signifier of the complex, Union-threatening ensemble of conflicts and discourses temporarily halted by the 1850 Compromise, it could not escape getting caught up in similar ineffectual displacements and prophetic ironies. Essentially using the plantation to gloss northern home and workplace relations, the minstrel show witlessly though constantly and uniquely focused attention on the great conflicts of national life at midcentury. If by the late 1840s minstrelsy had assumed a cultural centrality one would scarcely have predicted for it, its popularity seems in retrospect a token of its curious, polysemous insistence on matters that much contemporaneous discourse evaded. And if history gave it moment, Stephen Foster's emergence as a composer of popular "Plantation Melodies" gave blackface performance an aesthetic charge potent in its historical consequences. The national self-fashioning that took place with the aid of songs such as "Oh! Susanna" revealed not only the significance of racial and sectional questions for the nation's future but also the fact that precisely that future was at stake.

170

TWO-TONE

The rapid increase in the popularity of blackface minstrelsy after around 1846 suggests that whatever else it may have been, it was a remarkably good business. There is every indication that the minstrel show, like other elements of New York's downtown amusement scene, was beginning to make a lot of people a lot of money, and in a variety of ways, according to its various modes of dissemination. A quick scan of George Odell's *Annals of the New York Stage* for the postdepression years discloses a whole battery of newly professional blackface performers, now with this company and now with that, assembling and reassembling with a fluidity for which only volumes of ready cash can be assumed to account. The minstrel show's stars, such as T. D. Rice, Charles White, E. P. Christy, and George Harrington (pseudonymously George Christy), were apparently able to take home astronomical weekly paychecks, as the many contemporary references to their salaries indicate (never mind that many of these men died destitute).[2] Christy's Minstrels' seven-year run at New York's Mechanics' Hall (from March 1847 to July 1854) was only the most notable example of the many kinds of steady work to be had selling "blackness" as a commodity. "Mass" entertainment publishers (Dick and Fitzgerald in New York, T. B. Peterson and Turner and Fisher in Philadelphia) yearly cranked out dozens of dime songbooks in the names of famous minstrel stars or companies (see Fig. 11); these books, usually only printed lyrics without music—little lyric volumes of mass-produced racist caricature—evidently allowed fans of blackface to sing the words at home to tunes they knew by heart from the theater, and were therefore advertisement, a symbol of product loyalty, as much as entertainment.[3] Nor did the sheet-music business lag behind. Firth and Pond, Stephen Foster's New York publisher, employed twenty men to engrave and print its annual output of over two hundred pieces of music (a good deal of it culled from "low" realms such as the minstrel show), the selling of which occupied another ten men and brought in a revenue of $70,000.[4] In this form blackface minstrelsy entered the middle-class parlor, a development that soon led the *Journal of Music* to despair of all the

> "native compositions" and "composers" . . . who can *put together* notes and *make up* little pieces, that will sell. Inquire at the mills where all this grist is ground, inquire of the publishers who *snow* "sheet music" over all the land, as fast as it melts away, and they will tell you that the native crop is quite a vast affair, and pays the better as it is the more ephemeral. ("Native" 61)

The Adornian disgust responsible for this mix of metaphors completes the picture of an industry in ascendance.

At the center of this industry was the minstrel show's music, whose writers gave back in ritualized emotionalism what they received in capital investment. It is, then, to the music that I now turn, and to its sentimentalized images of plantation life, which were enlarged in this period into a mythology so enduring it

Why does dat Darkey follow me so ?

Composed by A. J. Phillips, for White's Band of Serenaders.

O why does dat darkey follow me so ?
  Like a cat dat is arter a mouse,
He is sure to be wid me whereber I go,
  An' always is watching my house.
      Follow me so.

Like a cat dat is arter a mouse,
  He is sure to be wid me wherebber I go,
  An' always is watching my house.
He winks, an' he whistles, an' squeezes my hand,
An' sometimes he kisses my glove,
But what is his meaning I can't understand,
But I tink dat de nigger 's in lub.
      Yah, ha !

Chorus : Why does dat darkey follow me so ?
    Like a cat dat is arter a mouse,
  He is sure to be wid me, whereber I go,
    An' always is watching my house.

My farder, he knows, thought fit to gib
  A cottage on purpose for me,
Wid a nice little garden, whar I might lib
  Like a bird quite as happy an' free.
He wishes to marry, I am sure dat's a fact,
  An' dat cottage wid me he would take,
But I tell dat same nigger he's on de wrong track,
  For dis darkey am wide awake.
      Yah, ha !

Chorus : Den back, go back, you're on de wrong track,
    You nebber can come it ober me,
  In dat cottage I'll lib, which my farder did gib,
    Like a bird quite as happy an' free.

Why were the Mexicans at the battle of Buena
Vista like good wine ? Because they both *run from
the grape.*

MAJOR. NY.

Fig. 11. Minstrel Songbook, 1848.
Courtesy of the Butler Library, Columbia University

barely seems to have had a distinct beginning.[5] Surprisingly harsh and mournful when it was not cheerful and spry, this mythology was marketed in hundreds of cloying songs full of nostalgia, heartbreak, and death as much as winsome contentment, and its usefulness to a North marked by fracture and dissent will be of interest in this discussion. Yet the very coincidence of the music's popularity with what one might call its "industrial" character (some have suspected Stephen Foster of composing to formula, as lesser writers unquestionably did), together with its looming social and political importance, suggests that we first ought to find some mediating device that will account for the specific relations between minstrel music and its various socioeconomic determinations and consequences. The most likely *formal* bridge between such disparate realms is that of repetition. At once a principle of popular music and—as Theodor Adorno wrote—of the music industry, repetition is central to the human reception of music in its broadest social character. As Richard Middleton has written in a brilliant theoretical discussion from which the present analysis takes its lead, "The extent and nature of repetition in a given music [is] produced by and located at the point where several sets of determinations intersect," among them the political economy of production, the psychic and social economy of reception, technologies of musical creation and dissemination, and inheritances from musical traditions.[6] If the abuses of repetition as a mediating category in the hands of, say, Adorno are by now notorious, there nevertheless remain unexploited uses for its undeniable mediatory power.[7]

It is fitting that when Adorno set out to critique what he believed to be the regressive tendency of American jazz, its "crude unity"—that is, repetition—he seized upon an important antecedent: "[Jazz's] method, all declarations of propagandistic historians notwithstanding, has remained essentially unchanged; its prehistory dates back to certain songs from the first half of the nineteenth century, such as 'Turkey in the Straw' and 'Old Zip Coon'" ("Perennial" 121). From Adorno's perspective, the fact that the two named songs were actually one and the same might merely confirm his sense of popular music's standardization: who could tell them apart anyway? And if he knew that the song had come from the blackface theater, his charge had even more weight, for at least actual black music, while to Adorno "primitive," had some claim to a noncommodified authenticity. Authentic or not, however, the rhythmic repetition so crucial to commercial products derived from African-American music generally seemed to Adorno the internally rationalized result of a rationalized industry committed to the endless, cretinizing reproduction of the same under the ever-changing cover of fashion.[8] Certainly, as I have suggested, the blackface industry was taking off. One might assume that its racial repertoire was thus narrowed into easily replicable units of racist "common sense." But we ought neither to ascribe minstrelsy's rising popularity to culture-industry cunning nor read off its political results from industrial practice; recent studies have shown these assumptions to be rather too underdetermined.[9] We must somehow acknowledge the part played by commercial predictability in the writing, marketing, and consumption of minstrel music without disqualifying the place of audience responsiveness, disparate racial determinations, and historical consequence in our account. What political sense can we make of musical repetition in blackface minstrelsy? What racial antecedents did it organize and put on offer? Why did audience pleasure often take the form, as we saw in the last chapter, of repeated returns to the minstrel show, the desire, as the *Spirit of the Times* mimetically put it, "to go again, and again" (October 9, 1847)? How are we to understand audience demands in minstrel theaters for reprises of favorite songs, prompting exasperated theater managers to state in playbills that audiences "are PARTICULARLY REQUESTED NOT TO DEMAND A REPETITION"?[10] Let me begin to look for some answers in the formal properties of the songs themselves.

Richard Middleton distinguishes between two sorts of repetition in popular music: *musematic* and *discursive* repetition. Musematic repetition is based on the repetition of short units (musemes), such as the riffs or "shouts" in African-American music; a "purer" kind of repetition, it is likely to be unvaried and prolonged, and tends toward the "circularity" one associates with collective oral invention. Discursive repetition is based on the repetition of longer units, usually musical phrases, which are mixed in with contrasting units in a hierarchical framework; harmonic progressions give such repetition the more "narrative" character of written music of the Tin Pan Alley stripe. Yet, as Middleton cautions in "In the Groove," these are historical categories rather than crudely technological ones; they are "actively summoned into development and strongly mediated by the needs of distinct socio-economic configurations" (164). The link between individualist, literate musical composition and the development of bourgeois social formations, for example, has long been axiomatic.[11] By the same token, the two types are rarely mutually exclusive, particularly in the United States, and often coexist in a given popular form. The diversion of some of the impulses of written music into orally transmitted, black-influenced songs in nineteenth-century popular theater was itself summoned into being by the mix of classes in minstrel-show spectatorship, and by the mix of races in the antebellum North, quite apart from their paving the way for the earthshaking public emergence of African-American musical forms.

In terms of this basic distinction, nineteenth-century black secular song forms were usually (but not always) musematic, relying on short, repeated tags and refrains directly opposed to melodic narrativity—an eruption, as Max Roach has termed hip hop music, of "rhythm for rhythm's sake" (quoted in Owen 61). In *Recollections of a Southern Matron* (1838), for example, Caroline Gilman recounts a boat trip in South Carolina during which the slave oarsmen, led by one Juba, sing about the boat *Neely*, named for the young mistress on board with her suitor, Lewis:

Hi de good boat Neely?
She row bery fast, Miss Neely!
An't no boat like a' Miss Neely,
　Ho yoi'!

Who gawing to row wid Miss Neely?
Can't catch a' dis boat Neely—
Nobody show he face wid Neely,
　Ho yoi'!

Maybe Maus Lewis take de oar for Neely,
Bery handsome boat Miss Neely!
Maus Lewis nice captain for Neely,
　Ho yoi'![12]

The repetitions of "Neely" create a leveling, hypnotic effect, systematically broken up by "breaks" or "cuts" ("Ho yoi'!") that only intensify the repetitive flow once it is resumed.[13] This structure was highly elastic, shaped to the rhythm of work, and, as in this example, offered a perfect form for submerged, wry, or overtly bitter commentary about white people or their systematic abuses—among a great many other things. "I'm Gwine to Alabamy," notated by William Francis Allen and Lucy McKim Garrison for their edition of *Slave Songs of the United States* (1867), treats the forced separation of families under slavery (see Fig. 12):

I'm gwine to Alabamy,—Oh,
For to see my mammy,—Ah.

She went from Ole Virginny,—Oh,
And I'm her pickaninny,—Ah.

She lives on the Tombigbee,—Oh,
I wish I had her wid me,—Ah.

Now I'm a good big nigger,—Oh,
I reckon I won't git bigger,—Ah.

But I'd like to see my mammy,—Oh,
Who lives in Alabamy,—Ah.

(89)

The similarities between this song and Foster's "Oh! Susanna" are, paradoxically, striking evidence of the cultural changes that were rung on inherited forms, whether it was Foster who transformed the repeated cries into a conventional chorus or the slaves who broke down Foster's (already somewhat creolized) discursive structure into a sort of incantatory insistence.[14]

By contrast, the repetition in Anglo-American popular or music hall song was discursive, working at the largely melodic level of the phrase, and the repeats were either immediate, delayed, or some combination of the two. Middleton suggests that this kind of repetition was typified by the technique of sequence, the nearly identical repetitions of a musical phrase to fit changing harmonies, or that of

175

111.   I'M GWINE TO ALABAMY.

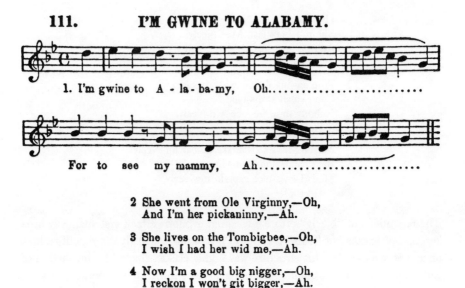

1. I'm gwine to A - la - ba - my,   Oh.............................

For   to   see   my mammy,   Ah............................

2 She went from Ole Virginny,—Oh,
  And I'm her pickaninny,—Ah.

3 She lives on the Tombigbee,—Oh,
  I wish I had her wid me,—Ah.

4 Now I'm a good big nigger,—Oh,
  I reckon I won't git bigger,—Ah.

5 But I'd like to see my mammy,—Oh,
  Who lives in Alabamy,—-Ah.

[A very good specimen, so far as notes can give one, of the strange barbaric
songs that one hears upon the Western steamboats.]

Fig. 12. From *Slave Songs of the United States*, 1867, ed. William Francis Allen,
Lucy McKim Garrison, and Charles Pickard Ware.
Courtesy of the Alderman Library, University of Virginia

phrase-structure repetition, in which the details change but leave intact a parallel-
ism or set of melodic analogies at the level of harmony and rhythm (see also
Maróthy 11–127). The following example, Henry Bishop's famous "Home! Sweet
Home!" (1823), represents the kind of song that was in the air when Stephen
Foster began to compose:

> 'Mid pleasures and Palaces though we may roam,
> Be it ever so humble there's no place like home!
> A charm from the skies seems to hallow us there,
> Which seek through the world, is ne'er met with elsewhere!
>
> Home! Home! sweet, sweet, Home!
> There's no place like home!
> There's no place like home!
>
> (Marrocco and Gleason 310–11)

This is perhaps the simplest type of discursive repetition, involving neither melodic analogies nor sequence. The first phrase is simply repeated immediately,
then a second occurs and is likewise repeated, before the chorus comes to cap it
all off. This type of repetition is clearly both repetitive and nonrepetitive, as the
repeated phrases are marshaled into the service of a broader narrative order.

Discursive repetition, Middleton argues, is thus in essence a way of deploying the power of repetition while taming it, of domesticating it by incorporation into other structural processes. Rather than marking time or even obliterating it, as musematic repetition often seems to do,[15] this type of repetition, as Middleton puts it, "makes us aware of rise and fall, a discursive hierarchy, and thus refers us to irreversible experiences" (165). This is an idea to which I will return.

It seems fairly clear that antebellum minstrel-show songs were situated at the intersection of these types of repetition. Historically there was a move away from the more "folk"-derived music (black, British, and Irish) imitated in early minstrelsy toward a more discursive, "bourgeois" (actually petit-bourgeois) song in the commercial era of the midcentury minstrel show, and from comic or novelty tunes to earnestly sentimental ones.[16] Yet well into the 1850s much of the blackface repertory was of a mixed character, in keeping with its general cultural mix as I have outlined it. Hans Nathan charts the convergence of cultural influences in the music along lines familiar from Middleton's discussion: "Excessive repetition of single tones and of phrases of narrow compass derives from the Negro; on the other hand, the symmetry of phrase structure is a white concept" (187). This blend is already present in "Old Zip Coon" (1834) (see Fig. 13), which, while it is related to two Irish hornpipes (Nathan 166–68), flattens out their complex figures in the repeated tones (and words) of its second and fourth bars; its chorus is then constructed out of a sequence, but feels more repetitive than it is because of its syncopated rhythm. A particularly good example of the cross between musematic and discursive modes of repetition from the most popular decade of blackface music is "De Blue Tail Fly" (1844) (see Fig. 14), which uses phrase-structure repetitions, but of phrases so brief and of such small interval that the effect is very flat indeed, with its refrain dunning after every verse. Nathan notes that minstrel songs came into their own in the 1840s by drawing less on European "folk" antecedents and more on just such multiple repetitions of brief phrases—the "chief structural principle" of the style of this period—now enhanced by a certain amount of rhythmic syncopation.[17]

This "racial" ambiguity in the makeup of minstrel songs was intensified by the range of song types most minstrel companies purveyed in the years I examine in this study, a range visible even in the course of a night's performance. On one side were the almost wholly musematic repetitions of Dan Emmett's 1843 "Old Dan Tucker":

> I come to town de udder night,
> I hear de noise den saw de fight,
> De watchman was a runnin roun,
> Cryin Old Dan Tucker's come to town,
>
> So get out de way!
> Get out de way!
> Get out de way! Old Dan Tucker,
> Your too late to come to supper.[18]

Fig. 13. "Zip Coon," 1834.
Courtesy of the Harvard Theatre Collection

There is scarcely any "discursivity" at all here; the attempt is to level out the song as much as possible through repeated tones and repeated shouts, in verse and chorus both. Of course, the impulse toward discursive repetition in most black-face songs was usually modified by at least some simulated presence of African-American elements. Yet on the other side were the many sentimental songs of the

178

Old Zip Coon is a very larned scholar, Old Zip Coon is a
very larned scholar, Old Zip Coon is a very larned scholar, He
plays on the Ban - jo Cooney in de hollar.

2
Did you ever see de wild goose sail upon de ocean,
O de wild goose motion is a very pretty notion,
For when de wild goose winks he beckon to de swallor,
An den de wild goose hollor, google, google, gollor.

3
Old suke Blueskin fell in love wid me,
She vite me to her house for to take a cup of tea,
What do you think Old Suke had for de supper!
Dare was chicken foot sparrow grass & apple sauce butter.

4
O my ole mistress is very mad wid me,
Because I wouldnt go wid her and live in Tennessee;
Massa built a barn dere and put all de fodder,
Dere was dis ting and dat ting and one ting an oder.

5
As I was a goine down a new cut road,
I met a little Tarrapin a looking at a Toad;
An jist at evry time de toad begin to jump,
De Tarrapin he hide himself behind a burnt stump.

6
Dat tarnal critter Crocket, he never say his prayers,
He kill all de wild cats de Coons and de Bears,
An den he go to Washington to help to make de laws,
An dere he find de Congress men sucking of deir paws.

7
If I was de President of dese United States,
I'd suck lasses candy and swing upon de gates,
An dose I didnt like I'd block em off de dockett,
An de way I'd block em off would be a sin to Crocket.

8
I tell you what's a goine to happen now very soon,
De United States bank will be blown to de moon,
Den all de oder bank notes will be mighty plenty,
An one silver dollar will be worth ten or twenty.

9
O glory be to Jackson, for he blow up de Banks,
An glory be to Jackson, for he many funny pranks,
An glory be to Jackson, for de battle of Orleans,
For dere he gib de enemy de hot butter beans.
Zip Coon

late 1840s lamenting the death of some "lady" or longing for the plantation past—
or both at once. These nostalgic "carry-me-back" songs, as Sam Dennison calls
them, were discursive structures out of a long tradition of "home songs" such as
"Home! Sweet Home!" however plaintively "black" they seemed (Austin 123–
62). Most typical of the songs that fell between these two kinds were some of
Foster's melodies, which often unfold by "discursively" repeating (or virtually
repeating) a single striking phrase, but betray little "narrative" musical development—as in "Oh! Susanna" (1848):

179

I came from Alabama wid
my banjo on my knee,
I'm g'wan to Lousiana,
My true love for to see,
It rain'd all night the day I left,
The weather it was dry,
The sun so hot I frose to death;
Susanna, dont you cry.

Oh! Susanna,
Oh! dont you cry for me,
I've come from Alabama,
wid my banjo on my knee.
(Jackson 89–91)

Cutting across all this variety was the tendency for minstrel troupes to identify themselves with a particular style. Hence the associations of vulgarity that dogged the Virginia Minstrels or Campbell's Minstrels, the somewhat more sentimental, "refined" affect of Buckley's Serenaders or the Ethiopian Serenaders, and the broadly middle-of-the-road appeal of Christy's Minstrels—though within such bounds, stylistic heteroglossia, as well as intimations of vulgarity, were the order of the day.

Generally, then, the overlapping types of repetition in "two tone" minstrel music (as in "Oh! Susanna") arose from a willed attempt to approximate as much as incorporate the effects one finds in slave songs such as "I'm Gwine to Alabamy." Adorno once scoffed at such "handicraft" devices for disguising the debased, mechanical character of the popular music that deployed them ("Popular" 308); and indeed, Foster's work is still often perceived, in a rather desperate racial euphemism, as genuine "folk" music. But a more Gramscian approach alerts us to the immediate social valences of the music's commercial miscegenation, the fairly direct kinds of cultural work, of both class and race, performed by its jumbling of racial signifiers. The disparate elements in blackface music were implicitly tied to different parts of its audience, and to multiple, overlapping meanings—not in any given or essential way, but in a process of articulation to groups and significances in the Jacksonian theater.[19] Counterfeited black "folk" elements no doubt undergirded sentimental or reactionary ideologies of plantation slavery (about which more shortly), but they also "represented" plebeian theatergoers, as I have suggested, and marked the literal encroachment of such people on the sanctums of respectable song. In this as in other ways, minstrelsy's racial meanings proved a cover story for class struggles, allowing working-class self-differentiation from petit-bourgeois respectability within minstrelsy itself, and perhaps urging intermittent interracial identifications through the (simulated) collectivist ethos slave music shared with working-class culture. Blackface performance thus wrested space for plebeian representation from the patterns and traditions of mainstream American music, but only in partial and

De Blue Tail Fly

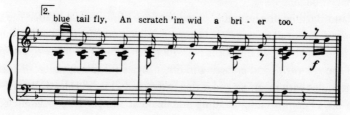

repeat from 𝄋

Fig. 14. "De Blue Tail Fly," 1844.
Courtesy of the Alderman Library, University of Virginia

contested ways; I would again remark the hegemonic cast of this insurgency (workingmen's "freedom" dependent on performative "blackness") as well as the class unevennesses of minstrel audiences. Indeed, the minstrel show's course in the 1850s revealed its possible counteruses as a mode of cultural embourgeoisement, its redirection of antithetical class impulses into a kind of imperiously bland, albeit racialized, gentility.[20] In any case, these racial cross-codings and internal contradictions in blackface music begin to clarify the ways repetition both dovetailed with and outstripped its frankly commercial uses. Likewise with the net "racial" effect of musical repetition in minstrelsy: a plundering of black music whose outcome was a hesitation between types, a tension between circularity and teleology, a wink at the counterfeit alongside a nod toward "blackness"—a struggle within minstrel music of the kind that would characterize appropriations of black culture to the present day.

Yet despite these social contradictions, there would still appear to be a close fit, as Fredric Jameson suggests, between the whole enterprise of musical repetition and reified modes of musical apprehension under capitalism.[21] Notwithstanding a certain atavistic, communal *joie d'esprit* in the minstrel show, the iterative practices in blackface music—rhythmic repetition, repeated tags and phrases, the recycling of lines in different songs, the recycling of songs themselves—can hardly have induced the same effects in newly commodified situations of music making or listening as in the precapitalist oral cultures (black or white) from which they provided a transition. The popular association of repetition with what Adorno terms "distraction," mere sensation, the trance, all the mindless investments allegedly called forth by the numbing calculations of pop music, argues poorly for any but the most degraded and "obedient" responses to this cultural mode, if not to the popular generally ("Popular" 310, 312). As I mentioned in chapter 6, however, such a loss of the subject has recently become a privileged category of pleasure in the writings of many postmodern theorists. Although, as Tania Modleski has pointed out, these writers are no more friendly to the popular than was the Frankfurt School, they may nonetheless help us view more complexly the collective "absence" induced by pop-musical repetition in the minstrel show—as more than merely the tyranny of capitalist, white-supremacist banality.[22]

Roland Barthes, for instance, posed the idea of *jouissance* against the inferior (and "mass" cultural) enjoyments he together denoted *plaisir*, an attempt to find a language for the bliss "in the course of which the 'subject' of the text, escaping the logic of the *ego-cogito* and engaging in other logics (of the signifier, of contradiction), struggles with meaning and is deconstructed ('lost')" (Heath 10). *Plaisir* is a shoring up, a "comfortable" reading practice that affirms the consistency of one's selfhood, making available, in Stephen Heath's words, "the cultural enjoyment of identity . . . a homogenizing movement of the ego" (9); conversely, *jouissance*, on the model of the orgasm, "seeks [the ego's] loss" through disruptions and crises in one's relation to signifying practice itself (Barthes, *Pleasure* 14).

182

Yet the vulgar, ego-mastering *plaisir* of a musical compulsion to repeat is, critically speaking, at odds with the unselving distraction supposedly attendant on popular pleasure. Indeed, from another angle, Middleton suggests, the latter looks a lot like *jouissance*, perhaps brought on by even "industrial" music—which, as with all music, in Henri Lefebvre's words, "communicates corporeality" and "renders the body into social practice" ("Musique"). That is all it does, say its harshest critics. But in doing so it delivers up Barthes's "grain of the voice," the materiality of the musical signifier. Blackface patrons, rendered unto the body, spoke of "plaintive" and "affectionate" minstrel songs that went "directly to the heart," while J. S. Dwight spoke mordantly of them as the "melodic *itch* of the times."[23] And such music delivers up the signifier's fleshly coordinates—we have seen minstrel-show patrons requested in playbills "not to beat time" (repetitively) "with their feet"—where one had expected only the rule of the same, the mechanical pleasure of the next. One musicologist has argued that because the psychogenetic origins of music lie in the relationship of baby to mother, in, for instance, the aural and tactile repetitions of heartbeat and breathing—a relationship that preexists the emergence of a subject—the experience of even rigidly structured music may well call up pre-oedipal moments whose disruptions are the hallmark of *jouissance*.[24] The popular vocabulary of "rapture" and its related terms in nineteenth-century musical parlance surely indicates something of this blissful emptying out of the self. We are, then, left with an apparent ambiguity. Did blackface musical repetition produce a merely pleasurable girding of the (racial) ego, as in Freud's notion of the repetition compulsion; or did it open up a space in the listener for ego loss, rupture, *jouissance?*

It is an ambiguity that resides in Freud's own account of repetition. On the one hand, the *fort/da* game of *Beyond the Pleasure Principle* appears as a way of mastering reality; the child delights in the disappearance and repeated return of small objects in order to overcome the pain of separation from the mother. This is a game of self-preservation, and the repetitions based on it in cultural products might be seen as an attempt to buffer the ego against reality's shocks and jolts (8–11). On the other hand, such repeated stagings of obviously unpleasurable experiences led Freud to the much more far-reaching theory of the death instinct, in which an inherent urge toward inertia in all organic life, overriding or preceding the pleasure principle, becomes the ultimate object of repetition (30). From this perspective, repetition would appear to tend toward a final loss of the subject, originating on some presubjective level and resulting, perhaps, in moments of *jouissance*. But it is soon clear that the death instinct's purpose is itself to fulfill the ego's instinctual wishes (to die), a purpose at variance with a relaxation or disruption of ego functions. Over against the death instinct, however, Freud constructs sexuality, eros; disrupter and disturber of all inertia, it accounts for sources of pleasure not tied even to repetition's cessation of tension, and may be seen, Middleton points out, as the root of Barthes's *jouissance*.

But we have not simply returned here to the initial ambiguity of ego preservation, death, repetition, *plaisir* over against ego loss, sexuality, rupture, *jouissance*. For sexuality and the death instinct, Freud avers in *The Ego and the Id*, are not mutually exclusive; they are articulated together as what Paul Ricoeur calls "coextensive domains" (292). They are undifferentiated forces each of which may serve either the libido or the ego. The wires are often crossed. Think, for instance, of narcissistic forms of sexuality; or consider the paradox Freud observes, that sex (dependent in its very essence on repetitive motion) results in miniature forms of the self's extinction (*Ego* 37), a process evoked musically, of course, by heavily incantatory patterns of repetition. What all this suggests is that the seemingly opposed interpretations of repetition are in fact bound up with one another—that the effects of musical repetition are very precisely ambiguous and range over a spectrum of meanings depending on given mixes of musical elements.

By this I mean that the ambiguity regarding the outcome of musical repetition per se was overdetermined by the minstrel show's use of two different kinds of repetition, musematic and discursive, each of which, Middleton argues, produces or makes available a different psychological "set." Middleton writes that the effects of repetition may vary widely according to its specific form; "its precise effects [owe] to the nature of what is repeated [rhythms and short refrains or more extended musical phrases] and the extent to which it is mixed up with other elements (channelling repetition in particular directions)" (173). Breaking down the twin tendencies in minstrel music toward ego dispersal and self-identity, one might say that its use of musematic repetition, seemingly closer to primary psychic processes, was most congenial to momentary losses of ego boundaries, while its use of discursive repetition, as in János Maróthy's account of bourgeois song, permitted egoistic self-affirmation. These tendencies were stitched up together in a host of musical combinations, so that, far from being only an epiphenomenon of the commercial bottom line—the racist, ego-stroking cycle of novelty-boredom-novelty—blackface music constituted a variable field in which differing, even overlapping results might accrue to various stylistic mixes. The overdetermination of the psychological effects of repetition by confluences of repetitive musical type may indeed have garnered complex and equivocal calibrations of response. Above all, the "racial" mixtures in minstrel music may mean that the conflicted energies making blackface minstrelsy an institution to contend with in these years were determined in part at the formal level of its song craft.

For it follows that libidinal and ego functions as they were manifested in blackface musical repetition had specific racial effects. Without attempting very closely to examine instances of blackface music for the sorts of response their complexities may have brought forth, I submit that musematic repetition in the minstrel show was linked in purely formal terms to blissful, "unraced" moments of ego loss, and discursive repetition to ego-preserving feelings of racial mastery and self-assurance. The surface details of minstrel song types bear out this speculation, the "blacker" structures immersing whites in boundary-crossing affairs of racial Otherness and the "whiter" folk or ballad structures making

184

opportunistic use of the black mask. Of course these types were crossed not only with each other but also with other racial and cultural determinations; the perceived "blackness" of miscegenated blackface performance still warred with (at best) a widespread condescension toward black arts, just as sentimental "slave" laments that were patently derived from European music sometimes performed liberatory racial work. These contradictions, indeed, are my point: they took shape in accordance with the structure of racial feeling impressed by a moment of evidently widening cracks in the social bloc. Not that there was any immediate link between racial feeling and national conflict, nor that the resurgence of the slavery controversy in late-1840s America represented any new consensus (on either side) about racial matters. This period's uncontainable "social motion," however, did not fail to pervade either the subjectivities of those who lived it or the cultural products it sponsored. The same pressing conflicts underlay both the minstrel show's popularity and the American 1848; minstrelsy responded at the (emotional and representational) level of commercial racial ritual to political and economic conflicts that were fought out in legislatures, boardrooms, and streets.[25] In *Noise: The Political Economy of Music* Jacques Attali argues for the predictive value of music, its capacity to register at very deep levels the goings-on of the social surround. Something similar was beginning to occur in the way blackface minstrelsy, through musical repetition and other devices, mediated between social conflict and national racial ambivalence.

In other words, I credit the minstrel show with a sudden new capacity to turn vast knots of social turbulence into conflicted stagings of racial subjectivity, and vice versa, to shuttle between racial drama and social trauma. The fact that the depression had passed and theatrical venues were in the black again did not in itself account for the new range of song styles in minstrelsy, nor for the frisson of trouble that clung to the minstrel show. No doubt its makers' purposes, though various, amounted to a hegemonizing effort, coincident with Democratic party policy, on behalf of things as they were: racist self-assurance, then sectional compromise, then white-supremacist Unionism. But once the act was off and running, it was difficult to rein in resonances and images that grew up seemingly out of nowhere to map, as political allegory and as racial feeling, the course of events. The minstrel show was now a national presence; and its evocation of garden-variety racial disdain as well as paranoid racial fantasizing, complacent white-Negroism as well as humanitarian interest, indicates its effortless ability to operate in the realms of racial subjectivity and national self-reflection at one and the same time.

It is indeed in the context of the slavery controversy that the racist and populist positions on minstrelsy fully emerged. Thus an antislavery *New York Tribune* writer spoke of blackface music's "truth to the humanity of which it assumes to be the exponent" and linked it to "the true originators of this music—the negroes themselves": "Plaintive and slow, the sad soul of the slave throws into his music all that gushing anguish of spirit which he dare not otherwise express" ("Black"

107). Conversely, J. K. Kennard imagined the minstrel show to be a springboard for cultural insurrection: "At no time does the atmosphere of our planet cease to vibrate harmoniously to the immortal songs of the negroes of America. At this present moment, a certain ubiquitous person"—"Dan Tucker"—"seems to be in the way of the whole people of these United States simultaneously" (335). Meanwhile, sometime b'hoy Walt Whitman's skittery involvement in antislavery politics coincided with a nervous seesawing between infatuation and disgust in his view of the minstrel show. As always, and owing partially to institutions such as the minstrel show, variousness in facts of racial feeling bore an uncertain and indirect but unmistakable relation to political turmoil.[26]

The minstrel show's constituency was itself beginning to demonstrate its racial ambivalences in the political arena. Most historians have observed a new antislavery interest among workingmen in the late 1840s, though insistently deteriorating working conditions closer to home certainly paced the turn toward a new politics. As the issue of territorial expansion moved to the foreground, an undertone of impatience with slavery emerged in many labor newspapers and platforms; in 1846, for instance, the New England Association of Mechanics, Farmers, and other Workingmen resolved "to secure to all others those rights and privileges for which we are contending ourselves." The Wilmot Proviso's injunction that slavery be excluded from newly acquired territory was in many ways more attractive to workers than abolitionism; the Proviso's concern with free *white* labor emphasized how they might theoretically benefit in the form of public lands. Wilmot or no, the New England Industrial League in 1850 condemned the Fugitive Slave Law outright, and northern workingmen's general disdain for slavery in this period outweighed their distaste for the abolitionists themselves. By the same token, however, it was no less possible for a leading federation of workers, the Industrial Congress, to bypass slavery in its political efforts although it was antislavery in its platform.[27] Labor's increasing antislavery gestures, in other words, were shot through with racial hostility, political cross-purposes, and sheer indifference, and can be read as an index of racial feeling only with the greatest caution.

Yet I hope to show that these political and affective confusions were precisely what the formal ambiguities of blackface music and performance symbolically harmonized. As both cultural register and cultural agent, performance genres have as one of their chief tasks the translation of social cleavages into cultural form. Formal specificities indicate the shape of a culture's understanding of such conflicts, if not that of the conflicts themselves.[28] This is why the minstrel show's most elaborate invention, the plantation mythology that came to fruition in the late 1840s, was also the most revealing picture of a social order coming apart at the seams.

HOMESICKNESS

To move from blackface minstrelsy's dance, humor, and music to its social imagery of plantation slavery is to be struck immediately by an unremitting and largely unremarked emphasis on death, nostalgia, and doom. Relief was ready to hand, of course, in the (by then) conventional mode of plantation gaiety—darkies perennially ready to sing, Massa to be pleased, heels to be kicked up, lovers to be pursued. The reigning tonality of the minstrel show in its most popular years was of course upbeat. But there was a gaping sore at the heart of all this cheer. The early work of Stephen Foster (a sort of one-man research and development team) alone contained the main elements of sentimentalized plantation distress on which most minstrel companies capitalized forthwith. Some of these songs, to be sure, mourned good times on the plantation now gone, most explicitly Foster's "Massa's In de Cold Ground" (1852). But it seems to me revealing that even tributes to the plantation took the form of keening its loss, and very often this tonality brushed against the grain of proslavery ideology. In his exhaustive content analyses of blackface songbooks, Robert Toll found the minstrel show in this period as contradictory an affair as its musical devices have led us to believe, criticisms of slavery running roughly equal to sympathetic representations of it (66).

Foster's "Plantation Melodies," for instance, feature sweethearts or whole families who are separated by the slave trade and long to reunite, yearning for the glad days past and never to return, as in "Old Folks at Home" (1851) or "Farewell My Lilly Dear" (1851). Young men lament the death of their chosen ones in youth's full bloom, as in "Nelly Was a Lady" (1849). Slaves do backbreaking work and wait for death to carry them home, as in "My Old Kentucky Home, Good-Night!" (1853), or breathe their last after years of toil, as in "Old Uncle Ned" (1848). I mimic the cloying unrestraint of these songs only to convey how heavy their effects were—heavy but effective, for they touched commentators of every kind—W. M. Thackeray, for example:

> I heard a humorous balladist not long ago, a minstrel with wool on his head and an ultra-Ethiopian complexion, who performed a negro ballad that I confess moistened these spectacles in a most unexpected manner. I have gazed at thousands of tragedy queens dying on the stage, and expiring in appropriate blank verse, and I never wanted to wipe them. They have looked up, be it said, at many scores of clergymen without being dimmed, and behold! a vagabond with a corked face and a banjo sings a little song, strikes a wild note, which sets the heart thrilling with happy pity. (quoted in Wittke 53)

Sentimental plantation songs moistened their share of spectacles, and for good reason. Their generic projection of death and sorrow onto female or "feminized" male black victims, which coincided with the encroachment in the late 1840s of a larger female spectatorship on the minstrel show's generalized masculinism, pushed all the right buttons for the midcentury culture of feeling, preternaturally alive to tales of virtuous suffering and familial disintegration:

> Nelly was a lady
> Last night she died,
> Toll de bell for lubly Nell
> My dark Virginny bride.[29]

I would incidentally emphasize the vanguardism of this strategy. It is true that milking sentiment by way of black characters was a practice of long standing, reaching back to at least the "noble Negro" types of the late eighteenth-century stage (from which sentimental blackface songs indeed partly descended). But historical and theatrical contexts had changed enough for "blackness" to be unorthodox territory for the evocation of strong feeling, and only the minstrel show's innovations in this area helped establish "blackness" as one fundamental source of the sentimental. Stephen Foster's family was probably embarrassed by rather than proud of his plantation songs, and Charles Hamm goes so far as to argue that mainstream sentimental music was itself the product, not the motive, of minstrelsy's maudlin strain (Austin 95; Hamm 136–39). As I suggested in chapter 1, the consequences of this feminization of "blackness" for black representation and domestic ideology both can scarcely be overstated; the two would soon come crashing together, as though for the first time, in Stowe's *Uncle Tom's Cabin*.[30]

More specifically, these songs cemented the popular preoccupation with death which Ann Douglas has argued was one cornerstone of sentimentalism. A controlled luxuriance in grief amounting to what Douglas calls "therapeutic self-indulgence" (245), this emphasis on the departing and the departed nonetheless had the useful outcome of endowing black people with human emotion, indeed the perpetual sorrow of life under slavery. That it is also one of minstrelsy's most insidious legacies—issuing today in, say, pious tributes to Martin Luther King, Jr., the hushed tears and whispers of greatness masking a lot of business as usual—should not allow us to overlook its Christian exaltation of the powerless in the nineteenth century.[31] Indeed, one outcome of this attempt to keep up with white concerns was that it produced a new and very different kind of black figure along with the better-known goofs and simps. Yet the morbid opportunism inherent in the vogue of the dear departed does lead one to suspect that these undeniably racially positive songs were also doing other, less charitable kinds of work, and this in turn reminds us of their "white," ego-shoring, discursive form. The death instinct so central to musical repetition now manifested itself at the mournful level of content, as though this whole genre longed thematically for the pleasurable cessation of tension that is the death instinct's hallmark; and in this sense the "narrative" cast of discursive, sentimental minstrel songs does indeed "refer us to irreversible experiences" (165), as Richard Middleton has it.

We are in the province of Poe's "most poetical topic in the world" (486)—the dead woman—and surcease was visited not upon an audience willing to forego its racial ranking but upon the hapless female or feminized blacks who populated the plantation melodies. For this reason it is difficult to shake the feeling that what was being repeated in these songs amid a sympathetic emotional agenda was, simply, racial and sexual aggression, that is, metaphorical murder. Into the pantheon of blackface social figurations (the black dandy, the childlike trickster) must be admitted the elegized dead black woman (or feminized man). The elegy, according to Jahan Ramazani, so depends for its existence on the death of the person being memorialized that elegists can in some sense be said to will the death they lament (17–26). There is a self-evident ambiguity in this situation. Narrating desire by absenting the loved one—desire being structured around a lack, in Lacan's account—such cultural products, in Ramazani's words, "enact a symbolic rite of presence and absence" (18); seeking to master grief, not unlike in Freud's *fort/da* game, they seem to relish the loved one's removal as much as mourn it. And where poets are occasionally self-conscious about this dynamic, meditating on it over the course of a poem, minstrel writers exploited it with a vengeance.

In short, laments for the dead in minstrel songs were very often occasions for symbolic violence and hostility. Here, for instance, is the Charles White song "Emma Snow" (1848), in which an idyllic Alabama love story turns harsh:

> Now that happy time hath sorrow,
>   The day is turned to night;
> I lost my dearest Emma
>   By the poison adder's bite.
> We miss'd her in de evening,
>   And we hunted far and wide,
> And we found her in the meadows,
>   Whar she sicken'd and she died.[32]

Not only is Emma Snow's death portrayed and lingered over (the adder's bite a rococo if not naughty embellishment), but there is a kind of jokey straitjacketing of the lines that actually serves to distance rather than entrance the listener. But it is with more than representations of racial cruelty that we are dealing here; the unease relaxed by this generic death drive was ultimately social, and it was rooted in the most pressing racial questions of the day. One might say that while such songs needed the recurring deaths of black people in order to exist, they also repeatedly wished away the existence of blacks altogether. Mournful enough on the face of things, the general run of such songs supervised the elimination of black characters rather than marked their passing away. And it seems to me that what was being symbolically eliminated and put to rest was the whole lamented business of slavery in the United States, by means of the elimination of black people themselves. Consider the sold-down-the-river sadness of Foster's "My Old Kentucky Home, Good-Night!":

> They hunt no more for the possum and the coon
> On the meadow, the hill and the shore,
> They sing no more by the glimmer of the moon,
> On the bench by the old cabin door.
> The day goes by like a shadow o'er the heart,
> With sorrow where all was delight:
> The time has come when the darkies have to part,
> Then my old Kentucky Home good-night!
>
> (Jackson 71)

It would be perverse to deny empathic glimmers, moonlit or otherwise, in such a hegemonic form; and these lines glare rather than glimmer. But there is no greater qualification of the seemingly positive nature of romantic racialism's sentimental ethos than that so much of it centers on black misery, death, indeed disappearance. Stowe, like Lincoln himself in the 1850s, would send George Harris to Africa to realize his fortunes, and good riddance.

Thus, as this example begins to show, minstrelsy's plantation mythology in effect mediated between different social agendas and social feelings. Simultaneously lamenting and killing off the black victim, it condensed ambivalences of racial feeling into a single complex figure, implicitly connecting such ambivalences to the antislavery impulse—which, indeed, was increasingly of a racially unsympathetic character. At the same time, and for all its ambivalence, this mythology backed the minstrel show into putting broken-family sentimentalism at the service of antislavery, as the abolitionists themselves did. (And did, often enough, with blackface songs: the abolitionist Hutchinson Family Singers performed Foster's "Old Folks at Home" with Foster's own words [Austin 35].) It was much the same with the nostalgic longing at the heart of these songs, which focused the sentimental appeal and in sublimated ways took up social conflicts underlying or adjacent to the slavery crisis. Minstrel-show nostalgia, usually for home and family life on the plantation, strikes me (again) as a condensed, fortuitous mapping of white desire in dark skin.

> Way down upon de Swanee ribber,
> Far, far away,
> Dere's wha my heart is turning ebber,
> Dere's wha de old folks stay.
>
> All up and down de whole creation,
> Sadly I roam,
> Still longing for de old plantation,
> And for de old folks at home.[33]

Alexander Saxton argues that nostalgic blackface songs spoke at once to restless migrants moving west, recently transplanted rural folk in cities, and rootless urban dwellers beginning to experience the anomie of modern metropolitan life; turning the South into a kind of timeless lost home, a safe, imaginary childhood, these songs proved supremely satisfying to a wide variety of white audiences.[34] Certainly this view complements my argument in chapter 6 about blackface's world of the child; and nostalgia was so rife in late 1840s blackface songs as to indicate a rather widespread preoccupation with traumatic parting, distance, temporal and geographic breaks. This is also, perhaps, minstrelsy's strongest connection with Irish-American audiences and performers, whose displaced self-masking in minstrelsy (as I have interpreted it) involved, further, a lament for home and circumstance that deepened and extended the minstrel show's sentimentalism. Whatever the case, audiences everywhere fell hugely for this aspect of minstrelsy. One fan wrote to the *Journal of Music* that the Swedish singing sensation Jenny Lind's performance of "Home! Sweet Home!" had caused "such an emotion as I never before experienced; it might be *exquisite home-sickness,*" an effect this fan also said was strikingly achieved by Foster's "Old Folks at Home."[35]

What interests me here is the allusive elasticity of nostalgia as a mode, its ability to join, through what Saxton calls "psychological identity," the facts of metropolitanization, the frontier, immigration, and urban weightlessness—to bring these together and to suggest by way of the black mask their relationship to racial matters. It is not merely that, at one time or another, blackface songs took up these facts as explicit themes. Minstrel nostalgia intimated by emotional antidote all the forces in American life that seemed to be pulling the country apart. As an affective category it was occasionally of racially positive value, a rather dangerous formal move; as social allegory it was a superbly concise mediator, pinpointing if not insisting on the home sicknesses just then contributing to the slavery controversy, or at least making it harder to bear. We will see later how western migration was tied up with slavery, and how the minstrel show handled it; here I would pause over the way blackface nostalgia began through its peculiar racial logic to yoke slavery to the various divisions in the metropolis.

One might do worse than to start with the emotional profile of Stephen Foster himself. Born near Pittsburgh, Foster at the age of four moved with his family amid regrets and fears from the house in which he was born; at thirteen he left home to go to school under the protection of his brother William. He left again in his late teens, this time to work in Cincinnati with his brother Dunning, and soon after, at twenty-four, now with a young wife, Jane, he parted from his parents to go to New York and write songs. He separated temporarily from Jane three years later, and within a few more years his parents were dead. Foster was still only thirty-one. "From 1851," writes William Austin, "when he wrote 'Farewell! Old Cottage,' till he died, he continued to dream of the 'faithful shelter,' the 'guiding star,' the 'hospitable hearth,'" as his songs termed the various longings he felt. And Foster's case was hardly anomalous, at least with regard to geographic mobility; for working class as for middle class, Stuart Blumin shows, turnover rates in nineteenth-century cities were so high that the city was less a place than a process.[36]

The deracinating experience of modern life in the city underlay minstrelsy's brand of nostalgia, with tunes such as Christy and Wood's Minstrels' "Miller's Song" (1854) a dead giveaway: "The mill is torn away, / And a factory dark and drear / Rears its smoke o'er the clear blue sky."[37] And the fact that writers such as Foster cast this nostalgia in blackface form, that "blackness" was its best expression, indicated (among other things) the hidden but necessary social link between southern black life and the northern city dweller's own. The link is made with great clarity in the work of Richard Slotkin. In his magisterial study *The Fatal Environment*, Slotkin revises the traditional notion of a frontier safety valve continually reorienting prospects and possibilities in the congested metropolis, noting on the contrary a wholly reversed set of determinations, or at the very least the dialectical interdependence of city and frontier:

> Whereas the Frontier Thesis asserts that Metropolitan political economics are transformed by the intervention of an outside force or phenomenon—the discovery of a distant Frontier of superabundant natural wealth—it seems more plausible (and more consonant with economic and social facts) to consider an alternative hypothesis: that the particular forms taken by the developing political economy of the Metropolis—its modes of production, its system for valuing social and economic goods, its peculiar culture and history of social relations, its characteristic political institutions—inform the decision to seek Frontier wealth, and determine the kind of people that will go (or be sent) to the colonies, the kinds of resources they will be interested in, the ways in which they will organize their exploitation and governance of the territory, and so on. (42–43)

If the city determined the frontier equally if not more than the other way around, then it was the city's conflicts, perspectives, and politics—not to mention its psychic predispositions—that had prompted the continental expansion urging slavery back into the national debate. With an irony amounting to historical aptness, blackface songwriters hit upon a figuration—blackface nostalgia—that acknowledged this social relationship. The blooming, buzzing growth of the city, owing much to rural migration and, after the mid-1840s, to Irish and German immigration, allowed or encouraged "natives" to light out (or make the case for lighting out) for territories whose mode of labor became a dangerously open question. It is also true that "western" conflicts erupted in the city before manifesting themselves on the frontier. Industrialization North and South created political divisions in the metropolis over the extension of slavery and the protective tariff that in a very real sense determined the fate of the territories. Since slavery and the tariff, Slotkin writes, "were vital to the prosperity of businessmen in the two sections, and hence to politicians, the matter of territorial expansion in the West was increasingly held hostage to resolution of these Metropolitan issues" (113). The problems of the frontier, and therefore slavery, were bound up with the problems of the city; and blackface representations of slave nostalgia, for the indulgence of nostalgic city whites, recognized their inextricability.

Of course, this was only a specific instance of minstrelsy's general move from city to country within each night's show. Minstrel companies perfected the three-part structure of blackface performance in these years: first a group of songs, sometimes performed in whiteface, and often featuring the northern black dandy; an olio section comprising stump speeches and other novelties; and a full-blown burlesque skit set in the South. I believe this structure must be read as in every sense an attempt to *compass* city and frontier, or more precisely free metropolis and outland slavery. Most obviously a way of burlesquing as many black types as possible, the "narrative" performance practice of moving from the first part's North to the third part's South, from urban dandies to rural slaves, not only implied the necessary relationship of these realms but in a feat of cognitive mapping pursued their unity—their union—as a positive goal. One brisk black-face song by the name of "The Jolly Raftsman" (1849) literalized the connections. Imagining the road from bondage to freedom as a simple transplantation of slave customs to a northern urban setting, it metaphorically joined the fate of slavery to that of the city by asserting their identity:

> Oh, leabe your mammy, my deary lub;
> In New York we'll fry dem steaks;
> We'll feed de folks "up to de hub,"
> An' you shall "hurry up dem cakes!"
> • • •
> So good bye we bid to ole Virginny!
> Niggers, we bid you all farewell!
> Our massas dey may go to Guinea!
> In Free States we will dwell![38]

The nostalgia I have been discussing exemplifies in miniature the inability of minstrelsy's plantation mythology to avoid glossing social conflicts abutting the slavery crisis—a reckless referentiality aided by the tendency of minstrel products to air from behind the mask, as though live and direct from the white unconscious, just about anything that chanced to surface. Not only the city's relation to the West, as we shall see, but its inner life—the lives of workingmen and women, their lives together, their labor—made its way into representations of the plantation. And how could this not have been the case, if after all the minstrel show featured displaced and condensed portrayals of the white audience's concerns and desires? Alongside the arguments for and against slavery, alongside the (not simple) indulgences in the reputed ways of black folks, blackface inevitably offered a view of life in these United States among northern white folks, principally those aspects of it that weighed most on the public mind. Yet no one realized, when it came to more intimate conflicts, that the domestic ideologies of American institutional life—including those of slavery—would come under joking fire.

Domestic ideology was so ubiquitous an organizing metaphor in nineteenth-century America that its imagery allowed dangerously easy reference from sector to sector of the social formation. The familial underpinnings of late 1840s plantation songs were more than a necessary thematic device to hook increasingly "feminized" audiences, although they were that. Their sources were much deeper—deep enough, as I have noted, to run the risk of putting blackface's sentimental songs in a curiously supplementary relationship to the abolitionist appeal. Even when politics posed no danger, minstrel songs celebrated that emblematic familial grouping, the master and his slaves. Nor is it enough to say that this strategy was the obvious one in arguing on slavery's behalf. Taking its energy from the realities and ideologies of domestic life, the mythology of plantation paternalism became a figure for the family in America. Central to this figure was the master's strict but gentle management of the antic blacks who surrounded him. "Angelina likes de boys / As far as she can see dem, / She used to run old Massa round / To ax him for to free dem," goes a stanza from Foster's "Angelina Baker" (1850). Such pestering had little result, admitted Christy and Wood's Minstrels' "We'll All Make a Laugh" (1854): "Some massas love dar darkies well, and gib 'em what dey want—/ Except it is dar freedom—and *dat* I know, dey won't: / Howeber, *we* am happy, and contented whar we am, / As a serenading party, and a scientific band."[39] From one angle, the slavemaster was proof of the benignity of the Law, of a patriarchy that ruled with a feather touch. Goaded and run around he might be, but lovingly serenaded he always was, firm father to the last.

Indeed, needling asides like this one, minstrel songs hinted, were a sort of family joke, a touch of plantation jocularity meant to lighten the load of a just and necessary hierarchy. Rather than posing threats to the regime, they evinced the security of the system that indulged them. Yet throughout the plantation songs the various pesterings continue, suggesting that something less assured was also going on here. Foster's "Ring, Ring de Banjo!" (1851) confirms this hunch:

> Once I was so lucky,
> My massa set me free,
> I went to old Kentucky
> To see what I could see:
> I could not go no farder,
> I turn to massa's door,
> I lub him all de harder,
> I'll go away no more.
>
> • • •
>
> Early in de morning
> Ob a lubly summer day,
> My massa send me warning
> He'd like to hear me play.
> On de banjo tapping,
> I come wid dulcem strain;
> Massa fall a napping—
> He'll nebber wake again.
>
> • • •
>
> My lub, I'll hab to leabe you
> While de ribber's running high
>
> • • •

194

> I's guine to make some money;
> But I'll come anodder day—
> I'll come again my honey,
> If I hab to work my way.
> (Jackson 113)

This was of course the standard blackface argument against freeing the slaves, that they could not stand on their own two feet; and it comports comfortably enough with the aggression perhaps attributed here to slave music—the death that may be a murder but is just as surely an unfortunate orphaning. Yet however one adjudicates the mixed impulses in some of these songs, which do briefly or obliquely kick against plantation authority, their contradictions unexpectedly serve to foreground the whole issue of the master class's power. Rather than taking this power for granted, blackface songs selling the notion of the happy plantation offered an extended focus on the purview, limits, and operations of paternal authority. Attempting to narrate a supposedly untroubled instance of racial ideology, they revealed its gaps, or "unspokens" in Pierre Macherey's term, let loose signifiers of unsaid, unconscious misgivings (85–89). Weirdly apposite to songs of plantation misery, these cheerful tunes registered disturbances or instabilities in the plantation mythology such that the master's control was made as much a question as an answer.

Putting aside for the moment the question of what effects these representations had on the antebellum racial status quo, their obsession with the father at a time of extreme tension within the working-class family urges us to see them as social figurations of white northern life. And there is another reason as well. As the early republican agrarian ethos sank into industrialized obsolescence, the universal valorization of the mythic deferential yeoman, as we have seen, gave way to an ideal of the manly mechanic, from whom all dependence, docility, and domesticity were now projected onto women and blacks—the predominant part of the proletariat, which workingmen were (often unsuccessfully) bent on remaining above (Slotkin 139). I have noted continuities in the representation of blacks and women, chiefly in the sentimental writing that used the equation for liberatory purposes; and the often feminized character of slaves on the minstrel-show plantation doubly suggests we read the latter as in part a fictive mediation of women in the northern home. What, we might ask, was the attraction of the plantation's "natural" hierarchy of master and happy slaves to a northern male working population not always, perhaps, unduly agitated about the state of affairs under slavery? And how do we account for the teasing threats to that hierarchy within minstrel songs themselves? One answer may be found in the development of the working-class family in these years, which, under pressure from the emergent sexual division of labor, betrayed growing instabilities in the traditional sex/gender system.

Amid new patterns of wage earning, men and women began to renegotiate the whole question of gender and its particular capacities and responsibilities within the family. Men with sharply reduced opportunity in the postdepression years had perforce to relinquish some patriarchal control over the home, while work options for women gave them some measure of autonomy. Ancient varieties of exploitation lived on, of course, whether in the sexualized inequality of encounters on the street or the reconstructed household dependencies of women's (chorelike) "outwork." But male workers appear to have felt quite unmanned by the trajectory of family life. Finding it difficult to shore up their power in the straitened and unreliable circumstances of wage earning, men clung to at least the ideology of female dependency. In their labor organizations they spoke on behalf of a rejuvenated patriarchal family, with men in the workplace and women in their rightful and natural place—the home.[40] This vision only partly mimicked the middle-class domestic ideology of women's "influence." It was a proud code of the provider, according to which women would perform the duties of the household in a firmly protected atmosphere of working-class dignity, not one of (powerfully feminized) bourgeois respectability. Radical workingmen's masculinist opposition to women's labor outside the home resisted rather than capitulated to bourgeois norms, since workers thought the very necessity of female wage work was evidence of the class oppression they protested. As was often the case in plebeian culture, patriarchal assertion provided the primary avenue of workingmen's self-respect. In the end these men were far more concerned about female competition within the trades than they were about women's well-being, and the working-class version of separate spheres obviously perpetuated real constrictions for women, though it also had the refreshing effect, as Christine Stansell argues, of acknowledging them as indispensable if frankly subordinate members of the working community (141).

This ideology plainly salved men's anxieties rather than addressed women's needs. So did ideological tropes such as the much-excoriated, sexually immoral (read: self-sufficient) "factory girl" of male labor rhetoric, reform tracts, and urban journalism, a transparent attempt to halt the drift in the domestic balance of power (Stansell 125–28, 139). Blackface gags brayed their support: "Why is a man that's taking a popular medicine like a man that's whipping his wife? Because he takes an' *he licks her,* (elixer)."[41] The well-ordered minstrel plantation seems a choice picture of the family for men who felt less and less firmly at the helm, so precisely are its scope, energy, and primary concerns reminiscent of working-men's fantasied "family of labor," as the labor leader John Commerford called it (quoted in Wilentz 253)—quite as much as the disturbances attending this imaginary minstrel-show hierarchy mirrored workingmen's own experience of family life. The class specificity of the wish-fulfilling plantation mythology is clear in its benevolent male-centeredness, its loving obeisance to the gentle planter's power—something of a departure from middle-class domestic ideology, whose ideal man was ambitious in the world but retiring at home; and a new turn on middle-class fictional representations of the plantation, whose masters were largely declining or ineffectual.[42] In so imaging the family, however—more accurately, in celebrating the paternalist imagery that structured so much American life, including both the family and slavery—blackface minstrelsy could not elude an emphasis on its troubling "unspokens." By unconsciously taking up and representing the Real of the family in plantation form, the minstrel show allowed instabilities in domestic life to become contradictions in the much-heralded familial basis of slavery—the anguish of its forced separation of families, the dubious legitimacy of the master. Of course it goes without saying that other factors also shaped and pressured the unsettled outlines of the blackface plantation. Yet minstrel songs, in forming what look like unintended dream-work resolutions to familial conflicts, registered the turbulence of the home and revealed men's version of domestic ideology for what it was, in any sphere: a utopian fantasy of household control trying desperately to ignore its own encroaching obsolescence.

Here again, then, one confronts in blackface a certain narrative compromise formation of conflicts in the North that were, in this case ideologically, tied to slavery. But how does this argument square with what I have said about the tendency of spectators to identify with black characters onstage, with the slaves themselves? What inducements would there have been for men to project themselves into the role of master, a figure only obliquely represented in these songs and, even in the racial worst of times, anathema to northern workingmen? In *The Ideology of Power and the Power of Ideology* Göran Therborn argues that ideologies always have a dual character, insofar as they represent both one's own (imaginary) position as well as this position over against an Other. Therborn therefore splits ideologies into ego-ideologies and alter-ideologies: whereas ego-ideologies outline the role one imagines oneself inhabiting, alter-ideologies determine the place of the Other in that ideology, most often the position of the dominated (27–28). In the minstrel show, I have argued, workers' ego-ideology was confused and distorted; white workingmen indulged in displaced blackface versions of themselves, "went black," even as they were engaged in racist ridicule. In terms of ego-ideology, the male spectator was alternately his "black" self and black people's "manly" white superior, when, of course, "blackness" did not simply underscore a resistant sense of white "manliness," as in the rhetoric of "wage slavery." It was in terms of his alter-ideology that he became a planter. The spectator may intermittently have identified with black characters—he had to if the minstrel show was to have its impact—but he always knew what he was *not:* a slave, whether of wages or of the plantation; *he* was no feminized (proletarian) subaltern. Here was a convenient fiction born in part of male panic, a gendered fantasy of renewed mastery over inferiors whose blandishments the mechanic enjoyed and whose pleasures he commanded.

It must be said that there was another available view, even within the minstrel-show audience. At least one writer made it clear that women might experience this mythology, and these same associations, in precisely opposite ways. If for workingmen the plantation was implicitly an ideal image of the family, for women the family felt, well, like a plantation. M. W. Tyler's remarkable novel of 1855, *A Book Without a Title*, draws the parallel from a woman's perspective—and it is not a pretty sight.[43] Mira Dana, the novel's protagonist, goes to work in the famous Lowell factories in order to help finance her brother's education. She fiercely resists the harshness of factory life (not to mention the social logic that makes her work for her brother's benefit), and eventually leads a "Lowell girls" strike. Sometime after, she marries a southern planter and moves to the South, where family life brings to her mind the equation not only of wife and slave but of wife and wage slave as well. Tyler implies that women's experience of the family *was* their version of (wage) slavery—that plantation, factory, and home were interchangeable metaphors for one another—and her novel indicates the possibility of women's less conflicted identification with the slaves than that which workingmen felt. Proslavery propagandists may have used the family as a rationalizing image for the plantation, just as factory representatives used it for the workplace, but the suggestion here is that, far from a neutral or "natural" grid useful in mapping the social world, the family was continuous with—even determined by—extrafamilial forms of exploitation. From the evidence of Tyler's novel it appears that some women, in discerning the real continuities between these spheres, understood the ways in which paternalist familial ideologies (such as those of slavery) infected freedom in the home. The vogue of the mournful plantation song seems in more than its sentimental appeal a subtle product of women's identification with (blackface) slaves. Not for nothing did Stowe and other feminists rename the peculiar institution the "patriarchal institution." The famous women's rights meeting at Seneca Falls looms here as part of the unfinished business of the American 1848, conspicuous by the minstrel show's fear—or, what is the same thing, its burlesques—of it.[44]

As for the equation of family and factory, more women than Tyler, it is safe to say, made the connection. This is clear from the English hatter James Dawson Burn's observations of working women in New York. During his three years of living there, Burn noted sourly that female workers had neither due deference toward their husbands nor a proper mastery of the rudiments of housekeeping: "They will not be instructed by their husbands; and as proof of their obstinacy, one of their common remarks to each other when speaking of their husbands is that they would like to see a man who would boss them" (85). Such, one realizes, was often the true nature of the laboring family—patriarch-bosses and unwilling minions. Throwing that relationship into relief against a plantation background, moreover, Tyler's novel insists on the familiar notion of wage slavery that workingmen themselves, those righteous masters, occasionally pondered in blackface portraits of slave life. Such an appreciation on the part of men was not at all inconsistent with the minstrel plantation's happier figuration of the family, given the metaphorical capaciousness of ideological narratives, the subjective

198

workings of ideology itself, or the gendered likenesses of men's self-images: "planter" heads of the family on one hand, manly mechanics resisting their descent into wage slavery on the other.

So, finally, the nature of northern work for both men and women was at issue in minstrelsy's pricking of the southern boss. From another angle—the angle of white ego-ideology—the plantation mythology, for all its contentment, was the most elaborated version of the industrial imagery housed in the phrase "wage slavery," and took its (unconscious) lead from struggles at work. Once again, that is to say, the minstrel show in these its most popular years figured as a racialized mediator of northern conflicts in southern guise, willy-nilly joining national dissatisfactions about northern and southern work. Indeed, as a kind of upbeat American feudalism the minstrel-show South appreciably enlarged the metaphorical "blackness" that, I have argued, became a figure for the "Europeanizing" of working conditions, the bluntly medieval nature of lower-class work under capitalism. In such terms it was far from accidental that some "Plantation Melodies" unceremoniously, even jubilantly, killed off the beloved master—an occurrence less exceptional than one has any right to expect in songs devoted to, as people in the nineteenth century would have said, "nonagitation" in regard to slavery. We have seen an instance already in Foster's "Ring, Ring de Banjo!" but the baldest, most loving account of the master's demise is the popular "De Blue Tail Fly" (1844):

> O when you come in summertime,
> To South Carlinar's sultry clime;
> If in de shade you chance to lie,
> You'll soon find out de blue tail fly,
> An scratch 'im wid a brier too.
>
> • • •
>
> When I was young, I used to wait
> On Massa's table an hand de plate;
> I'de pass de bottle when he dry,
> An brush away de blue tail fly,
> An scratch 'im wid a brier too.
>
> Den arter dinner massa sleep,
> He bid me vigilance to keep;
> An when he gwine to shut he eye,
> He tell me watch de blue tail fly,
> An scratch 'im wid a brier too.
>
> When he ride in de arternoon,
> I foller wid a hickory broom;
> De poney being berry shy,
> When bitten by de blue tail fly,
> An scratch 'im wid a brier too.
>
> One day he rode aroun de farm,
> De flies so numerous did swarm;

One chance to bite 'im on de thigh,
De debble take dat blue tail fly,
   An scratch 'im wid a brier too.

De poney run, he jump, an pitch,
An tumble massa in de ditch;
He died, an de Jury wonder why,
De verdict was de "blue tail fly,"
   An scratch 'im wid a brier too.

• • •

Ole Massa's gone, now let him rest,
Dey say all tings am for de best;
I neber shall forget till de day I die,
Ole Massa an de blue tail fly,
   An scratch 'im wid a brier too.
             (quoted in Nathan 429–31)

What, in fact, but the slave's own "negligence" kills his master? The sped-up jubilance of the penultimate line conveys the song's sense of its own mischievousness. In moments such as this, blackface performance, energized by a felt cynicism toward the boss in popular life, stumbled into hyena laughs at the muted victory of slaves, a brief subversion whose reach may have extended toward both white women and white men in the workplace and the family.

As we have seen, however, the earlier trains of thought and metaphor within working-class culture which had allowed certain direct links to be made between shop floor and cotton field had broken down as northern working conditions declined—to say nothing of the fact that white men were always of at least two minds about the equation of workers with slaves. The ideological climate changed with the onset of depression; and by the late 1840s the emancipatory uses of "wage slavery" as a rhetorical device, if not wholly superseded, were at least outrun by other investments—the interest in western homesteading, for example, or the heating up of the slavery issue. As I have noted, the move toward antislavery did not depend on any developed sense of the shared fate of black and white labor (such as had sometimes been implied in the rhetoric of wage slavery) or on labor abolitionism; as we shall see, it was other social questions, chiefly the issue of "free soil," that sparked a concomitant and intense degree of antislavery. Mostly concern about the status of work at home took precedence. Said the labor reformer William West of workingmen in 1846: "They do not hate chattel slavery less, but they hate wages slavery more."[45]

The minstrel show's idioms of defiance were furnished not by a close connection between worker resistance and blackface (wage) slaves but by a generalized sense of cultural opposition that in certain instances made creative links to "blackness" available. Certainly the boss/planter was villainized in working-class culture; a typical image, for instance, was the likening of Whiggish eastern capitalists to the feudal overlords of the Spanish conquest in Mexico. During the Mexican War of 1846–48, the *Democratic Review* deployed this analogy in order to rebuke capitalist speculation on the labors of the American "pioneer army," though it also connected the religious opposition to slavery in America with the fanaticism of Spanish Catholic priests.[46] And yet a George Lippard could draw the parallel between lords of the loom and lords of the lash—and thus slaves and workingmen—in *The Quaker City* (1844): "Then came the slaves of the city, white and black, marching along one mass of rags and sores and misery huddled together. . . . Chains upon each wrist and want upon each brow. Here they were, the slaves of the cotton Lord and the factory Prince; above their heads a loom of iron, rising like a gibbet in the air, and by their sides the grim overseer" (389). The blackface plantation mythology resided somewhere in this broad set of resistant images and impulses. It was here that extraordinary apparitions such as heroic plantation firemen would appear in 1848, songs of blackface "sons of freedom" and a blackface Mose which clearly spoke in the accents of the white popular classes.[47] The "freedom" was of course conveyed through racial carica-ture, and much of the time white self-assertion depended on the representation of black subjugation. But it is difficult to deny the brief, subterranean identifications across the boundaries of race or the broadly antithetical stances that could occur on the minstrel-show plantation, such was the tendency for lower-class cultural pride, forced into the peculiar dramatic shape of blackface, to result in unruly racial meanings. Here was labor abolitionism as an unbidden social fantasy, an imaginary and largely unconscious alliance of white and black against all the lords of labor.

This series of conflicts, duplicities, and false moves in the mythology of the plantation confirms Richard Slotkin's argument that paternalist ideology at-tempted "to mask the changes that were in fact transforming relations between proprietors and dependents both inside and outside the family" (140). As the minstrel show made use of it, the plantation mythology also tried to manage the changing relations between the nation's two principal sections, and the social and affective ambiguities that resulted, finally persisting in the illusion that for half the country American feudalism could go on indefinitely. One notes, however, that the mask was cracking. In working so hard to efface the conflicts from which it took its energy, the plantation mythology bared them.

FACING WEST

If we can now see blackface minstrelsy to have thrived on a remarkably complex and extensive involvement—an allusive ease, a sense almost of "collaboration," in T. S. Eliot's term—with its audiences' lives and desires, we must yet account for perhaps the strangest fact of all. I mean that these years of its peak popularity coincided with the greatest surge of antislavery feeling the United States had yet experienced. The easy explanation is that the minstrel show meant to stanch national racial divisions with calculated racist counterpressure; indeed, we know that printed proslavery propaganda began to accumulate only when antislavery ideology became more insistent. Another possibility, that the minstrel show existed quite happily in its time alongside antislavery politics, given the latter's own often problematic racial attitudes, seems more correct historically if less satisfying analytically. It could also and more interestingly be argued that, with the increase in antislavery feeling, minstrel performers, like their legislative counterparts, incorporated certain antislavery images and arguments into their generally complacent acts in order to achieve a sense of national balance on dangerous racial divisions in the republic; on this view, minstrelsy becomes the Compromise of 1850 plus banjo. No doubt all of these explanations have their partial truth. But I would suggest another view of the broad fit between blackface minstrelsy and the events leading up to the Compromise.

Inevitably taking up notable issues and conflicts in white popular life, the minstrel show, I have argued, made correlate glosses on the slavery issue, sometimes backing itself into dangerous racial ideologies. Perhaps the central, most defining instance was the way it became a major national signifier of western migration. To understand this process requires us to know about popular investments in the land issue—the issue, in a word, of California gold. We have seen that the collapse of autonomous working-class politics in the aftermath of the 1837 panic deflected attention from class enemies, uniting white working class and emergent petite bourgeoisie around campaigns of racial, religious, and ethnic opposition: antiabolitionism, temperance, nativism. Curiously, the South itself was about to become the prime "preindustrial" enemy, as one of the popular reform schemes that had hampered labor abolitionism earlier in the decade began to push the popular classes into resisting the enlargement of the area of slavery. Owing in part to the huge gain of southwestern land that seemed the likely outcome of the conflicts with Mexico, and perhaps owing even more to the activities of free-land groups such as George Henry Evans's National Reform Association (NRA), the spread of slavery was now increasingly a concern of the laboring population. Where Evans had in 1844 invoked the notion of wage slavery to rebut the abolitionist defense of southern slaves and to argue on behalf of northern "white slaves" (a retreat from his own earlier position), it was soon evident that the interest in free-white homesteading would bring the issue of slavery into the center of public controversy.[48]

In 1845, for instance, the NRA and the New England Workingmen's Association issued the call for a New York convention to galvanize a new general movement of labor. Although the workingmen explicitly stated their desire to "abolish slavery" along with other social ills, this desire seems in retrospect almost the result rather than the cause of their proposed remedy for "the slaves of wages and all other slaves forever": free public lands, not abolitionism (quoted in Lofton 279). Many workers saw in the land issue—whether as explicit reform program or as generalized ideological tendency—a more sensible response to northern and southern working conditions than abolitionism, which they often felt was a single-issue campaign. Yet, however uninterested in antiracist politics the free-land positions may have been, the notion of free land for free (white) labor vivified popular disdain for slavery.[49] Again, this effect came as much from distaste for the presence of black slaves in the territories as it did from hatred of the institution itself.[50] In any case, the politically undetermined character of western land was what made it possible for many workingmen's organizations to stake their claim with the banner of antislavery. Indeed some, following the Van Burenite wing of the Democratic party, criticized the Mexican War as an attempt to get more land for southern slaveholders, and in May 1848 a mass meeting in Boston's Faneuil Hall celebrated the recent revolutionary success of the French, crying down southern despotism and northern oligarchy and urging "the destruction of white and black slavery" (quoted in Lofton 282). By the circuitous route of land reform, workingmen were ever more publicly invested in halting slavery. Facing west, they brought the slavery crisis back over the eastern horizon.

And the slavery crisis, of course, cast long shadows over the nation; the gaze west was portentous, as the writer for the *Southern Quarterly Review* sensed but did not fully understand. It threatened to spark the sort of "European" conflict on American soil that the western surge was supposed to have rendered impossible. By the late 1840s agitation around the issue of western lands was such that every invocation of westward movement brought with it the bitter question of whether newly acquired territory would be slave or free, a rather ominous fact given the importance of "Manifest Destiny" (as *Democratic Review* editor John O'Sullivan called it in 1845) to northern social aspiration. It is in every respect striking, therefore, that blackface minstrelsy should have moved to the cultural center at precisely this moment, and, as we shall see, by means of the matter of the West. The emphasis and outline of blackface acts revealed the political unconscious of Manifest Destiny. However ironically, the minstrel show became the badge of northern sectional formation and its developing struggles over slavery. One might even say that the backhanded antislavery politics of these years, which avoided civil rights in favor of land and other matters only to see issues of race return to startling centrality, were best represented in minstrelsy's mapping of white men's move west. Blackface tunes, especially those of Stephen Foster, became the very theme songs of the popular republic and California gold. The story of "Oh! Susanna's" recruitment into the politics of America's 1848 is very simple, but the song's repercussions were as large as the crisis that a legislative compromise could only temporarily stall.

In many ways "Oh! Susanna" is the summation of blackface song craft. For one thing, it contains most of the elements I have identified as central to the plantation mythology—lost love, separated families, death, home, nostalgia—themselves, of course, signifying a wide variety of contemporary social facts and facts of feeling:

I came from Alabama wid
my banjo on my knee,
I'm g'wan to Lousiana
My true love for to see,
It rain'd all night the day I left,
The weather it was dry,
The sun so hot I frose to death;
Susanna, dont you cry.

Oh! Susanna,
Oh! dont you cry for me,
I've come from Alabama,
wid my banjo on my knee.

I jumped aboard de telegraph,
And trabbelled down de riber,
De Lectrie fluid magnified,
And killed five hundred Nigger
De bullgine bust, de horse run off,
I realy thought I'd die;
I shut my eyes to hold my breath,
Susanna, dont you cry.

I had a dream de odder night
When ebery ting was still;
I thought I saw Susanna,
A coming down de hill.
The buckwheat cake war in her mouth,
The tear was in her eye,
Says I'm coming from de South,
Susanna, dont you cry.

I soon will be in New Orleans,
And den I'll look all round,
And when I find Susanna,
I'll fall upon the ground.
But if I do not find her,
Dis darkie'[ll] surely die,
And when I'm dead and buried,
Susanna, dont you cry.

(Jackson 89–91)

Perhaps it was this compression of so many of the minstrel show's favorite themes into an unarguably infectious tune that made "Oh! Susanna" a hit. The song that a twenty-one-year-old Foster first saw performed at a Pittsburgh ice cream saloon in 1847 was immediately pirated by Nelson Kneass, a local, eventually quite well known blackface performer, and Christy's Minstrels were soon singing it at Mechanics' Hall in New York City (several of the first sheet versions of the song claimed Christy's authorship).[51]

It was, of all things, a polka—the rhythm of a rising generation marking itself off from the discarded elegances of the formerly audacious waltz. For our purposes it is important to note the nationalist accents of the polka. "For the fighters of 1848," William Austin observes, the polka "fitted exuberant hopes for national freedom—no matter whether the nation was Polish, Bohemian, German, French, Irish, or American." If Foster's song found itself caught up in an ambiguous tussle of American nationalisms—to which "nation" did it refer, the northern, the southern, or the black?—the urgent connotations of its rhythm no less than its context strike me as responsible. All the more so in light of the fact that, as Austin further writes, the attempt to cross this rhythm with sources closer to home was quite unforced, the "polka pigeon-wing" or "Jim Crow Polka" a seemingly natural (though terribly ambiguous) expression of youthful American hope and desire (9). All of this—the West, northern social desire, musical nationalism—was about to cohere around a most singular event.

On November 26, 1848, amid a complex series of political developments crucial to the slavery controversy—among them the Free-Soil insurgency within the Democratic party and that year's presidential campaign—the *Baltimore Sun* broke the story that gold had been discovered in California. Through December and January newspapers headed "Ho! for California!" began to hit the stands; the *New York Herald*'s special California edition of December 26 sold out in one hour. The promise of land thus entangled with the prospect of fortune, thousands of the inspired credulous began the rush west for gold. Three gold rushers, preparing in late December to sail from Salem, Massachusetts, on board the bark *Eliza*, set their own words to a brand-new blackface tune:

> I come from Salem City,
> With my washbowl on my knee;
> I'm going to California,
> The gold dust for to see.
>
> • • •
>
> I jumped aboard the Liza ship,
> And traveled on the sea,
> And every time I thought of home
> I wished it wasn't me!
> The vessel reared like any horse
> That had of oats a wealth,
> It found it couldn't throw me,
> So I thought I'd throw myself.
>
> • • •
>
> I'll scrape the mountains clean, my boys,
> I'll drain the rivers dry,
> A pocket full of rocks bring home,
> So brothers, don't you cry!
>
> Oh, California!
> That's the land for me,
> I'm going to Sacramento,
> With my washbowl on my knee.
> (Minnigerode 323–24)

This version of "Susanna," like those that followed it, plainly salvages the giddiness of the original lyrics and exists on that slim margin alone. Yet Foster's song, with many variations on the migration theme, was embraced in ways its young author could hardly have predicted. No fewer than eight different copyright claims for "Susanna" were registered within fourteen months of its first hearing. Very soon a sentimental ditty about two black lovers probably separated by slavery and trying to find their way back to each other became the national anthem of westward expansion. In *Eldorado*, his 1850 account of a trip to California, Bayard Taylor remembered watching Sacramento blackface bands nightly play "Susanna," and noted "the curious expressions of satisfaction and delight in the faces of the overland emigrants, who always attended in a body." To this day the song's original content is obscured by its association with westward pioneering.[52]

As though in direct response to the nationalist tones of "Susanna," and as though in acknowledgment of the social logic behind their choice, westward migrants had seized upon the song as their own. From behind the mask of a slave determined to overcome the peculiar institution's breakup of families, they celebrated America's move west.[53] No matter that political containment had been the intended result of blackface shows: such white self-masking, in this context, implicitly connected the North's westering impulse and its growing distaste for southern slavery, in the process turning "Susanna" into a rather mordant comment on the desperate problem of American nationalism at midcentury. Small wonder its original lyrics were so often suppressed! Blackface writers, no mean examples of market cunning, proceeded to contribute many different versions of "Susanna," but the adoption of these "black" songs by Free-Soil northerners only reiterated the racial subtext of their pursuit of the new Eldorado. Although the songs recounted a variety of tales, chief among them were oblique references to westward migration and national expansion, such as "Lilla dear, Good Bye"—

> Tho' I am going far away,
> Beyond the dark blue sea,
> I leave my heart with Lilla dear
> In good old Tennessee.

or explicit musical boosterism, as in "California Song":

> This country's all excited,
> 'Bout the Californy gold,
> And every one's delighted
> With the stories that are told;
> Then, the steamers bring such glorious lines,
> And such monstrous junks, to boot—
> Oh! for happy California mines,
> We, one and all, will scoot![54]

Once in motion the drift was hard to stop, and minstrel tunes became an outright venue for northern nationalism. "De Mexicans dey fled before us, / And Taylor he took Matamoras," goes "General Taylor," a song whose infatuation with Zachary Taylor (the slaveholding Whig general turned more or less antislavery president) marks both the antislavery promise and the political ambiguity of liberal nationalism in blackface.[55]

Nor should it come as any particular surprise that "Susanna" was stridently appropriated by the b'hoys, especially in the melodramas featuring Mose. *Mose in California*, an 1849 play capitalizing on recent events, features a set piece in which the most widely known "California" version of "Susanna" is hooted to all assembled:

> Oh! California!
> That's the land for me!
> I'm going to Sacramento,
> With my wash-bowl on my knee!
> (quoted in Dorson 291)

It is scarcely an overstatement to say that "Susanna," and by extension blackface minstrelsy, had become a sectional signifier, a potent popular figure for the North and "all its emigrations, colonizations and conquests," as Bayard Taylor put it (275). The shape and function of commercial blackface acts, that is to say, had been transformed by historical developments they had had some hand in bringing about. Less and less a vehicle of racist alignment between the sections, the minstrel show, now in its guise as a mask for the North, actually began to mark their difference—a much larger and more dangerous division than those for which it had previously provided a stage. The aforementioned "narrative" character of a typical night's show, joining city to country, North to South, seemed an ever more futile attempt to disguise the sectional break that Zip Coon the northern dandy and Jim Crow the southern slave now inevitably suggested. Things were falling apart, for reasons of race, and the foremost racialist entertainment of its time was taking—if not serving—notice.

One must therefore argue that it is almost beside the point whether or not the b'hoys directly expressed antislavery (let alone antiracist) views. Their use of minstrelsy to further northern ends, to figure northern society generally, made the case for them, and with the sort of ambiguity that—as we have seen in its doubled, two-tone songs and in its contradictory plantation mythology—forcefully mirrored the northern antislavery thrust. When, in other words, this case involved a certain sympathy for the slaves, as in "Oh! Susanna" or other, even more sentimental songs, the minstrel show may be said to have intensified the North's racially equivocal agenda, pressing an implicitly antislavery point even as it lampooned and wished away the blacks who would be its prime beneficiaries. In the very broadest sense, nationalism in blackface was an ironic, shadow black nationalism, particularly when northern white men expressed their nationalist pride—a pride that would result a dozen years later in the extinction of slavery—through the black mask: "Oh, we are de Cowbellogers, / An de General Taylor sojers, / . . . We'll ring dese bells all ober de land, / From Newtown creek to de Rio Grande."[56] This *despite* the racism that marked the general run of blackface productions, for, as I note in conclusion, these dubious attitudes infected institutionalized antislavery as well.

This condensation of working-class and racial impulses, as for instance in the marriage of blackface and Mose, gestured toward the largest meanings of the American 1848. The congested intersection of these twin social desires has, of course, informed much of my historical narrative. Their convergence here is of immense significance. On the one hand, blackface was clearly useful in figuring class struggle. Officially buried for several years by the late 1840s, class demands reemerged as one motive for the popular surge west. Making "blackness" their mask, men of the popular classes called on current (racial) languages of social division to manifest their distaste for the class-riven realities that going west was meant to redress. Thus was class desire expressed in the racial modality of blackface, whose usefulness as a "vulgar" class signifier and as an ugly vision of white working-class supremacy—as well as a sublimated antislavery herald—has been starkly clear. True enough, this whole set of figurations met up with the post-panic graphing of class in ethnic or other terms, the overall effect of which was to submerge class dissent. Here, however, the expression of interclass northern pride in a vision of nationalist western pioneering not only did not tame class desires but turned the struggle against "preindustrial" formations (the Irish, blacks, drinkers) into a drama of sectional division. In short, the working-class white man in blackface figured both the division between classes and that between class systems as a whole, as though to gloss the one would naturally gloss the other.[57] While there is some truth in the argument that the united northern fight against the South effectively destroyed class dissent, in one respect this fight brought class and racial agendas, which had always been tense partners, suddenly and strikingly together.[58] It did so most clearly in the Free-Soil movement, the closest the United States ever got to a labor abolitionism.

Eric Foner has argued that the Free-Soil movement was founded on precisely the resolution of the antinomy of labor and abolitionism. Bringing together radical Democrats, antislavery Whigs, and much of the antislavery Liberty party, it settled (temporarily and in compromised form) the old arguments between workers and abolitionists, the competing claims of class and race. The Free-Soilers made antislavery "a respectable element in politics," in the words of William Seward, by disseminating the moral equivalent of abolitionism—antislavery—yet abandoning the agitation for black civil rights; they criticized northern capitalist relations (in the form of free-land arguments) yet asserted that the real threat to northern labor lay in the South's desire to extend slavery.[59] This critique would not soon go away, though the Free-Soilers lost their bid for the presidency in 1848; half a decade later it formed the ideology of the early Republican party.

The question was whether, in achieving this unprecedented alliance between antislavery and labor, the Free-Soil party was in any way emancipatory for black people. The degree of prejudice within its ranks was extreme: Joshua Giddings, a major antislavery advocate and Free-Soil leader who had on several occasions defended black suffrage in the House, still refused to state unambiguously his belief in the equality of white and black people, and similar contradictions characterized other antislavery stalwarts such as Salmon P. Chase, Charles Sumner, and Horace Mann. The *National Era*, the Liberty and then Free-Soil party organ (in which, a few years later, *Uncle Tom's Cabin* would be serialized), termed the presence of the Negro race an "inconvenience," supported voluntary black emigration to Africa or to public land in the United States, and complained that "the real evil of the Negro race" was that they were "so fit for slavery"—though the paper was equally capable of criticizing the prejudice of some former New York Democrats within the Free-Soil party. For these reasons and others, some abolitionists refused to support the Free-Soilers, among them Gerrit Smith and Samuel R. Ward. Yet Frederick Douglass, urging the vote in 1848 for Free-Soil presidential candidate Martin Van Buren, believed that, however ambiguous their antislavery positions, the Free-Soilers were the only if not the best game in mainstream political life, and most free blacks in the North appear to have agreed. That black civil rights had been struck off the roll as an issue—that racism generally was much more visible within the party than its positions would lead us to believe—even as it injected racial-sectional questions into politics, was not the least of Free-Soil's parallels with blackface minstrelsy. As Foner has concluded, the party's platform was so broad that it received support from those who abhorred the presence of fugitive blacks in the North and slaves in the territories, as well as veteran antislavery spokesmen and those more abstractly concerned with the South's influence on the national government.[60] This list is probably not a bad taxonomy of the minstrel show's own audience.

But it will not do to leave the matter there, with blackface minstrelsy as the cultural equivalent of Free-Soil. For it was equally a harbinger of the Compromise of 1850: it derided the slave more than it advanced the North's pallid version of antislavery, and its plantation mythology indicated that it was dedicated to keeping the Union together with slavery or without it. Stasis was its social ideal. In 1851 Stephen Foster wrote a campaign song in support of the Democratic Bigler brothers, to the tune of his own "Camptown Races": "The Constitution is our theme, Hurrah! Hurrah! / And Union is our cherished dream, / Hurrah for the Bigler boys!"[61] If in the late 1840s minstrelsy provided a space where, in disguised ways, the conflicts between white workers and black might be resolved, its very existence kept those conflicts alive. Indeed, the latter constituted minstrelsy's "live social intelligibility," to use V. N. Volosinov's phrase, its hosting of sharply contradictory social aims and desires (23).

As the national art of its moment, the minstrel show harmonized a variety of impulses. It represented a return of the racial repressed that did indeed follow the American empire in all its migrations and colonizations. It figured a nationalist urge to nation building whose inevitable result was sectional conflict. And, by way of the consolatory mask, white folks' other, "black" self, it lamented and denied the strife of its time. At one stroke it revealed the sectional divide that lay behind the "national" veil and tried to close it up. In doing so, the minstrel show provided the soundtrack for the American 1848.

8

Uncle Tomitudes:
Racial Melodrama and
Modes of Production

It is a sad blunder; for when our stage shall become the deliberate agent in the cause of abolitionism, with the sanction of the public, and their approbation, the peace and harmony of this Union will soon be ended.

—*New York Herald* (1852)

In January 1854 T. D. Rice took the Bowery Theatre stage as Tom in one of the numberless dramatic productions of Harriet Beecher Stowe's *Uncle Tom's Cabin*. Rice's path from celebrated Jim Crow in the early 1830s to sympathetic Uncle Tom twenty years later highlights the improbable political geometry of blackface minstrelsy. Surely Rice's Bowery appearance in a more or less antislavery play registered a series of changes: changes in the theater's social position, now as close to lower million as to upper ten; changes in theatrical production, as melodrama was now spliced to blackface performance; and changes, evidently, in racial representation itself. Even half a dozen years earlier it would have seemed preposterous thus to cast Rice, an originator of blacking up. We ought not, however, let these changes obscure the extent to which the great midcentury vogue of "Tom shows" owed precisely to the blackface tradition. The stage conventions of such productions, which included minstrel tunes and blackface makeup, were clearly those of minstrelsy; dramatizations of *Uncle Tom* foregrounded not only sectional conflict but also the blackface forms that had shadowed it. "He is decidedly the best personator of negro character who has appeared in any drama," wrote the *Spirit of the Times* of Rice as Uncle Tom, obliterating the distinction between the play and the minstrel show (January 21, 1854). *Uncle Tom's Cabin* onstage was in one sense minstrelsy's logical antebellum conclusion, and by the 1850s casting Rice as Uncle Tom followed a train of thought. It confirms the equivocal character of racial representation—of blackface minstrelsy and *Uncle Tom's Cabin* both—just prior to the Civil War.

One might say this state of affairs issued from the Compromise of 1850. With party politics nearly swallowed up by sectional feeling, Congress attempted

211

through legislation to forestall an ultimate crisis of sectional division. Compromise designer Henry Clay's chief provisions for "the peace, concord, and harmony of the Union" amounted to a sort of sectional balancing act: the admission of California as a free state but no restrictions regarding slavery in other territories gained from Mexico; the prohibition of the slave trade in the District of Columbia but no abolition of slavery there. The gravest item, which threw off the balance, was a call for the more effectual capture and remittance of fugitive slaves, eventuating in the Fugitive Slave Law in 1851. Compromise fever extended from Clay of Kentucky to Daniel Webster of (it seemed) all New England; Webster's famous Seventh of March speech clinched the deal.[1] For his acceptance of slavery in the name of Compromise and Union, Webster was excoriated far and wide (from Emerson's disdain to Whittier's "Ichabod"), and Stowe composed first "The Freeman's Dream" (1850) and then *Uncle Tom's Cabin* (1851–52) in outrage over his efforts.[2] America's most popular nineteenth-century novel made sectional conflict an inescapable cultural matter. Turning this conflict into affecting tableaux, *Uncle Tom*'s dramatists deepened sectional discord; for every one of the three hundred thousand who bought the novel in its first year, many more eventually saw the play.[3] Yet to varying degrees the stage versions followed from the Compromise in another sense: they attempted to match its sectional tact. This was particularly so in the fence-sitting dramatizations that tried to make antislavery a stroke for Union; but even in the version most faithful to Stowe's novel, *Uncle Tom's Cabin* was itself a compromise between antislavery politics and established entertainment conventions.

The reader will have noticed the equivocation in my account: *Uncle Tom's Cabin* as a break from but also a continuation of blackface minstrelsy; minstrelsy and *Uncle Tom* as of equally uncertain provenance. I have found this ambiguity an unavoidable product of the revolutionary 1850s. The fact is that the Tom plays fully revealed this decade's social and racial contradictions, and thus finished off what the minstrel show had unintentionally begun. Not only were there versions of the play written from antislavery, moderate, and proslavery positions—the lot of them informed by the devices of the minstrel show—but they all took up in their very formal structures the sectional division, based on competing economic systems, that would soon culminate in civil war. Indeed, "modes of production" is a doubly resonant phrase, aptly invoking both theatrical forms and economic formations. Onstage each sectional mode had its characteristic tone, politics, and regime of racial representation, and these were visible in the competing productions of *Uncle Tom*, if not indeed in a single production. To produce the play was by definition to engage in a divisive cultural struggle. While the plays tried to tame down their material with melodrama, their political consequence was heated journalistic and street debate, sometimes conducted right outside the theater. The cultural manifestations of America's competing modes of production warred within the shared language of *Uncle Tom's Cabin*—the precise condition, writes Fredric Jameson, of cultural revolution (*Political* 89–100). *Putnam's Monthly* in

1853 termed this situation "Uncle Tomitudes," which it could not have known would result in a prelude to civil war on the stage.

"A WONDERFUL 'LEAPING' FISH"

After a forty-week run in the Free-Soil *National Era, Uncle Tom's Cabin* was published in book form on March 20, 1852. Something of the immediacy of its impact may be gauged from the fact that its first stage production occurred during its serialization, before the book appeared. Since no law existed copyrighting fictional material for stage use, adapters were free to appropriate at will. In January 1852 a short-lived anti-Tom play, *Uncle Tom's Cabin as It Is; The Southern Uncle Tom,* was produced at the Baltimore Museum. The telling echo of Bowery melodrama (most evidently the 1848 Mose vehicle *New York As It Is*) fixes the social cast of this adaptation no less than the more successful ones that followed it. Pursuing emotionally wrought narrative with a racial theme, stage adapters of *Uncle Tom's Cabin* simply conjoined the forms they found appropriate to the attempt at hand, melodrama and blackface, for audiences already more than familiar with them.[4]

When the novel was published, Asa Hutchinson of the reform-oriented Hutchinson Family Singers approached Stowe about a possible stage adaptation, which the author, Puritan antitheatrical prejudices intact, declined.[5] Particularly with no approval from Stowe forthcoming to even the most congenial of adapters, the way was opened for the canny professional. The first serious attempt at a stage version was that of C. W. Taylor, which ran at New York's Purdy's National Theatre for about ten performances in late August and early September 1852. Reaching haphazardly for the novel's coattails, this hour-long *Uncle Tom's Cabin* shared the bill with a T. D. Rice burlesque of Shakespeare called *Otello* and other minor acts. The rather bald attempt to mute sectional controversy with blackface parody, and Taylor's reckless editorial hand (St. Clare, Eva, and Topsy were absent), did not prevent the *New York Herald* among others from finding in this *Uncle Tom* a disturbing abolitionist portent.[6] But it was two competing dramatizations, those of George Aiken and H. J. Conway, that would rule the market in *Uncle Tom's Cabin.*

Even as Taylor's production gave halting visibility to the Tom show, the Aiken and Conway versions were gestating in Troy, New York, and Boston, respectively. Like Taylor, Aiken appears to have been overcome by the weight of Stowe's material, and omitted Tom's story in his *Uncle Tom's Cabin,* which premiered in Troy on September 27, 1852. Having given all his attention to Little Eva (partly in deference to the child star of the George C. Howard acting family, Cordelia Howard), Aiken was soon forced by his play's popularity and its sins of omission to write a sequel, *The Death of Uncle Tom, or The Religion of the Lowly.* The sequel's odd detachment from the rest of the story is probably what persuaded Aiken and his company to make the daring move of combining the two parts into a single play, a whole night's show of six acts, eight tableaux, and thirty scenes—the first full-length, night-long dramatic production to date (Ames 1045–52). Aiken's adaptation is the one that has come down to us as the definitive dramatic treatment of Stowe's work, in part because it is the only one for which we have an authoritative script, and in part because it is so attentive to Stowe's intentions and even her words, though there are certainly lapses in dramatic efficacy. Aiken does conjure much theatrical excitement out of scenes such as the battle between the George Harris escape party and the slave traders, but he deemphasizes or omits some characters and scenes crucial to Stowe's message and invents others with unclear motivation. Aiken does not dramatize the self-conscious trickery of Sam and Andy, for instance, erasing some of the novel's more telling instances of black agency under slavery.[7] Miss Ophelia, however, is supplied with a love interest in the person of one Deacon Perry, and much of this subplot devolves into trivial farce. Aiken also leans heavily on two low-comedy types, a Quaker frontiersman lifted from Stowe and a callow Yankee called Gumption Cute. In other major respects, however, Aiken follows Stowe's story and vents her chief arguments against slavery.[8] This *Uncle Tom* played a record-breaking one hundred nights in Troy before opening at Purdy's National Theatre in New York on July 18, 1853.

Meanwhile, Conway's adaptation was taking shape at Kimball's Museum in Boston, opening there as the full-length Aiken opened in Troy on November 15, 1852.[9] This dramatization departs from Aiken's on a number of counts, most notably in its relatively complacent politics. Its criticism of slavery is voiced largely by another invented Yankee figure, Penetrate Partyside, a sort of roving reporter in the South à la Dickens or Frederick Law Olmsted; Conway's ambivalence about such observers is manifested in the curious doubleness of Partyside, who may one moment harshly criticize slavery and the next question Eva's "taste" in wanting her father to buy Uncle Tom (2.2). Conway depicts at great length a slave auction in which Legree rigs the bidding so that he can capture Tom, but this only weakens Stowe's case against slavery's contractual ordinariness. In any event a variety of minstrel gags and cracks softens Conway's mild antislavery perspective. Conway, unlike Aiken, avoids any too inflammatory feeling by setting Tom free in the play's happy ending (George Shelby has meanwhile freed Chloe and the children), and a confounding final address to the audience sends best wishes to "our" Uncle Tom, hoping "his life may be happy, though it be life among the lowly" (6.3). P. T. Barnum got wind of the Conway version's impressive run and Compromise politics and booked it for the American Museum beginning November 7, 1853.

These two major adaptations aired in the giddy atmosphere of other, almost incidental versions of *Uncle Tom;* a rewritten version by Taylor at the National and a Bowery Theatre version by H. E. Stevens starring T. D. Rice, for instance, premiered in January 1854.[10] The theatrical world was soon crowded with off-
214

shoots, parodies, thefts, and rebuttals of every imaginable kind—a "magic lantern" version (tableaux from the play) at the Franklin Museum, innumerable blackface lampoons such as Charles White's *Uncle Dad's Cabin* (1855), Christy and Wood's Minstrels' full-scale *Uncle Tom's Cabin, or, Hearts and Homes* (1854), the former Virginia Minstrel Frank Brower's *Happy Uncle Tom* (1854), George Christy's *Lights and Shadows of Southern Life or, Uncle Tom's Cabin* (1858), Irish parodies such as *Uncle Pat's Cabin* (by H. J. Conway) and *Uncle Mike's Cabin* (1853), and so on ad nauseam.[11]

As even this casual and incomplete list suggests, *Uncle Tom's Cabin* very quickly dominated northern popular culture, and did so for several years.[12] How much so may be gleaned from one of the play's early patrons, Henry James. James's remarks in *A Small Boy and Others* concerning his youthful trips to both the Conway version of *Uncle Tom* at Barnum's Museum and the Aiken version at the National have been taken for the swipes at Stowe they are, but the swipes also serve James's half-articulated notion that *Uncle Tom's Cabin* was a new kind of cultural artifact, a sign of change in the character of American culture. "We lived and moved at that time, with great intensity, in Mrs. Stowe's novel . . . my first experiment in grown-up fiction." In this and other observations, James's memory of Stowe's book is saturated with a sense of its nontextual nature, its pithy and immediate provision of flesh-and-blood life—"less a book than a state of vision, of feeling and of consciousness, in which [readers] didn't sit and read and appraise and pass the time, but walked and talked and laughed and cried and, in a manner of which Mrs. Stowe was the irresistible cause, generally conducted themselves" (167). The gush of this sentence so exceeds the studied gentle irony of *A Small Boy* that we may be sure of Stowe's early effect on James. And its brief antiliterary enthusiasm is the context for what follows:

> Appreciation and judgment, the whole impression, were thus an effect for which there had been no process—any process so related having in other cases *had* to be at some point or other critical; nothing in the guise of a written book, therefore, a book printed, published, sold, bought and "noticed," probably ever reached its mark, the mark of exciting interest, without having at least groped for that goal *as* a book or by the exposure of some literary side. Letters, here, languished unconscious, and Uncle Tom, instead of making even one of the cheap short-cuts through the medium in which books breathe, even as fishes in water, went gaily round about it altogether, as if a fish, a wonderful "leaping" fish, had simply flown through the air. This feat accomplished, the surprising creature could naturally fly anywhere, and one of the first things it did was thus to flutter down on every stage, literally without exception, in America and Europe. If the amount of life represented in such a work is measurable by the ease with which representation is taken up and carried further, carried even violently furthest, the fate of Mrs. Stowe's picture was conclusive: it simply sat down wherever it lighted and made itself, so to speak, at home; thither multitudes flocked afresh and there, in each case, it rose to its height again and went, with all its vivacity and good faith, through all its motions. (168)

215

James's metaphor of *Uncle Tom's Cabin* as one of Barnum's oddities—a performing fish—communicates in form and in content that he is speaking in these lines of the culture industry itself. Stowe surely suffers a good deal of condescension here, but from another angle she seems the co-inventor with Barnum of a new ubiquity of popular culture. Uncle Tom leaps from the page, evading his textual confinement and springing into national consciousness as an aerial fact with no apparent links to the mechanics of production ("printed, published, sold, bought and 'noticed'") or of form ("simply [flying] through the air"). Indeed, James's hesitancy in the final sentence between *Uncle Tom* as a work of fiction, a "measurable" "representation," and *Uncle Tom* as a living being, "ma[king] itself, so to speak, at home" and going "through all its motions," indicates an eye-rubbing uncertainty about the precise status of this new cultural force. More than in its taking a full evening's performance time, *Uncle Tom's Cabin* was revolutionary in its effortless and near-immediate replication everywhere; rousing for its politics but apprehended as pop-culture iconography, the story so transcended the usual media of culture that it put an uncanny new spin on one's *relation* to the culture. Uncle Tom was at once all places and specifiably nowhere. It was this quality as much as anything else to which Lincoln referred when he famously attributed the Civil War to Stowe.

A résumé of the scene-ending tableaux in the Bowery Theatre production of the play (starring Rice) gives the rhythm and flavor of *Uncle Tom*'s melodramatic reproducibility: Eliza's escape; Eliza's peril on the ice; Eliza's preservation; the freeman's defense; the death of Eva; the death of St. Clare; the murder of Tom; the death of Chloe; and the "realms of bliss" (Moreau vol. 1). This is very nearly *Uncle Tom* as silent film—which it would indeed become quite early in cinematic history.[13] Dramatists crafted *Uncle Tom's Cabin* into an allegorical series, a set of holy pictures. To this extent the story carried the religious aura with which Stowe had invested it but lost the precise political import Stowe's intrusive and pointedly abrasive narrative voice had been able to enforce. Where in the novel there was melodrama pinned to a politics of antislavery domestic feminism, onstage there were free-floating trademark pictographs with greater or lesser political bite, according to the production. Throw in a little blackface activity, the "cultural dominant" in antebellum racial portrayal, and one has the recipe for an extremely uncertain political play.

BLACKFACE UNCLE TOM

The proximity of *Uncle Tom's Cabin* shows to blackface performance is suggested in a *New York Daily Times* account of the Aiken adaptation, "'Uncle Tom' Among the Bowery Boys." When a blackfaced G. C. Germon made his entrance in the role of Uncle Tom, the *Times* reported, the audience geared up for a laugh,

for he had "that accent which, in the theatre, is associated always with the comic."
He might easily have been taken, said the reviewer, for

> a camp-meeting preacher [who would] overdo the matter, or he would be so
> ignorant as to make his religious sentiments ridiculous. His very first words,
> however, showed that a good hand had his part. The accent, a broad and
> guttural negro accent, but the voice deep and earnest—so earnest, that the first
> laugh at his nigger words, from the pit, died away into deep stillness. "No,"
> said he, "I can't run away. Let *her* [Eliza] go—it's her right! If I must be sold,
> le'b me [be] sold—Mass'r allers found me on the spot. I nebber hab broke my
> trust, and nebber will." (July 27, 1853)

One historian alleges that Germon had feared tainting his career by playing a
"Jim Crow darkey," and while this is probably only speculation, it does specify the
theatrical convention that any Uncle Tom inherited (Birdoff 42). Indeed, the
lines quoted in the *Times* at first glance only reinforce the association of *Uncle
Tom's Cabin* dramas with minstrel-show sentimentalism. Strikingly, while Uncle
Tom in Stowe's novel had been a strong and reasonably young man, Uncle Tom
in successive productions of the play grew older and older, no doubt owing to the
influence of minstrelsy's pathetic elderly men such as Stephen Foster's "Old
Uncle Ned."[14]

The changes Stowe's tale underwent in making the transition from page to
stage underscore its indebtedness to the minstrel tradition. Both Aiken and
Conway, as Bruce McConachie observes, generally gutted the novel's gender
politics, cutting such major female moral exemplars as Rachel Halliday and Mrs.
Bird, and reducing the roles of Eliza and Aunt Ophelia to passive victim and
comic old maid, respectively ("Out" 10–11). By and large, the plays turn the fight
for black freedom into male combat; Conway substitutes George Harris's gun-
fight with Haley, Loker, and Marks for Eliza's crossing of the Ohio, and in both it
is the return of young George Shelby and various others to the Legree plantation,
not Stowe's matrifocal polis, that really tips the scales.[15] Without the female axis
on which Tom and other blacks in the novel are aligned, and are thereby (at least
in intention) enhanced—Stowe's "romantic racialism"—the black types in the
Uncle Tom dramas drift free, veering between the devoted and the daft, one hardly
better than the other. Nor is this effect countered by any truly sustained critique
of slavery, as in the novel.[16]

What remains in both adaptations are moments straight from Christy. In
Aiken, Legree enjoins Sambo and Quimbo to "sing and dance one of their
dances" (6.3); Topsy and little Harry do so at the playwright's behest. Whereas
Stowe wryly references "Jim Crow" in regard to these characters (44, 352), in
Aiken, St. Clare's description of Topsy as "rather a funny specimen in the Jim
Crow line" is not only much less ironized but right on target (2.2). Mrs. G. C.
Howard's Topsy—"I 'spects I's de wickedest critter in de world" (2.4)—was a
departure from the minstrel show's typical female types, whose ridicule depended

on their overripe aptitude or special inaptness for courtship and love; Topsy, by contrast, was Miss Ophelia's mischievous, unruly sidekick, a sort of female match for the rustic Jim Crow.[17] "Destined to become for Anglo-Saxon millions the type of the absolute in the artless," as James wrote, Howard's Topsy set the standard for future stage Topsys as well as for the character's pictorial representation in nineteenth-century engravings and illustrations (172). Conway's *Uncle Tom* actually begins with a minstrel show. In a remarkable diversion from both Stowe's novel and Aiken's version of it, in which Eliza and George Harris's bitter and terrified conversation about the imminent separation of their family sets the plot in motion, Conway foregrounds slaves singing blackface choruses: *"Sam Solo:* Come lay it out you niggers, / Come hoe it down with me, / The way we'll heel and toe it out / Will be a sight to see" (1.1). In this version Sam and Andy are highlighted but function as virtual endmen of the group, straightaway beginning a minstrel dialogue about some horses which is sustained when Mrs. Shelby enters the conversation in the interlocutor's role.

Yet the fact that minstrelsy itself in the early 1850s was no unitary political phenomenon makes the stage *Uncle Tom* a startlingly ambiguous text. The knotted inextricability of minstrel-show trappings from the *Uncle Tom* tradition begs the question of the work's influence on the minstrel tradition. Stephen Foster's "My Old Kentucky Home, Good-Night!" (1853), with its Kentucky cabin and separating family, was directly inspired by Stowe (its working title was "Poor Uncle Tom, Good Night"); Foster's song became a staple of the plays, as did his "Old Folks at Home" (1851). The emergent sentimental strain of blackface minstrelsy took heart from *Uncle Tom's Cabin* and infused it in turn. William Austin writes that Foster's sense of his work was "thrown into some confusion" when *Uncle Tom*'s stage adaptations began to give his blackface songs a more respectable gloss than they or even his genteel compositions had previously received; certainly his reputation was enhanced by his association with *Uncle Tom* (236). In this respect, Austin argues, the blackface plantation-song tradition and the *Uncle Tom* tradition "overlapped and nearly coalesced" (235), and Harry Birdoff goes so far as to lament that no production of *Uncle Tom's Cabin* scored by Foster ever occurred (138).

Tempting though the prospect may be, *Uncle Tom's Cabin* cannot be written off as just another minstrel show. The *Uncle Tom* stage plays were surely versions of minstrelsy, but to that extent they were infected by the minstrel show's own ambiguities. Lampooning Topsy one minute and lamenting Tom's fate the next, *Uncle Tom* was nearly as duplicitous as blackface performance—which is to say that it raised hackles on both sides of the slavery question. No doubt the play, like the book, compromised the abolitionist agenda. As Wendell Phillips had said of the novel's sentimentalism, "There is many a man who weeps over Uncle Tom and swears by the [proslavery] *Herald.*"[18] *The Liberator* in turn derided Conway's dramatic version: "Barnum has offered the slave-drivers the incense of an expurgated form of Uncle Tom. He has been playing a version of that great story at his

Museum, which omits all that strikes at the slave system, and has so shaped his drama as to make it quite an agreeable thing to be a slave" (December 16, 1853). And yet the *Herald* itself found the first, catchpenny production of C. W. Taylor's *Uncle Tom's Cabin* at the National Theatre a dangerous premonition. This version was replete with minstrel-show importations; much like the Conway version, the show began with a minstrel tune, "Nigga in de Cornfield," and a "Kentucky Breakdown Dance." But its suggestion of what *Herald* editor James Gordon Bennett termed "the imaginary horrors of Southern slavery" was enough to convince him that *Uncle Tom* marked "a new epoch and a new field of abolition authorship—a new field of fiction, humbug and deception, for a more extended agitation of the slavery question—than any that has heretofore imperiled the peace and safety of the Union." For Bennett, compromise was the order of the day:

> The institution of Southern slavery is recognized and protected by the federal constitution, upon which this Union was established, and which holds it together. But for the compromises on the slavery question, we should have no constitution and no Union—and would, perhaps, have been at this day, in the condition of the South American republics, divided into several military despotisms, constantly warring with each other, and each within itself. The Fugitive Slave law only carries out one of the plain provisions of the constitution. When a Southern slave escapes to us, we are in honor bound to return him to his master. And yet, here in this city—which owes its wealth, population, power, and prosperity, to the Union and the constitution, and this same institution of slavery, to a greater degree than any other city in the Union—here we have nightly represented, at a popular theatre, the most exaggerated enormities of Southern slavery, playing directly into the hands of the abolitionists and abolition kidnappers of slaves, and doing their work for them. (September 3, 1852)

Bennett had reason for his rage. The *Uncle Tom* shows' great achievement was to put even the worst elements of blackface minstrelsy into a narrative—no longer merely an implied context—of sectional debate. Wherever in its politics a particular production might fall, sectional division made up *Uncle Tom*'s storyline. *Uncle Tom* often slouched back into the ambit of minstrel-show japery, but it also, as the *Times* intimated, turned minstrelsy toward the prospect of black redemption.

The chief *Uncle Tom's Cabin* dramas, then, both were and were not minstrel shows. The plays could not in any case have avoided making use of blackface devices: minstrelsy was the current material condition of theatrical production in the representation of racial matters. But in doing so they made the minstrel show's duplicities outright contradictions, to some extent redeploying blackface acts for explicit antislavery purposes. The results were never less than equivocal, as we have seen; but we must begin to see this quality as a mark of the period in question. As social contradiction was the historical theme of the 1850s, so the *Uncle Tom's Cabin* plays made the theme their own. They did so, as I have said, by making this contradiction visible specifically at the level of popular stage representation. I now want to go further and argue that the play's way of introducing sectional controversy into the theater was by foregrounding and even thematizing the vagaries of racial representation. Here it makes sense to isolate for discussion the two competing versions of *Uncle Tom's Cabin*. Aiken and Conway each took up one of the minstrel show's contradictory representational strategies in regard to blacks—Conway its hard-edged ridicule, Aiken its sentimentalism. It could scarcely have been the stated politics of either version that won over the *New York Daily Times* or offended the *Liberator,* for the explicit antislavery content in both was roughly the same. Rather, it was the reigning racial tonality of each play that put the message across, the way its particular iconography did or did not suggest an irreverence for the plight of the slaves. Conway earned low marks from the *Liberator* because his version took over wholesale the minstrel show's racial meanness; Aiken's Tom succeeded, the *Times* was careful to point out, because he escaped the comic, falling instead into a Fosteresque pathos. This is not at all to say that Conway exploited only the comic and Aiken only the sentimental; true to the plays' ambiguous minstrel legacy, they were crossed-hatched by a variety of devices. But, by and large, Conway left the minstrel show's worst contributions intact, while Aiken brought out the radical uses lurking in it. This in fact was the ground of theatrical controversy: *Uncle Tom's Cabin* onstage was the site of competing attempts to capture the authority of blackface.

MODES OF PRODUCTION

Althusserian social theorists have suggested that every social formation resides not in a single mode of economic production but in a complex overlay of several modes at once, with residual modes now subordinated to the dominant one and emergent modes potentially disruptive of it.[19] Fredric Jameson argues that every ensemble of such overlapping modes has its own "cultural dominant," or specific, defining cultural sensibility. To the extent that competing economic modes (and their networks of ideological self-representation) coexist at any given moment, so will clash and conflict occur in the realm of culture, dominant or not, and even in the space of a single text. Jameson writes that moments when the "coexistence of various modes of production becomes visibly antagonistic, their contradictions moving to the very center of political, social, and historical life," constitute situations of cultural revolution (*Political* 95–96). The advent or consolidation of any mode of production is accompanied by a cultural revolution specific to it, and the emergence of the bourgeois state in America was no exception. Without entering into the long-standing debate on the antebellum South's precise mode of production, we can see clearly that the sections at midcentury—northern industrialists and western farmers on the one hand, southern slaveholders and their unlanded allies on the other—were engaged in a major effort of economic struggle and eventual national consolidation, as observers from Karl Marx to David Potter have stressed.[20] In the stage versions of *Uncle Tom's Cabin* one sees aspects of a

220

cultural revolution fully equal to this revolutionary political moment. Not only did their thematic content make visible the antagonism between America's two modes of production or regimes of economic organization, but in formal terms they staged sectional difference as a contest between the comic and the sentimental aspects of the minstrel show. Although these racial discourses did not arise in any essential or unitary way from economic modes of production, competing versions of *Uncle Tom's Cabin* turned them into sectional cultural dominants.

The lines the *Times* quoted from the Aiken version illustrate how much Tom sets the tone for that play's politics. "I ain't going," says Tom when he hears of Eliza's escape plan. "If I must be sold, or all the people on the place, and everything go to rack, why, let me be sold. . . . [T]he Lord's given me a work among these yer poor souls, and I'll stay with 'em and bear my cross with 'em till the end" (1.3). As in Stowe's novel, Tom is a sacrificial figure, a black Christ. He has much to bear, for Aiken emphasizes the Harris family's breakup and Eliza's trials, while Eva is shown fading fast in Tom's spiritual glow. To Aiken's credit, much of Topsy's role is taken up with Eva's effect on her, not her antics only; her conversion and her regret at Eva's passing pile on more sentimentalism. In this sense the strategic sounding of "Old Folks at Home" when Tom has been sold down the river hardly comes as a shock to the attentive reader (5.3). Legree in this version, moreover, figures the bad conscience of the slaveholder, not the pure malignancy he becomes in the Conway adaptation; whereas Conway's Cassy must taunt Legree with his sins, Aiken's Legree knows that his alienation from maternal affection is his problem but cannot quite find his way back. "Curse me if I think there's any such thing as forgetting anything, any how," he says, meaning his dead mother, but just as well speaking of the acts of barbarity he has committed since his antisentimental rejection of her (6.3). The *Tribune* wrote of Aiken's version, "The play is a veritable *pièce de mouchoir*, a *comédie larmoyante*—for tears were freely shed by the audience" (August 8, 1853). "Of the lightness and gayety of the book there was no sign," confirmed Francis Underwood, who accompanied Stowe on a visit to this dramatization. Topsy must have been the exception, for Mrs. Howard was in that role, and Stowe was apparently delighted by her. Stowe's engagement with this stage Topsy suggests that the Aiken adaptation was in other respects able to hold a tone of sentimental gravity, on which Underwood himself plays when he writes that Howard and Stowe appeared to exchange glances during the performance: "Mrs. Stowe's face showed all her vivid and changing emotions, and the actress must surely have divined them. The glances when they met and crossed reminded me of the supreme look of Rachel when she repeated that indescribable *Hélas!*" Throughout the play Underwood saw Stowe display "smiles and tears succeeding each other."[21]

By contrast, Conway's version opens, according to a Barnum advertisement, with an "amusing and appropriate Ethiopian Medley Overture," and makes enthusiastic use of the minstrel show's comic mode.[22] I have already said that Sam and Andy become major characters in this version, and not as the sometimes self-conscious ironists they are in Stowe but as jokey buffoons. For his part, the Yankee Penetrate Partyside occasions as much mirth as indignation at the spectacle of slavery. Walking along the plank to board the boat going south, Partyside feels his feet slipping and sliding and wonders whether he is stepping on eels; these turn out to be slaves in chains, whom the comparison, so close to many we have seen in minstrel songs, does its best to make light of (2.1). If this moment of complacency does not belong to Partyside, many others do, such as when Partyside jokes about the "niggers" on whose behalf he is evidently writing, or when he ridicules Adolph, St. Clare's valet (3.1). Indeed, it is a mark of this play that its antislavery mouthpiece makes most of its comic minstrel japes, as though in the single figure of Partyside the desperate social symptom and its theatrical antidote were joined. Revealingly, whenever Conway stoops to sentimentalism, he deploys its safer side—not "Old Folks at Home" when Tom is sold but "Massa's in de Cold Ground" when St. Clare dies (5.1). Thus did Barnum falsely advertise when he said of the Conway play that "it does 'nothing extenuate nor set down aught in malice'"—quoting, pointedly and obnoxiously, Othello's final address—and speak more accurately when he said that "it does not foolishly and unjustly elevate the negro above the white man in intellect or morals" (quoted in Birdoff 89).

These dominant representational approaches fit precisely the differing political intentions of Aiken and Conway. The sectional division their separate strategies arose from and acknowledged was thematized in other ways as well, again through figures derived from the minstrel stage: the southern rustic and the "northern" dandy. Even in Stowe's novel, Uncle Tom and Topsy on the one hand and St. Clare's Adolph on the other are surely inheritances from the minstrel show; in the Tom shows they become displaced markers of sectional dispute. Aiken gives Topsy an entrance during which she excoriates the dandified blacks who evidently call her "nigger": "[*Without.*] You go 'long. No more nigger dan you be! [*Enters—shouts and laughter without—looks off.*] You seem to think yourself white folks. You ain't nerry one—black *nor* white. I'd like to be one or turrer" (2.4). (These events result in one of the more pathos-driven moments Topsy is allowed, a tearful pledge to Eva that she will try to be, as Eva puts it, "one of those spirits bright Uncle Tom sings about!") Given the way Zip Coon and Jim Crow had come to seem sectional signifiers, condensing northern urbanity and southern rusticity into black figures that referenced the source of the struggle, such moments are difficult to detach from a context of *national* controversy. Despite the fact that condescension toward Topsy and disdain for black dandies are both projected onto black characters—as though this were not generated elsewhere— these minstrel-show attitudes are aligned, by way of minstrel types, with sectional matters. The tug-of-war between Topsy and the dandified blacks which Topsy describes indeed seems just that, complete with rhetorical combat ("Miss Rosa— she gives me lots of 'pertinent remarks"), symbolic violence (Topsy destroys

Jane's earrings and dumps dirty water on all the dandies), and actual violence (Topsy lays a trap of scalding water for Miss Rosa) (2.4).

Conway is even more invested in such displaced struggles. Through Partyside, Conway dwells on the differences between Adolph and Tom; Partyside is stunned to learn that Adolph, with his light skin and adorned in St. Clare's vest, is not part of the family, while Tom's status is never questioned. Partyside makes the dichotomy particularly clear in his references to Adolph and Topsy, whose respective jobs (valet for Adolph, "danc[ing] breakdowns" for Topsy) record similar proclivities to those we have seen in the two chief minstrel types (3.1). Later Conway secures this theme by depicting a pointless fight between Adolph the dandy and Sam the plantation hand (5.1)—pointless, that is, unless we recognize the social energies making such a fight necessary. Not for nothing does St. Clare die in both versions of the play from knife wounds Legree inflicts while lunging at a Yankee disputant; Legree's Vermont origins notwithstanding, he represents the South, making St. Clare a passive victim of sectional animus.

The fact is that in using these dramatic strategies, the *Uncle Tom's Cabin* plays institutionalized the social divisions they narrated. Sectional debate henceforth became theatrical ritual, part of the experience of *Uncle Tom*. To examine the partisan discourse around the two major versions of the play is to witness a situation in which stage devices have sparked a dramatic rivalry which in turn effortlessly invokes political upheaval. Accordingly, the phrase "modes of production" in this context takes on a highly condensed and overdetermined set of meanings. Barnum may be said to have raised the stakes on opening Conway's version of the play in obviously direct competition with the Aiken–National Theatre version, which was then in its fourth month of performances. Barnum's ad for the American Museum *Uncle Tom*, in addition to the aforementioned crowing about his refusal to "unjustly elevate the negro," promised that his was the "only just and sensible dramatic version of Mrs. Stowe's book that has ever been put upon the stage." As if this claim were not pointed enough, Barnum dismissed his rival, though not by name: "And instead of turning away the audience in tears, the [American Museum] author has wisely consulted dramatic taste by having Virtue triumphant at last, and after all its unjust sufferings, miseries and deprivations, conducted to happiness by the hand of Him who watches over all." He thus notably denounces the Aiken version's very mode—sentimentalism's tears— while piously (and falsely) claiming the same sentimental values for his own "happy" production. The National shot back in its ad: "Which is the humbug version of *Uncle Tom's Cabin?* Not that played at the National Theatre!" The gauntlet had been thrown down.[23]

There are grounds for thinking the small war that followed surprising and significant. It is true that, coming a few short years after the Astor Place riot and nowhere approaching the intensity of that conflagration, the *Uncle Tom* feud seems like petty cash. Yet in this case, as in the case of a whole tradition of theater disturbances, ideologies of the state and of the stage intertwined, charging the theatrical realm's every gesture. Significantly, too, the ideologies in question had to do not with competing *class* productions of the play—one typical cause of theatrical riots—but with national and racial questions. Both productions inhabited a broadly popular arena of reference, discourse, and audience; it was the sectional perspective of the plays that filled the air and made dramatic theory fair game for political discussion. Taking its lead from Barnum's ad, the *Morning Express* rationalized Conway's ending by appealing to the play's popular public:

> There is no good reason why Uncle Tom should be whipped to death by a brute in a moral drama, because from the popular character of the drama itself, such a closing triumph for vice and defeat of virtue would leave a most pernicious impression upon the general mind. Hence the astonishing success of the sumptuous version of Uncle Tom at Barnum's Museum, where the hero, after all his tribulations, is restored to his freedom and his family. (quoted in Birdoff 89–90)

Through this critic's convenient resort to the melodramatic categories of good and evil, one again glimpses the competing aesthetics of the sentimental and the comic. Presumably the "pernicious impression" the *Morning Express* feared was the rousing, lachrymose effect of Tom's fatal whipping on Conway's "sumptuous" work of what one can only call Compromise formation.[24]

The *New York Atlas* indeed thought Conway's version violated the spirit of Stowe's text, and, pointing to the dramatist's English birth, spoke in a lexicon of national service:

> It may be well enough, perhaps, for the mendicants of the state, if they belong to the "home squadron," to vitiate the works of authors of *their* own country; but, is it to be endured that an imported scion of Cripplegate should be allowed to falsify and misrepresent such an author as Mrs. Stowe, to pander to the appetites of a few mercenary toadies, who would misrepresent a moral and enlightened community? *Uncle Tom's Cabin*, as played at the American Museum, has few charms for us; and yet, it is the popular drama of that establishment. It calls in immense audiences; and, of course, is most vociferously applauded.

Readers interested in an authentic version were directed to the National Theatre, for there the play did not "pander to the fears of the timid, nor gratify a perverted taste" (November 20, 1853). The rhetoric of territorial rights and community representation alerts us to the fact that in the case of *Uncle Tom's Cabin*, theatrical taste and political devotion had once again become one and the same. To misrepresent Stowe as Conway does, the argument goes, is to allow a "few mercenary toadies" to misrepresent the nation. Observers of *Uncle Tom's Cabin* understood perfectly clearly that struggles over the text mediated struggles over sectional allegiance.

That is why it repays our attention to note the public relations gambits launched all around this curious rivalry between theaters. One feels the gravity of what under normal circumstances would be culture-industry business as usual. Barnum hung a fifty-foot sign along the cornice of the American Museum bearing the play's title, some five hundred yards of cotton muslin; in accord with Conway's hedging politics, one end showed a black dancer and the other a fight between fugitive slaves and their now legal hunters. Three days after Barnum opened the Conway version, A. H. Purdy celebrated the one-hundredth performance of the Aiken version at his National Theatre with a "Grand Jubilee Festival," complete with brass band on the balcony (incidentally a Barnum innovation), fireworks, and Drummond light on the roof (Odell 6:309). When Barnum had some success with a play called *Little Katy, or the Hot Corn Girl,* Purdy in December 1853 mounted his own production at the National starring Aiken's Little Eva, Cordelia Howard. Despite its attempt to represent New York street life after the fashion of the Mose plays, the drama so resembled *Uncle Tom's Cabin* (it was indeed dramatized by one of *Uncle Tom's* first adapters, C. W. Taylor) that it too took on some of the energies of the rivalry. Purdy claimed that Cordelia Howard had read the story of Little Katy—which would soon appear in novel form as Solon Robinson's *Hot Corn* (1854)—in the (antislavery) *Tribune,* and had pledged to save a dollar per night from her *Uncle Tom's Cabin* performances to give to some real Katy. A proslavery newspaper attacked this ploy and the theater that sponsored it: "There is not a greater rendezvous for prostitution and iniquity of every sort than this same National Theatre," wrote the *New York Observer:*

> Undoubtedly the moral character of the play which has for the last few months been nightly exhibited on its stage [*Uncle Tom's Cabin*], and with so much success, has been the means of enticing hundreds of innocent souls within its halls and on the road to ruin. But Satan has indeed put on the double garb of an angel of light when, as a means of alluring a still larger number of them into his snares, he clothes himself thru the column of that same N.Y. *Tribune* with the eminently righteous work of devoting a dollar a night for the support of a charity to which the National Theatre with the above zealous aid is nightly adding its victims. (quoted in Birdoff 94–95)

Braving this challenge, the editor of the *New York Atlas* on the contrary found the National iniquity-free—or, as one patron put it, demystifying the editors' code, "this 'ere theatre is one that goes in for religion, virtue, morality—and *liberty!*" (Birdoff 96).

So intense did the late 1853 rivalry become that it eventually found its way back into the play. At one point in the Aiken version the Yankee Gumption Cute engages Topsy in a (minstrel) dialogue:

Cute: Don't you be too severe, now, Charcoal; I'm a man of genius. Did you ever hear of Barnum?
Topsy: Barnum! Barnum! Does he live out South?
Cute: No, he lives in New York. Do you know how he made his fortin?
Topsy: What is him fortin, hey? Is it something he wears?

225

> *Cute:* Chowder, how green you are!
>
> *Topsy:* [*Indignantly.*] Sar, I hab you to know I's not green; I's brack. . . .
>
> *Cute:* . . . Well, as I was saying, Barnum made his money by exhibiting a *woolly* horse; now wouldn't it be an all-fired speculation to show you as the woolly gal? (5.2)

Topsy refuses, but one feels the damage has been done. In any case, the Yankee Barnum is here pegged as the "southerner" his version of the play revealed him to be. In this and other ways the play thrived on the political stir it had generated and kept it going beyond the proscenium. Legend has it that the controversy was carried forth into the street, where fevered debate took place under the gaslights and where, on Chatham Street, near the National, two clothing stores allied themselves with the warring productions of *Uncle Tom,* one store calling itself Horton and Barnum's, the other Brown and Purdy's, and each respectively hawking the latest fashions of the South and the North (Birdoff 96–97).

By way of the play, sectional feeling had seeped into the half-conscious gestures of everyday life; and the new political space *Uncle Tom* opened up did not close again when these particular versions ended their runs. Further Tom shows, C. W. Taylor's (and others') dramatization of Stowe's *Dred,* J. T. Trowbridge's abolitionist *Neighbor Jackwood,* Dion Boucicault's melodrama *The Octoroon,* the John Brown-inspired *The Insurrection,* and other plays in the 1850s attested to the cultural revolution of which the minstrel show had been one portent. Bruce McConachie is thus only partly correct in charging the stage adaptations of *Uncle Tom's Cabin* with "normalizing" Stowe's novel, "smoothing away the radical challenges to the dominant culture implicit in its mystical and matrifocal values" ("Out" 7). The plays emptied *Uncle Tom* of Stowe's feminism and her partial critique of capitalism, but they translated her antislavery (*not* antisouthern) convictions into sectional barbs. The increasingly uneasy coexistence of economic systems worked its way into a tussle of sign systems that productions of *Uncle Tom's Cabin* only dimly realized they were developing. Based on a narrative of sectional ideologies in conflict, the plays exuded sectionally loaded incidents and devices, and rather than symbolically resolving these, the Tom plays blew apart the happy ambiguities of the minstrel shows from which they had come. It was at this level of intervention that *Uncle Tom* did its work; the comic and the sentimental, the cornerstones of minstrelsy, no longer seemed entirely compatible. The divergent productions of *Uncle Tom's Cabin* had given them a sectional gloss, and as long as there was friction in the street, there would be disruption on the stage.

WAGE SLAVERY ONCE MORE

For many observers the play held an importance beyond its explicit political message. This lay in its specifically popular audience, whom abolitionists had often perceived to be hostile to their cause. "Oh! Susanna" may have intimated a working class ready to hear a different tune regarding the extension of slavery; *Uncle Tom's Cabin*, it was widely noted, actively recruited the b'hoys. William Lloyd Garrison liked Aiken's version better than he had liked the novel, not least because *Uncle Tom* was beginning to secure the Free-Soil alliance of workers and slaves that had hitherto been only inchoate:

> If the shrewdest abolitionist amongst us had prepared the drama with a view to make the strongest anti-slavery impression, he could scarcely have done the work better. O, it was a sight worth seeing, those ragged, coatless men and boys in the pit (the very *material* of which mobs are made) cheering the strongest and the sublimest anti-slavery sentiments! The whole audience was at times melted to tears, and I own that I was no exception. (September 9, 1853)

To which the skeptic will reply: and then they went out and bought the *Herald.* There is wish fulfillment here, but it is buttressed by a great variety of opinion noting the new class of spectators Aiken's dramatization roped into this ideological arena. The *New York Atlas* called on a now familiar code to make its case: "The gallery was filled with a heroic class of people, many of them in red woollen shirts, with countenances as hardy and rugged as the implements of industry employed by them in the pursuit of their vocations" (October 16, 1853). Their silence at the moment Eliza crosses the Ohio causes the writer to look around, only to find the whole audience, b'hoys included, in tears. No doubt the foreign visitor Adolphus Hart was partly correct when he noticed in the balconies and pit a "class intent on every scene in the drama that could gratify their morbid love of cruelty, and make them gloat over pictures of human wretchedness and misery." Yet this ruder interest in mere sensation resulted perforce, Hart wrote, in much "shouting and holloing as Eliza was crossing the Ohio, or George Harris was shooting his pursuers" (5–6). The *New York Tribune,* remembering the 1834 antiabolitionist rioting, made essentially the same point about this new venue for rowdiness:

> No mob would have dared to disturb the Abolition part[y] at the National Theatre. It was composed largely of the stuff which demagogues acting under oligarchs have used for the purpose of burning down halls, destroying printing presses, assaulting public speakers, intimidating, striking [interesting ambiguity], killing. Now that is changed, at least in Chatham-st.

Its conclusion was that "[t]he 'b'hoys' were [now] on the side of the fugitives. The pro-slavery feeling had departed from among them. They did not wish to save the Union. They believed in the higher law" (August 8, 1853). One notes indeed that one month into the run of Aiken's adaptation, the National began accommodating black spectators, though in a separate part of the theater (Odell 6:238).

Adaptations of *Uncle Tom's Cabin* were perfectly situated to infiltrate this cultural sphere in a way Stowe's novel had been unable to do. Their chief theaters, such as the National, the Bowery, the American Museum, and the Franklin Museum, were well known for their ability to cater to the million. Henry

James remembered the National as a "playhouse till then ignored by fashion and culture . . . deep down on the East side, whence echoes had come faintest to ears polite" (169). The same, of course, might have been said of the other theaters as well.[25] If, as James suggests, *Uncle Tom's Cabin* marked a time when more than one class would again enter a single theater, it also made possible a decisive shift in concern among the popular classes in particular. *Little Katy*'s continuities with Aiken's *Uncle Tom* already indicated the popular cultural sphere into which this antislavery material had been inserted. Aiken himself had been a "sensation" dramatist before embarking on the Howards' version of Stowe's tale, having done up stories from the *New York Ledger* for the Albany stage (*The Gun-Maker of Moscow* and others); in the early 1860s he became the American Museum's house dramatist, and he later wrote dime novels for the George Munro publishing house (including *A New York Boy Among the Indians* [1872]).[26] Selected cast members of Conway's version at Barnum's Museum were none other than veterans of the Mose vehicles and other such melodramas; Emily Mestayer, James's favorite in the part of Eliza, had on more than one occasion played Mose's Lize. Sure enough, there is a bit part in Conway's *Uncle Tom* for a slave called Little Mose. These overlaps had the effect of reaching the popular classes where they lived. Rather than talking down to them from the abolitionist's lofty perch, *Uncle Tom* dramas spoke in the idiom of popular melodrama, wedding new political concerns to familiar forms.

New political concerns did not always amount to new politics, of course; the ideological slant of Conway's version alone saw to that. Any too optimistic view of this new popular interest in antislavery melodrama is tempered by other sorts of common responses to *Uncle Tom*—by which I mean, in part, the parodies of blackface minstrelsy. Christy's Minstrels, for instance, soon turned the burlesque third part of their show into "Life Among the Happy," and Christy and Wood's Minstrels in 1854 devised an operatic burlesque of *Uncle Tom* in which Tom was not sold, Legree was not present, and a general plantation frolic substituted for the pathos of melodrama.[27] Frank Brower's "Happy Uncle Tom" (rehearsed for at least a decade) was a huge hit; based for the most part on extremely tired hard-of-hearing jokes (Tom is deaf), the piece apparently also featured a jig and banjo dance (Brower 5–8). Sam Sanford also performed a "Happy Uncle Tom" act, which he claimed brought in $11,000 in nine weeks:

> Oh, white folks, we'll have you to know
> Dis am not de version of Mrs. Stowe;
> Wid her de Darks am all unlucky
> But we am de boys from Old Kentucky.
> (quoted in Toll 94–95)

The most telling ripostes, however, pitted the condition of the slave against that of the white worker in the North, as in "Take Care of Number One":

But don't come back, Aunt Harriet; in England make a fuss,
Go talk against your country, put money in your puss;
And when us happy darkies you pity in your prayer,
Oh, don't forget de WHITE SLAVES dat's starvin' ober dar!
(Dixey 64–65; see also *Pop* 211)

This was obviously a charge that had not gone away; as the Irish parodies (one by Conway himself) make particularly clear, the competing constituencies for liberation were still in competition. The *Irish American* printed a scathing piece (interestingly titled "Mrs. Stowe in Cork") that argued the case of "Father Pat" against that of Uncle Tom, and held up the sufferings of the white peasant to the hypocritical antislavery Stowe, "the female Barnum" (Birdoff 183–84). This critique arose in part from the ways the dramas themselves handled the tension between antislavery and working-class concerns. In St. Clare's comparisons of slaves and workers as well as in other moments of the play, conflict over the notion of "wage slavery" emerged again, not to be resolved so easily by a single "abolitionist" drama.

There is, of course, a great deal of room in the story of *Uncle Tom's Cabin* for mechanic accents, to borrow Michael Denning's phrase. Right off the bat George Harris loses his job in the factory to which his master has hired him out; the master has decided that George's lease on independence is getting too dear, and wants him to come back to the plantation and, despite his marriage to Eliza, an arranged marriage. This demotion is transparently a shift from artisan (George is an inventor) to slave, and in conjoining the two, the action everywhere invokes George's status as put-upon "wage slave." In the dramas George's speeches about his lack of freedom thus take on a specifically artisanal cast, making the freedom in question a matter of both black and working-class relevance. George's mixed racial heritage reinforces this equation in a literal way and allows him to mediate between the worlds of white audience and black slave. Significantly, Aiken makes much more of George's plight than does Conway. Aiken's George and Eliza begin the play, agonizing at length over their fate. "I'm a poor, miserable, forlorn drudge," says George, wishing he were dead; Eliza counters, "I know how you feel about losing your place in the factory, and you have a hard master; but pray be patient" (1.1). The multiaccentuality of these lines, pointing at once to southern slave and northern artisan, is self-evident, as is the familiar appeal of George's righteous "manliness." His declaration of independence is a workingman's "republican" manifesto: "I'll fight for my liberty, to the last breath I breathe! You say your fathers did it; if it was right for them, it is right for me!" (2.3). (The *Times* reported that such speeches got "great cheers" [July 27, 1853].) In the Conway version, by contrast, the first scene between Eliza and George is buried in the middle of act one, just after the minstrel-show opening, and George's plan to escape has apparently already been discussed between them, for George assumes rather than announces it, decisively diminishing the impact

(1.2). George does get to make his stirring declaration (1.5) and shoot at Loker, Haley, and Marks when they pursue him, but Conway's conflation of the escapes of Eliza and George, both of them complete by the end of act one, gives George much less stage time. Already in the George Harris subplot Aiken proved himself much more attentive to the potential links between slave and worker; he accordingly earned the approval of antislavery portions of the working class and their journalistic friends, and perhaps, as the *Spirit of the Times* wrote, "made converts to the abolition doctrine many persons, we have no doubt, who have never examined the subject" (March 11, 1854). Conway's version, shrinking the role of George and downplaying the power of sympathy, left significantly more space for derision and dismissal than for alliance politics.

This was no less the case with St. Clare's disquisitions on the relative conditions of southern slaves and "British" workers. In the novel St. Clare assesses the slaves to be "better off than a large class of the population of England" (341). St. Clare's conservative labor critique is softened by Stowe's portrayal of him as fatally flawed rather than mean; he has no illusions regarding the slaves' contentment with their enslavement and even has a certain sympathy for both wage slave and black slave (339). But he makes essentially John C. Calhoun's argument about the greater oppressions of the North: "[The English laborer] is as much at the will of his employer as if he were sold to him."[28] Considering the Tom shows' rather different audience from that of the novel, this was a position requiring sensitive handling by the dramatist: pushed too hard, it would compromise the story's antislavery politics; pushed too little, it might alienate the working class.[29] Aiken interestingly chooses to bypass this thorny issue, giving St. Clare no chance to air his opinions on the subject of workers and slaves. St. Clare makes his sectional case by mocking Ophelia's personal disdain for Topsy in light of her missionary zeal, and otherwise ridicules the "lovely rule of woman"; but the rest is silence (2.2; 3.1). Conway, however, exploits St. Clare's brief on behalf of the white worker. Penetrate Partyside, taking on the function of Miss Ophelia in the novel, criticizes St. Clare for trafficking in slaves, and St. Clare gets to make his labor critique in full: "The English aristocracy, and capitalists . . . are only doing in another form what the American planter does" (2.2). This apology for slavery is lifted nearly verbatim from the novel, as is St. Clare's assertion that while the slave can be whipped to death, the worker can be starved to death. Labor oppression under slavery is the same as labor oppression the world over, says St. Clare. To this small extent Conway equates the condition of worker and slave; but, the argument goes, at least the South is forthright about its economic regime. Partyside himself defends the white worker when he comes across a law requiring manumitted elderly slaves to be provided with food, clothing, and shelter by their deceased masters' estates: "Pity it weren't more general. Guess it wouldn't do much harm to some of the rich folks in the North if they was obliged to provide for all those who have gotten grey and superannuated in their service" (6.1). Thus, despite the vacillation between prolabor and generally antiaristocratic

230

views, Conway endorses Calhoun—or, closer to home, Mike Walsh—and the white-egalitarian reading of "wage slavery."[30]

Together with Aiken's foregrounding of George Harris, his refusal to enter the swampy terrain of labor's racial politics has the effect of a hopeful gesture in the direction of a labor abolitionism. Restricting St. Clare's diatribes, Aiken avoids even an echo of the nettled cry of "white slavery." Conway, in allowing St. Clare free reign, offers a sharp response from within a putatively antislavery play to the long-standing abolitionist denial of the pinched circumstances of northern workers. There are in Conway no characters and little rhetoric with labor-abolitionist potential; since George Harris is a marginal figure at best and Penetrate Partyside a deeply suspect antislavery spokesman, the play efficiently blocks most liberatory political entries. The differing positions in the Tom shows and in related dramatic productions therefore suggest that the *Uncle Tom's Cabin* plays did not at all mark something so unequivocal as a turn in working-class racial perspective. Rather, they intensified the racial terms of working-class debate. There were now "northern" and "southern" portions of the northern popular classes; the perennial conflicts over labor's racial politics intersected with struggles over sectional policy, each giving spark to the other. Put another way, national controversy over slavery disrupted alliances between workers even as conflicts over labor's proper racial alignments furthered sectional dislocation. Not the least of *Uncle Tom's Cabin*'s stage achievements was to force together these different realms of feeling—one local, diurnal, a matter of daily bread and racial responsiveness; one national, broadly political, a situation of major historical significance.

This was, of course, also the purpose of mid–nineteenth-century political parties, and the competing versions of *Uncle Tom* soon had their party equivalents.[31] Two months into the *Uncle Tom's Cabin* stage feud, in January 1854, Stephen A. Douglas introduced his Kansas-Nebraska bill into congressional debate. The purpose of the bill was to grant to local governments the right to declare slavery legal in territory formerly established as free by the 1820 Missouri Compromise. The bitter fight over Kansas-Nebraska was the revolutionary centerpiece of the 1850s, dramatically confirming sectional divisions, destroying the major political parties, and—in the actual combat in "Bleeding Kansas" between those favoring and those opposing Douglas's "popular sovereignty"—foreshadowing the war to come. Douglas's bill was widely perceived as a test of party loyalty for those Democrats who persisted in their Free-Soil sympathies. The 1848 Free-Soil presidential run of erstwhile Democrat Martin Van Buren, in opposition to what the radical Barnburners perceived to be Polk's pandering to the South and proslavery expansionism, had already weakened national party ties; despite the Compromise and the overwhelming Democratic victory of Franklin Pierce in 1852, Van Buren's attempt made the Democratic defections in the wake of Douglas's bill that much easier.[32] Where before there had been an uneasy cross-sectional Democratic coalition enlisting a majority of workers under a banner of southern appeasement, there was now no party consensus at all on the issue of slavery. Together with factional conflict over other issues (temperance, nativism, internal improvements, patronage), the slavery controversy dealt a hard blow to the Democrats, producing an electoral debacle in 1854. The two-party system was breaking down, evidenced most succinctly by Whig editor Horace Greeley's proposal that Democratic editor William Cullen Bryant, no friend of Greeley's, head the 1856 New York State ticket of the newly formed Republican party.[33] The *Uncle Tom* controversy was both product and portrait of the social energies that gave rise to this political upheaval, as the *Spirit of the Times,* among others, perceived. "The slavery agitation has been augmented by the passage of the Nebraska-Kansas bill, and a little zest is given to the votaries of negro freedom by an attendance at the Bowery or National. . . . We have nothing to do here with the matter, politically, but we can perceive what the drama may do to foster or eradicate passions and prejudices of high or low degree" (March 11, 1854).

Sectional thinking had come alive in the North. Party politics had been for decades a way of keeping sectional tension out of the public sphere; the coming of the Civil War witnessed the displacement of national politics by sectional insurgency. The Democratic defectors' contribution to the Republicans, for example, was stunning; one Democrat wrote to the *New York Tribune* that he had voted for Pierce, Cass, and Polk in the previous three elections but was calling in 1854 for a fusion of elements to oppose the Nebraska bill. The House vote on the bill made clear the northern Democratic split: forty-four Democrats voted for, forty-three against.[34] (This fact alone calls into question some writers' easy equation of northern workingmen with the Democratic party and therefore the prosouthern stance in these years.)[35] Specifically sectional perspectives produced the Republican party in 1854–56 out of a coalition of Liberty party members, liberal Whigs, and anti–Nebraska bill Democrats. The Republicans came together around a belief in the northern way of life: "free labor," antiexpansionism, and rather ambivalent racial feeling. The achievement of the Republicans was to turn adherence to a renovative ideal of capitalist labor into a sectional critique of the South and the extension of slavery, bringing together the interests of workers and abolitionists (and, to be sure, racists) in a way that seemed synonymous with northern well-being. Aiken's version of *Uncle Tom's Cabin* clearly resembled this fusion of ideas, beliefs, and feelings, and it struck a chord among the northern popular classes. Of course, it is impossible to know the influence of Aiken's play on Republican party formation, parallel development though it may have been; but in the increasingly visible and sophisticated sphere of popular culture it gave great emotional weight to the divisions that had begun to occur. In an era in which, as Eric Foner has observed, politics was itself becoming part of the culture industry, the ubiquity of *Uncle Tom* and its unavoidable sectional emphasis surely played its part (*Politics* 30–31). Not least among Aiken's adherents, perhaps, were those who rejected the "white slavery" call of southern-sympathizing New York

Democrats—the specter of free blacks clamoring for white men's rightful jobs. In the 1856 election the Republicans indeed appealed to workers by publicizing southern proslavery figures' derogatory remarks about northern wage earners, nicely joining sectional and labor critiques.[36] At the very least, *Uncle Tom's Cabin* registered these changes in sectional alignment and the vicissitudes in labor's racial politics; as the foremost racial melodrama of the day, it brought political and social change into the realm of feeling and crystallized it into memorable and irrecusable images.

But of course there was no end to class struggle, as the continued supersession of racial concerns by class anxiety suggests. Class energies had themselves reemerged after a decade of slumber; the New York tailors' strike of 1850 led to the first state-sponsored violence in history against urban American workers (Wilentz 380). I have noted that the Industrial Congress, after 1850 a leading coalition of the trades, was antislavery in its platform but in the ensuing decade remained indifferent to its agitation, preferring "to abolish Wages Slavery before we meddle with Chattel Slavery" (quoted in Wilentz 382). These no doubt were Conway's partisans, as were all those workers Iver Bernstein has described as disgusted with centralized Republican party politics in New York City and determined to flout them (96–97). Conway's play mediated upheaval in the nation's party organizations, but it flowed even more directly from the class resentments responsible for the rhetoric of "white slavery." Union at all costs, indifference to slavery, the immediacy of northern working-class oppression: these were the pressing concerns hardly veiled in the background and foreground of Conway's play, and they resonated with portions of the working class ready to refuse the rule of reforming Republican politicians.[37] Whether craftsmen desiring wage earners to mount a distinctively working-class influence outside the major parties or proletarianized artisans less put off by middle-class reformers' interventions in Congress, many workers still demurred from slavery agitation. Their party was the Democracy, and wage labor their reality.[38]

The terrific conflicts among and within the *Uncle Tom's Cabin* plays root us in the national-popular struggles of the 1850s. A peculiarly fissured text in all of its dramatic versions, *Uncle Tom* relied on strategies of blackface representation that unsettled the plays even as the differing dramas put such stage conventions to largely conflicting uses. The sectional divide to which the competing versions of the play bore witness abutted questions of popular racial alliance and testified to cracks in the national bloc that only a state apparatus imposed during a great civil war would at last address.[39] There was ultimately to be just one reigning mode of production, but it would have to be won in a long and bitter conflagration. The final stage directions of Aiken's *Uncle Tom's Cabin* provide grim commentary on that battle: *"Impressive music.—Slow curtain."*

Afterword

I have located contradictions in blackface performance and in nineteenth-century racial ideologies that combined to produce a variety of unsuspected political effects. What I have called the social unconscious of blackface suggests that the whites involved in minstrelsy were far from unenthusiastic about black cultural practices or, conversely, untroubled by them, continuous though the economic logic of blackface was with slavery. As often as not, this involvement depended on an intersection of racial and class languages that occasionally became confused with one another, reinforcing the general air of political jeopardy in minstrel acts. The vernacular rowdiness of such acts helped turn them into acknowledged, if unlikely, representatives of a peculiarly American culture. At every turn blackface minstrelsy has seemed a form in which transgression and containment coexisted, in which improbably threatening or startlingly sympathetic racial meanings were simultaneously produced and dissolved. Neither the social relations on which blackface delineations depended, the delineations themselves, their commercial setting, nor their ideological effects were monolithic or simply hegemonic. The question then arises: what were the immediate cultural and historical results of this "seeming counterfeit"?

As the nation edged toward civil war, Herman Melville issued a meditation on this subject in the June 1855 *Putnam's Monthly*, a journal founded two years earlier out of the collapse of Young America's literary nationalism. Where Young America had paid remarkably superficial attention to race—the Neddy Mellish–Pompey Smith subplot in Cornelius Mathews's *Big Abel and the Little Manhattan* (1845) is a perfect example—Melville had from his earliest work highlighted the victims of slavery and Manifest Destiny, and in "Benito Cereno" foregrounded the problem of racial representation itself.[1] We might indeed see the story as Melville's version of the minstrel show, in which he ingeniously brings together the narrative paradigm of slave insurrection with the ironies and conundrums of minstrel acts. The slaves-turned-mutineers disguised as slaves aboard the *San Dominick* are in virtual blackface, performing for the liberal northern visitor too blinkered to know better. The implication is that Captain Delano's inadequate responses to the slaves in secret revolt have been so conditioned by forms such as minstrelsy that the blacks are reduced to instances of white fantasy about them, a fact the insurrectionaries use to their advantage. Yet Melville's pessimism about

234

the effects of white racial discourse is revealed in the way the rebelling slaves are, for most of the story, stuck in mid-drama, frozen in the midst of revolutionary activity. In Melville's view there is apparently no possible emergence from behind the minstrel mask even in the act of revolt, which is to say that the mask itself interrupts the attempt to throw it off. "Benito Cereno" implicates the minstrel show in what it sees as the grim course of racial politics and indeed of American history in the 1850s.

Melville's peers among the northern liberal bourgeoisie were more sanguine if less thoughtful about the representation of black people and black culture. Following upon the romantic-racialist vogue of *Uncle Tom's Cabin* and Stephen Foster's songs, and celebrated by Harriet Beecher Stowe herself, a black singer named Elizabeth Greenfield enjoyed a brief renown in the 1850s. Greenfield, known as the "Black Swan" (no doubt in mimicry of Jenny Lind, the "Swedish Nightingale"), seemed to Stowe and others to capture the promise of blackface minstrelsy's cultural "blackening." Though noted particularly for her classical repertoire (Handel, Bellini, Donizetti), Greenfield was known to sing not only "Home! Sweet Home!" but also Foster's "Old Folks at Home." Stowe's memory of one Greenfield concert indicates the uncertainties surrounding this attempt to turn Stephen Foster to the account of a black people's tradition. For the "choicest of the *elite*" of London, surrounded by other singers bent on national illustration, Greenfield sings as a representative of her race:

> Miss Greenfield's turn for singing now came, and there was profound atten-tion. Her voice, with its keen, searching fire, its penetrating vibrant quality, its *"timbre,"* as the French have it, cut its way like a Damascus blade to the heart. It was the more touching from occasional rusticities and artistic defects, which showed that she had received no culture from art.
>
> She sang the ballad, "Old folks at home," giving one verse in the soprano, and another in the tenor voice.

One enraptured English lord, according to Stowe, declared the "use of these halls for the encouragement of an outcast race, a *consecration.*" The reverent response to Greenfield pressed upon Stowe the realization that "there really is no natural prejudice against colour in the human mind."[2]

But the fascination with the "Black Swan's" artless and pitiable persona, not to mention her proximity to blackface, sounded a distinct note of condescension, and easily flipped over into contempt. One spectator at a New York performance, Alfred Bunn, heaped derision on Greenfield, and, turning to a discussion of a women's rights advocate, he ventured to describe "Miss Lucy Neale (Stone, we beg the lady's pardon)," invoking the minstrel "wench" character (Lucy Neale) the "Black Swan" had suggested to him (61). Indeed, the immediately ensuing history of black stage representation indicates the highly problematic status of such performances. Black organizations such as the Fisk Jubilee Singers took the stage in the 1870s to perform black "sorrow songs," or spirituals, to astonished ears; but, like Elizabeth Greenfield, they included Foster songs in their repertoire, confounding the notion of a distinctive African-American people's tradition. In fact the group had already been mistaken for minstrel performers and had taken the name Jubilee Singers to differentiate themselves from such acts. Soon after, both black and white blackface minstrel troupes began assuming the rubric of "jubilee" singing groups, mixing minstrel songs with spirituals and effectively muddying the traditions. The people's-culture gambit, once infected by the minstrel tradition, would remain a highly ambiguous one into the twentieth century (Toll 236–37).

Perhaps sensing this impure confluence of traditions, Martin Delany's black-nationalist novel *Blake: or, The Huts of America* (1859–61) devises a complex reinvention of the minstrel tradition. Delany refuses to settle for Melville's liberal despair. Similar to "Benito Cereno," *Blake* narrates a planned slave uprising, and here, too, insurrectionary energies intersect with minstrel forms. But Delany makes guerilla appropriations of Stephen Foster plantation melodies, gives them new and often parodic lyrics, and in this way furnishes his rebels with songs of revolution. Foster's pathetic "Old Uncle Ned" (1848), for example, which mourns the passing of the slave Old Ned, arms Delany with a song that wishes good riddance upon the master:

> Hang up the shovel and the hoe o o o!
> I don't care whether I work or no!
> Old master's gone to the slaveholders rest—
> He's gone where they all ought to go!
>
> (105–6)

Blake writes black agency back into history through blackface songs taken "back" from those who had plundered black cultural practices. Rather than reject the cultural territory whites had occupied by way of minstrelsy, Delany recognizes that occupation as fact and occupies it in turn. In Delany's novel, black claims on the national culture, given distorted but influential shape in the minstrel show, come home to roost. Through a vivifying irony, *Blake* transforms the impact of black cultural practices on American culture into the political movement they had augured—anticipating with relish the imminent conflict so many northern white intellectuals would mourn.[3]

These three moments from the tail end of my history capture the range of minstrelsy's cultural results. The conflicts they signify, like most cultural conflicts, held a tenuous relation to concrete social turbulence, but they were ultimately those of a social order in the midst of a great renegotiation of the character and color of labor. The overwhelming working-class white (and, when legalized, black) enlistment in the Union cause was one worldly outcome of these cultural ideas, feelings, and acts, which blackface tunes sometimes acknowledged by putting the Union in blackface: "For soon we'll stop each rebel raid / When I march along wid de Black Brigade" (Brower 9). But there were other, bleaker responses, as is suggested by the northern popularity of Dan Emmett's famous

236

"Dixie" (1859), a blackface plantation melody in the traditional mold adopted by the Confederacy as its theme song.[4] As the Civil War entered its third year, New York was beset by racial rioting on a scale hitherto unequaled in American history. In response to an 1863 federal conscription act intended to bolster flagging volunteer Union armies, unskilled Irish workers revolted, dealing death and destruction to blacks and black property throughout the city. Draftees included all men aged twenty to thirty-five (if unmarried twenty to forty-five). Those able to hire a substitute or pay a $300 fee could be legally exempted from service; poorer men perceiving themselves to be fighting someone else's war rebelled against the Republican law with arson, looting, machine-breaking, sabotage of railroad and telegraph lines, and murder and public sexual mutilation of blacks. The cost was at least one hundred and five lives and over $1 million in property.[5]

This violence, too, was part of the cultural milieu that nurtured blackface performance. One blackface song, "The Bonny Green Flag," expressed the rioters' sentiments outright: "They say that the Irish need not apply, / But when soldiers they want, in the front Pat is seen."[6] At the same time, I have hoped to emphasize the terrific variability in class and racial feeling surrounding such events. As W. E. B. Du Bois perceived, the racial violence of the draft riots was inseparable from a class context that was manipulated to serve the ruling elites, and in which pinched class circumstances forestalled interracial recognitions and solidarity.[7] Capitalism was ultimately the enemy, but racial feeling the immediate obstacle; energies directed against the state apparatus might too easily join those focused on black people. This dialectic has provided the principal themes of my study. Class straits may energize interracial cooperation, but they are also often likely to close down the possibility of interracial embrace. In the 1830s upper-class reformers alien to the proletarian public sphere were apt to interrupt the incipient solidarity marked by the radical slogan "wage slavery." When the existence of any wages at all became an open question in the depression years, a racial scapegoat was quite convenient to a white-egalitarian alliance of workers and employers. The variability of white racial feeling reemerged in the years of America's 1848, though the North largely backed by way of class-based struggles into the conflicts over slavery that were to produce the Civil War. The social contradictions issuing from a national entity based on competing modes of economic production, together with labor's conflicts over whether to oppose wage slavery or chattel slavery, confirm that the question of American labor in the broadest sense could be addressed only after the demise of slavery.

The charge has been leveled by some historians that the antislavery movement deflected attention from northern working conditions and forestalled a rigorous critique of capitalist wage relations—precisely the charge of some workers in the antebellum North.[8] But, as David Roediger has observed, it is more accurate to say that *slavery*, not antislavery, prevented the full-circle critique of capitalism on behalf of all workers which could emerge (if in intermittent fashion) only after the war. Neither the abolitionists, the labor movement, nor even the Republicans fully developed the interracial prolabor argument that the Civil War for the first time made available, if not exactly inevitable (*Wages* 87, 174). Shortly after the war, in 1867, Karl Marx wrote that in the "United States of North America, every independent movement of the workers was paralysed so long as slavery disfigured a part of the Republic. Labour cannot emancipate itself in the white skin where in the black it is branded."[9] How could any but these words from *Capital* form the appropriate ending to my story? Marx's image of labor as a great Blakean body, with certain of its parts immobilized owing to the shackling of others, gestures to the immensity of the "emancipation" these words invoke: not mere trade union unity—even less bourgeois "tolerance"—but a visionary conception of human collectivity.

Notes

Introduction

1. Alexander Saxton, "Blackface Minstrelsy and Jacksonian Ideology" 27.
2. Since this work is still in the process of formation, any listing of it must be eclectic and inexhaustive: John Szwed, "Race and the Embodiment of Culture"; Barbara Fields, "Ideology and Race in American History" and "Slavery, Race, and Ideology in the United States of America"; Homi Bhabha, "The Other Question" and "Of Mimicry and Man"; Barbara Johnson, "Metaphor, Metonymy, and Voice in *Their Eyes Were Watching God*" and "Mirror Stages"; the essays in Henry Louis Gates, Jr., ed., *"Race," Writing, and Difference;* Stuart Hall, "Gramsci's Relevance for the Study of Race and Ethnicity"; Hazel Carby, *Reconstructing Womanhood;* Paul Gilroy, *"There Ain't No Black in the Union Jack";* Philip Cohen, "Tarzan and the Jungle Bunnies"; the essays in Kobena Mercer, ed., *Black Film/British Cinema;* Richard Dyer, "White"; the essays in Cheryl Wall, ed., *Changing Our Own Words;* Andrew Ross, "Ballots, Bullets, or Batmen"; David Roediger, *The Wages of Whiteness;* Tania Modleski, *Feminism Without Women* 115–34; Lauren Berlant, "National Brands/National Body"; Kobena Mercer, "Skin Head Sex Thing" and "'1968'"; bell hooks, "Representing Whiteness in the Black Imagination"; Vron Ware, *Beyond the Pale;* Michael Rogin, "Blackface, White Noise"; Toni Morrison, *Playing in the Dark;* and Christopher Looby, "'As Thoroughly Black as the Most Faithful Philanthropist Could Desire.'"
3. I am thinking here of Stuart Hall, "The Meaning of New Times" and "New Ethnicities"; Dick Hebdige, *Hiding in the Light;* Andrew Ross, *No Respect;* Mary Childers and bell hooks, "A Conversation about Race and Class"; and others.
4. This point is made forcefully in David Roediger, "'Labor in White Skin,'" and Stanley Aronowitz, "Writing Labor's History."
5. For some acute remarks on this missed chance, see Mike Davis, *Prisoners of the American Dream* 18–29.
6. On Lincoln's enjoyment of minstrelsy in Chicago, see Jesse Weik, *The Real Lincoln* 75, 85–86, and Albert Beveridge, *Abraham Lincoln* 1:536, 597–98.
7. For a reading of *Black Like Me,* see Eric Lott, "White Like Me."
8. Michael Rogin, "Blackface, White Noise" 417–19.
9. Robert Cantwell, *Bluegrass Breakdown* 249–74; Robert Dawidoff, "Some of Those Days"; Armond White, "The White Albums" 21.
10. Robert Winans, "The Folk, the Stage, and the Five-String Banjo in the Nineteenth Century" and "The Black Banjo-Playing Tradition in Virginia and West Virginia." Those interested in hearing historical recreations of antebellum minstrelsy are directed to the recordings *Popular Music in Jacksonian America* and *The Early Minstrel Show.*
11. Raymond Williams, *Marxism and Literature* 133–34, emphasis in original. I use

Williams's phrase "structures of feeling" to refer, as he does, to a "structured formation which, because it is at the very edge of semantic availability, has many of the characteristics of a pre-formation, until specific articulations—new semantic figures—are discovered in material practice" (134). Williams's concept is far more useful, it seems to me, than conventional, functionalist ideas of racial "relations" or "pathologies" because it inquires into the social and historical "lived" quality of meanings and values, and into the complex and historically variable relation between these and more formally held beliefs or ideologies.

12. In this I follow Stuart Hall's argument against the misleading view that "because racism is everywhere a deeply anti-human and anti-social practice . . . therefore it is everywhere *the same*—either in its forms, its relations to other structures and processes, or its effects." See "Gramsci's Relevance for the Study of Race and Ethnicity" 23.

13. It may be that by the 1920s an imaginary proximity to "blackness" was so requisite to white identity and to the culture industry which helped produce that identity—witness the sudden vogue of the suntan—that the signifier of blackface had become redundant; the apposite development of forceful public black cultural production in the Harlem Renaissance also made itself felt. The death of minstrelsy as a (professional, not college fraternity) stage activity, however, does not speak to blackface's lingering presence on the motion picture screen—minstrelsy's somewhat baffling afterlife. I am grateful to Harry Stecopoulos for confirming my hunch about racial subjectivity in the 1920s; on blackface in the movies, see Joseph Boskin, *Sambo* 148–63, and Tania Modleski, *Feminism Without Women* 115–34.

14. The locus classicus for this view is Carl Wittke, *Tambo and Bones*, with its elision (but for assurances about the character of the "darky") of racial politics altogether. More recent examples of such nostalgia have been furnished by the United States Congress, with the disclosures that Representative Robert Michel (R-Illinois) and Senator Alan Simpson (R-Wyoming) respectively enjoyed and performed in minstrel shows.

15. For excellent exceptions, see Berndt Ostendorf, *Black Literature in White America* 65–94, and Robert Cantwell, *Bluegrass Breakdown* 249–74.

16. See, for example, Eve Sedgwick on the relation of representations of sexuality to social power in *Between Men* 7.

17. For examples of the first tendency, see Hans Nathan, *Dan Emmett and the Rise of Early Negro Minstrelsy* (on minstrel music and dance), or William Mahar, "Black English in Early Blackface Minstrelsy" (on dialect), both excellent pieces of research; for examples of the second tendency, see Carl Wittke, *Tambo and Bones*, Constance Rourke, *American Humor* 77–104, and Robert Toll, *Blacking Up*.

18. For a view of American Studies as a "cautionary example" to cultural studies (one the writer himself might have heeded), see Patrick Brantlinger, *Crusoe's Footprints* 26–33; on American Studies scholarship as radical cultural criticism, see Alan Trachtenberg, "Myth and Symbol"; on its relationship to British cultural studies and Marxism, see, for instance, Leo Marx, "The Long Revolution"; Gary Hentzi and Jon Anderson, "An Interview with Jonathan Arac" 7; Michael Denning, "'The Special American Conditions'"; Joel Pfister, "The Americanization of Cultural Studies"; and Cary Nelson, "Always Already Cultural Studies."

19. Raymond Williams, *Culture* 92–93.

20. For an extended discussion, see Michael Denning, "'The Special American Conditions.'"

21. For examples of this tendency (notably the work of Lawrence Grossberg and John Fiske) and a partial exoneration, see Joel Pfister, "The Americanization of Cultural Studies" 205.

22. This possibility was suggested to me by a reading of Donna Haraway, "A Manifesto for Cyborgs"; see esp. 91.

23. For an analysis of Reagan-Thatcher "authoritarian populism," see Stuart Hall, *The Hard Road to Renewal;* on the social context of recent cultural theory, see Michael Denning, "The End of Mass Culture."

24. For examples in which disgruntled blacks obstruct the development of a reconstructed welfare state, see J. Anthony Lukas, *Common Ground;* William Julius Wilson, *The Truly Disadvantaged;* Shelby Steele, *The Content of Our Character;* Jim Sleeper, *The Closest of Strangers;* Thomas Byrne Edsall and Mary D. Edsall, *Chain Reaction.*

25. Stanley Aronowitz, "Writing Labor's History" 172–73.

Chapter 1

1. Each of these positions is of course underwritten by an intellectual tradition as old as "mass" culture itself. The view of capitalist popular culture as a "culture industry" that systematically cretinizes and depoliticizes an ever more passive populace is best articulated in the writings of the Frankfurt School; its classic expression is Theodor Adorno and Max Horkheimer, "The Culture Industry." The populist view of mass culture as a less mediated phenomenon of "the people" is perhaps most forcefully argued by Leslie Fiedler in *What Was Literature?*

2. My theoretical framework is indebted to Stuart Hall, "Notes on Deconstructing 'the Popular'"; Michael Denning, *Mechanic Accents;* and T. J. Clark, *The Painting of Modern Life* 205–39. More generally these formulations, and many that follow, are drawn from work on culture industry phenomena by scholars associated with the Birmingham Centre for Contemporary Cultural Studies, including Richard Hoggart, *The Uses of Literacy;* Stuart Hall et al., *Policing the Crisis;* Richard Johnson, "What is Cultural Studies Anyway?"; Paul Gilroy, *"There Ain't No Black in the Union Jack";* and Dick Hebdige, *Hiding in the Light.* Like-minded work in the United States includes Fredric Jameson, "Reification and Utopia in Mass Culture"; Jean Franco, "What's in a Name?"; Tania Modleski, *Feminism Without Women;* and Hazel Carby, *Reconstructing Womanhood.* The pervasive influence of the work of Steven Marcus should also be acknowledged here, especially his pioneering effort in *The Other Victorians* to make cultural sense of dubious text.

3. As does this minstrel conundrum: "Why are minstrel companies like midnight robbers? Because they live by their deeds of darkness" (*White's New Book* 31).

4. "Cuff"—a kind of common-denominator figure of nineteenth-century white fantasy about black people—shows up again in Harriet Beecher Stowe's "Parson's Horse Race" (1878), in which cultural appropriation is revealed to be a one-way street: "Cuff was the doctor's nigger man, and he was nat'lly a drefful proud critter! The way he would swell and strut and brag about the doctor and his folks and his things! The doctor used to give Cuff his cast-off clothes, and Cuff would prance round in 'em and seem to think he was a doctor of divinity himself, and had the charge of all natur" (472). Obviously this scene is insufficiently ironized—precisely *because* cultural appropriation is a one-way street; black borrowings from the dominant culture, according to whites, result by definition in absurdity. The scene affords a rather bleak, though probably unconscious, commentary on Reconstruction from the author of *Uncle Tom's Cabin.*

5. Mrs. Anne Mathews, *A Continuation of the Memoirs of Charles Mathews, Comedian* 1:239.

6. Carl Wittke, *Tambo and Bones* 75; *New York Herald* January 1, 1848.

7. Among these are Al Field, *Watch Yourself Go By* 113, and "Reminiscences" (I am

indebted to Robert Toll, *Blacking Up* 38, for these references). See also P. T. Barnum's *Struggles and Triumphs* (1869), in which a backstage altercation arises because the young Barnum in blackface is mistaken for an impudent black man (90).

8. Mark Twain, *Autobiography* 62, 60.

9. On the purposes and value of the genealogy, see Michel Foucault, "Nietzsche, Genealogy, History." Concerted attempts to narrate a minstrel-show "ancestry" include Olive Logan, "The Ancestry of Brudder Bones"; Brander Matthews, "Rise and Fall of Negro Minstrelsy"; and George Rehin, "Harlequin Jim Crow." These attempts are mistaken because, while illuminating—I have called on them to produce my genealogy—they finally make no room for historical discontinuity in the wearing of blackface, positing a kind of linear development; and they tend to underplay the central racial dimension—even, in the case of Rehin, to argue its only secondary importance.

10. There is a second, subsidiary purpose to this genealogy, which Cornel West has clarified in a position paper regarding the study of race in Marxist cultural studies. That is briefly to elucidate some specific American resonances of the various western white-supremacist discursive logics: Judeo-Christian (blackness as divine curse), scientific (blackness as anthropological object), and psychosexual (blackness as vengeful father, carefree child, dirt, excrement). See West, "Marxist Theory and the Specificity of Afro-American Oppression" 22–24; see also, in this regard, Joel Kovel, *White Racism.*

In my genealogy I have purposely tried not to privilege literary representations of black people, to respect the relative autonomy of broadly "theatrical" ones. Literary representations, in any case, largely reiterate the contradictions and problems I note in this discussion. For analyses of such literary representations, see Francis Gaines, *The Southern Plantation;* Sterling Brown, *The Negro in American Fiction;* Jean Fagan Yellin, *The Intricate Knot;* William Van Deburg, *Slavery and Race in American Popular Culture* 31–39; and, more generally, William Taylor, *Cavalier and Yankee.* As for artistic representations, see Albert Boime, *The Art of Exclusion,* and Sue Bridwell Beckham, "By 'N' By Hard Times."

11. Harlequin, for instance, was a rustic with a strong dialect, whose role, according to Marmontel, was "that of a patient servant, loyal, credulous, greedy, always amorous, always getting his master or himself into a scrape" (quoted in Nicoll 73–74): a description very close to those of some minstrel types. Indeed, in certain late eighteenth-century theatrical productions a slave is turned into a harlequin by a wizard, and after marrying his master's daughter lives happily ever after (Gates, *Figures* 52). Both the outrage and the amusement of such activities were to be found in the minstrel show. (Pantomime and minstrelsy, Harlequin and Jim Crow, were literally conjoined at New York's Kemp's Lyceum in 1848. George Odell, *Annals of the New York Stage* 5:494).

For slave tricksters, see Lawrence Levine, *Black Culture and Black Consciousness* 102–33. For earlier blackface figures on the stage, see Charles Baskervill, *The Elizabethan Jig* 286–88; Pierre Duchartre, *The Italian Comedy* 124, 135; David Mayer, *Harlequin in His Element* 44; Allardyce Nicoll, *The World of Harlequin* 73–74; Henry Louis Gates, *Figures in Black* 51–53; and George Rehin, "Harlequin Jim Crow."

12. George Rehin, "Harlequin Jim Crow" 687. In *Figures in Black* Henry Louis Gates argues that in minstrel representations the black and white mask of the Harlequin is split into the black "Tambo" and the white "Bones" (52). While some interesting observations follow from this idea, it strikes me as mostly fanciful. It is even unclear whether the interlocutor of the early minstrel show appeared in whiteface; and I know of no accounts of the endmen which indicate that one was white and the other black.

13. S. Foster Damon, *Series of Old American Songs* no. 16.

14. Huggins suggestively but rather too hastily assimilates all early minstrel figures to those of Mike Fink, Davy Crockett, and (their northern counterpart) Yankee Doodle

(*Harlem Renaissance* 249). That there was significant overlap is uncontroversial, as John Blair makes clear in "Blackface Minstrels in Cross-Cultural Perspective" 55. But this overlap neither accounts for the varied cultural effects such figures could produce nor for the songs that do not feature such types. Robert Cantwell somewhat overingeniously argues that minstrel performers who called on such types were involved in a multilayered act of *self*-parody—that minstrel types resembled Fink and Crockett because they parodied black styles that originated in parody of white men (*Bluegrass Breakdown* 261).

15. In *Black Literature in White America* Berndt Ostendorf talks about the minstrel show as a kind of compromise formation between the poles of "intermixture and insurrection" (69).

Nathan Huggins and Sylvia Wynter have produced psychosexual arguments that extend Ellison's critique in interesting ways. Huggins reads minstrel figures as projections of all that the dominant culture deemed undesirable (albeit fascinating) (244–301); Wynter gives them a Lacanian gloss, seeing in the qualities attributed to the (b)lack the inverse of what the dominant culture considered human ("Sambos and Minstrels"). For this line of thinking in regard to the *longue durée* of western colonialism and slavery, see Frantz Fanon, *Black Skin, White Masks* 141–209, and George Rawick, *From Sundown to Sunup* 128–33.

16. Damon, *Series of Old American Songs* no. 14.

17. In "Mirror Stages" Barbara Johnson remarks that if the (Lacanian) phallus is almost by definition white, the penis must be black—which accounts for its unruly and threatening potential. I am grateful to Michael Rogin for a similar point in regard to my project. In *Black Skin, White Masks*, Frantz Fanon remarks that in the white imagination, "the Negro . . . is a penis" (170; emphasis in original).

18. In *Vested Interests* Garber pursues this thesis rather singlemindedly; see also Natalie Zemon Davis, *Society and Culture in Early Modern France* 132. I return to blackface cross-dressing in chapters 2 and 6.

19. As Carroll Smith-Rosenberg has demonstrated in "Davy Crockett as Trickster," another would surely be the various 1830s and 1840s Crockett almanacs, revealing compendiums of misogynist and male homosexual fantasy. "Wench" characters were cut from the same cloth.

20. *Christy and Wood's New Song Book* 85–86.

21. See Claudia Johnson, "That Guilty Third Tier" for a discussion of antebellum theater prostitution; see also Patricia Cline Cohen, "Unregulated Youth."

22. Susan Davis, "'Making Night Hideous'" 187–92 and *Parades and Power* 77–111, esp. 106. I have also learned much from Dale Cockrell, "The Early Blackface Minstrel and His World."

23. Davis, "'Making Night Hideous'" 192; see also Paul Gilje, *The Road to Mobocracy* 258–60.

24. Alexander Saxton introduces the useful phrase "white egalitarianism" to describe the adherence of the popular classes in this period to both white supremacy and democratic (class) ideals. See *The Rise and Fall of the White Republic* 221. This is Saxton's version of what Pierre van der Berghe has termed "herrenvolk democracy." On van der Berghe, see George Fredrickson, *The Black Image in the White Mind* 65, 84, 90–94.

25. For an argument about race in which this is an ever-present possibility, see Stuart Hall, "New Ethnicities" 28–29.

26. This song on the Kensington nativist riot of 1844 *might* be considered a tenuous vindication of minstrelsy in regard to Jacksonian rioting:

Oh, in Philadelphia folks say how,
Dat Darkies kick up all de rows,
But de *riot* up in *Skensin'ton*
Beats all de darkies twelve to one.

An' I guess it wasn't de niggas dis time.
I guess it wasn't de niggas dis time,
I guess it wasn't de niggas dis time, Mr. Mayor,
I guess it wasn't de niggas dis time.
("Philadelphia Riots," Dennison 134)

In any case, this song is ambiguous in precisely the ways I have been outlining.

27. This tradition includes Margaret Fuller, "Entertainments of the Past Winter"; "Letter from a Teacher at the South"; "The Black Opera"; "Negro Minstrelsy—Ancient and Modern"; "Songs of the Blacks"; W. E. B. Du Bois, "The Negro in Literature and Art"; Francis Gaines, *The Southern Plantation* 95–111; James Weldon Johnson, *Black Manhattan* 87; Constance Rourke, *American Humor* 77–104; S. Foster Damon, "The Negro in Early American Songsters"; Stanley Edgar Hyman, "American Negro Literature and Folk Tradition"; Hans Nathan, *Dan Emmett;* George Rehin, "The Darker Image"; Orrin Clayton Suthern, "Minstrelsy and Popular Culture"; William Austin, *"Susanna," "Jeanie," and "The Old Folks at Home";* David Grimsted and William Stowe, "White-Black Humor"; Robert Winans, "The Folk, the Stage, and the Five-String Banjo"; Berndt Ostendorf, *Black Literature in White America* 65–94; Robert Cantwell, *Bluegrass Breakdown* 249–74; William Mahar, "Black English in Early Blackface Minstrelsy" and "'Backside Albany' and Early Blackface Minstrelsy"; W. T. Lhamon, "Constance Rourke's Secret Reserve"; and Carl Bryan Holmberg and Gilbert Schneider, "Daniel Decatur Emmett's Stump Sermons."

28. Ralph Ellison, "Change the Joke" 50. In "Twain's 'Nigger' Jim" Bernard Bell marshalls much evidence of Mark Twain's "socialization in the ethics of Jim Crow": his love of minstrelsy, his brief enlistment in a Confederate militia, the racism of some early (private and published) letters, his apprenticeship in the racism of southwestern humor, and internal evidence from *Huck Finn* itself, obviously the underside of Clemens's complex investment in black culture.

29. See also Fredrick Woodard and Donnarae MacCann's *"Huckleberry Finn* and the Traditions of Blackface Minstrelsy." As they point out, the unfinished "Tom Sawyer's Conspiracy" includes a scene in which Tom goes to his aunt's garret to find "our old nigger-show things" and plan a "nigger" disguise (11–13, n.4). Mark Twain's imaginative encounters with race seem to have been unavoidably bound up with blackface minstrelsy. Soon after leaving Hannibal for New York in 1853, Twain wrote his mother about free blacks in the North: "I reckon I had better black my face, for in these Eastern States niggers are considerably better than white people" (quoted in Bell 11).

30. Guy Cardwell, *Twins of Genius* 105. I have benefited from Steven Mailloux's discussion of this issue in *Rhetorical Power* 57–99 and from Forrest Robinson, *In Bad Faith* 111–211.

31. Quoted in Fredrickson, *The Black Image in the White Mind* 102. This is the contradictory "other half" of the image of the potent and frightening black male. These two images, as John Blassingame observes, existed together in a kind of dialectical relationship, the one assuaging fears that the other raised. Both images certainly haunted the minstrel show. See *The Slave Community* 223–38, and, more generally, Fredrickson, *Black Image* 43–129.

32. Quoted in Fredrickson, *Black Image* 107.

33. Delany quoted in Wilson Moses, *The Golden Age of Black Nationalism* 46; Douglass quoted in Waldo Martin, *The Mind of Frederick Douglass* 235–36.

34. This tradition includes R. P. Nevin, "Stephen C. Foster and Negro Minstrelsy"; T. A. Brown, "The Origin of Negro Minstrelsy"; H. D. Stone, *Personal Recollections of the Drama* 240–41; Olive Logan, "The Ancestry of Brudder Bones"; N. M. Ludlow, *Dramatic Life as I Found It* 392–93; H. P. Phelps, *Players of a Century* 165–67; Brander Matthews, "The Rise and Fall of Negro Minstrelsy"; J. G. Burtnett, "National Elements in Stephen Foster's Art"; Dailey Paskman and Sigmund Spaeth, *"Gentlemen, Be Seated!"*; and Carl Wittke, *Tambo and Bones*.

35. This revived tradition includes M. H. Winter, "Juba and American Minstrelsy"; Bernard Wolfe, "Uncle Remus and the Malevolent Rabbit"; Frank Davidson, "The Rise, Development, Decline, and Influence of the American Minstrel Show"; Ralph Ellison, "Change the Joke and Slip the Yoke"; Kenneth Lynn, *Mark Twain and Southwestern Humor* 100–111; Cecil Patterson, "A Different Drum"; LeRoi Jones, *Blues People* 82–86; James Dorman, "The Strange Career of Jim Crow Rice" and "Shaping the Popular Image of Post-Reconstruction American Blacks"; Alan Green, "'Jim Crow,' 'Zip Coon'"; Russell Nye, *The Unembarrassed Muse* 162–69, 308–15; Nathan Huggins, *Harlem Renaissance* 244–301; Robert Toll, *Blacking Up;* Alexander Saxton, "Blackface Minstrelsy and Jacksonian Ideology"; Charles Hamm, *Yesterdays* 109–40; Sylvia Wynter, "Sambos and Minstrels"; Sam Dennison, *Scandalize My Name* 27–186; Jean Baker, *Affairs of Party* 213–43; William Van Deburg, *Slavery and Race in American Popular Culture* 17–24, 39–49; Joseph Boskin, *Sambo* 65–94; Robert Dawidoff, "Some of Those Days"; Houston Baker, *Modernism and the Harlem Renaissance* 17–24; David Roediger, *The Wages of Whiteness* 95–131; Jan Pieterse, *White On Black* 132–56; and Roger Abrahams, *Singing the Master* 131–53.

36. Stuart Hall, "New Ethnicities" 28–29.

37. Mark Twain, *Huckleberry Finn* 26. Indeed, in *Chants Democratic* Sean Wilentz argues that "the real object of scorn in these shows was less Jim Crow than the arriviste, would-be aristo—either the white interlocutor or the dandified black, both parodies of unmerited self-satisfied condescension" (259). Wilentz names the right targets, but I would insist with David Roediger that class meanings were always imbricated with working-class racial feeling ("Labor" 294; *Wages* 123)—though not, to be sure, in simple or politically guaranteed ways, as I argue throughout.

38. James Monroe Trotter, *Music and Some Highly Musical People* 271, 274. For more on the Georgia Minstrels, see Richard Waterhouse, *From Minstrel Shows to Vaudeville* 47–80.

39. Douglass was acutely aware of this problem. On tour in England in 1846, he found himself relentlessly exoticized—minstrelized. As he wrote to an abolitionist friend: "It is quite an advantage to be a nigger here. I find I am hardly black enough for British taste, but by keeping my hair as wooly as possible I make out to pass for at least half Negro at any rate" (quoted in Martin 116). Douglass's wicked irony depends on the fact that he was, precisely, "half Negro"—born of a black mother and a white father.

40. In *Incidents in the Life of a Slave Girl* Harriet Jacobs's escape to the shed where she would spend seven years is made in a blackface disguise; even "the father of [her] children" does not recognize her (437).

Chapter 2

1. On minstrelsy's northern aura and its threat to territory undergoing sectional tension (i.e., 1850s Kansas as well as the South), see Carl Wittke, *Tambo and Bones* 82–83.

2. For a similar point regarding Hoagy Carmichael's place in a twentieth-century commercial context, see Roger Hewitt, "Black Through White." I have also found useful Catherine Gallagher's discussion of Marx's analysis of the commodity in her review of Rachel Bowlby, *Just Looking,* and N. N. Feltes, *Modes of Production of Victorian Novels,* in addition to Bowlby and Feltes themselves.

3. Berndt Ostendorf observes that "the lower class folk in Western society, and blacks among them, have served the dominant classes in two ways: first in setting up the material basis of high civilization, second in healing the injuries of that civilization by maintaining alternative life styles and cultures" (77–78). The result, as John Szwed points out, is often that the dispossessed become bearers of the dominant classes' "folk" culture (30).

4. This is also the view of John Szwed, to whom I owe the coinage "minstrelization." See "Race and the Embodiment of Culture."

5. Many scholars have made a strong case for the existence of an identifiable black culture in the antebellum North, among them Leon Litwack, *North of Slavery* passim, esp. 187–213; Eileen Southern, *The Music of Black Americans* 53–59, 97–127; Theodore Hershberg, "Free Blacks in Antebellum Philadelphia"; Dena Epstein, *Sinful Tunes and Spirituals* 127ff.; Ira Berlin, "Time, Space, and the Evolution of Afro-American Society" 45–54 and "The Revolution in Black Life"; Sterling Stuckey, *Slave Culture* 73–83, 141–46; and Shane White, *Somewhat More Independent* 92–106, 150–206.

6. The first verses of "Backside Albany," also known as "The Siege of Plattsburg," go as follows:

Back side Albany stan' Lake Champlain,
One little pond, half full a' water
Plattebug dare too, close pon de main,
Town small—he grow bigger do hereater.
On Lake Champlain
Uncle Sam set he boat,
An Massa M'Donough he sail 'em;
While Gen'ral M'Comb
Make Plattebug he home,
Wid de army, who courage nebber fail 'em.

On 'lebenth day of September
In eighteen hund'ed an fourteen,
Gubbener Probose, and he British soger,
Come to Plattebug a tea party courtin;
An he boat come too
Arter Uncle Sam boat,
Massa 'Donough do look sharp out de winder—
Den Gen'ral M'Comb,
(Ah! he always a home,)
Catch fire too, jis like a tinder.

The battle follows, in which General Sir George Prevost is very patriotically defeated, as indeed he was in the Battle of Plattsburg (1814). See William Mahar's "'Backside Albany' and Early Blackface Minstrelsy" for this song and an analysis of it in regard to the battle it versifies.

7. These words are Herbie Hancock's, and he is talking about break dancing in the 1980s (36).

8. For accounts of the African Grove Theatre see Simon Snipe, *Sports of New York;* George Odell, *Annals of the New York Stage* 3:34–37, 70–71; Roi Ottley and William

Weatherby, ed., *The Negro in New York* 72–73; Herbert Marshall and Mildred Stock, *Ira Aldridge* 28–47; Errol Hill, *Shakespeare in Sable* 11–16; and Russell Sanjek, *American Popular Music and Its Business* 2:156–58.

9. "Stump speeches" do appear to have grown out of white observation of black churches and black street oratory, other fairly common theaters of racial interaction. Whites were clearly nonplussed by black religious practices. In part because of its demonstrative character, black worship put whites in mind of secular culture. One observer noted that hymns "were lengthened out with long repetition choruses" and sung "in the merry chorus-manner of the southern field harvest, or husking-frolic method of black slaves," generally including the foot stomping and thigh slapping that invoked "negro dancing in Virginia"—the sort of Sunday morning vehemence, he wrote, that prematurely awakened neighboring white workingmen sleeping off a Saturday night binge (quoted in Nash, *Forging* 223).

10. For a good sketch of Mathews in America, see Walter Blair, "Charles Mathews and His 'A Trip to America'"; see also Sam Dennison, *Scandalize My Name* 505–14.

11. For work on Pinkster, Election Day, and John Canoe festivities, see Edwin Olson, "Social Aspects of Slave Life in New York" 71–72; Eileen Southern, *The Music of Black Americans* 53–59; Lynne Emery, *Black Dance* 30–34, 140–45; Dena Epstein, *Sinful Tunes and Spirituals* 66–68; Ira Berlin, "Time, Space, and the Evolution of Afro-American Society" 53–54; Joseph Reidy, "'Negro Election Day'"; James Eights, "Pinkster Festivities in Albany Sixty Years Ago"; Lorenzo Greene, *The Negro in Colonial New England* 245–48; Ira Reid, "The John Canoe Festival"; Sterling Stuckey, *Slave Culture* 73–83, 142–44; Shane White, *Somewhat More Independent* 95–106; and Dale Cockrell, "The Early Blackface Minstrel and His World."

12. Not to mention of racial politics itself. Cincinnati, for example, home in the late 1830s and 1840s of Stephen Foster, Harriet Beecher Stowe, and the humanitarian lecturer Alexander Kinmont, has the odd distinction of being simultaneously the promised land to which Eliza Harris escapes in *Uncle Tom's Cabin* and the composition site of Foster's idyllic "Plantation Melodies."

13. See Mechal Sobel, *The World They Made Together,* for evidence (in Virginia) of the kinds of interracial cultural practices that develop in conditions of extensive racial contact; see also Carter Woodson, "The Negroes of Cincinnati Prior to the Civil War" and Howard and Judith Sacks, "Way Up North in Dixie" 421–25.

14. The crowning example is the work of Newman White. See "White Man in the Woodpile" and *American Negro Folk-Songs.*

15. Edward LeRoy Rice's *Monarchs of Minstrelsy*, though often sketchy, is the most comprehensive source for profiles of blackface performers.

16. See Saxton's "Blackface Minstrelsy and Jacksonian Ideology" 5–7, 15–16; see also Saxton's "George Wilkes" for some of the other activities of the milieu that nourished blackface performers. These articles have been incorporated into Saxton's study *The Rise and Fall of the White Republic.*

17. T. Allston Brown, *History of the American Stage* 202.

18. Consider an 1844 song called "Polko Foco Poetics," aimed at James K. Polk's vice president, G. M. Dallas, a longtime supporter of Nicholas Biddle's Bank of the United States:

> If DALLAS now turn *anti* Bank
> Or what the Loco Polkos *axes*,
> His next Jim Crowish, wheel about prank,
> May TEXAS turn to doleful TAXES!

> And DALLAS then by permutation,
> Will turn ALL-SAD in this great nation.
>> (*Kentucky* 11)

For another reading of blackface as Democratic party ideology, see Jean Baker, *Affairs of Party* 249–58.

19. See the notable account of French bohemia by Arnold Hauser, *The Social History of Art* 4:189–93; see also Richard Miller, *Bohemia* 29–78.

20. Morrison Foster, *My Brother Stephen* 83. In *"Susanna," "Jeanie," and "The Old Folks at Home"* William Austin disputes and complexifies this claim (238–39).

21. As J. S. Dwight's *Journal of Music* put it: "In [the black's] wild bursts of melody he seems to be giving utterance to that exultant liberty of soul which no chains can bind, and no oppression subdue. . . . Let us not be ashamed to learn the art of happiness from the poor bondman at the South" ("Songs" 51).

22. That this feeling was a little more than business as usual is indicated by the following blackface verse, in which a black man seems to acknowledge the surplus value being generated from expropriated black practices:

> [Jim] gwan to de Bowery to see Rice a actin,
> He tink he act de brack man much better dan de white 'un . . .
> [Rice] cut de pigeon wing, an he do de handsome ting,
> Wheel about and turn about, an' bring de money in.
>> ("De New York Nigger," *De Susannah* 74)

This subtly acknowledged guilt suggests a certain amount of unexpected self-consciousness on the part of the expropriators.

23. In *Across the Atlantic* (1851) John Delaware Lewis observes that young men wishing to be comical would greet others on the street with an imitation of "the peculiar chuckle of the sable race" they had learned from the minstrel show (22). I am grateful to Bluford Adams for bringing this to my attention. Elizabeth Blackmar has suggested to me that this appropriation of black masculinity may also have allowed imaginary access to black women apart from white men's assumed prerogative of rape, providing an outlet for white male desire not fully accounted for by stereotypes of black female "looseness." I thank her for this suggestive notion, to which I return intermittently in part II.

24. Revising René Girard's triangulated model of heterosexual desire in *Deceit, Desire, and the Novel*—in which men fighting over a woman engage in a more intense bond than either of the men share with the woman—and drawing on Gayle Rubin's reaccentuation (in "The Traffic in Women") of an anthropological tradition that views women as objects of exchange in a male economy, Eve Sedgwick explores some of the ways men maintain patriarchal domination by bonding through mediating women. "Homosocial" bonds are those heterosexual, homophobic relations that consolidate men's interests. But, as we shall see, homosocial and homosexual desire are, in Sedgwick's words, "remarkably cognate" ("Beast" 246). See *Between Men* 1–27.

In the minstrel show, as will become clear, this dynamic extended in several directions. In addition to the traffic in women effected by minstrelsy's "wench" characters, white male bonding occurred over the bodies of black men as well. This homosocial bonding was, oddly, mediated by white men's *appropriations* of "black" maleness—a peculiar kind of traffic in black men.

25. Quoted in Robert Toll, *Blacking Up* 142; see also the *New York Clipper* September 20, 1873, on the "songstress" Ernest Linden, as well as Marjorie Garber, *Vested Interests* 275–81.

26. For the best account of Elvis's racial contradictions, see Greil Marcus, *Mystery*

Train 141–209; see also George Lipsitz, *Class and Culture in Cold-War America* 195–225. An acute reading of 1950s intellectual white-Negroism can be found in Andrew Ross, *No Respect* 65–101; see also Steve Shoemaker, "Norman Mailer's 'White Negro.'" White-Negroism appears particularly to have afflicted the many Irish-American men who became minstrel performers; indeed, Mailer's essay is a sort of extension of this ethnic subtext. There is, as Werner Sollors has observed, a long tradition in America of ethnic artists figuring themselves or other "white" ethnicities as black (or Native American) ("Literature" 656). If in the twentieth century, as Mailer's essay implicitly suggests, the men most identified—and most in conflict—with African-Americans have been American Jews, in antebellum America the Irish had a similar relationship to "blackness." I outline this history in chapter 4; we need only note here the extensive Irish investment in early minstrelsy, including performers such as Dan Bryant, Dan Emmett, Joel Walker Sweeney, and E. P. Christy—a tradition inherited by Jewish men from Al Jolson and George Gershwin to bebopper Mezz Mezzrow, some of the Beat writers, and Lou Reed, whose "I Wanna Be Black" (1978) may be taken as a provisional, self-conscious end point (but not the end) of this tradition. For a brilliant analysis of the surplus symbolic value generated by Jews out of black culture, see Michael Rogin, "Blackface, White Noise."

27. In his attributing agency to the blackface artist and leaving "negro melody" disembodied and uncopyrighted, and in the language of cost accounting, one senses here as elsewhere that Hutton and other such writers would prefer that the question remain open. See also Charley White, "Origin of Negro Minstrelsy."

28. This discussion owes much to Edward Said, *Beginnings* chap. 2, and to J. F. Lyotard's reflections on the function of "legitimating narratives" (*Postmodern* 18–20). The many accounts of the rise of minstrelsy, some briefer than others, include "Origins of Jim Crow"; James Kennard, "Who Are Our Negro Poets?" 332; F. C. Wemyss, *Theatrical Biography* 178–79 and *Theatrical Biography of Eminent Actors* 122; G. W. Curtis, "Editorial Notes" 572; "Letter from a Teacher at the South"; "E. P. Christy: Originator of Ethiopian Minstrelsy"; Sol Smith, *The Theatrical Journey* 53; "Obituary, Not Eulogistic"; R. P. Nevin, "Stephen C. Foster" 608–9; T. A. Brown, *History of the American Stage* 310 and "The Origin of Negro Minstrelsy"; H. D. Stone, *Personal Recollections* 240–41; Olive Logan, "Ancestry of Brudder Bones"; H. P. Phelps, *Players of a Century* 166–67; Noah Ludlow, *Dramatic Life as I Found It* 392–93; E. S. Conner, "An Old Actor's Memories"; J. J. Jennings, *Theatrical and Circus Life* 368; Walter Leman, *Memories of an Old Actor* 92; Laurence Hutton, "The Negro on the Stage"; E. L. Rice, *Monarchs of Minstrelsy* 7–10; M. B. Leavitt, *Fifty Years in Theatrical Management* 23–24; Brander Matthews, "The Rise and Fall of Negro Minstrelsy" 755; Arthur Hornblow, *A History of the Theater in America* 2:107ff.

29. "Negro Minstrelsy—Ancient and Modern" 72.

30. I have been inspired here by the art historian T. J. Clark, who has read mid-nineteenth-century French painting through "symptomatic" analyses of its contemporaneous critics, and in this way—by a kind of historical ethnography—reconstructed the concerns of an art form's "public." Clark makes an analogy with Freudian theory: if the unconscious is visible only in slips, silences, and (in)admissions in conscious life, so the political unconscious of the public, though usually hidden by official representations that are made of it in the discourse of the critic, can erupt out of gaps in this discourse:

> Like the analyst listening to his patient, what interests us, if we want to discover the [public], are the points at which the rational monotone of the critic breaks, fails, falters; we are interested in the phenomena of obsessive repetition, repeated irrelevance, anger suddenly discharged—the points where the criticism is incomprehensible are the keys to

> its comprehension. The public, like the unconscious, is present only where it ceases; yet it determines the structure of private discourse; it is the key to what cannot be said, and no subject is more important. (*Image* 12)

Clark's remarks are evidently (though not explicitly) based on Pierre Macherey's *Theory of Literary Production*, to which I am also indebted. See Richard Dyer's *Heavenly Bodies* for a similar practice of reconstructing the racial and sexual discourses in which, for example, movie stars become intelligible.

31. I mean, of course, to imply again the threatening alternatives of intermixture and insurrection in my formulation of minstrel-show origin narrative paradigms. I am using a model of narrative analysis that has been developed out of a long tradition of Marxist theories of mediation by scholars associated with the Birmingham Centre for Contemporary Cultural Studies, most notably Stuart Hall (see, for instance, Hall et al., ed., *Resistance Through Rituals* 9–74); see also Fredric Jameson, "Reification and Utopia in Mass Culture" and *The Political Unconscious* 77–80. Drawing on the work of Claude Lévi-Strauss in *Structural Anthropology*, these theorists suggest that the function of cultural forms is not only to mediate but symbolically or "magically" to resolve lived social contradictions.

32. "Negro Minstrelsy—Ancient and Modern" 73–74; see also *New York Herald* January 6, 1848.

33. Marx writes:

> Could commodities themselves speak, they would say: "Our use-value may be a thing that interests men. It is no part of us as objects. What, however, does belong to us as objects, is our value. Our natural intercourse as commodities proves it. In the eyes of each other we are nothing but exchange-values." (*Capital* 83)

And Dreiser:

> Fine clothes to her were a vast persuasion; they spoke tenderly and Jesuitically for themselves. When she came within earshot of their pleading, desire in her bent a willing ear. The voice of the so-called inanimate! Who shall translate for us the language of the stones?
>
> "My dear," said the lace collar she secured from Partridge's, "I fit you beautifully; don't give me up."
>
> "Ah, such little feet," said the leather of the soft new shoes; "how effectively I cover them. What a pity they should ever want my aid." (75)

What allows commodities to talk is precisely their exchange value; it is this that masks their social character as labor and gives them a life of their own. Under slavery the opposite happens: self-owning human beings become voiceless things, pure socioeconomic values. "Lending oneself" occupies a strange middle ground between the two, suggesting both self-ownership and an invitation to self-enslavement, particularly given the uses to which Cuff's loan is put. It is in any case Nevin's ambivalence toward black labor that is represented here, for he is comfortable with neither slavery nor free labor; this ambivalence accounts for the shifting displacements going on in his narrative.

34. Carolyn Karcher has argued forcefully that the confidence man's race is finally a riddle, that Melville's manipulations leave us no way of knowing whether he is "really" white (here in blackface) or black. While her argument is generally persuasive, and I agree with Karcher that the issue of slavery is at the heart of *The Confidence-Man*, the specific implications of blackface are central to Black Guinea's first appearance; in the sixth chapter Melville himself invokes the minstrel show, and it is only later that race is successively destabilized. This fact hardly calls Karcher's point into question; indeed, it is probably central to it. See Karcher, *Shadow over the Promised Land* 186–257.

35. Eric Sundquist links Melville's view of benevolence to abolitionism in *"Benito Cereno* and New World Slavery" 102.

Chapter 3

1. The title of Lippard's last novel was *New York: Its Upper Ten and Lower Million* (1853). Huyssen's term comes from his study *After the Great Divide*. For gendered accounts of the divide that have influenced the shape of my project, see Huyssen, "Mass Culture as Woman"; Tania Modleski, "The Terror of Pleasure"; and Ann Douglas, *The Feminization of American Culture*.

2. George Rehin, "The Darker Image" 371. For a similar argument, see Albert McLean, *American Vaudeville as Ritual*.

3. "Pompey's Rambles," *White's New Book of Plantation Melodies* 15–16; see also "Broadway Song," *Buckley's Song Book for the Parlor* 43, and "Coney Island," *Budsworth's New Comic Ethiopian Songster* 54.

4. Quoted in David Grimsted, *Melodrama Unveiled* 52–53.

5. See Bruce McConachie, "The Theatre of Edwin Forrest." Forrest, a great fan of minstrelsy, was also certainly one of the first to "black up"—as "Cuff, a Kentucky negro," in Cincinnati in 1823 (Rice 23).

6. For accounts of the Astor Place rioting, see the *New York Herald* May 11, 1849; "Opinions of the Press on the Late Occurrences in Astor Place," *New York Herald* May 16, 1849; William Northall, *Before and Behind the Curtain* 123–51; Alvin Harlow, *Old Bowery Days* 323–332; Richard Moody, *The Astor Place Riot;* David Grimsted, *Melodrama Unveiled* 68–74; Peter Buckley, *To the Opera House* 3–83 (quotation at 20); and Lawrence Levine, *Highbrow/Lowbrow* 63–68.

7. For this diversity, see, among others, Richard Stott, *Workers in the Metropolis* 37–67, 214–16, and Buckley, *To the Opera House* 147, 294–409.

8. See Buckley, *To The Opera House* 346–53, 370–76; Stott, *Workers in the Metropolis* 222–29, 247–76. Erik Olin Wright's *Classes* is to date the best theoretical discussion of class. Wright makes a distinction between class *structure* and class *formation.* "Class structure refers to the structure of social relations into which individuals (or, in some cases, families) enter which determine their class interests" (9). "Class formation . . . refers to the formation of organized collectivities within that class structure on the basis of the interests shaped by that class structure" (10). Classes, then, "have a structural existence which is irreducible to the kinds of collective organizations which develop historically (class formations), the class ideologies held by individuals and organizations (class consciousness) or the forms of conflict engaged in by individuals as class members or by class organizations (class struggle), and . . . such class structures impose basic constraints on these other elements in the concept of class" (28).

My concern is minstrelsy's role in antebellum class formation. I am assuming that structurally the minstrel show was at all times part of a class-inflected culture which began to emerge after 1830 and which underwent an increasing separation from the dominant culture; and that while the people who made up minstrelsy's audiences often employed a populist language of the "industrious" or "producing" classes to describe themselves, they nevertheless had a sense of belonging to this class-inflected culture. By class formation, then, I mean the ways minstrelsy participated in or redirected class conflict or contributed shifting languages of race for such conflict.

9. F. C. Wemyss, *Theatrical Biography; or, The Life of An Actor and Manager* 178–79.

10. *Journal of Music* September 17, 1853, 191. Wrote the *New York Tribune:* "We may be at fault in comprehending the sinuosities of a score, and quite out in our *majors* and

minors, but we would not exchange the profound reverence with which a Yorker receives 'Lilly Dale,' or 'Woodman Spare that Tree,' or 'The Old Folks at Home,' as, in some sort, a stammering utterance of his best hopes and sweetest reminiscences, for all the sensuous and deliquescent raptures of southern shores" ("Popular" 99).

William Austin notes that these lines appear in Walt Whitman's "Salut au Monde!" as it stood from 1856 to 1876: "[T]he Virginia plantation chorus of negroes of a harvest night . . . the strong baritone of the 'long-shoremen of Manahatta . . . the stevedores unlading the cargoes, and singing" (63)—a series whose associations clearly depend on those of the minstrel show, particularly as it moves from slaves to white workingmen, with perhaps a hint of the interracial character of dockwork.

11. For a similar point, see David Roediger, *The Wages of Whiteness* 110, 116.

12. It is time, one would think, to put the somnolent idea of American exceptionalism to bed. Recent labor historians have certainly demonstrated striking class parallels between the American and European contexts. Indeed, in *Prisoners of the American Dream* Mike Davis pointedly argues that, far from being a fundamental American essence, the lack of class consciousness relative to that of Europe has actually been temporarily created—and then, with a vengeance, undone again—at various historical junctures, most recently in the "failure of the labor movements of the 1930s and 1940s to unify the American working class on either the economic or the political planes" (8). This history might also account for the veneration of the idea of American exceptionalism by the cold war generation of U.S. intellectuals. For a first-rate discussion of this matter, see Eric Foner, "Why Is There No Socialism in America?"

13. Paul Johnson, *A Shopkeeper's Millennium* 42; see also the fascinating account of the origins of "boss" in Roediger, *The Wages of Whiteness* 50–54.

14. Stuart Blumin, "The Hypothesis of Middle-Class Formation" 313–16.

15. I have drawn most on the following sources for these historical developments: Herbert Gutman, *Work, Culture, and Society in Industrializing America* 3–78; David Montgomery, "The Shuttle and the Cross"; Paul Faler, "Cultural Aspects of the Industrial Revolution"; Alan Dawley, *Class and Community;* Dawley and Faler, "Working-Class Culture and Politics in the Industrial Revolution"; Paul Johnson, *A Shopkeeper's Millennium;* Susan Hirsch, *Roots of the American Working Class;* Bruce Laurie, "'Nothing on Compulsion,'" *Working People of Philadelphia*, and *Artisans into Workers* 15–112; Edward Spann, *The New Metropolis;* David Gordon, Richard Edwards, and Michael Reich, *Segmented Work, Divided Workers* 1–17, 48–99; Mary Blewett, "Work, Gender, and the Artisan Tradition in New England Shoemaking"; Sean Wilentz, *Chants Democratic* 23–142; Steven Ross, *Workers on the Edge* 3–192; Stuart Blumin, "The Hypothesis of Middle-Class Formation"; Kerby Miller, *Emigrants and Exiles* 263–79, 293–344; Amy Bridges, "Becoming American"; Christine Stansell, *City of Women* 43–62; Elizabeth Blackmar, *Manhattan for Rent;* Richard Stott, *Workers in the Metropolis;* and Patricia Cline Cohen, "Unregulated Youth."

16. In "Ideology and Race in American History" Barbara Fields concurs that a new discourse of race was a result of "the unfolding of bourgeois social relations" generally (152). But for a "prehistory" of working-class whiteness, see Roediger, *The Wages of Whiteness* 31–36.

17. See, among others, Bernard Mandel, *Labor* 65–70; Leon Litwack, *North of Slavery* 158–68; John Runcie, "'Hunting the Nigs'" 197, 203; Leonard Richards, *"Gentlemen of Property and Standing"* 151–55; Emma Jones Lapsansky, "'Since They Got Those Separate Churches'" 61; Bruce Laurie, *Working People of Philadelphia* 63–66, 156–58; Paul Gilje, *The Road to Mobocracy* 165–66; and Iver Bernstein, *The New York City Draft Riots* 27–31.

18. Robert Ernst, *Immigrant Life in New York City* 105–6; Litwack, *North of Slavery* 162–66; Richard Slotkin, *The Fatal Environment* 149; Kerby Miller, *Emigrants and Exiles* 267; Dale Knobel, *Paddy and the Republic* 88–103; Roediger, *The Wages of Whiteness* 133–163. I pursue this equation in chapters 4 and 6.

Minstrel skits portrayed the Irish in terms identical to those in which they portrayed blacks; see, for example, "Paddy Conner's College," *Billy Birch's Ethiopian Melodist* 11.

19. In *The Politics and Poetics of Transgression* Peter Stallybrass and Allon White insist that discourses and discursive hierarchies owe much to the specific social locations or ideological topography in which they are produced (194–95).

20. Theodore Schank, "The Bowery Theatre" 282; Elliott Gorn, *The Manly Art* 133–34; Neil Harris, *Humbug* 40–41; Stott, *Workers in the Metropolis* 212–35, 242–46.

21. Recent labor historians have elaborated the ways in which the American working class reworked republican principles, descended from Enlightenment figures such as Tom Paine, into an "artisan republican" rhetoric designed to resist the emerging capitalist order. Broadly speaking, this scholarship includes Alfred Young, *The Democratic Republicans of New York;* Edward Pessen, *Most Uncommon Jacksonians;* Eric Foner, *Tom Paine and Revolutionary America;* Sean Wilentz, *Chants Democratic;* and much of the work cited in note 15.

22. I am, of course, invoking one of the central ideas of Edmund Morgan's *American Slavery—American Freedom,* a profound work of paramount importance to my own. David Roediger, "'Labor in White Skin,'" and Stanley Aronowitz, "Writing Labor's History," offer useful sustained critiques of the new labor history; both argue the inextricability of white workingmen's freedom and American slavery and racism. This view has begun to be substantiated by, among others, Richard Slotkin, *The Fatal Environment;* Alexander Saxton, *The Rise and Fall of the White Republic;* and Roediger, *The Wages of Whiteness.*

23. Charles Haywood, "Negro Minstrelsy and Shakespearean Burlesque" 86 (quotes *Hamlet* parody); Lawrence Levine, *Highbrow/Lowbrow* 11–82; Ray B. Browne, "Shakespeare in American Vaudeville and Negro Minstrelsy" 382 and "Shakespeare in the Nineteenth-Century Songsters" 215–18; Tilden Edelstein, *"Othello* in America" 187–88; William Mahar, "Ethiopian Skits and Sketches" 248–54; Gary Engle, ed., *This Grotesque Essence.* In addition to Peter Buckley's *To the Opera House* (3–409), Robert Allen, *Horrible Prettiness* 51–76 and Bruce McConachie, *Melodramatic Formations* 65–155 offer fine accounts of antebellum theatrical culture.

24. Bruce Laurie, *Working People of Philadelphia* 55.

25. For studies of the saloon in nineteenth-century working-class life, see Jill Seigel Dodd, "The Working Classes and the Temperance Movement in Antebellum Boston"; Jon Kingsdale, "The 'Poor Man's Club'"; Roy Rosenzweig, *Eight Hours for What We Will* 35–64; Gorn, *The Manly Art* 133–36; and Stott, *Workers in the Metropolis* 217–222.

26. For accounts of Walsh's career, see Robert Ernst, "The One and Only Mike Walsh"; Wilentz, *Chants Democratic* 326–35; Saxton, "George Wilkes"; and Roediger, *The Wages of Whiteness* 75–77. The Free-Soilers, said Walsh, were "traitors who, at a pepper-and-salt convention, held in Buffalo in 1848, fraternized, with pertinacious assumption of well-dissembled sincerity, with disappointed and disloyal Whigs, rampant Abolitionists, and long-heeled Negroes, pampered by the traitorous artifices of demagogues, whose hearts and purposes were blacker than the faces of the poor dupes they were deluding in doing so" (quoted in Ernst, "Walsh" 60–61).

27. This decline is implied, for instance, in Constance Rourke's essay on Barnum in *Trumpets of Jubilee* 276–319. For earlier incarnations of the museum in America, see Thomas Bender, *New York Intellect* 47, 83–87.

28. In "P. T. Barnum's Double Bind," Richard Herskowitz argues that Barnum's

typically outrageous publicity foregrounded advertising itself as a kind of "metamessage," reconciling spectators to the deceptions being worked upon them: "Barnum's *oeuvre* operated to carry the spectator away from the frustration of events that were falsely advertised, towards an identification with the process of advertising" (139)—and, by implication, with Barnum himself, who candidly shared the mechanisms of his "humbugs." Spectators' feelings of being "insiders," undeceived yet intrigued by the enormity of false claims, were bought with capitulation to the advertising that nonetheless manipulated them.

29. M. R. Werner, *Barnum* 204. Apparently it was not Barnum but black showmen who invented this trick. Ira Berlin observes that 1790s Baltimore was a hotbed of black entertainment enterprises: Robert Wilson, a free Negro, paid one dollar to hold a three-month exhibit; a license was granted to a "Negro Rope Dancer"; and permission was given to exhibit "a Negro turned White as a Show" (*Slaves* 62).

30. Lydia Maria Child's "Mary French and Susan Easton" (1834) also instances the peculiar attraction antebellum whites had to fantasies of racial transmutation. Mary is kidnapped, stained black, and sold into slavery; the climactic moment comes when her weeping washes the black away, triumphantly revealing her unbesmirched identity. I am indebted to Karen Sánchez-Eppler's fine analysis of this story in "Bodily Bonds" 36, 38–39.

31. For the mulatto figure as a fictional device of racial mediation, see Werner Sollors, "Literature and Ethnicity" 656; Hazel Carby, *Reconstructing Womanhood* 88–91, 171–73; and Mary Dearborn, *Pocahontas's Daughters* 131–58.

32. Alexander Saxton, "Problems of Class and Race" 232–33.

33. Walt Whitman, *Uncollected Poetry and Prose* 1:236. For the 1858 remark, and for more on Whitman and race, see Daniel Aaron, *The Unwritten War* 59–62.

34. William Austin, *"Susanna," "Jeanie," and "The Old Folks at Home"* 61; Walt Whitman, *Uncollected Poetry and Prose* 1:236; Eric Foner, "Racial Attitudes of the New York Free Soilers" 92. See also Joseph Jay Rubin, *The Historic Whitman* 278–86 and passim; this chapter's epigraph is quoted at 279.

35. *New York Mirror* December 29, 1832.

36. Here as elsewhere Peter Buckley's *To the Opera House* has been indispensable (139–61).

37. T. Allston Brown, *History of the New York Stage* 1:284.

38. Antebellum volunteer fire companies approximated gangs or fraternal organizations as much as fire-fighting units. Sporting names such as Lady Washington and Old Maid, they not only involved themselves in party politics but also engaged in intense intercompany conflict, often neglecting a raging fire to combat or sabotage a rival company in the street. For work on the fire companies, see Lowell Limpus, *History of the New York Fire Department;* Alvin Harlow, *Old Bowery Days* 201–15; Bruce Laurie, "Fire Companies and Gangs in Southwark"; and Richard Stott, *Workers in the Metropolis* 229–31.

39. For accounts of Mose and the Bowery milieu generally, see George Foster, *New York in Slices* 43–47 and *New York by Gas-Light* 101–9; William Bobo, *Glimpses of New York* 162–67; Charles Haswell, *Reminiscences of an Octogenarian* 270–71; Harlow, *Old Bowery Days* 190–215; Richard Dorson, "Mose the Far-Famed and World-Renowned"; John Jentz, "Artisans, Evangelicals, and the City" 238–55; Buckley, *To the Opera House* 294–409; Sean Wilentz, *Chants Democratic* 257–71; Christine Stansell, *City of Women* 89–100; Elliott Gorn, *The Manly Art* 129–36; David Reynolds, *Beneath the American Renaissance* 463–66; Stott, *Workers in the Metropolis* 222–29; and Luc Sante, *Low Life*.

40. Alexander Saxton also notes the overlapping of class and racial concerns in the

blackface version of Mose. See "Blackface Minstrelsy and Jacksonian Ideology" 9–11. Jules Zanger, "The Minstrel Show as Theater of Misrule," makes a similar point but parcels out class and racial satire to different characters—the haughty interlocutor and the black endmen—and thus to some extent simplifies their meaning.

41. "Wake Up, Mose!" M. Campbell, *Wood's Minstrels' Songs* 25; *White's New Illustrated Melodeon Songbook* 72; *White's New Book of Plantation Melodies* 24. See also "The Fireman's Boy," *Beadles Dime Song Book No. 3* 34. A daguerreotype of T. Prendergast and Dan Bryant (c. 1850–56) shows the two in full blackface "b'hoyisme"—cocked stogeys, canes, stovepipe hats (Harvard Theatre Collection).

42. This was not an unusual occurrence; there are other recorded instances of black involvement in minstrelsy this early in its history. Francis Johnson, a prominent black Philadelphia composer and bandleader, made an arrangement of the minstrel tune "Dandy Jim," and apparently performed it with a (probably white) Mr. Creely, "the celebrated Negro Melodist," in 1844. Eileen Southern speculates further that Johnson may have had direct contact with Dan Emmett's Virginia Minstrels, as the title page of Johnson's arrangement suggests. See Southern, "Black Musicians and Early Ethiopian Minstrelsy" 80 and *The Music of Black Americans* 107–10.

43. *New York Herald* May 12, 1849.

44. Gorn, *The Manly Art* 140–44 and "'Good-Bye Boys'" 403, 409; Stansell, *City of Women* 89–101; and Stott, *Workers in the Metropolis* 253–56, 270–76.

45. As I have noted, Eve Sedgwick defines homosocial bonds as heterosexual, homophobic relations between men, mediated by women, which consolidate men's interests. Because homosocial and homosexual desire are closely related, however, there is built in to homosocial bonds a constant sexual instability and consequent defensiveness with far-reaching implications. See Sedgwick, "The Beast in the Closet," for an analysis of this dynamic in Victorian fiction. I am also relying here on Louis Althusser's account of ideology. The function of ideology, says Althusser, is to represent (actually to *mis*represent) the subject's relation to his or her lived conditions of existence. It is thus an "imaginary" relation (in the Lacanian rather than the simply "false" sense), one that takes place in a realm of "misrecognition." Since the minstrel show was tantamount to an "ideological state apparatus," an institution with specific material rituals that produced (often contradictory) ideologies of race, class, and gender, this account of ideology is helpful in thinking about the ways white men's relation to black men was structured by the minstrel show in this period. See Althusser, *Lenin and Philosophy* 127–86.

46. The genesis of these concerns owed in part to the massive migrations of roving young workingmen to the city in the years of minstrelsy's greatest popularity. Country boys (and immigrant men) fled the commercial and cultural constrictions they had inherited and landed in towns and cities, where they lodged in boardinghouses, drank in saloons, and generally constituted an alarming new presence beyond the pale of conventional morality—at least according to moral reformers. As he was constructed by the most popular reformers (Henry Ward Beecher, John Todd, Sylvester Graham, O. S. Fowler), this endangered and dangerous species of young man was defined by an illicit attention to his own body which threatened to rend the body politic. One need not submit to the reformers' valuation of this phenomenon to allow the general validity of their perception. See Carroll Smith-Rosenberg, *Disorderly Conduct* 79–108; Allan Horlick, *Country Boys and Merchant Princes;* Stuart Blumin, "Mobility and Change in Ante-Bellum Philadelphia" and "Residential Mobility Within the Nineteenth-Century City"; Richard Stott, "The Geography of Gender in Nineteenth-Century America"; and Sam Bass Warner, *The Private City* 49–78.

Chapter 4

1. This story has been told best in Perry Miller's wonderful study *The Raven and the Whale.*

2. I am indebted to T. J. Clark's suggestive use of this essay in his discussion of the French *café concert* in *The Painting of Modern Life* 216–17. Gramsci's term "national-popular" is an analytical device of variable definition in the *Prison Notebooks*. Politically it was developed to conceptualize the ways in which the fascist ascendancy in Italy might be combated, not by directly seizing power (which was impossible) but by securing a cross-class alliance in a mass party that would contest its hegemony—a transitional stage ultimately leading to socialist democracy. Culturally it sought to articulate elements of an indigenous culture to a national will or mass desire for historical change. My use of the term emphasizes this connection between indigenous cultural forms and political formations—between, in particular, vernacular elements and the idea of the nation—though it will become clear how many contradictions accrue to such a notion in the American context. That, indeed, is one reason for my use of it. See Gramsci, *Selections from Cultural Writings* 196–286, and David Forgacs, "National-Popular."

3. Eliot, however, might have; in a deeply felt moment he said that his "nigger drawl" owed to his closeness to his native St. Louis. See Terence Hawkes, *That Shakespeherian Rag* 86.

4. For a similar point, see Andrew Ross, "Ballots, Bullets, or Batmen" 41–44.

5. See the essays in Tony Bennett et al., *Popular Culture and Social Relations*. I take this particular emphasis from Bennett's essay "The Politics of 'the Popular'" 8, 19.

6. For a theoretical inquiry into the problem of constructing "indigeneity," see Bill Ashcroft, Gareth Griffiths, and Helen Tiffin, *The Empire Writes Back* 133–45; see also Timothy Brennan, "The National Longing for Form," and Homi Bhabha, "DissemiNation."

7. Anderson links the rise of both the newspaper and the novel to the formation of national self-consciousness (28–40). See also Alexander Saxton, "Problems of Class and Race in the Origins of the Mass Circulation Press."

8. Charles Hamm, *Yesterdays* 115; Hans Nathan, *Dan Emmett* 159–88, 194–213, 70–97; Robert McDowell, "Bones and the Man"; Marshall Stearns and Jean Stearns, *Jazz Dance* 49–54; M. H. Winter, "Juba and American Minstrelsy" 42. Ralph Ellison and Albert Murray, of course, have insisted on the "mulatto" character of American culture for a generation or more. See particularly Murray, *The Omni-Americans*, but also Ellison, *Shadow and Act* and *Going to the Territory.*

9. It might be noted here that many scholars' overattention to textual evidence—primarily songsters (without music), in effect written "scores" for interactive affairs of performance—has skewed their view both of minstrelsy's inauthenticity and of the varied effects minstrelsy might have produced in antebellum audiences. My attention to other media in addition to print is an attempt to redress this imbalance.

10. There was indeed a peculiar unevenness in whites' appropriations of black material, resulting in an art in which black dances survived relatively intact even amid the burlesque of the lyrics. The question is why the racist filter did not produce a more uniform parody of all the "black" elements. My own feeling is that this is evidence, again, of the contradictory relationship whites had to black people and to black culture.

11. For a survey of the debates on the origins of black secular (and religious) music, see Lawrence Levine, *Black Culture and Black Consciousness* 19–30.

12. Herbert Gutman, *Work, Culture, and Society* 59; Frederick Douglass, *My Bondage and My Freedom* 76 and *Life and Times* 54.

13. The former song can be found in *The Negro Forget-Me-Not Songster* 33, and the latter is mentioned in Carl Wittke, *Tambo and Bones* 224; Wittke lists Irish-nationalist titles at 200. On the Irish-black identification in Harrigan and Hart, see Robert Toll, *Blacking Up* 247, 249. A song called "The Darkey's Lament," according to one 1847 playbill, was a parody of "The Irish Emigrant's Lament" (Winans, "Minstrel-Show" 72).

14. Michael Feldberg, *The Turbulent Era* 44–45, 50–51; John Runcie, "'Hunting the Nigs'" 199–200; Bruce Laurie, *Working People of Philadelphia* 124–25; and David Roediger, *The Wages of Whiteness* 133–137.

15. See Osofsky's excellent "Abolitionists, Irish Immigrants, and the Dilemmas of Romantic Nationalism," as well as Robert Ernst, *Immigrant Life in New York City* 153, and Kerby Miller, *Emigrants and Exiles* 263. For the best exposition of the contradictions that faced the attempted abolitionist–working-class alliance in these years, see Eric Foner, "Abolitionism and the Labor Movement in Ante-Bellum America." See also chapters 5 and 6.

16. As I noted earlier, a similar argument might be made for the twentieth-century Jewish involvement in black culture, from minstrelsy to jazz. See Irving Howe, *World of Our Fathers* 562–63; Michael Rogin, "Blackface, White Noise" and "Making America Home"; and Charles Musser, "Ethnicity, Role-Playing, and American Film Comedy." In addition, see Robert Ernst, *Immigrant Life in New York City* 135–37, 181–84, and David Roediger's splendid account of the making of working-class Irish "whiteness" in *The Wages of Whiteness* 133–63. There was, to be sure, plenty of anti-Irish nativism registered in the minstrel show (though even this could in certain cases be a strategy of Irish "Americanization"). Consider this verse from "Old Paddy Whack" (early 1850s):

> Dan [O'Connell] scolds de Yankee's wid a big figger,
> Kase dey take care ob us poor nigger,
> But slave holders am not worse by smash,
> Dan he dat fobs de repealer's cash.
>
> (*Negro* 91–92)

See Robert Toll, *Blacking Up* 175–80, for a review of minstrelsy's shifting portrayals of the Irish.

17. "Dem Niggers am Dead an Gone," *White's New Illustrated Melodeon Songbook* 59.

18. William Austin, *"Susanna," "Jeanie," and "The Old Folks at Home"* 44; see also the *Journal of Music*'s equation of minstrelsy with national music ("National" 140). As one blackface songster put it, the cry of America's lack of a native music was "tauntingly reiterated, until our countrymen found a triumphant, vindicating APOLLO in the genius of E. P. Christy." *Christy's Plantation Melodies No. 4* v.

19. *New York Herald* November 1, 1842.

20. As I observed in chapter 1, Stowe's Uncle Tom and Stephen Foster's sentimental slaves, the former arguably "radical" and the latter often reactionary, are *as types* nearly indistinguishable. The point is that the type had publicly emerged for the first time; what remained to be fought out were its political meanings. See William Stanton, *The Leopard's Spots;* William Gossett, *Race* 54–83; George Fredrickson, *The Black Image in the White Mind* 51–164; and Reginald Horsman, *Race and Manifest Destiny* 116–57.

21. See also *Broadway Journal* July 12, 1845, 13–14. Imagine patrician diarist George Templeton Strong's dismay when at Castle Garden, "instead of the accustomed orchestra, out came five hideous savages with black faces, who called themselves Nigger Serenaders, and began singing something about Miss Juliana Johnson" (Lawrence 372). Mid–twentieth-century British observers called on the very same equations to criticize the

deluge of American mass-cultural products—equations by then about a century old. See Dick Hebdige, *Hiding in the Light* 45–76.

22. I am indebted to Bruce Franklin's provocative discussion of this article, and of the relation of black arts to America's national culture, in *The Victim as Criminal and Artist* 73–123. Franklin's book had a formative influence on my project.

23. I have lifted this apt phrase from Berndt Ostendorf, *Black Literature in White America* 67.

24. "Negro Minstrelsy in London" 67.

25. Robert Faner, *Walt Whitman and Opera* 40; Walt Whitman, *An American Primer* 24.

26. Bayard Taylor, *Eldorado* 275. The famed American pianist and composer Louis Moreau Gottschalk wrote in 1853 a *Grand National Symphony*, which, performed solo as *American Reminiscence* or *National Glory*, included quotations of "Oh! Susanna" and "Old Folks at Home," perhaps the beginning of those tunes' lengthy middle-class institutionalization as national exemplars—and, simultaneously, of "black" culture's recruitment as an American "folk" culture. See William Austin, *"Susanna," "Jeanie," and "The Old Folks at Home"* 22. For interesting treatments of the minstrel show in different national contexts, see Dale Cockrell, "Of Gospel Hymns, Minstrel Shows, and Jubilee Singers"; George Rehin, "Blackface Street Minstrels in Victorian London"; Simon Frith, "Playing with Real Feeling"; Michael Pickering, "White Skin, Black Masks"; J. S. Bratton, "English Ethiopians"; and Richard Waterhouse, *From Minstrel Show to Vaudeville*.

27. Antonio Gramsci, *Selections from Cultural Writings* 349. The "historical origin" or "artistic aspect" of cultural material, Gramsci wrote of popular music, matters less than that a certain group of people has adopted it because it "conform[s] to their way of thinking and feeling" (*Cultural* 195). In this sphere of popular counterfeits, as Tony Bennett argues in "Marxism and Popular Fiction," nothing matters but the way certain artifacts momentarily secure their adherents and inspire various popular formations.

28. By contrast, very little cultural appropriation took place in the written form of the slave narrative. Mattie Griffith's fraudulent 1857 slave narrative, *Autobiography of a Female Slave* (by a planter's daughter), is a rare exception. Even if we include Harriet Beecher Stowe's work as an example of such appropriation—her use, for example, of the slave narratives of Henry Bibb and Josiah Henson in writing *Uncle Tom's Cabin*—suffice it to say that this was a second-order attempt at cultural incorporation, a kind that was far less pervasive than the formal consequences of minstrelsy, which, as we shall see, influenced the stage productions of *Uncle Tom's Cabin* itself.

29. Smith-Rosenberg has demonstrated that the Crockett almanacs, which began to appear after 1835, can be read as a kind of fictional management, through the medium of the body, of antebellum American social dislocation. An out-of-hand adolescent in rebellion against paternal authority, Crockett as he is portrayed in the almanacs is a paragon of orality, scatology, and violent sexuality. Posed in all respects against the formation of an emergent bourgeois respectability, the almanacs nevertheless, according to Smith-Rosenberg, ultimately formed a "paean to the free individual" at a time when America was witnessing the most thoroughgoing institutionalization in its history (107–8) rebelliousness, in short, embodied (provided a Barthesian mythology for) the bourgeoisie's belief in uncontained, unfettered selves even as they resisted the material historical developments underwriting this ideology.

30. In addition to Stuart Hall, I am indebted here to T. J. Clark's study *The Painting of Modern Life* 205–39.

31. "Negro Minstrelsy—Ancient and Modern" 73; "Who Writes Our Songs?" 52;

William Austin, *"Susanna," "Jeanie," and "The Old Folks at Home"* 79; T. W. Higginson, "Negro Spirituals" 685.

32. Stanley Aronowitz, "Defining the Popular"; see also Dominick LaCapra, *History and Criticism* 45–69, for some cautions in regard to Ginzburg's project, particularly its implicit formulation of peasant culture as a fully reconstructed, static whole. For discussions of the appropriation of English and Native American oral traditions, see Gene Bluestein, *Voice of the Folk* 1–15, and Arnold Krupat, "Native American Literature and the Canon."

33. See Iain Chambers, *Popular Culture* 140–44, for the ways the color bar was broken in radio; see, among others, Jules Tygiel, *Baseball's Great Experiment*, or C. L. R. James, *Beyond a Boundary*, for the world-historical struggles that may obtain in the world of sport.

34. Quoted in David Roediger, "'Labor in White Skin'" 293.

35. Karl Marx, "A Criticism of American Affairs" 211; Marx is referring specifically to the progress of the Civil War. The first sections of Greil Marcus, *Lipstick Traces* (1–152), constitute an extended meditation on punk music's relation to its late-1970s social history.

36. In *Subversive Genealogy* Rogin brilliantly reads Melville's career through political developments that roughly parallel the European context; but for brief explicit statements on that context, see 15–23, 102–6. See also Larry Reynolds, *European Revolutions and the American Literary Renaissance*.

37. Rogin, *Subversive Genealogy* 148, 130; Frederick Merk, *Manifest Destiny and Mission in American History* 180–201.

Chapter 5

1. For Rice's career, see Molly Ramshaw, "Jump Jim Crow!"

2. See, for example, Nathan Huggins, *Harlem Renaissance* 270, 273, and Jules Zanger, "The Minstrel Show as Theater of Misrule."

3. Uncatalogued playbills in the Harvard Theatre Collection.

4. Another writer, the theater historian Laurence Hutton, noted in 1889 that many blackface performers had made names for themselves, "to say nothing of the bands of veritable negroes who have endeavored to imitate themselves in imitation of their white brethren in all parts of the land" (144). As if in response to this cultural effect, in *Uncle Tom's Cabin* Stowe has Mr. Shelby hail George and Eliza Harris's little boy as "Jim Crow" (44).

5. S. Foster Damon, *Series of Old American Songs* no. 13.

6. "Negro Minstrelsy—Ancient and Modern" 73.

7. Richard Dyer, *Heavenly Bodies* 138–39; emphasis in original.

8. S. Foster Damon, *Series of Old American Songs* no. 17.

9. Insurrection was no small concern in the 1830s and early 1840s, as an editorial in the *New York Sun* makes clear. When Joshua Giddings introduced a resolution in Congress that commended the slaves who revolted aboard the *Creole* and steered it to Britain, the *Sun* (March 25, 1842) compared him to "Robespierre, Brissot and Marat," who "set themselves up as champions of the freedom of speech and of the negroes, and led the way to deeds of blood, the history of which will appall the world throughout all time to come" (quoted in Saxton, "Problems" 233). For an excellent treatment of the ironies attending the issues of slavery and revolution in these years, see Eric Sundquist, "Slavery, Revolution, and the American Renaissance"; for a brilliant analysis of the overdetermined proximity in T. W. Higginson, *Army Life in a Black Regiment* (1867) of black male bodies, weapons, and the sort of homoerotic interest I review in this discussion, see Christopher

Looby, "'As Thoroughly Black As the Most Faithful Philanthropist Could Desire.'"

10. S. Foster Damon, *Series of Old American Songs* no. 14.

11. *White's New Illustrated Melodeon Songbook* 82.

12. For this depressing but infinitely suggestive excerpt from the history of sexual relations, see Leonore Davidoff, "Class and Gender in Victorian England"; a provocative analysis is also to be found in Peter Stallybrass and Allon White, *The Politics and Poetics of Transgression* 154–56. More generally, see Steven Marcus, *The Other Victorians* chap. 3, as well as Christine Stansell, *City of Women* 125–27, 139, 161–65, 175.

13. Philip Cohen, "Tarzan and the Jungle Bunnies" 27. Tania Modleski has argued that the extreme ambivalence toward women in Hitchcock's films arises from a similar dialectic of misogyny and identification—the identification so threatening that it *requires* misogyny (*Women* 5, 13). Aptly in the present context, psychoanalytic theorists and their film-theory epigones have speculated that perceptual contradictions, the play of belief and nonbelief, the disavowal of things one knows on other levels to be true, originate in castration anxiety. The (male) shock at seeing the "castrated" mother gives rise to two thoughts: all human beings are endowed with a penis (primal belief), and some human beings do not have a penis (evidence of the senses). This "lasting matrix," as Christian Metz calls it, is the "affective prototype of all the splittings of belief which man will henceforth be capable of" (70). The minstrel show's blackface counterfeits capitalized on the proximity of these two structures—the origins of belief and disavowal in castration anxieties about black men. See Sigmund Freud, "Fetishism"; in *Black Skin, White Masks* Frantz Fanon also notes this interplay of identification and disavowal (141–209).

14. Michael Rogin argues this point at length in *Subversive Genealogy* 236–56.

15. The phrase "play of pronoun function" comes from Mark Nash, *"Vampyr* and the Fantastic" 37. The notion is brilliantly elaborated in Carol Clover, "Her Body, Himself."

16. Michael Denning, *Mechanic Accents* 176.

17. An early version of "Jim Crow" (published the same year as the illustration, 1833) suggests (derisively) that envy of black people is responsible for this identification:

> I'm so glad dat I'm a niggar,
> An don't you wish you was too
> For den you'd gain popularity,
> By jumping Jim Crow.
>
> Now my brudder niggars,
> I do not think it right,
> Dat you should laugh at dem
> Who happen to be white.
>
> Kase it dar misfortune,
> An dey'd spend ebery dollar,
> If dey only could be
> Gentlemen ob colour.
> (Dennison 54)

This charge is closer to the mark than the song would allow.

18. See, for example, Andrew Tolson, *The Limits of Masculinity* 63–64; Peter Stearns, *Be a Man!* 59–78; Sean Wilentz, *Chants Democratic* passim; Stansell, *City of Women* 77–78, 81, 95–96, 137–41; Denning, *Mechanic Accents* chap. 9; and David Montgomery, *Workers' Control in America* 13–14. Walt Whitman's bohemian bravado in the late 1840s and early 1850s—the "manly" bearing of a journeyman carpenter's son—derives at least in part from this dynamic.

19. For an excellent discussion of this imbalance, see Nancy Chodorow, "Mothering, Male Dominance, and Capitalism" 96–97. For an acute contemporary account and analysis of the construction of shop-floor masculinity, see Paul Willis, "Shop Floor Culture, Masculinity, and the Wage Form."

20. Freud's description of the deeply troubled moment of identification bears significantly on this discussion: "Identification, in fact, is ambivalent from the very first; it can turn into an expression of tenderness as easily as into a wish for someone's removal" (*Group Psychology* 37). I use "identification" loosely here to refer to both primary and secondary processes. (See also Mary Ann Doane, "Misrecognition and Identity.") Laura Mulvey has taken this dynamic several steps further. In a justly famous article on narrative film, Mulvey uses Freud to distinguish between a scopophilic, or objectifying, structure of looking (here, perhaps, a dominative fetishizing of the "black" performer) and a voyeuristic, or identificatory, one (here, interracial identification). My point is that there was in minstrelsy a more or less constant play between these two structures. See Mulvey, "Visual Pleasure and Narrative Cinema" 18. For some forceful observations on racial contradictions in white working-class subjectivity, see C. L. R. James et al., *Facing Reality* 124 and Martin Glaberman, *Wartime Strikes* 121–34. A powerful instance of antebellum white identification with blacks is a studio daguerreotype of blackface performer Charles White (c. 1850, Harvard Theatre Collection) in which all traces of irony have been expunged from White's rigidly forthright pose.

21. As I have mentioned, this model of cultural analysis, derived from the Claude Lévi-Strauss of *Structural Anthropology*, has been developed by theorists associated with the Birmingham Centre for Contemporary Cultural Studies, most notably Stuart Hall, as well as Fredric Jameson in "Reification and Utopia in Mass Culture" and *The Political Unconscious* 77–80 and passim.

22. For an analysis of America's "initial proletarianization," see David Gordon, Richard Edwards, and Michael Reich, *Segmented Work, Divided Workers* 1–17, 48–99. David Roediger is right to suspect the economic determinism of the job-competition argument (*Wages* 106, 147–50); as I try to show, this matter was heavily laden with race-specific associations and ideologies. But see also chapter 3.

23. See, for example, Linda Kerber, "Abolitionists and Amalgamators" 34, and John Runcie, "'Hunting the Nigs'" 196–202.

24. David Roediger dissents from this view of "wage slavery" rhetoric in "'Labor in White Skin'" 300–301 and in *Wages of Whiteness* 65–92, and Thomas Haskell has asked whether such rhetoric was not simply opportunist in "Capitalism and the Origins of Humanitarian Sensibility, Part I" 350. Skepticism about the radical usefulness of the idea of wage slavery stems, I think, from a failure to historicize it; conjunctural analysis reveals its potential use value in the 1830s and occasionally later, as is indicated in Williston Lofton, "Abolition and Labor" 277–83, and Eric Foner, "Abolitionism and the Labor Movement in Ante-Bellum America" 59–62 and "Workers and Slavery." I would argue, moreover, as the *American Whig Review* did in 1849, that labor's alliance with Calhoun was always "forced and unnatural," growing as much out of common enmities as proslavery principles. Much of the labor movement shared Calhoun's hatred of Martin Van Buren, and looked to the "Marx of the master class" (in Richard Hofstadter's phrase) for theoretical support of antimonopolistic "free trade." It certainly would not be long before radical democracy posed itself against the extension of slavery in the form of the Free-Soil movement. See Arthur Schlesinger, Jr., *The Age of Jackson* 406–8, 470; Hofstadter, *The American Political Tradition* chap. 4; and Sean Wilentz, *Chants Democratic* 327, 333.

25. Quoted in John Jentz, "Artisans, Evangelicals, and the City" 213.

26. Bernard Mandel, *Labor* 61–62, 74–75; Jentz, "Artisans, Evangelicals, and the

City" 193, 202–3, 234–76; Leonard Richards, *"Gentlemen of Property and Standing"* 140–41. Alan Dawley notes that while "white workers feared the competition of nonwhite laborers and shared the racism of a white-Anglo-Saxon-Protestant culture, they hated the institution of slavery, identified with the slave, and grouped overbearing Lynn manufacturers together with slavemasters as 'a set of lordly tyrants'" (65). I find rather overreaching the argument of David Roediger that working-class support for abolitionism arose from a wish to "follow middle class leaders who emphasized the *differences"* between white mechanic and black slave and thus distanced their relative conditions from each other (*Wages* 86).

27. In fact the two traditions often contradicted each other, the presence of Paineite artisans frightening evangelical antislavery supporters away. Jentz, "Artisans, Evangelicals, and the City" 208–15.

28. Jentz, "Artisans, Evangelicals, and the City" 215; Joseph Rayback, "The American Workingman and the Antislavery Crusade" 153.

29. Jentz, "Artisans, Evangelicals, and the City" 213–14; Bernard Mandel, *Labor* 82. This is to argue strongly against Lorman Ratner, *Powder Keg,* which assumes labor's hostility toward both organized abolitionism and antislavery views generally; labor was often hostile to the former but usually in agreement with the latter. For a nice riposte to Ratner, see Jentz, "Artisans" 232. For a succinct summary of the contradictions in the relationship of abolitionism and labor, see W. E. B. Du Bois, *Black Reconstruction in America* 17–26; see also Bruce Laurie, *Working People of Philadelphia* 66; Herbert Shapiro, "Labor and Antislavery"; and Bruce Levine, *Half Slave and Half Free* 156–59. In "Ideology and Race in American History," Barbara Fields insists on the contradictory nature of popular racial feeling: "[Racial] attitudes . . . are promiscuous critters and do not mind cohabiting with their opposites. Indeed, they sometimes seem to be happier that way" (155).

30. Alexander Saxton, "Problems of Class and Race" 232. See Arthur Schlesinger, *The Age of Jackson* 424–27, for a quick summary of the Democratic splits over slavery.

31. A labor pamphlet from 1850, for instance, indicts the abolitionists for being, simply, the "Hollow-Hearted Swindlers of Labor": "These men know by experience the preference of CHEAP HIRED LABOR over Chattel" (quoted in Rayback, "American" 154). See also Bernard Mandel, *Labor* 62.

32. John Jentz, "The Anti-Slavery Constituency in Jacksonian New York City" 108; Rayback, "The American Workingman and the Antislavery Crusade" 153. For the class connotations of the mutually reinforcing movements of abolitionism and evangelicalism see Schlesinger, *The Age of Jackson* 136–40, 350–60; Bertram Wyatt-Brown, *Lewis Tappan and the Evangelical War Against Slavery;* Lawrence Friedman, "Confidence and Pertinacity in Evangelical Abolitionism"; Paul Johnson, *A Shopkeeper's Millennium;* Eric Foner, "Abolitionism and the Labor Movement"; and Sean Wilentz, *Chants Democratic* 145–49, 305. Had workers in New York City and other northeastern centers converted like their counterparts in the Burned Over District of upstate New York, one might suppose the lessened opposition to evangelicalism to have contributed to the antislavery vanguard. At least in New York City, writes Sean Wilentz, workers did not in any great number sign on to the evangelical cause (279–80). Yet this produced no firm ideological result; secular traditions of antislavery persisted as much as did the reaction to "Tappanism"—itself perhaps the result of evangelicalism's organizational headquarters' being housed in New York City.

33. Foner, "Abolitionism and the Labor Movement" 66.

34. *De Susannah, and Thick Lip, Melodist* 73; Bruce McConachie, "'The Theatre of

the Mob'" 35. See Wilentz, *Chants Democratic* 180–81, for a sense of the routineness of anti-Tappanism.

35. The impetus for this brief investigation is, of course, the extraordinary work on popular rioting and mobbing produced by George Rudé (*The Crowd in History*), E. P. Thompson ("The Moral Economy of the English Crowd"), and others. I have drawn my narrative from these accounts: Gustave de Beaumont, *Marie*, "Appendix"; Alvin Harlow, *Old Bowery Days* 289–93; Linda Kerber, "Abolitionists and Amalgamators"; Leonard Richards, *"Gentlemen of Property and Standing"* 113–22; Jentz, "Artisans, Evangelicals, and the City" 245–55; Paul Weinbaum, *Mobs and Demagogues* 23–27; Wilentz, *Chants Democratic* 264–65; Peter Buckley, *To the Opera House* 184–90; and Paul Gilje, *The Road to Mobocracy* 162–70.

36. Richards, *"Gentlemen of Property and Standing"* 151–55; Jentz, "Artisans, Evangelicals, and the City" 247–48.

37. Peter Buckley carefully notes that these separate actions "became part of a seamless organism" in the minds of contemporary observers (190), given the "mobocratic" spirit (as a young Abraham Lincoln was to call it) of those days. See Lincoln's 1838 "Address to the Young Men's Lyceum of Springfield."

38. Quoted in Jentz, "Artisans, Evangelicals, and the City" 249.

39. Jentz, "Artisans, Evangelicals, and the City" 251–55 (the quote is from Jentz, "The Anti-Slavery Constituency in New York City" 117); David Roediger, *The Wages of Whiteness* 110.

40. The text here is reprinted in Gary Engle, ed., *This Grotesque Essence* 1–12. It dates from 1856, but Hans Nathan observes that it derives from the original. Although no plot summary survives from the early performances, the playbill synopsis of a companion piece, *Bone Squash*, is in almost complete agreement with its 1856 printing, and the names of the characters in *O Hush!* are virtually identical with the earlier play's. See Nathan, *Dan Emmett* 67.

41. Richards, *"Gentlemen of Property and Standing"* 114–15. In Gustave de Beaumont's *Marie* (1835), whose pivotal episode is based on the July riots, the antiabolitionist violence interrupts the wedding ceremony of a Frenchman and a mulatto, rather nicely underscoring the link between the rioters' motives and fears of amalgamation.

42. Emma Jones Lapsansky's "'Since They Got Those Separate Churches'" is very good on the emergence of the black dandy as an ideological fiction—its class sources and its regulation of black behavior. Black responses to the fiction included an 1838 Philadelphia *Colored American* article that asserted, "The same class of vagabonds who mob abolitionists, would as readily mob . . . the aristocracy could they do it with the same impunity" (72), casually making clear the class resonance of abolitionism. See also Gary Nash, *Forging Freedom* 254–59.

43. Indeed, Lapsansky observes that in Philadelphia it was not amalgamation per se but amalgamation for the purposes of *upward mobility* to which rioters objected (62).

44. Jentz, "Artisans, Evangelicals, and the City" 192 and "The Anti-Slavery Constituency in Jacksonian New York City" 110.

Chapter 6

1. Emmett's account, a more elaborated and convincing narrative than those of Billy Whitlock and G. B. Wooldridge, appeared in the *New York Clipper* May 19, 1877; the other accounts were published there a year later (April 13, 1878). Despite Hans Nathan's assessment, the evidence may support E. P. Christy's claim of having organized (in Buffalo, New York) the first minstrel band, though Emmett's was no doubt the first in New

York City. See *Dan Emmett* 116–18, 143–46; more generally, see C. B. Galbreath, *Daniel Decatur Emmett*.

2. On charivari, and for further references, see E. P. Thompson, "'Rough Music'"; Natalie Zemon Davis, *Society and Culture in Early Modern France* 97–123; and Peter Stallybrass and Allon White, *The Politics and Poetics of Transgression* 24.

3. The argument of this chapter has been influenced by the brilliant analysis by Stuart Hall et al. in *Policing the Crisis* of the British "mugging" scare of the early 1970s— an attempt on the part of "law and order" to regain lost ground in the wake of the "crisis" of the 1960s.

4. *New York Herald* February 6, 1843.

5. Hans Nathan is very precise about the makeup of the first minstrel shows. See *Dan Emmett* 118–34, 143–53.

6. This assertion is still perhaps a controversial one, based as much on guesswork as on insurmountable evidence. About all that can be adduced on the matter is the recollection of the late nineteenth-century performer Lew Dockstader that the early interlocutor's lack of "darky dialect" contrasted with his black makeup; on the basis of this statement, Robert Toll concludes in *Blacking Up* (63, n.63) that interlocutors generally appeared in blackface. Certainly there is a considerable *lack* of evidence of a whiteface interlocutor in this period, much less songbook illustrations featuring blackface companies with a sole whiteface performer. Reminiscences such as that of Mark Twain, which does support the claim of a white interlocutor, seem influenced both by regional particularity (Twain saw shows in Hannibal) and by minstrelsy's later incarnations—more accurate in spirit than in all their facts. The ease with which the mask accommodated a variety of dialects—Irish brogues, the b'hoy's slang, even parodic, German-inflected English—perhaps indicates less of a contradiction between the blackface mask and genteel dialect than one might have expected. The white interlocutor, at least in urban centers, appears to have been a later development.

7. In this respect the minstrel show is not unrelated to television situation comedy; see Patricia Mellencamp, "Situation Comedy, Feminism, and Freud." For some interesting remarks on the minstrel show's structure, see W. T. Lhamon, "Constance Rourke's Secret Reserve" xxxiv.

8. See, for instance, George Rehin, "Harlequin Jim Crow"; Robert Winans, "Early Minstrel-Show Music"; Gary Engle, "Introduction," *This Grotesque Essence;* and William Mahar, "Ethiopian Skits and Sketches."

9. By "right-minded black comedy" I mean anything from Spike Lee's films to Bill Cosby to the unfortunate "In Living Color."

I have been oriented in this project by several excellent discussions of pleasure: Roland Barthes, *The Pleasure of the Text;* Laura Mulvey, "Visual Pleasure and Narrative Cinema"; Fredric Jameson, "Pleasure"; and Colin Mercer, "Complicit Pleasures" and "A Poverty of Desire." Also helpful are John Lowe, "Theories of Ethnic Humor" John Morreall, *Taking Laughter Seriously* 27–37; and Werner Sollors, *Beyond Ethnicity* 131–41.

10. *Knickerbocker* 16, 1 (July 1840), 84.

11. If the symbolic depends on reflection and lack, writes Christian Metz, "the cinema is a body . . . a fetish that can be loved" (57). Barbara Freedman's *Staging the Gaze* argues that the same might be said of the actor's presence in the theater (47–77).

12. "Peabody's Lecture, On the Great Soger Camp-Meeting," *White's New Book of Plantation Melodies* 79.

13. *White's New Book of Plantation Melodies* 13; *White's New Illustrated Melodeon Songbook* 31.

14. S. Foster Damon, *Series of Old American Songs* no. 37.

15. Steven Marcus, *The Other Victorians* 266–86. Edward James's *Amateur Negro Minstrel's Guide* advises that three quarters of an inch of lipstick will "make the face look all mouth when opened to its full extent" (8).

16. S. Foster Damon, *Series of Old American Songs* no. 39.

17. *Popular Music in Jacksonian America*, side 2.

18. "Now Hold your Horses, will You!" *Christy and Wood's New Song Book* 9; see also George Christy, *Essence of Old Kentucky* 46–47.

19. A third possibility is that some audience members experienced a marginally more positive nostalgia for nurture rather than infant rage; this was true, we shall see, for the wave of sentimental black images that would soon begin to flood the minstrel stage. I have been influenced here by Michael Rogin's psychohistorical interpretation of white attitudes toward Native Americans in the antebellum period. See *Fathers and Children* 3–15, 114–25; see also Sander Gilman, "Black Bodies, White Bodies" 256.

20. Peter Stallybrass and Allon White, *The Politics and Poetics of Transgression* 192. This argument refines ideas drawn from symbolic anthropologists such as Mary Douglas, who have written of the body as a symbolic representation of the social forces that produced it—bodily functions and boundaries, points of entry and of exit signifying societal relations and values. See, for example, Douglas, *Natural Symbols* esp. 65–81.

21. Paul Faler, "Cultural Aspects of the Industrial Revolution" and *Mechanics and Manufacturers* 100–138; Paul Johnson, *A Shopkeeper's Millennium* 55–61, 79–83; Sean Wilentz, *Chants Democratic* 271, 277–84, 305.

22. For a similar argument, see David Roediger, *The Wages of Whiteness* 97, 100, 110, 118, and, regarding theatrical portrayals of the Irish, Bruce McConachie, "The Cultural Politics of 'Paddy.'"

23. Slavoj Žižek, "Eastern Europe's Republics of Gilead" 57; see also Sylvia Wynter, "Sambos and Minstrels" 152–54.

24. F. C. Wemyss, *Theatrical Biography; or, The Life of An Actor and Manager* 179.

25. Roediger, *The Wages of Whiteness* 133–34, 150–54; Kerby Miller, *Emigrants and Exiles* 267.

26. Peter Stallybrass and Allon White make an excellent statement on how this formation comes about in *The Politics and Poetics of Transgression* 193–94. Julia Kristeva terms this predicament "abjection." Kristeva writes of the abject that "'unconscious' contents remain . . . *excluded* but in strange fashion," clearly enough "for a defensive *position* to be established" yet "not radically enough to allow for a secure differentiation between subject and object." Thus blackface's white spectator, in Kristeva's terms, "never stops demarcating his universe whose fluid confines . . . constantly question his solidity and impel him to start afresh" (7–8).

27. See Christian Metz, *The Imaginary Signifier*, for an account of how the castration threat is managed by replacing it with a fetish substitute: "The fixation on [the fetish's] 'just before' [castration] is thus another form of disavowal. . . . The fetish signifies the penis as absent, it is its negative signifier; supplementing it, it puts a 'fullness' in place of a lack, but in doing so it also affirms that lack" (70–71). The minstrel show exemplified and worked several permutations on this theme, as will become clear.

28. *Christy and Wood's New Song Book* 30; for further examples, see "Gal wid de Blue Dress on," *White's New Illustrated Melodeon Songbook* 65, and "White Cat and Black Cat," *White's New Ethiopian Song Book* 49.

29. Michael Denning, *Mechanic Accents* 146–48.

30. In thinking about racial and gender disguise, and about theater spectators' varying identifications with blackface characters, I am indebted once again to Carol Clover's "Her Body, Himself."

31. See, for instance, Amy Bridges, "Becoming American" 170–73, 176. On various aspects of the depression, see Samuel Reznick, "The Social History of an American Depression"; Robert Ernst, "Economic Nativism in New York City"; Ira Leonard, "The Rise and Fall of the American Republican Party"; and Sean Wilentz, *Chants Democratic* 299–359.

32. For this figure of "aristocratic" self-satisfaction, see Peter Buckley, *To the Opera House* 197–205.

33. In *Strangers in the Land,* John Higham conncects nativism with racism (4). Whereas single-minded class radicalism had had variable racial results in the 1830s, the complexities and constrictions of class feeling in the 1840s tended to produce a corollary sense of racial impatience and disdain.

34. See Bernard Mandel, *Labor* 79–80, 89–95; Eric Foner, "Abolitionism and the Labor Movement" 67–71; Williston Lofton, "Abolition and Labor" 254; and Joseph Rayback, "The American Workingman and the Antislavery Crusade" 152–53.

35. W. E. B. Du Bois, *Black Reconstruction in America* 21; Mandel, *Labor* 76–84; Rayback, "The American Workingman and the Antislavery Crusade" 155–56; Lofton, "Abolition and Labor" 269; Marcus Cunliffe, *Chattel Slavery and Wage Slavery* 19–31; David Roediger, *The Wages of Whiteness* 72–80.

36. Foner, "Abolitionism and the Labor Movement" 67–71; Lofton, "Abolition and Labor" 272.

37. Roediger, *The Wages of Whiteness* 97, 110, 116, 127.

38. In "Writing Labor's History," Stanley Aronowitz offers some excellent insights regarding what he sees as the internally split formation of the American working class, which encompassed not only an artisan republicanism developed in opposition to a consolidating bourgeoisie but also proletarian substrata resisting artisan culture itself (180–85). See also Roediger, *The Wages of Whiteness* 110.

39. See, for instance, Karen Halttunen, *Confidence Men and Painted Women.*

40. From an 1857 poster for a Boston performance of Christy's Minstrels (New York Public Library Theatre Collection).

41. On the internally contradictory (but finally conservative) character of the petite bourgeoisie, see Arno Mayer, "The Lower Middle Class as Historical Problem."

42. I rely here on "Heroes of the Burnt Cork," which includes one of the most detailed descriptions of antebellum cross-dressing.

43. See Christine Stansell, *City of Women* 78–80, 55–62, 89–100; Foster's remark is quoted at 94. Elsewhere, Foster makes the connection (without, I think, understanding it) between these women's work and their (resistant) sense of style: "The pretty book-folder and the pale seamstress, the buxom housemaid and the ambitious laundress, slave cheerfully all the week in the dreariest and most monotonous occupations, that they may obtain the means of making a handsome appearance at the Saturday night dance." See *New York in Slices* 111.

44. *New York Clipper* November 1, 1873; Olive Logan, "The Ancestry of Brudder Bones" 698; George Odell, *Annals of the New York Stage* 5:396; Robert Toll, *Blacking Up* 140; "The Dancing Lucy Long," *White's New Illustrated Melodeon Songbook* 46; Ralph Keeler, "Three Years as a Negro Minstrel" 77.

45. S. Foster Damon, *Series of Old American Songs* no. 31; *White's New Illustrated Melodeon Songbook* 47.

46. Robert Stoller, *Sex and Gender* 185, 176–86, 214–15; conversely, in "Transvestism" Ethel Person and Lionel Ovesey argue that transvestism seeks to allay separation anxiety, not castration anxiety, by using women's clothes as a substitute for the mother (308). See also Marjorie Garber's remarks on Stoller in *Vested Interests* 94–98.

47. Olive Logan, "The Ancestry of Brudder Bones" 698. The *New York Herald* wrote of one "wench" performance: "Such a strapping pair of colored ladies have not been seen for many a day. Fine fun may be expected" (November 7, 1842).

48. Lisa Jardine, *Still Harping on Daughters* 9–36; Katharine Eisaman Maus, "'Playhouse Flesh and Blood'"; Stephen Orgel, "Nobody's Perfect."

49. Lillian Schlissel, "Sexual Disguise"; Robert Toll, *Blacking Up* 144, 142. For searching discussions of the relationship of transvestism to homoerotic desire, see Marjorie Garber, *Vested Interests* 28–65, and Carole-Anne Tyler, "Boys Will Be Girls."

Chapter 7

1. I am indebted to Michael Rogin's excellent discussion of this article in *Subversive Genealogy* 104–5.

2. The *Journal of Music* noted that Christy's Minstrels performed 312 times in 1853 and netted $47,972 ("Black" 108); one songster boasted that Christy's Minstrels had given 69 concerts as early as 1842, yielding $1,847.52 (*Christy's No. 4* v); Robert Nevin wrote that Stephen Foster's commissions for "Old Folks at Home" alone totaled $15,000 (614); and in the *New York Herald*, a "card" published by Christy's Minstrels asserted that George Christy (who had ungratefully broken from the troupe) earned $19,680 in his two and a half years with them (November 7, 1853).

3. Not all of these lyrics, however, arose from minstrel performance; my guess (based partly on existing playbills) is that only a portion of the printed songs were ever performed onstage, though the ones that were probably supported songbook sales, and performed or not, songbook lyrics plugged the performers in whose names the books were published. In other words, to some extent the songbooks constituted an independent realm of literary production. While I have found little information concerning the circumstances of this production, minstrel songbooks did issue—voluminously—from urban dime novel or "fiction factory" publishing houses which depended on a highly organized system of speedy prose manufacture, and it is likely that much minstrel-show verse originated in the same way. It is even possible, given that many songs have a headnote marking their recent performance at such and such a music hall, that blackface artists used the verses fiction factories turned out rather than the other way around, perhaps setting them to tunes already in their repertoire—hence "De New Ole Dan Tucker" or "Old Tucker's Wedding" or even "Mrs. Tucker." (The fans at home, of course, could follow the same path.) Another interesting example of this culture industry collaboration is Tony Pastor, *George Christy: A Story of Minstrel Life* (1877), a dime novel extremely loosely based on the life of the famous blackface performer. The songs just mentioned are from the *Negro Forget-Me-Not Songster* 59, 110, and *White's New Illustrated Melodeon Songbook* 67. On the fiction factories, see Michael Denning, *Mechanic Accents*, chap. 2; Frank Schick, *The Paperbound Book in America;* and Madeleine Stern, ed., *Publishers for Mass Entertainment in Nineteenth-Century America* 35–50, 93–96, 101–14, 229–35.

4. William Austin, *"Susanna," "Jeanie," and "The Old Folks at Home"* 25. The *Journal of Music* eventually reprinted an 1854 article, "Obituary, Not Eulogistic: Negro Minstrelsy Is Dead," which sneered: "Fashion sent her cohorts to mingle with the unwashed million at the shrine of Gumbo, and negro sheet-music had immense sales, being found upon almost every piano in the land . . ." (118).

5. My use of "mythology" here is loosely derived from Roland Barthes's *Mythologies*, in which *myth* is defined as an instance of "depoliticized speech" (143), what Fredric Jameson would in certain cases call an "ideologeme"—in short ideology *narrated*, that is,

narrations of ideology presented as history or historical fact but from which history has been abstracted, evaporated, overthrown (*Political* 87–88).

6. Richard Middleton, "In the Groove, or Blowing Your Mind?" 160. Middleton's work has been indispensable to my thinking about repetition as a tool in the analysis of music and its relationship to society. An earlier version of his article, "Play It Again, Sam: Some Notes on the Productivity of Repetition in Popular Music," contains a few further examples and minor elaborations. All citations of Middleton are from "In the Groove."

In his introduction to Jacques Attali's *Noise*, Fredric Jameson incidentally suggests the importance of locating the kind of mediations I pursue here between music and socio-economic life: "Music . . . would seem to have the strongest affinities with that most abstract of all social realities, economics, with which it shares a peculiar ultimate object which is *number*" (vii).

7. In arguing that Adorno's pinched analysis still has merit, Bernard Gendron broaches the issue of repetition without, finally, saying much about its usefulness in social analyses of music. See "Theodor Adorno Meets the Cadillacs" 29–30. James Snead's acute "Repetition as a Figure of Black Culture," by far the best analysis I have seen of its subject, contributed much to the genesis of this discussion.

8. See Theodor Adorno, "On Popular Music" 306, 308–11, and "Perennial Fashion—Jazz" 121–27.

9. In this respect Richard Johnson's "What Is Cultural Studies Anyway?" has some helpful remarks on the necessity of taking the full cycle of production, artifact, and consumption into critical account, as does Dick Hebdige, *Hiding in the Light* 80–83; Janice Radway, "Reception Study," and Tania Modleski, "Some Functions of Feminist Criticism," are interesting discussions of ethnographic problems and possibilities.

10. Playbills in the Harvard Theatre Collection indicate that the demand for repeats became standard in the late 1840s, resulting in evenings so extended that managers began to institute a policy of no repetitions.

11. See, for instance, János Maróthy, *Music and the Bourgeois, Music and the Proletarian* 11–127.

12. Quoted in Lawrence Levine, *Black Culture and Black Consciousness* 11–12.

13. For a compelling discussion of the "cut," see Snead's "Repetition as a Figure of Black Culture" 67–70.

14. In *"Susanna," "Jeanie," and "The Old Folks at Home"* William Austin notes some other possible antecedents of Foster's song: on the one hand a slave ballad printed in the *Journal* of Edward Abdy, an English abolitionist who visited the United States in 1833–34; and on the other a Lowell Mason hymn (6, 10).

15. Stanley Crouch, in a paper called "Jazz and the Conquest of Time," has some apposite things to say about what Middleton calls musematic repetition.

16. Robert Winans charts this shift fairly conclusively in "Early Minstrel-Show Music."

17. Hans Nathan, *Dan Emmett* 180; chaps. 12 and 13, on early minstrel songs and banjo tunes, are unsurpassed.

18. S. Foster Damon, *Series of Old American Songs* no. 37.

19. "Articulation" has been used by Ernesto Laclau, Chantal Mouffe, and others in relation to the antiessentialist, not inherently class-specific character of cultural elements to emphasize their ties to particular social groups and social meanings as the result of extended processes of cultural work and struggle such as I described in chapter 3. See Laclau, *Politics and Ideology in Marxist Theory;* Mouffe, *Gramsci and Marxist Theory;* and Stuart Hall, "Some Paradigms in Cultural Studies" 38–48. In "Articulating Musical

Meaning/Re-Constructing Musical History/Locating the 'Popular,'" Richard Middleton uses this notion very effectively to discuss some formations of popular music.

20. Stephen Foster's last letter to E. P. Christy (1852) is perhaps the classic text here:

> As I once intimated to you, I had the intention of omitting my name on my Ethiopian songs, owing to the prejudice against them by some, which might injure my reputation as a writer of another style of music, but I find that by my efforts I have done a great deal to build up a taste for the Ethiopian songs among refined people by making the words suitable to their taste, instead of the trashy and really offensive words which belong to some songs of that order. Therefore I have concluded to reinstate my name on my songs and to pursue the Ethiopian business without fear or shame and lend all my energies to making the business live, at the same time that I will wish to establish my name as the best Ethiopian song-writer. But I am not encouraged in undertaking this so long as "The Old Folks at Home" stares me in the face with another's name on it. . . . (quoted in Austin 203)

21. Fredric Jameson, "Reification and Utopia in Mass Culture" 136–38. This is not the full extent of Jameson's position, which allows for complex impulses to be raised and symbolically resolved within the products of popular culture (138–48).

22. Tania Modleski, "The Terror of Pleasure" 156–60. In what follows I rely closely on Middleton's account of some of the effects of repetition in "In the Groove" 168–75.

23. J. S. Dwight, "Negro Minstrelsy" 124; William Austin, *"Susanna," "Jeanie," and "The Old Folks at Home"* 58.

24. For this idea, see Middleton's citation of and elaboration upon D. Avron's "Vers une metapsychologie de la musique" in "In the Groove" 170.

25. The phrase "social motion" comes from Jonathan Arac, *Commissioned Spirits.* For a similar argument in regard to bebop in 1940s New York, see Eric Lott, "Double V, Double-Time."

26. In 1846 there was broad agreement among British journalists that the Ethiopian Serenaders purveyed "the most beautiful combination of humour and pathos," but what they made of this now familiar mix is apparent in their range of response. On the one hand, there was the usual complacency and worse: "Five minstrels—niggers bred, we might almost swear, from the closeness of their copy of 'God's image carved in ivory,' though not niggers born," said the *Daily News;* "inexplicable and inhuman noises . . . strange up-heavings of the voice . . . snores, chokings, and whistles," cackled the *Herald.* Yet on the other hand, some extraordinary advocacy was thrown into the ring as well, such as this from the *Daily News*—which incidentally casts light on the ways antislavery cohabited with what we would regard as rather dubious racial feeling:

> Such was the effect produced, not alone upon ourselves, but manifestly upon a vast majority of the listeners by the songs we have instanced, as to banish any other than a feeling of deep commiseration for the unhappy misused beings who, under all the wrongs which they endure, can yet laugh and sing and dance gaily after their labours for the day are over. And, so far from feeling angry or indignant [at the Ethiopian Serenaders] . . . we feel extremely glad in being able to say that their exhibition is not only innocuous, as regards the poor helpless beings they represent, but calculated from its force, truthfulness, and mixture of the ludicrous with sentiment, to raise feelings which may at no distant period produce results that every friend of negro emancipation would hail with satisfaction. (March 18, 1846)

The press notices that the Ethiopian Serenaders received on their tour of England were collected in an 1846 pamphlet, *Ethiopian Serenaders;* the quotations are from 30–32.

27. Norman Ware, *The Industrial Worker* 225; Frederick Merk, *Manifest Destiny and*

Mission in American History 172–79; Bernard Mandel, *Labor* 115; Bruce Levine, *Half Slave and Half Free* 177–78; Williston Lofton, "Abolition and Labor" 278–79; Joseph Rayback, "The American Workingman and the Antislavery Crusade" 158, 160–62; Eric Foner, "The Wilmot Proviso Reconsidered"; Rayback, *Free Soil* 23–33; Sean Wilentz, *Chants Democratic* 382.

28. This is the great insight of Fredric Jameson's genre theory, and I have obviously recast it into broader form in this study. See Jameson, *The Political Unconscious* 103–50, and Michael Denning, *Mechanic Accents* 77.

29. Stephen Foster, "Nelly Was a Lady," in Richard Jackson, ed., *Stephen Foster Song Book* 82. Perhaps the most explicit of such songs was "Female Slave's Lament" (1851), *White's Serenaders' Song Book* 20. For *Putnam's Monthly* editor George William Curtis, minstrelsy and sentimentalism were virtually synonymous: "There is no people in the world so sentimental as we. Our only really popular songs are such negro melodies as those of Mr. Foster, ('Old folks at home,' 'Massa's in de cold ground,' &c.,) which are simply pathetic refrains adapted to what, in another sphere of literature, would be only extremely Laura Matilda-ish poetry, mainly dirges and desperate love songs" (572).

30. I have observed some of the implications of the feminization of blackness in chapter 1, but see also, for example, Karen Sánchez-Eppler, "Bodily Bonds," on senti- mentalist ideology's encounter with race, and George Fredrickson, *The Black Image in the White Mind* 97–129, on the vogue of sentimentalized "romantic racialism."

31. By extension the powerless included middle-class women and white working peo- ple; blackface sentimentalism might be seen as in part a "people's" version of the genteel sentimentalist discourse designed to equip or at least represent women disenfranchised by their distance from the centers of cultural power. I would stress, however, that this development was an uneven one, less a unitary phenomenon than a space within which class fractions grasped for the power to wield the cultural sign of feminized black victim. Sentimental minstrel songs were surely as indebted to, say, *Godey's Lady's Book* as they were to working-class melodrama's moments of female helplessness (Mose rescuing vic- tims from burning tenements), and they represented working-class whites only to the extent that they did not parrot the accents of genteel culture; they were hegemonic, an upwardly mobile gambit of show-biz respectability, to the extent that they did. Put another way, this trend was an attempted sentimentalist resolution of the growing class contradic- tions in minstrelsy's audience that would contribute to its substantial recomposition by the turn of the 1860s.

32. *White's New Illustrated Melodeon Songbook* 6.

33. Stephen Foster, "Old Folks at Home," in Richard Jackson, ed., *Stephen Foster Song Book* 101–2. For an account of this song's burial at the hands of Louis Armstrong, see Gary Giddins, "The Signifying Satchmo."

34. Alexander Saxton, "Blackface Minstrelsy and Jacksonian Ideology" 14–15; see also David Roediger, *The Wages of Whiteness* 119. The *New York Tribune* wrote in 1855: "Who has not often observed the tear of sensibility moistening the cheek of youth, while listening to the primitive strains of 'Uncle Ned'? . . . Ah, those tears constituted one of the blessings of that youth, which has now departed" ("Black" 107).

35. "Letter from a Teacher at the South" 164. For Irish homesickness, see Kerby Miller, *Emigrants and Exiles* 277; for an argument about the radical protest at the heart of popular nostalgia, see Alun Howkins and C. Ian Dyck, "'The Time's Alteration.'"

36. William Austin, *"Susanna," "Jeanie," and "The Old Folks at Home"* 119; John Tasker Howard, *Stephen Foster;* Gilbert Chase, *America's Music* 248–65; Stuart Blumin, "Residential Mobility Within the Nineteenth-Century City" and "Mobility and Change in Ante-Bellum Philadelphia"; Stephan Thernstrom and Peter Knights, "Men in Motion";

more generally, see, for example, Sam Bass Warner, *The Private City* 49–78, and Paul Johnson, *A Shopkeeper's Millennium* 37–55.

37. *Christy and Wood's New Song Book* 19.

38. *White's New Book of Plantation Melodies* 49.

39. Stephen Foster, *Minstrel-Show Songs* no. 1; *Christy and Wood's New Song Book* 43.

40. Christine Stansell, *City of Women* 137–41; Mary Blewett, "Work, Gender, and the Artisan Tradition in New England Shoemaking" 230–32.

41. *Christy and Wood's New Song Book* 29.

42. The image of middle-class domestic ideology that comes quickest to mind is Stowe's utopian Quaker family in *Uncle Tom's Cabin*. Wife and mother Rachel Halliday is the very model of domestic productivity and female influence, while husband Simeon is literally marginalized in the corner, "engaged in the anti-patriarchal operation of shaving" (222–25). One notes that in this scene even the surname is given to Rachel rather than to Simeon. For excellent discussions of this passage, and for auxiliary evidence of its antipatriarchal argument, see Leslie Fiedler, *What Was Literature?* 157–58, and Jane Tompkins, "Sentimental Power" 141–46.

On the fictional plantation, writes William Taylor, the southern gentleman "is not the master of his own house, to say nothing of his environment, and he is frequently patronized by the novelist himself. Often he has died before the story opens and exists only as a memory" (153). On the equivocal role of the planter in plantation fiction, see Taylor, *Cavalier and Yankee* 146–201.

43. I am indebted to Richard Slotkin's discussion of this text in *The Fatal Environment* 149.

44. Strikingly, Lydia Maria Child culled quotation upon quotation from the southern press illustrating the barbarism of slavery in *The Patriarchal Institution as Described by Members of Its Own Family* (1860). In *Life and Liberty in America: Sketches of a Tour in the United States and Canada in 1857–8*, Charles Mackay employed the more familiar locution—albeit with some qualification—writing that on a plantation he visited "the slaves are kindly treated, and . . . the patriarchal relation in all its best aspects exists between the master and his poor dependents" (207–8).

Particularly after Seneca Falls in 1848, burlesque stump speeches on women's rights were common in minstrel performances and songbooks.

45. Joseph Rayback, "The American Workingman and the Antislavery Crusade"; Williston Lofton, "Abolition and Labor" (William West's remark is quoted on 272); Eric Foner, "Abolitionism and the Labor Movement in Ante-Bellum America," "Racial Attitudes of the New York Free Soilers," and "Politics and Prejudice"; and Sean Wilentz, *Chants Democratic* 299–359.

46. Richard Slotkin, *The Fatal Environment* 178; see also Alan Dawley, *Class and Community* chaps. 2, 8.

47. See chapter 3.

48. Rayback, "The American Workingman and the Antislavery Crusade" 155–56; Lofton, "Abolition and Labor" 269; Eric Foner, "Workers and Slavery" 24–25; Bernard Mandel, *Labor* 84–86. Ronald Walters has demonstrated how the "erotic" South might have been particularly congruent with other preindustrial objects of republican distaste in *The Antislavery Appeal* 70–87.

49. In *Free Soil, Free Labor, Free Men* Eric Foner traces this logic through to its institutional conclusion in the founding of the Republican party in the mid-1850s. This impulse is perhaps the best riposte to David Roediger's dour view of the racial politics of "free labor" rhetoric, a view he takes despite considerable evidence of ambiguity regarding

working-class racial feeling, and despite the rhetoric's result in antislavery party politics, not to mention civil war. See *Wages of Whiteness* 80–81, 87.

50. Eugene Berwanger, *The Frontier Against Slavery*.

51. In *"Susanna," "Jeanie," and "The Old Folks at Home"* William Austin provides an authoritative account of the song's sources and its entry into the public domain (3–12); see also John Tasker Howard, *Stephen Foster* 134–56.

52. Meade Minnigerode, *The Fabulous Forties* 321, 323–24 (for the gold rush version of "Oh! Susanna"); Richard Jackson, ed., *Stephen Foster Song Book* 177; Bayard Taylor, *Eldorado* 275; Constance Rourke, *Troupers of the Gold Coast* 7–58.

53. It is no coincidence that William Wells Brown set radical lyrics to "Susanna," renamed "The Northern Star," in the *Anti-Slavery Harp* (1849). The chorus goes: "Oh! Star of Freedom, 'Tis the star for me; /'Twill lead me off to Canada, There I will be free" (quoted in Austin 36). It is in this form that "Susanna" appears to have entered black oral culture; both Harriet Tubman and Sojourner Truth sang it.

54. *Christy and Wood's New Song Book* 23, 68.

55. *White's New Book of Plantation Melodies* 30; see also Robert Johannsen, *To the Halls of the Montezumas* 230–40, 270–301.

56. "Bell Ringer's Medley," *White's New Illustrated Melodeon Songbook* 61–62. Bernard DeVoto stresses the emotional nation-building performed by minstrel melodies, specifically those of Stephen Foster, in "Stephen Foster's Songs." The most compelling accounts of the origins of the Civil War that emphasize the North's specifically *nationalist* impulses are Barrington Moore, *Social Origins of Dictatorship and Democracy* 111–55, and Eric Foner, "Politics, Ideology, and the Origins of the American Civil War."

57. I have been aided here once again by Alan Dawley and Paul Faler, "Working-Class Culture and Politics in the Industrial Revolution" 474–78.

58. The argument that northern class reform was thoroughly laid waste by the necessity of an interclass struggle against the South has been made by David Brion Davis, *The Problem of Slavery in the Age of Revolution* 251, and Alan Dawley, *Class and Community* 196, 238–39, though Eric Foner contests Dawley's implicit ascription of antislavery sentiment to northern capitalists in "Abolitionism and the Labor Movement" 74–76.

59. Eric Foner, "Racial Attitudes of the New York Free Soilers" 93 and "Abolitionism and the Labor Movement" 73–74; see also Joseph Rayback, *Free Soil* esp. 201–30.

60. Eric Foner, "Politics and Prejudice" 242, 247, 249–50 and "Racial Attitudes of the New York Free Soilers" 87–89, 91–92.

61. William Austin, *"Susanna," "Jeanie," and "The Old Folks at Home"* 33.

Chapter 8

1. Good accounts of Webster's (as well as Clay's) investment in the Compromise may be found in James Ford Rhodes, *History of the United States from the Compromise of 1850* 50–66; see also Irving Bartlett, *Daniel Webster* 240–53.

2. Christy's Minstrels managed both to support the Compromise and to lampoon Webster in a stump-speech parody of the Seventh of March speech:

> Do dese people want to tear up dat magnificent and magniglorious American flag what's ravelin' out in de breezes ob de atmosphere on de top ob de St. Nicholas Hotel? Eh? umph? Do dey want to strip it up and gib de stars to de Souf, and de stripes to de Norf? I answer you in clarion tones dat I hope may be heard from de risin' place ob de sun to de cheer in which he sets down. Dey can't do it, nor—nor any other man. ("Any Other Man," Christy, *New* 9–11)

See also "Or Any Other Man," *Frank Converse's "Old Cremona" Songster* 32.

3. Thomas Gossett, *Uncle Tom's Cabin and American Culture* 164, 260.

4. T. Allston Brown, *History of the New York Stage* 1:314; Harry Birdoff, *The World's Greatest Hit* 20–23. The primary, if somewhat dubious, sources for the history of the stage productions of *Uncle Tom's Cabin* are Harry Birdoff, *The World's Greatest Hit,* and Thomas Gossett, *Uncle Tom's Cabin and American Culture* 260–83. Birdoff is rather liberal with creative reconstructions of the past, and Gossett is wrong on several details (e.g., H. J. Conway, one of *Uncle Tom's Cabin's* chief adapters, is rechristened "Conroy"). I have also relied on newspaper accounts; George Odell, *Annals of the New York Stage;* J. N. Ireland, *Records of the New York Stage;* and T. Allston Brown, *History of the American Stage* and *History of the New York Stage.* See, in addition, Frank Rahill, *The World of Melodrama* 247–53; Vera Jiji, ed., *Showcasing American Drama;* and Robert Shipp, *"Uncle Tom's Cabin* and the Ethos of Melodrama."

5. "The world is not good enough yet for it to succeed," wrote Stowe to Hutchinson, evincing her commercial sense along with her piety. See Montrose Moses, "George L. Aiken's Dramatization of *Uncle Tom's Cabin"* 605–6, and Thomas Gossett, *Uncle Tom's Cabin and American Culture* 261.

6. James Gordon Bennett's *Herald* editorial (September 3, 1852) does reveal that the Taylor version, curiously enough, changed the names of George and Eliza Harris to Edward and Morna Wilmot—acknowledging, consciously or not, the part of the Wilmot Proviso and Free-Soil politics in giving rise to the story.

7. Readers still in doubt on this point should consult Christina Zwarg, "Fathering and Blackface in *Uncle Tom's Cabin"* 284–87.

8. David Grimsted's *"Uncle Tom* from Page to Stage" is an excellent account of the changes Aiken wrought on Stowe's novel; see also Barnard Hewitt, "Uncle Tom and Uncle Sam."

9. For a brief discussion of Conway's relationship with Kimball, see Bruce McConachie, "H. J. Conway's Dramatization of *Uncle Tom's Cabin."*

10. A New Orleans production called *Southern "Uncle Tom's Cabin"* was performed by the virulently antiabolitionist circus comedian Dan Rice, not, as is often stated, the minstrel performer T. D. Rice. Performed at Dan Rice's Amphitheatre in February 1854, the play was advertised as "a satirical quizzical burlesque by Mrs. Harriet Screecher Blow." See Joseph Roppolo, "Uncle Tom in New Orleans" 222, and Richard Moody, *"Uncle Tom's Cabin:* Introduction" 357.

11. For a fuller listing of these and related dramas, see Gary Engle, "The Atkinson Collection of Ethiopian Drama," and William Mahar, "Ethiopian Skits and Sketches."

12. Add to the theatrical list innumerable Uncle Tom songs (M. A. Collier's "Eva's Parting," John S. Adams's "I Am Going There, or, the Death of Little Eva," and so on); touring panoramic views and dioramas of *Uncle Tom's Cabin;* commemorative plates with scenes from the novel and bisque china busts of Tom and Eva; specially bound editions of the novel itself; St. Clare hats and Uncle Tom tippets; card games, picture books, and engravings. According to the *Liberator:* "It should be noted, among the favorable signs of the times, that artists, of all grades, now find it not only congenial, but a remunerative work, to represent the creations of Mrs. Stowe's genius in pictures and statues." See Thomas Riis, "The Music and Musicians in Nineteenth-Century Productions of *Uncle Tom's Cabin,"* and Stephen Hirsch, "Uncle Tomitudes" 311–20 (*Liberator* quoted at 316).

13. The first of many film versions of *Uncle Tom's Cabin* appeared in 1903; for this history, see Harry Birdoff, *The World's Greatest Hit* 392–410. For some very acute remarks on the development of film out of the surplus symbolic value of black representation, see Michael Rogin, "Blackface, White Noise."

14. Thomas Gossett, *Uncle Tom's Cabin and American Culture* 278–80.

15. The Aiken version has seen many reprintings; I have used the edition in Montrose Moses, ed., *Representative Plays by American Dramatists*. The Conway version has not been reprinted, was indeed considered lost until recently; a promptbook manuscript from an 1876 Boston Museum production is now held at the Harry Ransom Humanities Research Center at the University of Texas. There are some problems with this text: act four is largely reprinted from Aiken, and several of Conway's scenes in act three are missing. As Bruce McConachie has pointed out, these scenes can be supplemented by a Boston Museum program from December 7, 1852 (Boston Public Library), reference to which indicates that the 1876 production was in other respects virtually identical to the 1852 performances. See McConachie, "Out of the Kitchen and into the Marketplace" 25 n.2.

Stowe's construction of a female polis in *Uncle Tom's Cabin*, her "domestic feminism," has been illuminated by Ellen Moers, *Harriet Beecher Stowe and American Literature* 20–26; Leslie Fiedler, *What Was Literature?* 145–78; Jane Tompkins, "Sentimental Power"; Gillian Brown, "Getting in the Kitchen with Dinah"; Elizabeth Ammons, "Stowe's Dream of the Mother-Savior"; and Stephen Railton, *Authorship and Audience* 74–89. Such defenses of Stowe, however, usually entail the elision of racial matters, as Hortense Spillers argues in "Changing the Letter"; see also the critique of the feminist literature on *Uncle Tom's Cabin* in Rachel Bowlby, "Breakfast in America." For an argument that Stowe's novel was even more radical in its questioning of patriarchal structures than her partisans have recognized, see Christina Zwarg, "Fathering and Blackface in *Uncle Tom's Cabin*."

16. In the novel itself, as even some of its contemporaries remarked, Stowe's representations of blacks resemble those of minstrelsy. See *Literary World* December 4, 1852, 357.

17. Cf. H. J. Conway's remark in a letter to Moses Kimball: "We must [partially] depend for our comic parts on Topsy (hard thing to do as a female negro)" [*sic*]. Quoted in Bruce McConachie, "H. J. Conway's Dramatization of *Uncle Tom's Cabin*" 150.

18. *New York Herald* May 14, 1853.

19. Louis Althusser, "Contradiction and Overdetermination" and *Reading Capital;* Nicos Poulantzas, *Political Power and Social Classes*.

20. See Karl Marx, "The North American Civil War," "The Civil War in the United States," and "A Criticism of American Affairs"; Charles and Mary Beard, *The Rise of American Civilization* 2:3–7, 36–41; William Appleman Williams, *The Contours of American History* 284–319; Barrington Moore, *Social Origins of Dictatorship and Democracy* 111–55; David Potter, *The Impending Crisis* 32–35, 41–43.

21. Quoted in Montrose Moses, "George L. Aiken's Dramatization" 610–11.

22. Joseph Ireland, extra-illustrated edition of *Records of the New York Stage* 2:xvi.

23. In this and the next several paragraphs I am much indebted to Harry Birdoff, *The World's Greatest Hit*, for the detective work crucial to reconstructing the *Uncle Tom* feud (87–99, 107–26).

24. See Barnum's advertising copy alleging that, "while thoroughly anti-slavery in its sentiment, [Conway's play] contains not a single word calculated to offend those whose opinions on this topic favor its non-agitation." J. N. Ireland, extra-illustrated edition of *Records of the New York Stage* 2:xvi.

25. The *Knickerbocker* indulged its contempt for houses such as the National: "We went to the National Theatre the other evening, to behold the '*Rural Habitation of Uncle Thomas*,' vulgarly known as 'Uncle Tom's Cabin;' and we would n't go to see it again for a 'large sum of gold'" ("First" 210).

26. T. Allston Brown, *History of the American Stage* 6; Montrose Moses, "George L. Aiken's Dramatization" 608.

27. Playbill, June 2, 1854, Harvard Theatre Collection.

28. Harriet Beecher Stowe, *Uncle Tom's Cabin* 340. This conflict is submitted to lengthy and intelligent discussion in Charles Foster, *The Rungless Ladder* 49–57. Foster speculates that Stowe's portrait of St. Clare was inspired by Orestes Brownson's 1840 "The Laboring Classes," which equated the exploitative systems of capitalism and slavery and predicted class war eight years in advance of *The Communist Manifesto*. I believe Foster underemphasizes St. Clare's ultimate siding with the northern worker against the southern slave; and it is interesting to note that in Brownson's own development the positions of "The Laboring Classes" were soon elaborated into apologies for slavery. See, for example, Arthur Schlesinger, *The Age of Jackson* 299–304, 407–8, 425.

29. Of course the displacement of labor struggles onto Britain, in accordance with the abolitionist belief in American "free labor," might also have given working-class audiences trouble; but in most cases, as far as I can judge, the rhetoric of "European" working conditions seems to have functioned both as a figure for the northern states of America and as a useful fiction, in which workers still believed, that lifelong wage work was not yet an American affliction.

30. The *Tribune* did note that Barnum later altered this "deformity" of Conway's play, no longer defending so vehemently the white worker. Somewhat ambiguously, it added: "Now let him [Barnum] kill Uncle Tom and all will be right" (December 2, 1853).

31. Eric Foner, *Free Soil, Free Labor, Free Men* (on the Republican party) and Jean Baker, *Affairs of Party* (on the Democratic party), both enlarge on this purpose.

32. Foner, *Free Soil, Free Labor, Free Men* 156, 158, 154; Joseph Rayback, *Free Soil*. See the excellent review of northern intellectual response to the growth of sectional thinking in the North in George Fredrickson, *The Inner Civil War* 36–50.

33. Foner, *Free Soil, Free Labor, Free Men* 155, 237, 239, 165.

34. Foner, *Free Soil, Free Labor, Free Men* 157–58.

35. See, for example, Alexander Saxton, *The Rise and Fall of the White Republic* 127–82.

36. Helene Zahler, *Eastern Workingmen and National Land Policy* 102; see also Bernard Mandel, *Labor* 120–24. The title of one pamphlet said it all: *Slavery . . . To Be Made the Universal Condition of the Laboring Classes of Society. The Supporters of This Doctrine Vote for Buchanan* (Rayback, "American" 161).

37. See Iver Bernstein, *The New York City Draft Riots* 75–77, 85–86, 91–93, 99–100, 123–24.

38. See, for example, the white working-class anger expressed in the 1850s in John Hopkins, *The American Citizen* 132, and H. B. Mullins, *A Voice from the Workshop* 10–11; see also W. J. Rorabaugh, "Rising Democratic Spirits" 157.

39. For a reading of Lincoln's political rhetoric in the heat of this process, see Eric Lott, "The Eighteenth Brumaire of Abraham Lincoln."

Afterword

1. In an early letter to his brother, Michael Rogin notes, Melville signed himself "Tawney," and his first books mixed travel writing with anti-imperialist critique (*Subversive* 43). *Moby-Dick* (1851), written during the Compromise of 1850 debates, seems (as many have pointed out) an allegory of the Compromise itself. See Willie Weathers, "*Moby-Dick* and the Nineteenth-Century Scene"; Charles Foster, "Something in Emblems"; and Alan Heimert, "*Moby-Dick* and American Political Symbolism." For all three writers, the Union in Melville's allegory is destroyed by monomania: for Weathers, Ahab is William Lloyd Garrison, whose slogan was "No Compromise with Slaveholders"; for

Foster, Ahab is Daniel Webster, advocate of the Compromise and thus the betrayer of New England's moral hopes; and for Heimert, Ahab is John C. Calhoun, who would have preserved slavery not through compromise but at the expense of the Union.

2. Harriet Beecher Stowe, *Sunny Memories of Foreign Lands* 1:284, 43; for a similar view, see *Journal of Music* 5, 17 (1854), 134. For a brief account of Greenfield's career, see Eileen Southern, *The Music of Black Americans* 103–4.

3. Unfortunately this mournful, even nostalgic tone persists; one popular example is Ken Burns's television documentary "The Civil War" (1990).

4. For more on this ambivalence, see Caroline Moseley, "'When Will Dis Cruel War Be Ober?'"

5. Albon Man, "Labor Competition and the New York Draft Riots of 1863"; Robert Ernst, *Immigrant Life in New York City* 172–74; Bernard Mandel, *Labor* 189–94; Iver Bernstein, *The New York City Draft Riots* 3–42.

6. *Christy's Bones and Banjo Melodist* 57.

7. Du Bois wrote, "It was easy to transfer class hatred so that it fell upon the black worker" (*Reconstruction* 103–4).

8. David Brion Davis, *The Problem of Slavery in the Age of Revolution* 251; Alan Dawley, *Class and Community* 196, 238–39.

9. Karl Marx, *Capital* 301; see also the clarity of Bernard Mandel, *Labor* 204. For an excellent gloss on Marx's words, see David Roediger, "'Labor in White Skin'" 290–91.

Bibliography

Aaron, Daniel. *The Unwritten War: American Writers and the Civil War*. New York: Knopf, 1973.

Abrahams, Roger D. *Singing the Master: The Emergence of African-American Culture in the Plantation South*. New York: Pantheon, 1992.

Adorno, Theodor W. (with the assistance of George Simpson). "On Popular Music" [1941]. In *On Record: Rock, Pop, and the Written Word*. Ed. Simon Frith and Andrew Goodwin, 301–14. New York: Pantheon, 1990.

———. "Perennial Fashion—Jazz." *Prisms* [1967]. Trans. Samuel and Sherry Weber, 119–32. Cambridge, MA: MIT P, 1981.

Adorno, Theodor W., and Max Horkheimer. "The Culture Industry: Enlightenment as Mass Deception." In *Dialectic of Enlightenment* [1944]. Trans. John Cumming, 120–67. New York: Seabury Press, 1972.

Aiken, George L. *Uncle Tom's Cabin* [1852]. In *Representative Plays by American Dramatists* [1925]. Ed. Monstrose J. Moses, 2:605–93. New York: Benjamin Blom, 1964.

Allen, Robert C. *Horrible Prettiness: Burlesque and American Culture*. Chapel Hill: U of North Carolina P, 1991.

Allen, William Francis, Charles Pickard Ware, and Lucy McKim Garrison. *Slave Songs of the United States* [1867]. New York: Peter Smith, 1929.

Althusser, Louis. "Contradiction and Overdetermination." In *For Marx* [1965]. Trans. Ben Brewster, 87–128. London: Verso, 1977.

———. *Lenin and Philosophy and Other Essays*. Trans. Ben Brewster. New York: Monthly Review P, 1971.

Althusser, Louis, et al. *Reading Capital*. Trans. Ben Brewster. London: Verso, 1970.

"American Humor." *Democratic Review* 27.87 (1845): 212–19.

Ames, Edgar W. "First Presentation of *Uncle Tom's Cabin*." *Americana* 6.11 (1911): 1045–52.

Ammons, Elizabeth. "Stowe's Dream of the Mother-Savior: *Uncle Tom's Cabin* and American Women Writers Before the 1920s." In *New Essays on Uncle Tom's Cabin*. Ed. Eric J. Sundquist, 155–95. Cambridge: Cambridge UP, 1986.

Anderson, Benedict. *Imagined Communities: Reflections on the Origin and Spread of Nationalism*. London: Verso, 1983.

Arac, Jonathan. *Commissioned Spirits: The Shaping of Social Motion in Dickens, Carlyle, Melville, and Hawthorne* [1979]. New York: Columbia UP, 1989.

Aronowitz, Stanley. "Defining the Popular." CUNY Lecture Series on Bakhtin. New York, November 10, 1986.

———. "Writing Labor's History." *Social Text* 25/26 (1990): 171–95.

Ashcroft, Bill, Gareth Griffiths, and Helen Tiffin. *The Empire Writes Back: Theory and Practice in Post-Colonial Literatures*. London: Routledge, 1989.

Attali, Jacques. *Noise: The Political Economy of Music* [1977]. Trans. Brian Massumi. Minneapolis: U of Minnesota P, 1985.

Austin, William W. *"Susanna," "Jeanie," and "The Old Folks at Home": The Songs of Stephen C. Foster from His Time to Ours.* New York: Macmillan, 1975.

Babcock-Abrahams, Barbara. "'A Tolerated Margin of Mess': The Trickster and His Tales Reconsidered." *Journal of the Folklore Institute* 11.3 (1975): 147–86.

Baker, Benjamin. *A Glance at New York in 1848* [1848]. New York: n.d.

Baker, Houston A., Jr. *Blues, Ideology, and Afro-American Literature: A Vernacular Theory.* Chicago: U of Chicago P, 1984.

———. *Modernism and the Harlem Renaissance.* Chicago: U of Chicago P, 1987.

Baker, Jean H. *Affairs of Party: The Political Culture of Northern Democrats in the Mid-Nineteenth Century.* Ithaca: Cornell UP, 1983.

Bakhtin, Mikhail. *Rabelais and His World* [1965]. Trans. Helene Iswolsky. Bloomington: Indiana UP, 1984.

Barnum, P. T. *Struggles and Triumphs: or, Forty Years' Recollections of P. T. Barnum.* Hartford, CT: J. B. Burr, 1869.

Barthes, Roland. *Image-Music-Text.* Trans. Stephen Heath. New York: Hill and Wang, 1977.

———. *Mythologies* [1957]. Trans. Annette Lavers. New York: Hill and Wang, 1972.

———. *The Pleasure of the Text* [1973]. Trans. Richard Miller. New York: Hill and Wang, 1975.

Bartlett, Irving H. *Daniel Webster.* New York: Norton, 1978.

Baskervill, Charles Read. *The Elizabethan Jig and Related Song Drama.* Chicago: U of Chicago P, 1929.

Beadle's Dime Song Book No. 3. New York: I. P. Beadle, 1860.

Beard, Charles A., and Mary Beard. *The Rise of American Civilization.* 2 vols. New York: Macmillan, 1927.

Beaumont, Gustave de. *Marie, or Slavery in the United States* [1835]. Stanford: Stanford UP, 1958.

Beckham, Sue Bridwell. "By 'N' By Hard Times: Eastman Johnson's 'Life at the South' and American Minstrels." *Journal of American Culture* 6.3 (1983): 19–25.

Bell, Bernard. "Twain's 'Nigger' Jim: The Tragic Face Behind the Minstrel Mask." *Mark Twain Journal* 23.1 (1985): 10–17.

Bender, Thomas. *New York Intellect: A History of Intellectual Life in New York City.* New York: Knopf, 1987.

Bennett, Tony. "Marxism and Popular Fiction." *Literature and History* 7.2 (1981): 138–65.

———. "The Politics of 'the Popular' and Popular Culture." In *Popular Culture and Social Relations.* Ed. Tony Bennett, Colin Mercer, and Janet Woollacott, 6–21. Milton Keynes: Open UP, 1986.

Bennett, Tony, Colin Mercer, and Janet Woollacott, ed. *Popular Culture and Social Relations.* Milton Keynes: Open UP, 1986.

Bercovitch, Sacvan. *The American Jeremiad.* Madison: U of Wisconsin P, 1978.

Berlant, Lauren. "National Brands/National Body: *Imitation of Life.* In *Comparative American Identities: Race, Sex, and Nationality in the Modern Text.* Ed. Hortense Spillers, 110–40. New York: Routledge, 1991.

Berlin, Ira. "The Revolution in Black Life." In *The American Revolution: Explorations in the History of American Radicalism.* Ed. Alfred Young, 349–82. DeKalb: Northern Illinois UP, 1976.

———. *Slaves Without Masters: The Free Negro in the Antebellum South.* New York: Oxford UP, 1974.

———. "Time, Space, and the Evolution of Afro-American Society on British Mainland North America." *American Historical Review* 85 (1980): 44–78.

Bernstein, Iver. *The New York City Draft Riots: Their Significance for American Society and Politics in the Age of the Civil War.* New York: Oxford UP, 1990.

Berret, Anthony J. *"Huckleberry Finn* and the Minstrel Show." *American Studies* 27.2 (1986): 37–49.

Berwanger, Eugene W. *The Frontier Against Slavery: Western Anti-Negro Prejudice and the Slavery Extension Controversy.* Urbana: U of Illinois P, 1967.

Beveridge, Albert. *Abraham Lincoln, 1809–1858.* 2 vols. Boston: Houghton Mifflin, 1928.

Bhabha, Homi K. "DissemiNation: Time, Narrative, and the Margins of the Modern Nation." In *Nation and Narration.* Ed. Homi Bhabha, 291–322. New York: Routledge, 1990.

———. "Of Mimicry and Man: The Ambivalence of Colonial Discourse." *October* 28 (1984): 125–33.

———. "The Other Question: The Stereotype and Colonial Discourse." *Screen* 24.6 (1983): 18–36.

Billy Birch's Ethiopian Melodist. New York: Dick and Fitzgerald, 1862.

Birdoff, Harry. *The World's Greatest Hit.* New York: S. F. Vanni, 1947.

"The Black Opera." *New York Tribune,* June 30, 1855. Reprinted in *Journal of Music* 13.14 (1858): 107–8.

Blackmar, Elizabeth. *Manhattan for Rent: Housing and Property Relations in New York City.* Ithaca: Cornell UP, 1989.

Blair, John. "Blackface Minstrels in Cross-Cultural Perspective." *American Studies International* 28.2 (1990): 52–65.

Blair, Walter. "Charles Mathews and His 'A Trip to America.'" *Prospects* 2 (1976): 1–23.

Blassingame, John W. *The Slave Community: Plantation Life in the Antebellum South* [1976]. New York: Oxford UP, 1983.

Bledstein, Burton. *The Culture of Professionalism: The Middle Class and the Development of Higher Education in America.* New York: Norton, 1976.

Blewett, Mary. "Work, Gender, and the Artisan Tradition in New England Shoemaking, 1780–1860." *Journal of Social History* 17.2 (1983): 221–48.

Bluestein, Gene. *The Voice of the Folk: Folklore and American Literary Theory.* Amherst: U of Massachusetts P, 1972.

Blumin, Stuart M. "The Hypothesis of Middle-Class Formation in Nineteenth-Century America: A Critique and Some Proposals." *American Historical Review* 90.2 (1985): 299–338.

———. "Mobility and Change in Ante-Bellum Philadelphia." In *Nineteenth-Century Cities.* Ed. Stephan Thernstrom and Richard Sennett, 165–208. New Haven: Yale UP, 1969.

———. "Residential Mobility Within the Nineteenth-Century City." In *The Peoples of Philadelphia: A History of Ethnic Groups and Lower-Class Life.* Ed. Allen F. Davis and Mark H. Haller, 37–52. Philadelphia: Temple UP, 1973.

Bobo, William. *Glimpses of New York: By a South Carolinian.* Charleston, SC, 1852.

Boime, Albert. *The Art of Exclusion: Representing Blacks in the Nineteenth Century.* Washington, D.C.: Smithsonian, 1990.

Boskin, Joseph. *Sambo: The Rise and Demise of an American Jester.* New York: Oxford UP, 1986.

Bourdieu, Pierre. *Distinction: A Social Critique of the Judgment of Taste* [1979]. Trans. Richard Nice. Cambridge, MA: Harvard UP, 1984.

———. "Symbolic Power." *Critique of Anthropology* 4 (1979): 77–85.

Bowlby, Rachel. "Breakfast in America: *Uncle Tom*'s Cultural Histories." In *Nation and Narration*. Ed. Homi K. Bhabha, 197–212. New York: Routledge, 1990.

———. *Just Looking: Consumer Culture in Dreiser, Gissing, and Zola*. New York: Methuen, 1985.

Boyer, Paul. *Urban Masses and Moral Order in America, 1820–1920*. Cambridge, MA: Harvard UP, 1978.

Brantlinger, Patrick. *Crusoe's Footprints: Cultural Studies in Britain and America*. New York: Routledge, 1990.

Bratton, J. S. "English Ethiopians: British Audiences and Black-Face Acts, 1835–1865." *Yearbook of English Studies* z (1981): 127–42.

Brennan, Timothy. "The National Longing for Form." In *Nation and Narration*. Ed. Homi K. Bhabha, 44–70. New York: Routledge, 1990.

Bridges, Amy. "Becoming American: The Working Classes in the United States Before the Civil War." In *Working-Class Formation: Nineteenth-Century Patterns in Western Europe and the U.S.* Ed. Ira Katznelson, 157–96. Princeton: Princeton UP, 1986.

Brower, Frank. *Frank Brower's Black Diamond Songster and Ebony Jester*. New York: Dick and Fitzgerald, 1863.

Brown, Gillian. "Getting in the Kitchen with Dinah: Domestic Politics in *Uncle Tom's Cabin*." *American Quarterly* 36 (1984): 503–23.

Brown, Sterling. *The Negro in American Fiction* [1937]. New York: Arno Press, 1969.

Brown, T. Allston. *History of the American Stage* [1870]. New York: Benjamin Blom, 1969.

———. *History of the New York Stage* [1903]. 2 vols. New York: Benjamin Blom, 1969.

———. "The Origin of Negro Minstrelsy." In *Fun in Black; or, Sketches of Minstrel Life*. Charles H. Day, 5–10. New York: DeWitt, 1874.

Browne, Ray B. "Shakespeare in American Vaudeville and Negro Minstrelsy." *American Quarterly* 12.3 (1960): 374–91.

———. Shakespeare in the Nineteenth-Century Songsters." *Shakespeare Quarterly* 8.2 (1957): 207–18.

Buckley, Peter G. *To the Opera House: Culture and Society in New York City, 1820–1860*. New York: Oxford UP, in press.

Buckley's Song Book for the Parlor. New York: P. J. Cozans, 1855.

Budsworth's New Comic Ethiopian Songster. New York: F. A. Brady, 1861.

Bunn, Alfred. *Old England and New England*. Philadelphia: Hart, 1853.

Burn, James Dawson. *Three Years among the Working-Classes in the United States During the War*. London: Smith, Elder, 1865.

Burtnett, J. G. "National Elements in Stephen Foster's Art." *South Atlantic Quarterly* 21.4 (1922): 322–26.

"California Gold and European Revolution." *Southern Quarterly Review* 1.2 (1850): 273–313.

Campbell, M. *Wood's Minstrel Songs*. New York: Dick and Fitzgerald, 1855.

Cantwell, Robert. *Bluegrass Breakdown: The Making of the Old Southern Sound*. Urbana: U of Illinois P, 1984.

Carby, Hazel V. *Reconstructing Womanhood: The Emergence of the Afro-American Woman Novelist*. New York: Oxford UP, 1987.

Cardwell, Guy A. *Twins of Genius*. East Lansing: Michigan State College Press, 1953.

Chambers, Iain. *Popular Culture: The Metropolitan Experience*. New York: Methuen, 1986.

Channing, William Ellery. "Emancipation" [1840]. In *Works*. Vol. 6, 5–89. Boston: James Munroe, 1843.

Chase, Gilbert. *America's Music: From the Pilgrims to the Present.* 3d. ed. Urbana: U of Illinois P, 1987.

Child, Lydia Maria. "Mary French and Susan Easton." *Juvenile Miscellany* 3d ser., no. 6 (1834): 194–98.

———. *The Patriarchal Institution, as Described by Members of Its Own Family.* New York: American Anti-Slavery Society, 1860.

Childers, Mary, and bell hooks. "A Conversation about Race and Class." In *Conflicts in Feminism.* Ed. Marianne Hirsch and Evelyn Fox Keller, 60–81. New York: Routledge, 1990.

Chodorow, Nancy. "Mothering, Male Dominance, and Capitalism." In *Capitalist Patriarchy and the Case for Socialist Feminism.* Ed. Zillah R. Eisenstein, 83–106. New York: Monthly Review P, 1979.

Christy, E. Byron. *Christy's New Songster and Black Joker.* New York: Dick and Fitzgerald, 1868.

Christy, George. *George Christy's Essence of Old Kentucky.* New York: Dick and Fitzgerald, 1864.

Christy's Minstrels. *Christy's Bones and Banjo Melodist.* New York: Dick and Fitzgerald, 1867.

Christy's Minstrels. *Christy's Plantation Melodies No. 4.* Philadelphia: Fisher and Bros., 1854.

Christy and Wood's New Song Book. Philadelphia: T. B. Peterson and Bros., 1854.

Clark, T. J. *Image of the People: Gustave Courbet and the Revolution of 1848* [1973]. Princeton: Princeton UP, 1982.

———. *The Painting of Modern Life: Paris in the Art of Manet and His Followers.* Princeton: Princeton UP, 1984.

Clover, Carol. "Her Body, Himself: Gender in the Slasher Film." *Representations* 20 (1987): 187–228.

Cockrell, Dale. "Of Gospel Hymns, Minstrel Shows, and Jubilee Singers: Toward Some Black South African Musics." *American Music* 5.4 (1987): 417–32.

———. "The Early Blackface Minstrel and His World." Unpublished paper.

Cohen, Patricia Cline. "Unregulated Youth: Masculinity and Murder in the 1830s City." *Radical History Review* 52 (1992): 33–52.

Cohen, Philip. "Tarzan and the Jungle Bunnies: Race, Class, and Sex in Popular Culture." *New Formations* 5 (Summer 1988): 25–30.

Conner, Edmon S. "An Old Actor's Memories." *New York Times,* June 5, 1881. Reprinted in Marshall Stearns, *The Story of Jazz,* 111–12. New York: Oxford UP, 1956.

Converse, Frank. *Frank Converse's "Old Cremona" Songster.* New York: Dick and Fitzgerald, 1863.

Conway, H. J. *Uncle Tom's Cabin* [1852]. 1876 prompt-book ms. Harry Ransom Humanities Research Center, University of Texas-Austin.

Cooper, James Fenimore. *Satanstoe* [1845]. Lincoln: U of Nebraska P, 1962.

Cotton, Ben. "Interview with Ben Cotton." *New York Mirror,* July 3, 1897.

Crouch, Stanley. "Jazz and the Conquest of Time." Lecture, Columbia University, New York, April 1985.

Cunliffe, Marcus. *Chattel Slavery and Wage Slavery: The Anglo-American Context, 1830–1860.* Athens: U of Georgia P, 1979.

Curtis, George William. "Editorial Notes—Music." *Putnam's Monthly* 2.11 (1853): 571–74.

Damon, S. Foster. "The Negro in Early American Songsters." *Papers of the Bibliographical Society of America* 28 (1934): 132–63.

———, comp. *Series of Old American Songs*. Providence: Brown University Library, 1936.

Davidge, William. *Footlight Flashes*. New York: American News Company, 1866.

Davidoff, Leonore. "Class and Gender in Victorian England: The Diaries of Arthur J. Munby and Hannah Cullwick." *Feminist Studies* 5.1 (1979): 89–141.

Davidson, Frank C. "The Rise, Development, Decline, and Influence of the American Minstrel Show." Ph.D. diss., New York University, 1952.

Davis, David Brion. *The Problem of Slavery in the Age of Revolution, 1770–1823*. Ithaca: Cornell UP, 1975.

Davis, Mike. *Prisoners of the American Dream: Politics and Economy in the History of the U.S. Working Class*. London: Verso, 1985.

Davis, Natalie Zemon. *Society and Culture in Early Modern France*. Stanford: Stanford UP, 1975.

Davis, Susan G. "'Making Night Hideous': Christmas Revelry and Public Order in Nineteenth-Century Philadelphia." *American Quarterly* 34.2 (1982): 185–99.

———. *Parades and Power: Street Theater in Nineteenth-Century Philadelphia*. Berkeley: U of California P, 1986.

Dawidoff, Robert. "Some of Those Days." *Western Humanities Review* 41.3 (1987): 263–86.

Dawley, Alan. *Class and Community: The Industrial Revolution in Lynn*. Cambridge, MA: Harvard UP, 1976.

Dawley, Alan, and Paul Faler. "Working-Class Culture and Politics in the Industrial Revolution: Sources of Loyalism and Rebellion." *Journal of Social History* 9.4 (1976): 466–80.

Day, Charles H. *Fun in Black; or, Sketches of Minstrel Life*. New York: DeWitt, 1874.

Dearborn, Mary V. *Pocahontas's Daughters: Gender and Ethnicity in American Culture*. New York: Oxford UP, 1986.

Delany, Martin. *Blake: or, The Huts of America* [1859–61]. Ed. Floyd Miller. Boston: Beacon, 1970.

Denning, Michael. "The End of Mass Culture." *International Labor and Working-Class History* 37 (1990): 4–18.

———. *Mechanic Accents: Dime Novels and Working-Class Culture in America*. London: Verso, 1987.

———. "'The Special American Conditions': Marxism and American Studies." *American Quarterly* 38.3 (1986): 356–80.

Dennison, Sam. *Scandalize My Name: Black Imagery in American Popular Music*. New York: Garland Publishing, 1982.

De Susannah, and Thick Lip, Melodist. New York: T. W. Strong, 1850.

De Voe, Thomas F. *The Market Book* [1862]. New York: Burt Franklin, 1969.

DeVoto, Bernard. "Stephen Foster's Songs." *Harper's* 183.1093 (1941): 109–12.

Dickens, Charles. *American Notes* [1842]. New York: Penguin, 1972.

Dixey, Edward F. *Dixey's Essence of Burnt Cork*. Philadelphia, 1859.

Doane, Mary Ann. "Misrecognition and Identity." *Cine-Tracts* 11 (1980): 25–32.

Dodd, Jill Seigel. "The Working Classes and the Temperance Movement in Ante-Bellum Boston." *Labor History* 19.4 (1978): 510–31.

Dorman, James H. "Shaping the Popular Image of Post-Reconstruction American Blacks: The 'Coon Song' Phenomenon of the Gilded Age." *American Quarterly* 40.4 (1988): 450–71.

———. "The Strange Career of Jim Crow Rice." *Journal of Social History* 3.2 (1969–70): 109–22.

Dorson, Richard. "Mose the Far-Famed and World-Renowned." *American Literature* 15.3 (1943): 288–300.

Douglas, Ann. *The Feminization of American Culture*. New York: Knopf, 1977.

Douglas, Mary. *Natural Symbols: Explorations in Cosmology* [1970]. New York: Pantheon, 1982.

Douglass, Frederick. "Gavitt's Original Ethiopian Serenaders." *North Star,* June 29, 1849. Reprinted in *The Life and Writings of Frederick Douglass*. 5 vols. Ed. Philip S. Foner, 1:141–42. New York: International Publishers, 1950–75.

———. *Life and Times of Frederick Douglass* [1892]. New York: Collier, 1962.

———. *My Bondage and My Freedom* [1855]. Ed. William Andrews. Urbana: U of Illinois P, 1987.

———. *Narrative of the Life of Frederick Douglass* [1845]. Ed. Michael Meyer. New York: Modern Library, 1984.

Dreiser, Theodore. *Sister Carrie* [1900]. Ed. Donald Pizer. New York: Norton, 1970.

Du Bois, W. E. B. *Black Reconstruction in America, 1860–1880* [1935]. New York: Atheneum, 1969.

———. "The Negro in Literature and Art." *Annals* [1913]. Reprinted in *W. E. B. Du Bois: A Reader*. Ed. Meyer Weinberg, 231–36. New York: Harper and Row, 1970.

———. *The Souls of Black Folk* [1903]. In *Three Negro Classics*. Ed. John Hope Franklin, 207–389. New York: Avon, 1965.

Duchartre, Pierre Louis. *The Italian Comedy* [1929]. Trans. Randolph T. Weaver. New York: Dover, 1966.

Dunbar, Paul Laurence. *Sport of the Gods* [1901]. New York: Arno, 1969.

Dwight, J. S. "A Complaint on Behalf of Native Composers." *Journal of Music* 5.12 (1854): 94–95.

———. "Music for the People." *Journal of Music* 3.12 (1853): 94–95.

———. "Negro Minstrelsy." *Journal of Music* 1.16 (1852): 124.

Dyer, Richard. *Heavenly Bodies: Film Stars and Society*. New York: St. Martin's, 1986.

———. "White." *Screen* 29.4 (1988): 44–64.

"E.P. Christy: Originator of Ethiopian Minstrelsy." *New York Clipper,* August 19, 1854.

The Early Minstrel Show. New World Records NW 338, 1985.

Edelstein, Tilden G. "*Othello* in America: The Drama of Racial Intermarriage." In *Region, Race, and Reconstruction: Essays in Honor of C. Vann Woodward*. Ed. J. Morgan Kousser and James M. McPherson, 179–97. New York: Oxford, 1982.

Edsall, Thomas Byrne, and Mary D. Edsall. *Chain Reaction: The Impact of Race, Rights, and Taxes on American Politics*. New York: Norton, 1991.

Eights, James. "Pinkster Festivities in Albany Sixty Years Ago." In *Collection on the History of Albany*. 4 vols. Ed. Joel Munsell, 2: 323–27. Albany, 1865–71.

Elias, Norbert. *The Civilizing Process: The History of Manners* [1939]. Trans. Edmund Jephcott. New York: Urizen Books, 1978.

Eliot, T. S. "Marie Lloyd." In *Selected Prose of T. S. Eliot*. Ed. Frank Kermode, 172–74. New York: Harcourt, Brace, Jovanovich, 1976.

Ellison, Ralph. "Change the Joke and Slip the Yoke" [1958]. In *Shadow and Act* [1964], 45–59. New York: Vintage, 1972.

———. *Going to the Territory*. New York: Random House, 1986.

———. *Shadow and Act* [1964]. New York: Vintage, 1972.

Emery, Lynn Fauley. *Black Dance in the United States from 1619 to 1970*. Palo Alto: National Press Books, 1972.

Engle, Gary D. "The Atkinson Collection of Ethiopian Drama at the University of Chicago." *Resources for American Literary Study* 1.2 (1971): 181–99.

——, ed. *This Grotesque Essence: Plays from the American Minstrel Stage.* Baton Rouge: Louisiana State UP, 1978.

Epstein, Dena. *Sinful Tunes and Spirituals: Black Folk Music to the Civil War.* Urbana: U of Illinois P, 1977.

Ernst, Robert. "Economic Nativism in New York City During the 1840s." *New York History* 29.2 (1948): 170–86.

——. *Immigrant Life in New York City, 1825–1863* [1949]. Port Washington, NY: Ira J. Friedman, 1965.

——. "The One and Only Mike Walsh." *New-York Historical Society Quarterly* 36.1 (1952): 43–65.

Ethiopian Serenaders. *Music of the Ethiopian Serenaders.* Philadelphia: E. Ferrett, 1845.

Ethiopian Serenaders . . . from the St. James's Theatre, London. Harvard Theatre Collection, 1846.

Faler, Paul. "Cultural Aspects of the Industrial Revolution: Lynn, Massachusetts Shoemakers and Industrial Morality, 1826–1860." In *American Workingclass Culture: Explorations in American Labor and Social History.* Ed. Milton Cantor, 121–48. Westport, CT: Greenwood, 1979.

——. *Mechanics and Manufacturers in the Early Industrial Revolution: Lynn, Massachusetts, 1780–1860.* Albany: State University of New York P, 1981.

Faner, Robert D. *Walt Whitman and Opera.* Philadelphia: U of Pennsylvania P, 1951.

Fanon, Frantz. *Black Skin, White Masks* [1952]. Trans. Charles Lam Markmann. New York: Grove, 1967.

Feldberg, Michael. *The Turbulent Era: Riot and Disorder in Jacksonian America.* New York: Oxford UP, 1980.

Feltes, Norman N. *Modes of Production of Victorian Novels.* Chicago: U of Chicago P, 1986.

Fiedler, Leslie A. *Waiting for the End* [1966]. New York: Stein and Day, 1972.

——. *What Was Literature?: Class Culture and Mass Society.* New York: Simon and Schuster, 1982.

Field, Al G. *Watch Yourself Go By.* Columbus, 1912.

Fields, Barbara J. "Ideology and Race in American History." In *Region, Race, and Reconstruction: Essays in Honor of C. Vann Woodward.* Ed. J. Morgan Kousser and James M. McPherson, 143–77. New York: Oxford UP, 1982.

——. "Slavery, Race, and Ideology in the United States of America." *New Left Review* 181 (1990): 95–118.

"First Impressions of New York." *Knickerbocker* 43.2 (1854): 209–11.

Flynn, Joyce. "Melting Plots: Patterns of Racial and Ethnic Amalgamation in American Drama Before Eugene O'Neill." *American Quarterly* 38.3 (1986): 417–38.

Foner, Eric. "Abolitionism and the Labor Movement in Ante-Bellum America." In *Politics and Ideology in the Age of the Civil War,* 57–76. New York: Oxford UP, 1980.

——. *Free Soil, Free Labor, Free Men: The Ideology of the Republican Party Before the Civil War.* New York: Oxford UP, 1970.

——. *Politics and Ideology in the Age of the Civil War.* New York: Oxford UP, 1980.

——. "Politics and Prejudice: The Free Soil Party and the Negro, 1849–1852." *Journal of Negro History* 50.4 (1965): 239–56.

——. "Politics, Ideology, and the Origins of the American Civil War." In *Politics and Ideology in the Age of the Civil War,* 34–56. New York: Oxford UP, 1980.

——. "Racial Attitudes of the New York Free Soilers." In *Politics and Ideology in the Age of the Civil War,* 77–93. New York: Oxford UP, 1980.

———. *Tom Paine and Revolutionary America.* New York: Oxford UP, 1976.

———. "Why Is There No Socialism in America?" *History Workshop Journal* 17 (1984): 57–80.

———. "The Wilmot Proviso Revisited." *Journal of American History* 56.2 (1969): 262–79.

———. "Workers and Slavery." In *Working for Democracy: American Workers from the Revolution to the Present.* Ed. Paul Buhle and Alan Dawley, 21–28. Urbana: U of Illinois P, 1985.

Forgacs, David. "National-Popular: Genealogy of a Concept." In *Formations of Nation and People,* 83–98. London: Routledge, 1984.

Foster, Charles H. *The Rungless Ladder: Harriet Beecher Stowe and New England Puritanism.* Durham: Duke UP, 1954.

———. "Something in Emblems: A Reinterpretation of *Moby-Dick.*" *New England Quarterly* 34 (1961): 3–35.

Foster, George G. *New York by Gas-Light: With Here and There a Streak of Sunshine.* New York: DeWitt and Davenport, 1850.

———. *New York in Slices: By an Experienced Carver.* New York: William Graham, 1849.

Foster, Morrison. *My Brother Stephen* [1896]. Indianapolis: Foster Hall, 1932.

Foster, Stephen. *Minstrel-Show Songs.* New York: Da Capo, 1980.

Foucault, Michel. "Nietzsche, Genealogy, History." In *Language, Counter-Memory, Practice.* Ed. Donald Bouchard, 139–64. Ithaca: Cornell UP, 1977.

Fox, Charles H. *Charley Fox's Sable Songster.* New York: Frederic A. Brady, 1859.

Franco, Jean. "What's in a Name?: Popular Culture Theories and Their Limitations." *Studies in Latin American Popular Culture* 1 (1982): 5–14.

Franklin, H. Bruce. *The Victim as Criminal and Artist: Literature from the American Prison.* New York: Oxford UP, 1978.

Fredrickson, George M. The Black Image in the White Mind: The Debate on Afro-American Character and Destiny, 1817–1914. New York: Harper and Row, 1971.

———. *The Inner Civil War: Northern Intellectuals and the Crisis of the Union.* New York: Harper and Row, 1965.

Freedman, Barbara. *Staging the Gaze: Postmodernism, Psychoanalysis, and Shakespearean Comedy.* Ithaca: Cornell UP, 1991.

Freud, Sigmund. *Beyond the Pleasure Principle* [1920]. Trans. James Strachey. New York: Norton, 1961.

———. *The Ego and the Id* [1923]. Trans. Joan Riviere. Ed. James Strachey. New York: Norton, 1960.

———. "Fetishism" [1927]. In *On Sexuality,* 340–50. Harmondsworth, Eng.: Pelican, 1981.

———. *Group Psychology and the Analysis of the Ego* [1921]. Trans. James Strachey. New York: Norton, 1959.

———. *Jokes and Their Relation to the Unconscious* [1905]. Trans. James Strachey. New York: Norton, 1960.

Friedman, Lawrence J. "Confidence and Pertinacity in Evangelical Abolitionism: Lewis Tappan's Circle." *American Quarterly* 31.1 (1979): 81–106.

Frith, Simon. "Playing with Real Feeling: Making Sense of Jazz in Britain." *New Formations* 4 (1988): 7–24.

Fuller, Margaret. "Entertainments of the Past Winter." *Dial* 3.1 (1842): 46–72.

Gaines, Francis Pendleton. *The Southern Plantation: A Study in the Development and the Accuracy of a Tradition.* New York: Columbia UP, 1924.

Galbreath, C. B. *Daniel Decatur Emmett.* Columbus: F. J. Heer, 1904.

Gallagher, Catherine. Review of *Just Looking*, by Rachel Bowlby, and *Modes of Production of Victorian Novels*, by Norman Feltes. *Criticism* 29.2 (1987): 233–42.

Garber, Marjorie. *Vested Interests: Cross-Dressing and Cultural Anxiety*. New York: Routledge, 1992.

Gates, Henry Louis, Jr. *Figures in Black: Words, Signs, and the "Racial" Self*. New York: Oxford UP, 1987.

———, ed. *"Race," Writing, and Difference*. Chicago: U of Chicago P, 1986.

———. *The Signifying Monkey: A Theory of African-American Literary Criticism*. New York: Oxford UP, 1988.

Geertz, Clifford. *The Interpretation of Cultures*. New York: Basic Books, 1973.

Gendron, Bernard. "Theodor Adorno Meets the Cadillacs." In *Studies in Entertainment: Critical Approaches to Mass Culture*. Ed. Tania Modleski, 18–36. Bloomington: Indiana UP, 1986.

Giddins, Gary. "The Signifying Satchmo." *Village Voice*, May 23, 1989: 82.

Gilje, Paul A. *The Road to Mobocracy: Popular Disorder in New York City, 1763–1834*. Chapel Hill: U of North Carolina P, 1987.

Gilman, Sander L. "Black Bodies, White Bodies: Toward an Iconography of Female Sexuality in Late Nineteenth-Century Art, Medicine, and Literature." *"Race," Writing, and Difference*. Ed. Henry Louis Gates, Jr., 223–61. Chicago: U of Chicago P, 1986.

Gilroy, Paul. *"There Ain't No Black in the Union Jack": The Cultural Politics of Race and Nation*. London: Hutchinson, 1987.

Ginzburg, Carlo. *The Cheese and the Worms: The Cosmos of a Sixteenth-Century Miller* [1976]. Trans. John and Anne Tedeschi. Baltimore: Johns Hopkins UP, 1980.

Girard, René. *Deceit, Desire, and the Novel: Self and Other in Literary Structure*. Trans. Yvonne Freccero. Baltimore: Johns Hopkins UP, 1972.

Glaberman, Martin. *Wartime Strikes: The Struggle Against the No-Strike Pledge in the UAW During World War II*. Detroit: Bewick/ed, 1980.

Gordon, David M., Richard Edwards, Michael Reich. *Segmented Work, Divided Workers: The Historical Transformation of Labor in the United States*. New York: Cambridge UP, 1982.

Gorn, Elliot J. "'Good-Bye Boys, I Die a True American': Homicide, Nativism, and Working-Class Culture in Antebellum New York City." *Journal of American History* 74.2 (1987): 388–410.

———. *The Manly Art: Bare-Knuckle Prize Fighting in America*. Ithaca: Cornell UP, 1986.

Gossett, Thomas F. *Race: The History of an Idea in America*. Dallas: Southern Methodist UP, 1963.

———. *Uncle Tom's Cabin and American Culture*. Dallas: Southern Methodist UP, 1985.

Gramsci, Antonio. *Selections from Cultural Writings*. Ed. David Forgacs and Geoffrey Nowell-Smith. Trans. William Boelhower. London: Lawrence and Wishart, 1985.

———. *Selections from the Prison Notebooks*. Ed. and trans. Quintin Hoare and Geoffrey Nowell-Smith. New York: International Publishers, 1971.

Green, Alan W. C. "'Jim Crow,' 'Zip Coon': The Northern Origins of Negro Minstrelsy." *Massachusetts Review* 11.2 (1970): 385–97.

Greene, Lorenzo J. *The Negro in Colonial New England*. Port Washington, NY: Kennikat, 1966.

Griffith, Mattie [Martha Griffith Browne]. *Autobiography of a Female Slave* [1857]. New York: Negro Universities P, 1969.

Grimsted, David. *Melodrama Unveiled: American Theater and Culture, 1800–1850*. Chicago: U of Chicago P, 1968.

———. "*Uncle Tom* from Page to Stage: Limitations of Nineteenth-Century Drama." *Quarterly Journal of Speech* 56.3 (1970): 235–44.

Grimsted, David, and William F. Stowe. "White-Black Humor." Review of *Blacking Up: The Minstrel Show in Nineteenth-Century America*, by Robert Toll. *Journal of Ethnic Studies* 3.2 (1975): 78–96.

Gutman, Herbert. *Work, Culture, and Society in Industrializing America: Essays in American Working-Class and Social History*. New York: Vintage, 1976.

Hall, Stuart. "Gramsci's Relevance for the Study of Race and Ethnicity." *Journal of Communication Inquiry* 10.2 (1986): 5–27.

———. *The Hard Road to Renewal: Thatcherism and the Crisis of the Left*. London: Verso, 1988.

———. "The Meaning of New Times." In *New Times: The Changing Face of Politics in the 1990s*. Ed. Stuart Hall and Martin Jacques, 116–34. London: Verso, 1989.

———. "New Ethnicities." In *Black Film/British Cinema*. Ed. Kobena Mercer, 27–31. London: ICA, 1988.

———. "Notes on Deconstructing 'the Popular.'" In *People's History and Socialist Theory*. Ed. Raphael Samuel, 227–40. London: Routledge and Kegan Paul, 1981.

———. "Some Paradigms in Cultural Studies." *Annali* 21.3 (1978): 13–48.

Hall, Stuart, et al. *Policing the Crisis: Mugging, the State, and Law and Order*. London: Macmillan, 1978.

———. *Resistance Through Rituals: Youth Subcultures in Post-War Britain*. London: Hutchinson, 1975.

Halttunen, Karen. *Confidence Men and Painted Women: A Study of Middle-Class Culture in America, 1830–1870*. New Haven: Yale UP, 1982.

Hamm, Charles. *Yesterdays: Popular Song in America*. New York: Norton, 1979.

Hancock, Herbie. "Herbie Hancock Interview." *Musician* (February 1987): 36.

Haraway, Donna. "A Manifesto for Cyborgs: Science, Technology, and Socialist Feminism in the 1980s." *Socialist Review* 80 (1985): 65–107.

Harlow, Alvin F. *Old Bowery Days: The Chronicles of a Famous Street*. New York: D. Appleton, 1931.

Harris, Neil. *Humbug: The Art of P. T. Barnum*. Chicago: U of Chicago P, 1973.

Harrison, Jonathan Baxter. *Certain Dangerous Tendencies in American Life*. Boston, 1880.

Hart, Adolphus M. *Uncle Tom in Paris; or, Views of Slavery Outside the Cabin, Together with Washington's Views of Slavery*. Baltimore: Taylor, 1854.

Hartz, Louis. *The Liberal Tradition in America* [1955]. New York: Harcourt, Brace, Jovanovich, 1983.

Haskell, Thomas. "Capitalism and the Origins of Humanitarian Sensibility, Part I." *American Historical Review* 90.2 (1985): 339–61.

Haswell, Charles H. *Reminiscences of an Octogenarian of the City of New York*. New York: Harper's, 1897.

Hauser, Arnold. *The Social History of Art*. 4 vols. Trans. Stanley Godman. New York: Vintage, 1951.

Hawkes, Terence. *That Shakespeherian Rag: Essays on a Critical Process*. New York: Methuen, 1986.

Haywood, Charles. "Negro Minstrelsy and Shakespearean Burlesque." In *Folklore and Society*. Ed. Bruce Jackson, 77–92. Hatboro, PA: Folklore Associates, 1966.

Hearn, Lafcadio. *Selected Writings*. New York: Citadel, 1949.

Heath, Stephen. "Translator's Note." In Roland Barthes, *Image-Music-Text*, 7–11. New York: Hill and Wang, 1977.

Hebdige, Dick. *Hiding in the Light: On Images and Things*. New York: Routledge, 1988.

Heimert, Alan. "*Moby-Dick* and American Political Symbolism." *American Quarterly* 16 (1963): 498–504.

Henderson, Mary. *The City and the Theatre: New York Playhouses from Bowling Green to Times Square.* Clifton, NJ: James T. White, 1973.

Hentzi, Gary, and Jon Anderson. "An Interview with Jonathan Arac." *Critical Texts* 7.2 (1990): 1–23.

"Heroes of the Burnt Cork." In "Negro Minstrelsy in New York." Comp. Charles Moreau. Vol. 2. Harvard Theatre Collection, 1891.

Hershberg, Theodore. "Free Blacks in Antebellum Philadelphia: A Study of Ex-Slaves, Freeborn, and Socioeconomic Decline." *Journal of Social History* 5.2 (1971–72): 183–209.

Herskowitz, Richard. "P. T. Barnum's Double Bind." *Social Text* 2 (1979): 133–41.

Hewitt, Barnard. "Uncle Tom and Uncle Sam: New Light from an Old Play." *Quarterly Journal of Speech* 37.1 (1951): 63–70.

Hewitt, Roger. "Black Through White: Hoagy Carmichael and the Cultural Reproduction of Racism." *Popular Music* 3 (1983): 33–50.

Higginson, T. W. "Nat Turner's Insurrection" [1861]. In *Travellers and Outlaws: Episodes in American History,* 276–326. Boston: Lee and Shepard, 1889.

———. "Negro Spirituals." *Atlantic Monthly* 19.116 (1867): 685–94.

Higham, John. *Strangers in the Land: Patterns of American Nativism, 1860–1925.* New Brunswick: Rutgers UP, 1955.

Hill, Errol. *Shakespeare in Sable: A History of Black Shakespearean Actors.* Amherst: U of Massachusetts P, 1984.

Hirsch, Stephen A. "Uncle Tomitudes: The Popular Reaction to *Uncle Tom's Cabin.*" In *Studies in the American Renaissance, 1978.* Ed. Joel Myerson, 303–30. Boston: Twayne, 1978.

Hirsch, Susan. *Roots of the American Working Class: The Industrialization of Crafts in Newark, 1800–1860.* Philadelphia: U of Pennsylvania P, 1978.

Hobsbawm, E. J. *Primitive Rebels: Studies in Archaic Forms of Social Movement in the Nineteenth and Twentieth Centuries.* New York: Norton, 1959.

Hofstadter, Richard. *The American Political Tradition* [1948]. New York: Vintage, 1954.

Hoggart, Richard. *The Uses of Literacy: Changing Patterns in English Mass Culture.* New York: Oxford UP, 1957.

Holmberg, Carl Bryan, and Gilbert D. Schneider. "Daniel Decatur Emmett's Stump Sermons: Genuine Afro-American Culture, Language, and Rhetoric in the Negro Minstrel Show." *Journal of Popular Culture* 19.4 (1986): 27–38.

hooks, bell. "Representing Whiteness in the Black Imagination." In *Cultural Studies.* Ed. Lawrence Grossberg, Cary Nelson, and Paula Treichler, 338–46. New York: Routledge, 1992.

Hopkins, John H. *The American Citizen: His Rights and Duties According to the Constitution of the United States.* New York: Pudney and Russell, 1857.

Horlick, Allan. *Country Boys and Merchant Princes: The Social Control of Young Men in New York.* Lewisberg, PA: Bucknell UP, 1975.

Hornblow, Arthur. *A History of the Theater in America.* Philadelphia: J. B. Lippincott, 1919.

Horsman, Reginald. *Race and Manifest Destiny: The Origins of American Racial Anglo-Saxonism.* Cambridge, MA: Harvard UP, 1981.

Howard, John Tasker. *Stephen Foster, America's Troubadour.* New York: Thomas Y. Crowell, 1934.

Howe, Henry Warren. *Passages from the Life of Henry Warren Howe.* Lowell, MA: Courier-Citizen Company, 1899.

Howe, Irving. *World of Our Fathers: The Journey of the East European Jews to America and the Life They Found and Made* [1976]. New York: Schocken, 1989.

Howkins, Alun, and C. Ian Dyck. "'The Time's Alteration': Popular Ballads, Rural Radicalism, and William Cobbett." *History Workshop Journal* 23 (1987): 20–38.

Huggins, Nathan Irvin. *Harlem Renaissance.* New York: Oxford UP, 1971.

Hutton, Laurence. "The Negro on the Stage." *Harper's New Monthly Magazine* 79.469 (1889): 131–45.

Huyssen, Andreas. *After the Great Divide: Modernism, Mass Culture, Postmodernism.* Bloomington: U of Indiana P, 1986.

———. "Mass Culture as Woman: Modernism's Other." In *After the Great Divide: Modernism, Mass Culture, Postmodernism*, 44–62. Bloomington: U of Indiana P, 1986.

Hyman, Stanley Edgar. "American Negro Literature and Folk Tradition" [1958]. In *The Promised End: Essays and Reviews, 1942–1962*, 295–315. Cleveland: World Publishing, 1963.

Ireland, J. N. *Records of the New York Stage.* Extra-illustrated edition. 2 vols. New York: T. H. Morrell, 1867. Harvard Theatre Collection.

Irving, Washington. *Letters of Jonathan Oldstyle, Gentleman* [1824]. Ed. Bruce I. Granger and Martha Hartzog. Boston: Twayne, 1977.

Jackson, Richard, ed. *Stephen Foster Song Book.* New York: Dover, 1974.

Jacobs, Harriet [pseud. Linda Brent]. *Incidents in the Life of a Slave Girl* [1861]. In *The Classic Slave Narratives.* Ed. Henry Louis Gates, Jr., 333–515. New York: New American Library, 1987.

James, C. L. R. *Beyond a Boundary* [1963]. New York: Pantheon, 1983.

———. et al. *Facing Reality* [1958]. Detroit: Bewick/ed, 1974.

James, Edward. *The Amateur Negro Minstrel's Guide.* New York: James, 1880.

James, Henry. *A Small Boy and Others.* London: Macmillan, 1913.

Jameson, Fredric. "Pleasure: A Political Issue." In *The Ideologies of Theory, 1971–86*, 2:61–74. Minneapolis: U of Minnesota P, 1988.

———. *The Political Unconscious: Narrative as a Socially Symbolic Act.* Ithaca: Cornell UP, 1981.

———. "Reification and Utopia in Mass Culture." *Social Text* 1 (1979): 130–48.

Jardine, Lisa. *Still Harping on Daughters: Women and Drama in the Age of Shakespeare.* Totowa, NJ: Barnes and Noble, 1983.

Jennings, J. J. *Theatrical and Circus Life; or, Secrets of the Stage, Greenroom, and Sawdust Arena.* St. Louis: Sun Publishing, 1882.

Jentz, John B. "The Anti-Slavery Constituency in Jacksonian New York City." *Civil War History* 27.2 (1981): 101–22.

———. "Artisans, Evangelicals, and the City: A Social History of Abolition and Labor Reform in Jacksonian New York." Ph.D. diss., CUNY, 1977.

Jiji, Vera, ed. *Showcasing American Drama: George L. Aiken/Harriet Beecher Stowe: Uncle Tom's Cabin.* Brooklyn: Brooklyn College Humanities Institute, 1983.

Johannsen, Robert W. *To the Halls of the Montezumas: The Mexican War in the American Imagination.* New York: Oxford UP, 1985.

Johnson, Barbara. "Metaphor, Metonymy, and Voice in *Their Eyes Were Watching God.*" In *Black Literature and Literary Theory.* Ed. Henry Louis Gates, Jr., 205–19. New York: Methuen, 1984.

———. "Mirror Stages: Jacques Lacan and Frantz Fanon." Lecture, University of Virginia, October 30, 1991.

Johnson, Claudia D. "That Guilty Third Tier: Prostitution in Nineteenth-Century American Theaters." *American Quarterly* 27.5 (1975): 575–84.

Johnson, James Weldon. *Black Manhattan.* New York: Knopf, 1930.

Johnson, Paul E. *A Shopkeeper's Millennium: Society and Revivals in Rochester, New York, 1815–1837.* New York: Hill and Wang, 1978.

Johnson, Richard. "What Is Cultural Studies Anyway?" *Social Text* 16 (1986–87): 38–80.

Jones, LeRoi. *Blues People: Negro Music in White America.* New York: William Morrow, 1963.

Jordan, Winthrop D. *White over Black: American Attitudes Toward the Negro, 1550–1812.* Baltimore: Penguin, 1968.

Karcher, Carolyn L. *Shadow over the Promised Land: Slavery, Race, and Violence in Melville's America.* Baton Rouge: Lousiana State UP, 1980.

Keeler, Ralph. "Three Years as a Negro Minstrel." *Atlantic Monthly* 24.141 (1869): 71–85.

Kelley, Mary. *Private Woman, Public Stage: Literary Domesticity in Nineteenth-Century America.* New York: Oxford UP, 1984.

Kemble, Frances Anne [Fanny]. *Journal of a Residence on a Georgian Plantation in 1838–1839* [1863]. Chicago: Afro-American Press, 1969.

Kennard, James K., Jr. "Who Are Our National Poets?" *Knickerbocker* 26.4 (1845): 331–41.

The Kentucky Minstrel and Jersey Warbler. Philadelphia: Robinson and Peterson, 1844.

Kerber, Linda K. "Abolitionists and Amalgamators: The New York City Race Riots of 1834." *New York History* 48.1 (1967): 28–39.

Kingsdale, Jon M. "The 'Poor Man's Club': Social Functions of the Urban Working-Class Saloon." *American Quarterly* 25.3 (1973): 472–89.

Klein, Melanie. *Contributions to Psycho-analysis, 1921–1945.* London: Hogarth, 1948.

Kmen, Henry A. "Old Corn Meal: A Forgotten Urban Negro Folksinger." *Journal of American Folklore* 75.295 (1962): 29–34.

Knobel, Dale T. *Paddy and the Republic: Ethnicity and Nationality in Antebellum America.* Middletown: Wesleyan UP, 1986.

Kovel, Joel. *White Racism: A Psychohistory* [1970]. New York: Columbia UP, 1984.

Kristeva, Julia. *Powers of Horror: An Essay on Abjection* [1980]. Trans. Leon S. Roudiez. New York: Columbia UP, 1982.

Krupat, Arnold. "Native American Literature and the Canon." *Critical Inquiry* 10.1 (1983): 145–71.

LaCapra, Dominick. *History and Criticism.* Ithaca: Cornell UP, 1985.

Laclau, Ernesto. *Politics and Ideology in Marxist Theory.* London: Verso, 1977.

Lapsansky, Emma Jones. "'Since They Got Those Separate Churches': Afro-Americans and Racism in Jacksonian Philadelphia." *American Quarterly* 37.1 (1980): 54–78.

Laurie, Bruce. *Artisans into Workers: Labor in Nineteenth-Century America.* New York: Noonday, 1989.

———. "Fire Companies and Gangs in Southwark: The 1840s." In *The Peoples of Philadelphia: A History of Ethnic Groups and Lower-Class Life, 1790–1940.* Ed. Allen F. Davis and Mark H. Haller, 71–88. Philadelphia: Temple UP, 1973.

———. "'Nothing on Compulsion': Life Styles of Philadelphia Artisans, 1800–1850. *Labor History* 15.3 (1974): 337–66.

———. *Working People of Philadelphia, 1800–1850.* Philadelphia: Temple UP, 1980.

Lawrence, Vera Brodsky. *Strong on Music: The New York Music Scene in the Days of George Templeton Strong, 1836–1875.* Vol. 1. *Resonances, 1836–1850.* New York: Oxford UP, 1988.

Leavitt, M. B. *Fifty Years in Theatrical Management.* New York: Broadway Publishing, 1912.

Lefebvre, Henri. "Musique et semiologie." *Musique en jeu* 4 (1971).

Leman, Walter. *Memories of an Old Actor.* San Francisco: A. Roman Company, 1886.

Leonard, Ira M. "The Rise and Fall of the American Republican Party in New York City, 1843–1845." *New-York Historical Society Quarterly* 50.1 (1966): 151–92.

"Letter from A. W. T." *Journal of Music* 1.22 (1852): 170.

"Letter from a Teacher at the South." *Journal of Music* 2.21 (1853): 164.

Levin, Harry. *The Power of Blackness: Hawthorne, Poe, Melville.* New York: Vintage, 1958.

Levine, Bruce. *Half Slave and Half Free: The Roots of Civil War.* New York: Hill and Wang, 1992.

Levine, Lawrence W. *Black Culture and Black Consciousness.* New York: Oxford UP, 1977.

———. *Highbrow/Lowbrow: The Emergence of Cultural Hierarchy in America.* Cambridge, MA: Harvard UP, 1988.

Lewis, John Delaware. *Across the Atlantic.* London: G. Earle, 1851.

Lhamon, W. T. "Constance Rourke's Secret Reserve." In Constance Rourke, *American Humor* [1931], xiii–xli. Tallahassee: Florida State UP, 1986.

Limpus, Lowell M. *History of the New York Fire Department.* New York: Dutton, 1940.

Lincoln, Abraham. "Address to the Young Men's Lyceum of Springfield" [1838]. In *Collected Works.* Ed. Roy P. Basler, 1:108–15. New Brunswick: Rutgers UP, 1953–55.

Lippard, George. *New York: Its Upper Ten and Lower Million* [1853]. Upper Saddle River, NJ: Gregg P, 1970.

———. *The Quaker City; or, Monks of Monk Hall* [1844]. New York: Odyssey P, 1970.

Lipsitz, George. *Class and Culture in Cold War America: "A Rainbow at Midnight."* New York: Praeger, 1981.

Litvak, Joseph. "Back to the Future: A Review Article on the New Historicism, Deconstruction, and Nineteenth-Century Fiction." *Texas Studies in Language and Literature* 30.1 (1988): 120–49.

Litwack, Leon. *North of Slavery: The Negro in the Free States, 1790–1860.* Chicago: U of Chicago P, 1961.

Lofton, Williston. "Abolition and Labor." *Journal of Negro History* 33.3 (1948): 249–83.

Logan, Olive. "The Ancestry of Brudder Bones." *Harper's New Monthly Magazine* 58.347 (1879): 687–98.

Looby, Christopher. "'As Thoroughly Black as the Most Faithful Philanthropist Could Desire': The Erotics of Race in T. W. Higginson's *Army Life in a Black Regiment.*" In *Race and the Subject of Masculinities.* Ed. Harry Stecopoulos and Michael Uebel. Durham: Duke UP, 1994.

Lott, Eric. "Double V, Double-Time: Bebop's Politics of Style." *Callaloo* 11.3 (1988): 597–605.

———. "The Eighteenth Brumaire of Abraham Lincoln." *Clio* 22.2 (1993): 157–73.

———. "White Like Me: Racial Cross-Dressing and the Construction of American Whiteness." In *Cultures of U.S. Imperialism.* Ed. Amy Kaplan and Donald Pease, 474–95. Durham: Duke UP, 1993.

Lowe, John. "Theories of Ethnic Humor: How to Enter, Laughing." *American Quarterly* 38.3 (1986): 439–60.

Ludlow, N. M. *Dramatic Life as I Found It* [1880]. New York: Benjamin Blom, 1966.

Lukas, J. Anthony. *Common Ground: A Turbulent Decade in the Lives of Three American Families.* New York: Knopf, 1985.

Lynn, Kenneth. *Mark Twain and Southwestern Humor.* Boston: Little, Brown, 1960.

Lyotard, J. F. *The Postmodern Condition: A Report on Knowledge.* Trans. Geoff Bennington and Brian Massumi. Minneapolis: U of Minnesota P, 1984.

Macherey, Pierre. *A Theory of Literary Production* [1966]. Trans. Geoffrey Wall. London: Routledge, 1978.

Mackay, Charles. *Life and Liberty in America: Sketches of a Tour in the United States and Canada in 1857–8.* New York: Harper, 1859.

Mahar, William J. "'Backside Albany' and Early Blackface Minstrelsy: A Contextual Study of America's First Blackface Song." *American Music* 6.1 (1988): 1–27.

———. "Black English in Early Blackface Minstrelsy: A New Interpretation of the Sources of Minstrel Show Dialect." *American Quarterly* 37.2 (1985): 260–85.

———. "Ethiopian Skits and Sketches: Contents and Contexts of Blackface Minstrelsy, 1840–1890." *Prospects* 16 (1991): 241–79.

Mailer, Norman. "The White Negro" [1957]. In *Advertisements for Myself,* 311–31. New York: G. P. Putnam's, 1959.

Mailloux, Steven. *Rhetorical Power.* Ithaca: Cornell UP, 1989.

Man, Albon P. "Labor Competition and the New York Draft Riots of 1863." *Journal of Negro History* 36.4 (1951): 375–405.

Mandel, Bernard. *Labor: Free and Slave: Workingmen and the Anti-Slavery Movement in the United States.* New York: Associated Authors, 1955.

Marcus, Greil. *Lipstick Traces: A Secret History of the Twentieth Century.* Cambridge, MA: Harvard UP, 1989.

———. *Mystery Train: Images of America in Rock 'n' Roll Music* [1975]. New York: Dutton, 1982.

Marcus, Steven. *Engels, Manchester, and the Working Class* [1974]. Rev. ed. New York: Norton, 1985.

———. *The Other Victorians: A Study of Sexuality and Pornography in Mid-Nineteenth-Century England* [1966]. New York: Norton, 1985.

Maróthy, János. *Music and the Bourgeois, Music and the Proletarian.* Trans. Eva Rona. Budapest: Akademiai Kiado, 1974.

Marrocco, W. Thomas, and Harold Gleason, ed. *Music in America: An Anthology.* New York: Norton, 1964.

Marshall, Herbert, and Mildred Stock. *Ira Aldridge: The Negro Tragedian.* London: Rockliff, 1958.

Martin, Waldo E., Jr. *The Mind of Frederick Douglass.* Chapel Hill: U of North Carolina P, 1984.

Marx, Karl. *Capital: A Critique of Political Economy.* Vol. 1 [1867]. Trans. Samuel Moore and Edward Aveling. Ed. Frederick Engels. New York: International Publishers, 1967.

———. "The Civil War in the United States" [1861]. In *On America and the Civil War.* Ed. Saul K. Padover, 87–94. New York: McGraw-Hill, 1972.

———. *Class Struggles in France* [1850]. New York: International Publishers, 1964.

———. "A Criticism of American Affairs" [1862]. In *On America and the Civil War.* Ed. Saul K. Padover, 210–12. New York: McGraw-Hill, 1972.

———. "The North American Civil War" [1861]. In *On America and the Civil War.* Ed. Saul K. Padover, 69–78. New York: McGraw-Hill, 1972.

Marx, Leo. "The Long Revolution and the British Left," *Commentary* 32 (1961): 517–23.

Mathews, Mrs. Anne. *A Continuation of the Memoirs of Charles Mathews, Comedian.* 2 vols. Philadelphia: Lea and Blanchard, 1839.

Mathews, Cornelius. *A Pen-and-Ink Panorama of New York City.* New York: John S. Taylor, 1853.

Matthews, Brander. "The Rise and Fall of Negro Minstrelsy." *Scribner's Magazine* 57.6 (1915): 754–59.

Maus, Katharine Eisaman. "'Playhouse Flesh and Blood': Sexual Ideology and the Restoration Actress." *English Literary History* 46.4 (1979): 595–617.

Mayer, Arno. "The Lower Middle Class as Historical Problem." *Journal of Modern History* 47.3 (1975): 409–36.

Mayer, David. *Harlequin in His Element: The English Pantomime, 1806–1836.* Cambridge, MA: Harvard UP, 1969.

McConachie, Bruce A. "The Cultural Politics of 'Paddy' on the Midcentury American Stage." *Studies in Popular Culture* (1988): 1–13.

———. "H. J. Conway's Dramatization of *Uncle Tom's Cabin:* A Previously Unpublished Letter." *Theatre Journal* 34.2 (1982): 149–54.

———. *Melodramatic Formations: American Theatre and Society, 1820–1870.* Iowa City: U of Iowa P, 1992.

———. "Out of the Kitchen and into the Marketplace: Normalizing *Uncle Tom's Cabin* for the Antebellum Stage." *Journal of American Drama and Theatre* 3 (1991): 5–28.

———. "The Theatre of Edwin Forrest and Jacksonian Hero Worship." In *When They Weren't Doing Shakespeare: Essays on Nineteenth-Century British and American Theatre.* Ed. Judith L. Fisher and Stephen Watt, 3–18. Athens: U of Georgia P, 1989.

———. "'The Theatre of the Mob': Apocalyptic Melodrama and Preindustrial Riots in Antebellum New York." In *Theatre for Working-Class Audiences in the United States, 1830–1980.* Ed. Bruce A. McConachie and Daniel Friedman, 17–46. Westport, CT: Greenwood Press, 1985.

McDowell, Robert E. "Bones and the Man: Toward a History of Bones Playing." *Journal of American Culture* 5.1 (1982): 38–43.

McLean, Albert F. *American Vaudeville as Ritual.* Lexington: U of Kentucky P, 1965.

Mellencamp, Patricia. "Situation Comedy, Feminism, and Freud: Discourses of Gracie and Lucy." In *Studies in Entertainment: Critical Approaches to Mass Culture.* Ed. Tania Modleski, 80–95. Bloomington: Indiana UP, 1986.

Melville, Herman. *The Confidence-Man: His Masquerade* [1857]. New York: New American Library, 1954.

———. *Moby-Dick; or, The Whale* [1851]. Ed. Harold Beaver. New York: Penguin, 1972.

Mercer, Colin. "Complicit Pleasures." In *Popular Culture and Social Relations.* Ed. Tony Bennett et al., 50–68. Milton Keynes: Open UP, 1986.

———. "A Poverty of Desire." In *Formations of Pleasure.* Ed. Victor Burgin, 84–100. London: Routledge, 1983.

Mercer, Kobena, ed. *Black Film/British Cinema.* London: ICA, 1988.

———. "'1968': Periodizing Politics and Identity." In *Cultural Studies.* Ed. Lawrence Grossberg, Cary Nelson, and Paula Treichler, 424–38. New York: Routledge, 1992.

———. "Skin Head Sex Thing." In *How Do I Look?: Queer Film and Video.* Ed. Bad Object-Choices, 169–210. Seattle: Bay Press, 1991.

Merk, Frederick. *Manifest Destiny and Mission in American History.* New York: Random House, 1963.

Metz, Christian. *The Imaginary Signifier: Psychoanalysis and the Cinema* [1977]. Trans. Celia Britton, Annwyl Williams, Ben Brewster, and Alfred Guzzetti. Bloomington: Indiana UP, 1982.

293

Michaels, Walter Benn. *The Gold Standard and the Logic of Naturalism: American Literature at the Turn of the Century*. Berkeley: U of California P, 1987.

Middleton, Richard. "Articulating Musical Meaning/Re-Constructing Musical History/Locating the 'Popular.'" *Popular Music* 5 (1985): 5–43.

———. "In the Groove, or Blowing Your Mind? The Pleasures of Musical Repetition." In *Popular Culture and Social Relations*. Ed. Tony Bennett et al., 159–75. Milton Keynes: Open UP, 1986.

———. "Play It Again, Sam: Some Notes on the Productivity of Repetition in Popular Music." *Popular Music* 3 (1983): 235–70.

Miller, Kerby. *Emigrants and Exiles: Ireland and the Irish Exodus to North America*. New York: Oxford UP, 1985.

Miller, Perry. *The Raven and the Whale: The War of Words and Wits in the Era of Poe and Melville* [1956]. Westport, CT: Greenwood, 1973.

Miller, Richard. *Bohemia: The Protoculture Then and Now*. Chicago: Nelson-Hall, 1977.

Minnegerode, Meade. *The Fabulous Forties*. New York: Putnam's, 1924.

Modleski, Tania. *Feminism Without Women: Culture and Criticism in a "Postfeminist" Age*. New York: Routledge, 1991.

———. "Some Functions of Feminist Criticism, or The Scandal of the Mute Body." *October* 49 (1989): 3–24.

———, ed. *Studies in Entertainment: Critical Approaches to Mass Culture*. Bloomington: Indiana UP, 1986.

———. "The Terror of Pleasure: The Contemporary Horror Film and Postmodern Theory." In *Studies in Entertainment: Critical Approaches to Mass Culture*. Ed. Tania Modleski, 155–66. Bloomington: Indiana UP, 1986.

———. *The Women Who Knew Too Much: Hitchcock and Feminist Theory*. New York: Methuen, 1988.

Moers, Ellen. *Harriet Beecher Stowe and American Literature*. Hartford, CT: Stowe-Day Foundation, 1978.

Montgomery, David. "Labor in the Industrial Era." In *A History of the American Worker* [1976]. Ed. Richard B. Morris, 79–113. Princeton: Princeton UP, 1983.

———. "The Shuttle and the Cross: Weavers and Artisans in the Kensington Riots of 1844." *Journal of Social History* 5.4 (1972): 411–46.

———. *Workers' Control in America: Studies in the History of Work, Technology, and Labor Struggles*. New York: Cambridge UP, 1979.

———. "The Working Classes of the Pre-Industrial American City, 1780–1830." *Labor History* 9.1 (1968): 3–22.

Moody, Richard. *The Astor Place Riot*. Bloomington: Indiana UP, 1958.

———. "*Uncle Tom's Cabin*: Introduction." In *Dramas from the American Theatre, 1762–1909*. Ed. Richard Moody, 349–59. Boston: Houghton Mifflin, 1966.

Moore, Barrington, Jr. *Social Origins of Dictatorship and Democracy: Lord and Peasant in the Making of the Modern World*. Boston: Beacon, 1966.

Moreau, Charles C., comp. "Negro Minstrelsy in New York." 2 vols. Harvard Theatre Collection, 1891.

Morgan, Edmund S. *American Slavery—American Freedom: The Ordeal of Colonial Virginia*. New York: Norton, 1975.

Morreall, John. *Taking Laughter Seriously*. Albany: SUNY P, 1983.

Morris, Willie. *North Toward Home*. Boston: Houghton Mifflin, 1967.

Morrison, Toni. *Playing in the Dark: Whiteness and the Literary Imagination*. Cambridge, MA: Harvard UP, 1992.

Moseley, Caroline. "'When Will Dis Cruel War Be Ober?': Attitudes Toward Blacks in Popular Songs of the Civil War." *American Music* 2.3 (1984): 1–26.

Moses, Montrose J. "George L. Aiken's Dramatization of *Uncle Tom's Cabin.*" In *Representative Plays by American Dramatists* [1925]. Ed. Montrose Moses, 2:605–13. New York: Benjamin Blom, 1964.

———, ed. *Representative Plays by American Dramatists* [1925]. New York: Benjamin Blom, 1964.

Moses, Wilson Jeremiah. *The Golden Age of Black Nationalism, 1850–1925* [1978]. New York: Oxford UP, 1988.

Mouffe, Chantal. *Gramsci and Marxist Theory.* London: Routledge & Kegan Paul, 1979.

Mullins, H. B. *A Voice from the Workshop.* New York, 1860.

Mulvey, Laura. "Visual Pleasure and Narrative Cinema." In *Visual and Other Pleasures*, 14–26. Bloomington: Indiana UP, 1989.

Murray, Albert. *The Omni-Americans: Black Experience and American Culture* [1970]. New York: Vintage, 1983.

Musser, Charles. "Ethnicity, Role-Playing, and American Film Comedy: From *Chinese Laundry Scene* to *Whoopee* (1894–1930)." In *Unspeakable Images: Ethnicity and the American Cinema.* Ed. Lester D. Friedman, 39–81. Urbana: U of Illinois P, 1991.

Nash, Gary B. *Forging Freedom: The Formation of Philadelphia's Black Community, 1720–1840.* Cambridge, MA: Harvard UP, 1988.

Nash, Mark. "*Vampyr* and the Fantastic." *Screen* 17.3 (1976): 29–67.

Nathan, Hans. *Dan Emmett and the Rise of Early Negro Minstrelsy* [1962]. Norman: U of Oklahoma P, 1977.

"National Music." *Journal of Music* 6.18 (1855): 139–40.

"Native Musical Talent." *Journal of Music* 5.8 (1854): 61–62.

Negro Forget-Me-Not Songster. Philadelphia: Turner and Fisher, n.d. [early 1850s].

"Negro Minstrelsy—Ancient and Modern." *Putnam's Monthly* 5.25 (1855): 72–79.

"Negro Minstrelsy in London." *Journal of Music* 15.9 (1859): 67–68.

Nelson, Cary. "Always Already Cultural Studies: Two Conferences and a Manifesto." *Journal of the MMLA* 24.1 (1991): 24–38.

Nevin, Robert P. "Stephen C. Foster and Negro Minstrelsy." *Atlantic Monthly* 20.121 (1867): 608–16.

Nichols, Thomas Low. *Forty Years of American Life* [1864]. 2d ed. London: Longmans, Green, 1874.

Nicoll, Allardyce. *The World of Harlequin.* Cambridge: Cambridge UP, 1963.

Northall, William K. *Before and Behind the Curtain, or Fifteen Years' Observations among the Theatres of New York.* New York: W. F. Burgess, 1851.

Nye, Russell. *The Unembarrassed Muse: The Popular Arts in America.* New York: Dial, 1970.

"Obituary, Not Eulogistic: Negro Minstrelsy Is Dead" [1854]. Reprinted in *Journal of Music* 13.18 (1858): 118.

Odell, George C. D. *Annals of the New York Stage.* 15 vols. New York: Columbia UP, 1928–31.

Olson, Edwin. "Social Aspects of Slave Life in New York." *Journal of Negro History* 26.1 (1941): 66–77.

Orgel, Stephen. "Nobody's Perfect: Or Why Did the English Stage Take Boys for Women?" *South Atlantic Quarterly* 88.1 (1989): 7–29.

"Origins of Jim Crow." *Boston Transcript*, May 27, 1841.

Osofsky, Gilbert. "Abolitionists, Irish Immigrants, and the Dilemmas of Romantic Nationalism." *American Historical Review* 80.4 (1975): 889–912.

Ostendorf, Berndt. *Black Literature in White America.* Totowa, NJ: Harvester, 1982.

Ottley, Roi, and William J. Weatherby. *The Negro in New York: An Informal Social History.* New York: New York Public Library, 1967.

Owen, Frank. "Hip Hop Bebop." *Spin* (September 1988): 60–61, 73.

Parry, Albert. *Garrets and Pretenders: A History of Bohemianism in America* [1933]. New York: Dover, 1960.

Paskman, Dailey, and Sigmund Spaeth. *"Gentlemen, Be Seated!": A Parade of the Old-Time Minstrels.* Garden City, NY: Doubleday, Doran, 1928.

Pastor, Tony. *George Christy: A Story of Minstrel Life.* New York: George Munro, 1877.

Patterson, Cecil Lloyd. "A Different Drum: The Image of the Negro in the Nineteenth-Century Popular Song Books." Ph.D. diss., University of Pennsylvania, 1961.

Person, Ethel, and Lionel Ovesey. "Transvestism: New Perspectives." *Journal of the American Academy of Psychoanalysis* 6.3 (1978): 301–23.

Pessen, Edward. *Most Uncommon Jacksonians: Radical Leaders of the Early Labor Movement.* Albany: State U of New York P, 1967.

Pfister, Joel. "The Americanization of Cultural Studies." *Yale Journal of Criticism* 4.2 (1991): 199–229.

Phelps, H. P. *Players of a Century: A Record of the Albany Stage* [1880]. New York: Benjamin Blom, 1972.

Pickering, Michael. "White Skin, Black Masks: 'Nigger' Minstrelsy in Victorian Britain." In *Music Hall Performance and Style.* Ed. J. S. Bratton, 78–90. Milton Keynes: Open UP, 1986.

Pieterse, Jan Nederveen. *White On Black: Images of Africa and Blacks in Western Popular Culture.* New Haven, CT: Yale UP, 1992.

Poe, Edgar Allan. "The Philosophy of Composition." In *Selected Writings.* Ed. David Galloway, 480–92. New York: Penguin, 1967.

Pop Goes the Weasel Songster. Philadelphia: Fisher and Brother, n.d. [1853?].

Popular Music in Jacksonian America. MHS 834561, 1982.

"Popular Songs." *Journal of Music* 11.13 (1857): 99–100.

Potter, David. *The Impending Crisis, 1848–1861.* New York: Harper, 1976.

Poulantzas, Nicos. *Political Power and Social Classes.* Trans. Timothy O'Hagan. London: Verso, 1973.

Radway, Janice. "Reception Study: Ethnography and the Problems of Dispersed Audiences and Nomadic Subjects." *Cultural Studies* 2.3 (1988): 359–76.

Rahill, Frank. *The World of Melodrama.* University Park: Pennsylvania State UP, 1967.

Railton, Stephen. *Authorship and Audience: Literary Performance in the American Renaissance.* Princeton: Princeton UP, 1991.

Ramazani, Jahan. *Yeats and the Poetry of Death: Elegy, Self-Elegy, and the Sublime.* New Haven: Yale UP, 1990.

Ramshaw, Molly N. "Jump, Jim Crow!: A Biographical Sketch of T. D. Rice." *Theatre Annual* 17 (1960): 36–47.

Ratner, Lorman. *Powder Keg: Northern Opposition to the Anti-Slavery Movement, 1831–1840.* New York: Basic, 1968.

Rawick, George P. *From Sundown to Sunup: The Making of the Black Community.* Westport, CT: Greenwood, 1972.

Rayback, Joseph G. "The American Workingman and the Antislavery Crusade." *Journal of Economic History* 3.2 (1943): 152–63.

———. *Free Soil: The Election of 1848.* Lexington: UP of Kentucky, 1970.

Reed, Adolph, and Julian Bond. "Equality: Why We Can't Wait." *Nation* 253.20 (1991): 733–37.

Rehin, George F. "Blackface Street Minstrels in Victorian London and Its Resorts: Popular Culture and Its Racial Connotations as Revealed in Polite Opinion." *Journal of Popular Culture* 15.1 (1981): 19–38.

———. "The Darker Image: American Negro Minstrelsy Through the Historian's Lens." *Journal of American Studies* 9.3 (1975): 365–73.

———. "Harlequin Jim Crow: Continuity and Convergence in Blackface Clowning." *Journal of Popular Culture* 9.3 (1975): 682–701.

Reid, Ira D. "The John Canoe Festival." *Phylon* 3 (1942): 345–70.

Reidy, Joseph. "'Negro Election Day' and Black Community Life in New England, 1750–1860." *Marxist Perspectives* 3.1 (1978): 102–17.

Reising, Russell. *The Unusable Past: Theory and the Study of American Literature.* New York: Methuen, 1986.

"Reminiscences." July 26, 1902. Harvard Theatre Collection.

Reynolds, David S. *Beneath the American Renaissance: The Subversive Imagination in the Age of Emerson and Melville.* New York: Knopf, 1988.

Reynolds, Larry J. *European Revolutions and the American Literary Renaissance.* New Haven: Yale UP, 1988.

Rezneck, Samuel. "The Social History of an American Depression, 1837–1843." *American Historical Review* 40.4 (1935): 662–87.

Rhodes, James Ford. *History of the United States from the Compromise of 1850* [1907]. Ed. Allan Nevins. Chicago: U of Chicago P, 1966.

Rice, Edward LeRoy. *Monarchs of Minstrelsy from "Daddy" Rice to Date.* New York: Kenny, 1911.

Richards, Leonard L. *"Gentlemen of Property and Standing": Anti-Abolition Mobs in Jacksonian America.* New York: Oxford UP, 1970.

Ricoeur, Paul. *Freud and Philosophy.* New Haven: Yale UP, 1971.

Riis, Thomas. "The Music and Musicians in Nineteenth-Century Productions of *Uncle Tom's Cabin.*" *American Music* 4.3 (1986): 268–86.

Robinson, Forrest G. *In Bad Faith: The Dynamics of Deception in Mark Twain's America.* Cambridge, MA: Harvard UP, 1986.

Roediger, David. "'Labor in White Skin': Race and Working-Class History." In *Reshaping the U.S. Left: Popular Struggles in the 1980s.* Ed. Mike Davis and Michael Sprinker, 287–308. London: Verso, 1988.

———. *The Wages of Whiteness: Race and the Making of the American Working Class.* London: Verso, 1991.

Rogin, Michael Paul. "Blackface, White Noise: The Jewish Jazz Singer Finds His Voice." *Critical Inquiry* 18 (1992): 417–53.

———. *Fathers and Children: Andrew Jackson and the Subjugation of the American Indian.* New York: Knopf, 1975.

———. "Making America Home: Racial Masquerade and Ethnic Assimilation in the Transition to Talking Pictures." *Journal of American History* 79.3 (1992): 1050–77.

———. *Subversive Genealogy: The Politics and Art of Herman Melville.* New York: Knopf, 1983.

Roppolo, Joseph. "Uncle Tom in New Orleans: Three Lost Plays." *New England Quarterly* 27 (1954): 213–26.

Rorabaugh, W. J. "Rising Democratic Spirits: Immigrants, Temperance, and Tammany Hall, 1854–1860." *Civil War History* 22.2 (1976): 138–57.

Rosenzweig, Roy. *Eight Hours for What We Will: Workers and Leisure in an Industrial City, 1870–1920.* Cambridge: Cambridge UP, 1983.

Ross, Andrew. "Ballots, Bullets, or Batmen: Can Cultural Studies Do the Right Thing?" *Screen* 31.1 (1990): 26–44.

———. *No Respect: Intellectuals and Popular Culture.* New York: Routledge, 1989.

Ross, Steven. *Workers on the Edge: Work, Leisure, and Politics in Industrializing Cincinnati, 1788–1890.* New York: Columbia UP, 1985.

Rourke, Constance. *American Humor: A Study of the National Character* [1931]. Tallahassee: Florida State UP, 1986.

———. *Troupers of the Gold Coast or the Rise of Lotta Crabtree.* New York: Harcourt Brace, 1928.

———. *Trumpets of Jubilee.* New York: Harcourt, Brace, and World, 1927.

Rubin, Gayle. "The Traffic in Women: Notes on the 'Political Economy' of Sex." In *Toward an Anthropology of Women.* Ed. Rayna R. Reiter, 157–210. New York: Monthly Review P, 1975.

Rubin, Joseph Jay. *The Historic Whitman.* University Park: Pennsylvania State UP, 1973.

Rudé, George. *The Crowd in History: A Study in Popular Disturbances in France and England.* London: Lawrence and Wishart, 1981.

Runcie, John. "'Hunting the Nigs' in Philadelphia: The Race Riot of August 1834." *Pennsylvania History* 39.2 (1972): 187–218.

Ryan, Mary P. *Cradle of the Middle Class: The Family in Oneida County, New York, 1790–1865.* Cambridge: Cambridge UP, 1981.

Sacks, Howard L. and Judith R. Sacks. "Way Up North in Dixie: Black-White Musical Interaction in Knox County, Ohio." *American Music* 6.4 (1988): 409–27.

Said, Edward W. *Beginnings: Intention and Method* [1975]. New York: Columbia UP, 1985.

Sánchez-Eppler, Karen. "Bodily Bonds: The Intersecting Rhetorics of Feminism and Abolition." *Representations* 24 (1988): 28–59.

Sanjek, Russell. *American Popular Music and Its Business.* New York: Oxford UP, 1988.

Sante, Luc. *Low Life: Lures and Snares of Old New York.* New York: Farrar, Straus, and Giroux, 1991.

Saxton, Alexander. "Blackface Minstrelsy and Jacksonian Ideology." *American Quarterly* 27.1 (1975): 3–28.

———. "George Wilkes: The Transformation of a Radical Ideology." *American Quarterly* 33.4 (1981): 437–58.

———. "Problems of Class and Race in the Origins of the Mass Circulation Press." *American Quarterly* 36.2 (1984): 211–34.

———. *The Rise and Fall of the White Republic: Class Politics and Mass Culture in Nineteenth-Century America.* London: Verso, 1990.

Schank, Theodore. "The Bowery Theatre, 1826–1836." Ph.D. diss., Stanford University, 1956.

Schick, Frank L. *The Paperbound Book in America.* New York: R. R. Bowker, 1958.

Schiller, Dan. "From Rogues to the Rights of Men: Crime News and the *Police Gazette* (1845–1847)." *Media, Culture, and Society* 2.4 (1980): 377–88.

Schlesinger, Arthur M., Jr. *The Age of Jackson.* Boston: Little, Brown, 1945.

Schlissel, Lillian. "Sexual Disguise: Male/Female Impersonators in American Vaudeville, 1860–1920." American Studies Association Convention, New Orleans November 1990.

Sedgwick, Eve Kosofsky. "The Beast in the Closet: James and the Writing of Homosexual Panic." In *Speaking of Gender.* Ed. Elaine Showalter, 243–68. New York: Routledge, 1989.

————. *Between Men: English Literature and Male Homosocial Desire.* New York: Columbia UP, 1985.

Shapiro, Herbert. "Labor and Antislavery: Reflections on the Literature." *Nature, Society, and Thought* 2.4 (1989): 471–90.

Shipp, Robert H. *"Uncle Tom's Cabin* and the Ethos of Melodrama." Ph.D. diss., Columbia University, 1986.

Shoemaker, Steve. "Norman Mailer's 'White Negro': Historical Myth or Mythical History?" *Twentieth-Century Literature* 37 (1991): 343–60.

Sleeper, Jim. *The Closest of Strangers: Liberalism and the Politics of Race in New York.* New York: Norton, 1990.

Slotkin, Richard. *The Fatal Environment: The Myth of the Frontier in the Age of Industrialism, 1800–1890.* Middletown: Wesleyan UP, 1985.

Smith, Sol. *The Theatrical Journey.* Philadelphia: T. B. Peterson, 1854.

Smith-Rosenberg, Carroll. "Davy Crockett as Trickster: Pornography, Liminality, and Symbolic Inversion in Victorian America." In *Disorderly Conduct: Visions of Gender in Victorian America,* 90–108. New York: Oxford UP, 1985.

————. *Disorderly Conduct: Visions of Gender in Victorian America.* New York: Oxford UP, 1985.

Snead, James. "Repetition as a Figure of Black Culture." In *Black Literature and Literary Theory.* Ed. Henry Louis Gates, Jr., 59–80. New York: Methuen, 1984.

Snipe, Simon. *Sports of New York.* New-York Historical Society, 1822.

Sobel, Mechal. *The World They Made Together: Black and White Values in Eighteenth-Century Virginia.* Princeton: Princeton UP, 1987.

Sollors, Werner. *Beyond Ethnicity: Consent and Descent in American Culture.* New York: Oxford UP, 1986.

————. "Literature and Ethnicity." In *Harvard Encyclopedia of American Ethnic Groups.* Ed. Stephan Thernstrom, Ann Orlov, and Oscar Handlin, 647–65. Cambridge, MA: Harvard UP, 1980.

"Songs of the Blacks." *Journal of Music* 10.7 (1856): 51–52.

Southern, Eileen. "Black Musicians and Early Ethiopian Minstrelsy." *The Black Perspective in Music* 3.1 (1975): 77–83.

————. *The Music of Black Americans: A History* [1971]. New York: Oxford UP, 1983.

Spann, Edward K. *The New Metropolis: New York City, 1840–1857.* New York: Columbia UP, 1981.

Spillers, Hortense. "Changing the Letter: The Yokes, the Jokes of Discourse, or, Mrs. Stowe, Mr. Reed." In *Slavery and the Literary Imagination: Selected Papers from the English Institute, 1987.* Ed. Deborah E. McDowell and Arnold Rampersad, 25–65. Baltimore: Johns Hopkins UP, 1989.

Stallybrass, Peter, and Allon White. *The Politics and Poetics of Transgression.* London: Methuen, 1986.

Stansell, Christine. *City of Women: Sex and Class in New York, 1789–1860.* New York: Knopf, 1986.

Stanton, William R. *The Leopard's Spots: Scientific Attitudes Toward Race in America, 1815–1859.* Chicago: U of Chicago P, 1960.

Stearns, Marshall, and Jean Stearns. *Jazz Dance: The Story of American Vernacular Dance.* New York: Macmillan, 1968.

Stearns, Peter N. *Be a Man! Males in Modern Society.* New York: Holmes & Meier, 1979.

Stedman Jones, Gareth. "Class Expression Versus Social Control?: A Critique of Recent Trends in the Social History of 'Leisure.'" In *Languages of Class: Studies in English Working-Class History, 1832–1982,* 76–89. New York: Cambridge UP, 1983.

———. *Languages of Class: Studies in English Working-Class History, 1832–1982.* New York: Cambridge UP, 1983.

Steele, Shelby. *The Content of Our Character.* New York: St. Martin's, 1990.

Stern, Madeleine B., ed. *Publishers for Mass Entertainment in Nineteenth-Century America.* Boston: G. K. Hall, 1980.

Stoller, Robert J. *Sex and Gender: On the Development of Masculinity and Femininity.* London: Hogarth, 1968.

Stone, H. D. *Personal Recollections of the Drama* [1873]. New York: Benjamin Blom, 1969.

Stott, Richard B. "The Geography of Gender in Nineteenth-Century America: Youth, Masculinity, and the California Gold Rush." Organization of American Historians Convention, Louisville, April 1991.

———. *Workers in the Metropolis: Class, Ethnicity, and Youth in Antebellum New York City.* Ithaca: Cornell UP, 1990.

Stowe, Harriet Beecher. "The Parson's Horse Race." *Atlantic Monthly* 42.252 (1878): 470–74.

———. *Sunny Memories of Foreign Lands.* 2 vols. Boston: Phillips, Samson, 1854.

———. *Uncle Tom's Cabin; or, Life among the Lowly* [1852]. Ed. Ann Douglas. New York: Penguin, 1981.

Stuart, Isaac W. *Hartford in the Olden Time: The First Thirty Years* [1853]. In *Readings in Black American Music.* Ed. Eileen Southern, 48–49. New York: Norton, 1983.

Stuckey, Sterling. *Slave Culture: Nationalist Theory and the Foundations of Black America.* New York: Oxford UP, 1987.

Sundquist, Eric J. *"Benito Cereno* and New World Slavery." In *Reconstructing American Literary History.* Ed. Sacvan Bercovitch, 93–122. Cambridge, MA: Harvard UP, 1986.

———, ed. *New Essays on Uncle Tom's Cabin.* Cambridge: Cambridge UP, 1986.

———. "Slavery, Revolution, and the American Renaissance." In *The American Renaissance Reconsidered: Selected Papers from the English Institute, 1982–1983.* Ed. Walter Benn Michaels and Donald Pease, 1–33. Baltimore: Johns Hopkins UP, 1985.

Susman, Warren I. *Culture as History: The Transformation of American Society in the Twentieth Century.* New York: Pantheon, 1984.

Suthern, Orrin Clayton. "Minstrelsy and Popular Culture." *Journal of Popular Culture* 4.3 (1971): 658–73.

Szwed, John F. "Race and the Embodiment of Culture." *Ethnicity* 2.1 (1975): 19–33.

Taylor, Bayard. *Eldorado or Adventures in the Path of Empire* [1850]. New York: Putnam's, 1887.

Taylor, William R. *Cavalier and Yankee: The Old South and American National Character.* New York: George Braziller, 1961.

Thatcher, George. "The Only Thatcher's Autobiography." Thatcher Minstrel Program, New York Public Library Theatre Collection, n.d.

Therborn, Göran. *The Ideology of Power and the Power of Ideology.* London: Verso, 1980.

Thernstrom, Stephan, and Peter Knights. "Men in Motion: Some Data and Speculations about Urban Population Mobility in Nineteenth-Century America." In *Anonymous Americans: Explorations in Nineteenth-Century Social History.* Ed. Tamara Hareven, 17–47. Englewood Cliffs, NJ: Prentice-Hall, 1971.

Thompson, E. P. "The Long Revolution." Review of *The Long Revolution,* by Raymond Williams. *New Left Review* 9–10 (1961): 24–33, 34–39.

———. "The Moral Economy of the English Crowd in the Eighteenth Century." *Past and Present* 50 (1971): 76–136.

———. "'Rough Music': Le charivari anglais." *Annales* 27.2 (1972): 285–312.

———. "Time, Work-Discipline, and Industrial Capitalism." *Past and Present* 38 (1967): 56–97.

Thurman, Wallace. *The Blacker the Berry* [1929]. New York: Collier Books, 1970.

Tocqueville, Alexis de. *Democracy in America.* Vol. 2 [1840]. Ed. Phillips Bradley. New York: Vintage, 1956.

Toll, Robert C. *Blacking Up: The Minstrel Show in Nineteenth-Century America.* New York: Oxford UP, 1974.

Tolson, Andrew. *The Limits of Masculinity.* London: Tavistock, 1977.

Tompkins, Jane P. "Sentimental Power: *Uncle Tom's Cabin* and the Politics of Literary History." In *Sensational Designs: The Cultural Work of American Fiction, 1790–1860*, 122–46. New York: Oxford UP, 1985.

Trachtenberg, Alan. "Myth and Symbol." *Massachusetts Review* 25.4 (1984): 667–73.

Trotter, James Monroe. *Music and Some Highly Musical People.* Boston: Lee and Shepard, 1883.

Turner, Victor. *The Anthropology of Performance.* New York: PAJ Publications, 1986.

———. "Frame, Flow, and Reflection: Ritual and Drama as Public Liminality." In *Performance in Postmodern Culture.* Ed. Michel Benamou, 33–55. Madison, WI: Coda, 1977.

———. "Myth and Symbol." In *International Encyclopedia of the Social Sciences.* Ed. David L. Sills, 10:576–82. New York: Macmillan and Free P, 1968.

Twain, Mark. *The Adventures of Huckleberry Finn* [1884]. New York: Norton, 1977.

———. *The Adventures of Tom Sawyer* [1876]. New York: New American Library, 1979.

———. *The Autobiography of Mark Twain* [1924]. Ed. Charles Neider. New York: Harper and Row, 1959.

———. *Following the Equator: A Journey Around the World.* New York: Harper, 1897.

Tygiel, Jules. *Baseball's Great Experiment: Jackie Robinson and His Legacy.* New York: Oxford UP, 1983.

Tyler, Carole-Anne. "Boys Will Be Girls: The Politics of Gay Drag." In *Inside/Out: Lesbian Theories, Gay Theories.* Ed. Diana Fuss, 32–70. New York: Routledge, 1991.

Tyler, M. W. *A Book Without a Title; or, Thrilling Events in the Life of Mira Dana.* Boston: for the author, 1855.

"Uncle Tomitudes." *Putnam's Monthly* 1 (1853): 97–102.

Van Deburg, William L. *Slavery and Race in American Popular Culture.* Madison: U of Wisconsin P, 1984.

Volosinov, V. N. *Marxism and the Philosophy of Language* [1929]. Trans. Ladislav Matejka and I. R. Titunik. Cambridge, MA: Harvard UP, 1986.

Wall, Cheryl, ed. *Changing Our Own Words: Essays on Criticism, Theory, and Writing by Black Women.* New Brunswick: Rutgers UP, 1989.

Walters, Ronald G. *The Antislavery Appeal: American Abolitionism after 1830.* Baltimore: Johns Hopkins UP, 1976.

Ware, Norman. *The Industrial Worker, 1840–1860* [1924]. Chicago: Quadrangle, 1964.

Ware, Vron. *Beyond the Pale: White Women, Racism, and History.* London: Verso, 1992.

Warner, Sam Bass. *The Private City: Philadelphia in Three Periods of Its Growth.* Philadelphia: U of Pennsylvania P, 1968.

Waterhouse, Richard. *From Minstrel Show to Vaudeville: The Australian Popular Stage, 1788–1914.* New South Wales: NSW Press, 1990.

Weathers, Willie T. "*Moby-Dick* and the Nineteenth-Century Scene." *Texas Studies in Language and Literature* 1 (1960): 477–501.

Weik, Jesse W. *The Real Lincoln.* Boston: Macmillan, 1923.

Weinbaum, Paul O. *Mobs and Demagogues: The New York Response to Collective Violence in the Early Nineteenth Century.* Ann Arbor: UMI Research P, 1979.

Wemyss, F. C. *Theatrical Biography; or, The Life of An Actor and Manager.* Glasgow: R. Griffin, 1848.

———. *Theatrical Biography of Eminent Actors and Authors.* New York, 1852.

Werner, M. R. *Barnum.* New York: Harcourt, Brace, 1923.

West, Cornel. "Marxist Theory and the Specificity of Afro-American Oppression." In *Marxism and the Interpretation of Culture.* Ed. Cary Nelson and Lawrence Grossberg, 17–29. Urbana: U of Illinois P, 1988.

White, Armond. "The White Albums: Is Black Music under Siege?" *City Sun* 8.49 (1990): 19–21.

White, Charley. "Origin of Negro Minstrelsy." *New York Clipper,* June 24, 1854.

White, Newman I. *American Negro Folk-Songs.* Cambridge, MA: Harvard UP, 1928.

———. "The White Man in the Woodpile: Some Influences on Negro Secular Folk-Songs." *American Speech* 4.3 (1929): 207–15.

White, Shane. *Somewhat More Independent: The End of Slavery in New York City, 1770–1810.* Athens: U of Georgia P, 1991.

White's New Book of Plantation Melodies. Philadelphia: T. B. Peterson & Brothers, 1849.

White's New Ethiopian Song Book. Philadelphia: T. B. Peterson, 1850.

White's New Illustrated Melodeon Songbook. Philadelphia: T. B. Peterson & Brothers, 1848.

White's Serenaders' Song Book. Philadelphia: T. B. Peterson, 1851.

Whitman, Walt. *An American Primer* [early 1850s]. Madison, WI: Holy Cow!, 1987.

———. *The Gathering of Forces.* 2 vols. Ed. Cleveland Rogers and John Black. New York: Putnam's, 1920.

———. "The Old Bowery" [1885]. *The Collected Writings of Walt Whitman.* 2 vols. Ed. Floyd Stovall, 2:591–97. New York: New York UP, 1964.

———. "A Thought of Ours about Music in the United States." *Brooklyn Daily Eagle,* September 8, 1847. Reprinted in *The Gathering of Forces.* Ed. Cleveland Rogers and John Black, 2:345–46. New York: Putnam's, 1920.

———. *Uncollected Poetry and Prose.* Ed. Emory Holloway. New York: P. Smith, 1932.

"Who Writes Our Songs?" *Journal of Music* 15.7 (1859): 51–52.

Wilentz, Sean. *Chants Democratic: New York City and the Rise of the American Working Class, 1788–1850.* New York: Oxford UP, 1984.

Williams, Raymond. *Culture.* London: Fontana, 1981.

———. *Marxism and Literature.* New York: Oxford UP, 1977.

———. "Social Environment and Theatrical Environment." In *Problems in Materialism and Culture: Selected Essays,* 125–47. London: New Left Books, 1980.

Williams, William Appleman. *The Contours of American History* [1961]. Chicago: Quadrangle, 1966.

Willis, Paul. "Shop Floor Culture, Masculinity, and the Wage Form." In *Working-Class Culture: Studies in History and Theory.* Ed. John Clarke, Chas Critcher, and Richard Johnson, 185–98. London: Hutchinson, 1979.

Willis, Susan. "I Shop Therefore I Am: Is There a Place for Afro-American Culture in Commodity Culture?" In *Changing Our Own Words: Essays on Criticism, Theory, and Writing by Black Women.* Ed. Cheryl Wall, 173–95. New Brunswick: Rutgers UP, 1989.

Wilson, William Julius. *The Truly Disadvantaged: The Inner City, the Underclass, and Public Policy.* Chicago: U of Chicago P, 1987.

Winans, Robert B. "The Black Banjo-Playing Tradition in Virginia and West Virginia." *Journal of Virginia Folklore* 1 (1979): 7–30.

———. "Early Minstrel-Show Music, 1843–1852." In *Musical Theatre in America*. Ed. Glenn Loney, 71–97. Westport, CT: Greenwood, 1984.

———. "The Folk, the Stage, and the Five-String Banjo in the Nineteenth Century." *Journal of American Folklore* 89.354 (1976): 407–37.

Winter, Marian Hannah. "Juba and American Minstrelsy." In *Chronicles of the American Dance*. Ed. Paul Magriel, 39–63. New York: Henry Holt, 1948.

Wittke, Carl. *Tambo and Bones: A History of the American Minstrel Stage*. Durham: Duke UP, 1930.

Wolfe, Bernard. "Uncle Remus and the Malevolent Rabbit." *Commentary* 8 (1949): 31–41.

Woodard, Fredrick, and Donnarae MacCann. *"Huckleberry Finn* and the Traditions of Blackface Minstrelsy." *Interracial Books for Children Bulletin* 15.1, 2 (1984): 4–13.

Woodson, Carter G. "The Negroes of Cincinnati Prior to the Civil War." *Journal of Negro History* 1.1 (1916): 1–22.

Wright, Erik Olin. *Classes*. London: Verso, 1985.

Wyatt-Brown, Bertram. *Lewis Tappan and the Evangelical War Against Slavery*. Cleveland: P of Case Western Reserve U, 1969.

Wynter, Sylvia. "Sambos and Minstrels." *Social Text* 1 (1979): 149–56.

Yellin, Jean Fagan. *The Intricate Knot: Black Figures in American Literature, 1776–1863*. New York: New York UP, 1972.

Young, Alfred F. *The Democratic Republicans of New York: The Origins, 1763–1797*. Chapel Hill: U of North Carolina P, 1967.

Zahler, Helene S. *Eastern Workingmen and National Land Policy, 1829–1862*. New York: Columbia UP, 1941.

Zanger, Jules. "The Minstrel Show as Theater of Misrule." *Quarterly Journal of Speech* 60.1 (1974): 33–38.

Žižek, Slavoj. "Eastern Europe's Republics of Gilead." *New Left Review* 183 (1990): 50–62.

Zwarg, Christina. "Fathering and Blackface in *Uncle Tom's Cabin." Novel* 22.3 (1989): 274–87.

Index

Abjection, 265n.26

Abolitionism, 11–12, 29, 75, 96, 111, 127, 129–35, 155–56, 190, 194, 201–2, 207–10, 218–19, 226–28, 230–32, 237, 262n.31, 272n.53, 275n.29; and labor, 4, 75, 87, 104, 129, 131–32, 155–56, 186, 200–203, 208–10, 226–28, 230–31, 238, 250n.35, 262nn.26,29

Adorno, Theodor, 173, 180, 182, 241n.1

African Americans, 11–12, 15, 18–19, 20, 23, 29, 32–33, 35–36, 40–49, 50, 52–53, 57–58, 60, 71, 76–77, 84, 94–96, 99, 104, 112–13, 122, 127, 131, 134, 143, 149, 166, 174–75, 188–89, 193, 209, 227, 235–37, 246n.3, 250n.33, 254n.29, 255n.42, 263n.42; culture of, 38–62, 95, 99, 101, 103, 173–75, 178, 182, 185–86, 236, 247n.9, 248n.21, 272n.53; in North, 40, 246n.5, 247n.9. *See also* Race; Racism

African Grove Theatre, 44, 45

Agee, James, 3

Aldrich, Thomas Bailey, 31

Aldridge, Ira, 44, 45–46, 49

Allen, William Francis, 175

Althusser, Louis, 15, 220, 255n.45

Amalgamation. *See* Miscegenation

American exceptionalism, 69–70, 252n.12

American Museum, Barnum's, 72, 76–77, 214, 225, 227, 228

American Studies, 10–11, 240n.18. *See also* Cultural studies

Anderson, Benedict, 93

"Angelina Baker," 194

Antiabolitionism, 29, 112, 127–28, 130–35, 202, 227, 263n.41, 273n.10

Apollo Minstrels, 20

Aronowitz, Stanley, 103, 266n.38

Articulation, 180, 268n.19

Astaire, Fred, 5

"Astonishing Nose," 162–63

Astor Place Opera House, 9, 65, 66–67, 85, 88, 106, 154, 223

Astor Place riot, 9, 65, 66–67, 81, 85, 88, 106, 251n.6

Attali, Jacques, 185

Audiences: minstrel show, 64–65, 67–69, 80, 112–13, 124–26, 138–39, 151–53, 157–58, 165, 182, 191, 193, 201, 217; music hall, 91; theater, 44, 45, 81, 86, 157, 228; theorized, 249n.30. *See also* Minstrel show: reception

Austin, William, 191, 205, 218, 268n.14

Authoritarian populism, 11, 241n.23

Babcock-Abrahams, Barbara, 24, 27

"Backside Albany," 41, 46, 246n.6

Baker, Benjamin: *A Glance at New York in 1848*, 74, 83–84; *New York As It Is*, 74, 213

Bakhtin, Mikhail, 146

Baraka, Amiri. *See* Jones, LeRoi

Barnum, P. T., 72, 76–77, 112, 214, 216, 218, 222, 223, 224, 225, 242n.7, 253n.28, 274n.24. *See also* American Museum, Barnum's

Barthes, Roland, 141, 147, 182, 183, 267n.5

Bell, Bernard, 244n.28

Benedict, Ruth, 7

Bennett, James Gordon, 219

Bennett, Tony, 258n.27

Bercovitch, Sacvan, 69

Berlin, Ira, 40, 47

Bernstein, Iver, 233

Berret, Anthony, 31, 33

Berryman, John, 5

Bhabha, Homi, 6, 93

B'hoy, 67, 69, 81–89, 154, 158, 160, 186, 201, 207–8, 213, 216, 227–28, 255n.41. *See also* Bowery

Birdoff, Harry, 218

Birth of a Nation (Griffith), 5

Bishop, Henry, 176

Blackface: in art, 242n.10; and black penis, 25, 57–58, 121, 151–53, 243n.17; burnt cork, 26, 148, 229; and class, 27, 63–88, 123–35; and clowning, 22, 24–25; as com-

Blackface (*Cont.*)
   modity, 48–49, 60; as dream-work, 27, 135, 153, 197; and English stage, 22, 45–46, 68, 153, 242nn.11,12, 269n.26; in film, 5, 216, 240n.13; genealogy of, 22–29, 242nn.9,10; greasepaint, 26, 145, 148, 265n.15; in literature, 4–5, 31–35, 61–62, 123–24, 144–45, 163, 234–36, 242n.10, 245n.40; in public, 27–29; and rioting, 28–29, 84–85, 131–35, 237; and ritual inversion, 27–28, 148; and slave trickster, 22–23, 144, 189; and southwestern humor, 23–24, 242n.14. *See also* Minstrel show
Blackmar, Elizabeth, 248n.23
"Blackness," 7, 22, 25, 28, 32, 36–40, 51–52, 56, 62, 64, 68, 77, 80, 84, 87, 93, 96, 98, 100, 112–13, 116–17, 123, 126, 141–42, 145, 152, 171, 182, 185, 188, 192, 199, 200, 208, 240n.13, 249n.26
Black pageantry, 46–47
Black theater, 44–45. *See also* African Grove Theatre
Blair, John, 243n.14
Blassingame, John, 244n.31
Bledstein, Burton, 69
"Blue Tail Fly, De," 177, 181, 199
Blumin, Stuart, 69, 191
"Boatmen Dance," 162
Boaz, Franz, 7
Body, 19, 25–27, 57–58, 86, 112–35, 138, 140, 145–47, 153, 157, 159–68, 183, 243n.17, 265n.20
Bohemia, 50–51, 53–55, 260n.18
Bonaparte, Louis, 105, 106
Bond, Julian, 12
"Bonny Green Flag, The," 237
Booker, Johnny, 52
Boucicault, Dion, 226
Bourdieu, Pierre, 49, 158
Bowery, 64–69, 71–72, 76, 78–79, 81–84, 85–89, 136–37, 140, 157, 159, 213, 216. *See also* B'hoy
Bowery Circus, 136
Bowery Theatre, 72, 80, 85–86, 89, 132, 157, 211, 214, 227
Boyer, Paul, 69
Broderick, David, 75
Brooklyn Daily Eagle, 78, 98
Brower, Frank, 52, 136, 138, 215, 228
Brown, T. Allston, 61, 117
Brown, William Henry, 44
Brown, William Wells, 58, 79, 272n.53
Bryant, Dan, 95, 164
Bryant, William Cullen, 78, 232
Buckley, Peter, 66, 67, 72, 74, 76, 263n.37

Buckley's Serenaders, 180
Bull, Ole, 89, 97
Bunn, Alfred, 235
Buntline, Ned. *See* Judson, E. Z. C.
Burn, James Dawson, 198
Busch, Moritz, 97
Byron, George Gordon, Lord, 75

Cable, George Washington, 31
Calhoun, John C., 24, 156, 230, 231
"California Song," 206
Campbell's Minstrels, 180
"Camptown Races," 209
Cantwell, Robert, 48, 95, 96, 243n.14
Castle Garden, 68
Castration, 151–53, 161, 260n.13, 265n.27, 266n.46
Catholic church, 96
Channing, William Ellery, 32
Charivari, 136, 138
Chase, Salmon P., 209
Chatham Street Chapel, 131
Chatham Theatre, 69, 72, 74
Child, Lydia Maria, 33, 254n.30, 271n.44
"Ching a Ring Chaw," 119
Christy, E. P., 49, 51, 52, 141, 171, 263n.1, 269n.20
Christy, George (George Harrington), 15, 54, 95, 160, 164, 171, 215
Christy and Wood's Minstrels, 50, 192, 194, 215, 228
Christy's Minstrels, 20, 68, 84, 141, 144, 153, 171, 180, 204, 217, 228, 267n.2, 272n.2
Circus, 24–25, 112, 136, 140, 153
Civil War, 9, 105–6, 211–13, 216, 222, 224, 231–33, 236–38, 259n.35, 272n.49
"Clar de Kitchen," 22
Clark, T. J., 51, 103, 158, 249n.30
Clay, Henry, 50, 212
Clemens, Samuel Langhorne. *See* Twain, Mark
Clover, Carol, 265n.30
"Coal Black Rose," 117, 118, 127, 133
Cohen, Philip, 123, 126
Collins, John A., 155
Colonization, black, 132–33, 190, 209
Commerford, John, 196
Commodification of black culture, 39, 41–43, 48–62, 76–77, 100–105, 150, 171, 178, 250n.33
Compromise of 1850, 9, 37, 105, 170, 202–3, 209, 211–12, 224, 231, 272n.2, 275n.1
Connelly, Marc, 7
Conner, Edmon S., 61
"Cooney in de Holler," 84

Cooper, James Fenimore, 55
Cotton, Ben, 50, 52, 54
Crime, 70
"Cuff," 18, 57, 59, 60–61, 241n.4
Cullwick, Hannah, 122
Cultural revolution, 212, 220
Cultural studies, 10–11. *See also* American
  Studies
Culture industry, 8, 17–18, 63–88, 97, 100–
  105, 171–74, 180–84, 216, 225, 232, 241n.1.
  See also Popular culture
Curtis, George William, 270n.29
Cushman, Charlotte, 89

Daily Sentinel, 129
Dandy, black, 25, 107, 111–12, 120, 131–35,
  137, 140, 189, 193, 207, 222–23, 263n.42
Dandy Jim, 99
Dan Tucker, 58, 186
Davidge, William, 87
Davis, David Brion, 69
Davis, Mike, 96, 252n.12
Davis, Natalie Zemon, 27–28, 29
Davis, Susan, 28, 29
Dawley, Alan, 107, 130, 262n.41
Death instinct, 183–84, 188–90. *See also* Rep-
  etition
Delany, Martin, 4, 33, 50, 91, 236
Democratic party, 50, 79, 96, 130, 183, 203,
  205, 231–33, 262n.30
Democratic Review, 105, 200, 203
Denning Michael, 79, 135, 152, 229
Dennison, Sam, 179
Depression (1837–43), 107, 137, 153–54, 185,
  237. *See also* Panic of 1837
De Voe, Thomas, 41
Diamond, John, 112, 113, 115
Dickens, Charles, 113, 115, 116, 148
Dime novel, 64, 68, 78–80, 126, 134, 228,
  267n.3
"Dixie," 237
Dixon, George Washington, 111
Donne, John, 165
Dorman, James, 7
Dorson, Richard, 81
Douglas, Ann, 32, 62, 188
Douglas, Stephen A., 231
Douglass, Frederick, 4, 7, 15, 30, 33, 35–37,
  75, 95, 104, 127, 155, 209, 245n.39
Downing, Major Jack, 93
Draft riots (1863), 12, 94, 237
Dred Scott, 106
Dreiser, Theodore, 61, 250n.33
Du Bois, W. E. B., 16, 150, 237
Dunbar, Paul Laurence, 35

Dwight, J. S., 98, 99, 183
Dyer, Richard, 117, 118

1848: American, 9, 86–88, 105–7, 169–70,
  185, 203, 205, 208–10, 237; European, 105,
  169, 203, 205. *See also* Civil War
Election Day, 46–47
Elegy, 189
Elias, Norbert, 157
Eliot, T. S., 91, 201
Ellison, Ralph, 3, 4, 7, 25, 30, 38, 256n.8
"Emma Snow," 189
Emmett, Dan, 47, 49, 51, 95, 136, 138, 140,
  143, 177, 237, 263n.1
Engels, Friedrich, 55
Ethiopian minstrelsy. *See* Minstrel show
Ethiopian Serenaders, 153, 180, 269n.26
Evangelicalism, 129–31, 134, 262nn.27,32; re-
  ligious revivals, 74, 107; reformers, 111
Evans, George Henry, 129, 132, 155, 202
Evans, Walker, 7

Factory girl, 196
Faler, Paul, 107, 130
Family, 194–99
Fanon, Frantz, 152, 243nn.15,17
"Farewell My Lilly Dear," 187
"Farewell! Old Cottage," 191
Farrel, Bob, 128
Farren, George, 132
Faulkner, William, 122
Feejee Mermaid, 77, 113
Fiedler, Leslie, 5, 53, 241n.1
Fields, Barbara, 252n.16, 262n.29
Film, 91, 124, 140, 153, 216, 250n.30,
  260n.13, 261n.20, 264n.11, 273n.13; televi-
  sion, 264n.7
Finney, Charles Grandison, 131
"Fire, Fire, Fire," 84
Firth and Pond, Publishers, 171
Fisk Jubilee Singers, 235
Five Points, N.Y., 47, 84, 112, 116
"Folk," 7, 93, 101–3, 177, 180, 246n.3,
  258n.26
Foner, Eric, 47, 79, 129, 208, 209, 232,
  271n.49
Forrest, Edwin, 66, 89, 132, 251n.5
Foster, Charles, 275n.28
Foster, George, 84–85, 160
Foster, Stephen, 9, 16, 33, 47, 49, 50, 52, 95,
  170–71, 173, 175–76, 179–80, 187–91, 194,
  199, 203–4, 206, 209, 218, 235–36,
  247n.12, 266n.43, 269n.20
Franklin Museum, 227
Fredrickson, George, 32, 34, 244n.31

Free labor, 203, 232, 271n.49, 275n.29
Free Soil movement, 79, 200, 205–6, 208–10, 227, 231, 261n.24, 273n.6
Free Soil party, 106, 208–10, 272n.49
Freud, Sigmund, 142–45, 151, 162–63, 183–84, 189, 261n.20
Frontier, 38, 47–48, 101, 117, 170, 186, 191–93, 202, 206, 247n.12
Fugitive Slave Law, 9, 106, 169, 186, 212, 219
Fuller, Margaret, 7, 16, 20, 66, 97

"Gal from the South," 26, 152
Garber, Marjorie, 26
Garrison, William Lloyd, 75, 85, 111, 155, 227
Gates, Henry Louis, Jr., 242n.12
Gavitt's Original Ethiopian Serenaders, 36
Geertz, Clifford, 6, 40
"General Taylor," 206–7
Georgia Minstrels, 36
Germon, G. C., 216–17
"Gib Us Chaw Tobacco," 150
Giddings, Joshua, 209, 259n.9
Gilje, Paul, 149
Gilman, Caroline, 174
Ginzburg, Carlo, 103
Girard, René, 248n.24
Gliddon, George, 77
Gold rush, 106–7, 143, 169–70, 202–3, 205–10
Gramsci, Antonio, 11, 91, 101–2, 137, 256n.2, 258n.27
Greeley, Horace, 15, 155, 232
Greenfield, Elizabeth, 235
Griffin, John Howard, 5
Grimsted, David, 89

Haiti, 119
Hall, Stuart, 8, 11, 17, 70, 101, 240n.12, 264n.3
Halttunen, Karen, 69
Hamblin, Thomas, 72, 132
Hamlet, 45, 46, 73
Hamm, Charles, 188
Hancock, Herbie, 246n.7
Harmoneons, 78–79
Harrington, George. *See* Christy, George
Harris, Joel Chandler, 31
Harris, Neil, 76
Harrison. *See* One-Legged Harrison, 52
Hart, Adolphus, 227
Hartz, Louis, 69
Haven, Gilbert, 32
Hawkins, Micah, 41, 46

Hearn, Lafcadio, 48
Heath, Stephen, 182
"Hee Haw," 5
Herskowitz, Richard, 253n.28
Heth, Joice, 76–77, 113
Hewlett, James, 44
Higginson, Thomas Wentworth, 119, 259n.9
Higham, John, 266n.33
Hip hop music, 174; and break dancing, 246n.7 (*see also* Street dancing, black)
Hobsbawm, E. J., 27
Home Journal, 85
Homesickness, 191
"Home! Sweet Home!" 176, 179, 191, 235
Homosexuality. *See* Minstrel show: and homosexuality
Hone, Philip, 131
Horkheimer, Max, 241n.1
Howard, Cordelia, 213, 225
Howard, Caroline Fox (Mrs. G. C.), 217, 221
Howard, George C., 213
Howells, William Dean, 31
Howes, Uncle Nate, 136
Huggins, Nathan, 7, 23, 149, 242n.14, 243n.15
Hurston, Zora Neale, 7
Hutchinson, Asa, 213
Hutchinson Family Singers, 190, 213
Hutton, Laurence, 55, 259n.4
Huyssen, Andreas, 64

Imaginary, 5, 150, 152, 255n.45
"I'm Gwine to Alabamy," 175, 176, 180
Industrial morality, 74, 148–49
Insurrection: class, 85, 86–88; slave, 25, 45, 87, 119, 129, 186, 234, 236, 259n.9
"Ireland and Virginia," 95, 96
Irish, 35, 67, 70–71, 75, 94–96, 148–49, 154, 177, 191–92, 229, 237, 249n.26, 253n.18, 257n.13. *See also* Minstrel show: Irish
Irish American, 229
Irving, Washington, 66, 81

Jackson, Andrew, 24, 50
James, C. L. R., 3, 12
James, Henry, 76, 215, 218, 228
Jameson, Fredric, 22, 64, 147, 149, 182, 212, 220, 267n.5, 268n.6, 269n.21, 270n.28
Jazz, 173
Jazz Singer, The, 5
Jefferson, Thomas, 58
Jentz, John, 262n.29
Jews, 249n.26
"Jim Brown," 121

Jim Crow, 3, 7, 22–24, 51, 89, 99, 107, 115, 132, 137, 142, 205, 207, 211, 218, 222
"Jim Crow," 16, 56, 57, 59, 80, 111, 119, 217, 260n.17
John Canoe, 46
Johnson, Barbara, 243n.17
Johnson, James Weldon, 17
Johnson, Paul, 69, 70, 74
Johnson, Richard, 11
"Jolly Raftsman, The," 193
Jones, Gareth Stedman, 63, 69
Jones, LeRoi (Amiri Baraka), 7
Jordan, Winthrop, 28
Jouissance/plaisir, 182–84. *See also* Pleasure
Journal of Commerce, 131
Journal of Music, 68, 84, 98, 143, 171, 248n.21, 267nn.2,4
Juba. *See* Lane, William Henry
Judson, E. Z. C. (Ned Buntline), 66, 85
"Jumbo Jum," 120–21

Kansas-Nebraska controversy, 9, 105–6, 231, 232
Karcher, Carolyn, 250n.34
Keeler, Ralph, 52, 160
Kelley, Mary, 32
Kemble, E. W., 166
Kemble, Fanny, 95, 116–17
Kennard, James K., Jr., 57, 60, 99, 186
Kerouac, Jack, 50
King, Martin Luther, Jr., 188
Klein, Melanie, 145, 147
Kneass, Nelson, 204
Knickerbocker, 57, 99
Knobel, Dale, 95
Kotzebue, August von, 89
Kristeva, Julia, 265n.26

Lacan, Jacques, 152, 189
Land reform, 154, 186, 200, 202–3, 208
Lane, William Henry (Juba), 52, 113–16
Lapsansky, Emma Jones, 263n.43
Lefebvre, Henri, 183
Leon, Francis, 54, 164, 165
Levin, Harry, 123
Lewis, John Delaware, 248n.23
Liberator, 20, 44, 111, 218, 220, 273n.12
"Lilla Dear, Good Bye," 206
Lincoln, Abraham, 4, 190, 216
Lind, Jenny, 89, 191, 235
Lippard, George, 64, 79–80, 201
Little Katy, or the Hot Corn Girl, 225, 228
Litvak, Joseph, 57
Litwack, Leon, 38
Lize, 82–84, 160, 228. *See also* Bowery

Lloyd, Marie, 91
Logan, Olive, 53, 161
"Long Tail Blue," 25, 117, 120
Lower million. *See* Popular culture
"Lubly Fan," 145, 162
"Lucy Long," 49, 160–61, 166
Ludlow, Noah, 61

McAndrews, J. W., 43
MacCann, Donnarae, 244n.29
McConachie, Bruce, 217, 226
McDowell, Andrew, 50
Macherey, Pierre, 56, 195
Mackay, Charles, 271n.44
Macready, Charles, 66–67, 85
Macready, William, 95
Mailer, Norman, 5, 52, 54–55, 249n.26
Manifest Destiny, 105, 107, 203, 206–7, 234
Mann, Horace, 209
Marcus, Steven, 241n.2
Maróthy, János, 184
Marx, Karl, 55, 61, 105, 220, 238, 250n.33
Marx, Leo, 10
Masculinity, 9, 25, 35, 49–55, 86, 104, 122–23, 126–27, 152–53, 159–68, 195–99, 229, 248n.23, 255n.46, 258n.29, 260n.18
Mathews, Charles, 45, 49
Mathews, Cornelius, 74, 234
Matthews, Brander, 34
Mechanics' Hall, 68, 153, 171, 190, 207
Melodrama, 64, 72, 74, 83, 211–33, 270n.31
Melville, Herman, 67, 90, 234, 236; "Benito Cereno," 36, 62, 234–35; *The Confidence-Man,* 61–62, 123, 250n.34; *Moby-Dick,* 163, 275n.1
Mestayer, Emily, 228
Metz, Christian, 260n.13, 264n.11, 265n.27
Mexican War, 105, 169–70, 200, 202–3, 206–7
Middle class, 91, 196, 235, 258n.29; "boss," 70; formation of, 69–70, 81, 156–58; merchant capitalist, 70
Middleton, Richard, 173, 174, 177, 183, 184, 188, 268n.6
"Miller's Song," 192
Minstrelization, 40–55, 76
Minstrel show: and black men, 25, 51–55, 86, 97, 112–13, 115–22, 126–27, 131–35, 138, 146–47, 151–53, 162–64, 166, 187–89, 244n.31, 248nn.23,24, 260n.13; and black women, 26, 119–20, 127, 133, 145–47, 151–53, 187–89, 248n.23, 265n.19; blacks in, 36–37, 43, 104, 112–13, 115, 255n.42; and burlesque, 23–24, 73, 159–61, 198, 213, 215, 228–29; and class, 63–88, 123–35,

Women's party, 199

Wright, Paul John, 67, 251n 5

Winston-Salem, 253n 25